Power
At Play

Power At Play

A Memoir of Parties, Politicians and the Presidents in My Bedroom

Betty Beale

REGNERY GATEWAY
Washington D.C.

Library of Congress Cataloging-in-Publication Data

Beale, Betty.
Power at play : a memoir of parties, politicians, and the presidents
in my bedroom / Betty Beale.
p.   cm.
Includes index.
ISBN 0-89526-503-6
1. Beale, Betty.   2. Women journalists—Washington (D.C.)—Biography.
3. Celebrities—Washington (D.C.)—Biography.   4. Washington (D.C.)—
Social life and customs—1951–   I. Title.
PPN4874.B345A3   1993

070′.92—dc20   92-41187
[B]   CIP

Published in the United States by
Regnery Gateway
1130 17th Street, NW
Washington, DC 20036

Distributed to the trade by
National Book Network
4720-A Boston Way
Lanham, MD 20706

Printed on recycled, acid-free paper.
∞
Manufactured in the United States of America.

10   9   8   7   6   5   4   3   2   1

To my husband, without whose support and encouragement this book would never have been written.

Acknowledgments

I wish to express warm thanks to my editor Diana McLellan. It was such a joy to work with her. I looked forward to our meetings. I am also very appreciative of the efforts on my behalf of Peter Hannaford; and of the always ready and cheerful assistance of Megan Butler and Jennifer Reist of Regnery Gateway. I am grateful, too, to Al Regnery for his most congenial cooperation.

Contents

Power
At Play

CHAPTER 1

Hello, I'm Betty Beale

An Introduction

Throughout my long career as a journalist, my two sisters have scoffed that I don't have the faintest idea how ordinary people live. Perhaps they're right. After all, for over forty years I spent more time in the White House than in any house but my own.

As glamorous as it all was, I never planned to record those years in book form. But one day, columnist Walter Lippmann asked me what I intended to do with my papers. I told him the thought had never entered my head. I should leave them to a library, he said: "Anybody studying this period will have to read your columns to get a complete picture." He planted the idea that I might have something of interest to add to the history of my time.

During all the glittering hours I spent in the President's House I came to know—in addition to the presidential pair—the justices of the Supreme Court, the cabinet, the leaders of Congress, the heads of key agencies, the top military men, and scores of American, and occasionally foreign, celebrities. I achieved that status by being the only syndicated society columnist in Washington, and by earning the trust of those I covered.

Many of them became friends when they discovered that I would

3

not reveal their confidences if asked not to, and that I would conduct myself as a proper guest when attending one of their parties. I never subscribed to the media's adversarial attitude—i.e., if you want millions of readers, dig for the dirt and spread it around. For the investigative reporter it made sense. But for someone whose material depended on being invited to bigwig doings it would have been, quite simply, career suicide. Prior to Watergate, friendship with a president was considered a plus for members of the Fourth Estate. Former *Washington Post* Editor-in-Chief Ben Bradlee's closeness to Jack Kennedy resulted, he has affirmed, in several exclusives. By the same token, Bill White's personal relationship with Lyndon Johnson led readers to check his column for indications of which way the wind was blowing. But sometimes, even taking great care, I made powerful enemies.

Former Secretary of State Dean Acheson and I were at an election eve dinner in November of 1958, given by the Edward Foleys in their Kalorama Heights mansion. As he was the most newsworthy guest there I sought a quote from him when all the returns were in. The election had generally pleased the Democrats, except for Averell Harriman's loss of the New York governorship to Nelson Rockefeller. Said Acheson, "Harriman brought it on himself." How, I asked? "A commander is always responsible for a disaster that occurs under his command," he replied. I then asked him whom would he rather see run as the GOP presidential candidate in 1960, Nelson or Nixon? "It doesn't make any difference," responded the Democrat, who then said what he thought of each—in the most unflattering terms possible. Back home at my typewriter I took care to leave out the nasty comments in writing my lead: I quoted the only usable one. So I was surprised and hurt when I received a handwritten letter from him several days later which included these comments:

"I forget with people I like, that reporters are not people and should not be asked to occasions where friends relax and gossip. But we remain friends even though—if I can remember to do so—I [will] confine our talk to more enjoyable and less quotable gambits. I don't care in the least about anything except adding publicly to poor Averell's humiliation. As to Nelson and Nixon—poof!"

As I had been covering him considerably at parties for years and he knew it, I was furious at the arrogant assertions that put all the blame on me and none on himself. I wrote back that it was "very difficult for a reporter to know sometimes when and how to use the discretion for which the speaker has shown no concern." From then on I never approached him at parties and never spoke to him.

But in Washington, perhaps unlike other cities, there is an informal statute of limitations on such offenses.

Two years later, he came up to me and said, "Betty, why don't we be friends?"

"I did not know you wanted to be," said I. But then and there we buried the hatchet.

Sometimes, my glamorous tales from the Capital outraged readers—particularly those of some of the ninety-odd newspapers across the country who bought my syndicated column.

One "avid reader" in Memphis, Tenn., for example, informed me that he was amassing evidence against the next election.

"You may not realize what a great service you are rendering your country," he wrote. "The stuff you are reporting will do more to bring this nation to its senses, I believe, than any number of flag-waving, speech-making patriots. Every time I read one of your columns I feel like re-reading the whole history of ancient Rome, several chapters of the Holy Bible (especially the accounts of the destruction of Sodom and Gomorrah) then retiring to my closet for a couple of days of prayer . . . Haven't you people up there heard that the whole world is virtually sitting on a powder keg? . . .

"A great many people like myself, Betty, who work like a dog, sometimes eat worse than some dogs, are forever battling a rising tax burden and living costs . . . [and we] get pretty sick from some of the things we hear about in places of government . . . I hope that sometime . . . you can say some word to point the way back to a sense of responsibility toward the . . . jobs these people have."

Of course, I sympathized. But, I wrote, "I am at a loss to understand what satisfaction it could give anyone else or what advantages would result if the men who have been poring over their desks all day (and in Washington the top officials usually put in a 10 to 12-hour day) went straight home and moped all evening about the world situation. If someone asked you to a party would you decline because the world is in a bad situation? And if you did would it help the world any? . . ."

I went on to say that evening parties were an important channel for the business of diplomacy, that all such dinners were over by 11:00 P.M., and that the secretaries of State and Defense, for example, were at their desks at 7:30 A.M., worked till 7 or 7:30 P.M., then rushed home to change clothes for a diplomatic dinner. It was hardly Sodom and Gomorrah.

Still, I won't pretend it wasn't fascinating to cover the White House—moving amidst the charming-mannered guests in those elegant surroundings, eliciting comments on the national and international hottest news of the day.

But it was not always *comme il faut.*

I was there the night the wife of an assistant secretary of Defense felt her petticoat drop to her feet at a formal Eisenhower reception, then kicked it away only to watch with horror a military aide retrieve it and put it on the piano . . .

I was there the night of President and Mrs. Johnson's dance for Princess Margaret and Lord Snowdon when Christina Ford's strapless gown slipped below one bosom . . .

And the night of President and Mrs. Nixon's dinner for Duke Ellington which was followed by a jam session when the whole East Room became unglued . . .

And yet often the most fascinating, even spicy stories emerged from less promising venues.

I will never forget a tea held to publicize Ohio Senator Robert A. Taft's candidacy for president. It was in honor of the senator's energetic campaigning wife Martha, who was helping to carry the conservative banner against the more liberal General Eisenhower in the presidential race of 1952. The hostess was Louise Cromwell Heiberg—a remarkable woman whose husband, Alf, had originally courted her daughter, but ended up by becoming her own fifth husband. Louise, the daughter of rich, social Mrs. Edward P. Stotesbury of Philadelphia and Palm Beach, had been General Douglas MacArthur's first wife. She told me the general was never able to pass a mirror without pausing to admire his reflection therein. Alf gave Louise a parrot trained to say, "MacArthur, MacArthur."

Standing by the dining table in her Capitol Hill house, I looked down at the plates and was, at once, interested. They bore the American Eagle and looked so presidential I turned one over to determine their origin. On the back was the word "Harrison." I put it back, sidled up to Louise, and whispered, "Where did you get the White House china?" "That's an interesting story," she replied with a chuckle. "I'll tell you later."

She did. Then in her sixties or so and weighing, I would guess, over 300 lbs., Louise had once been a great beauty with a somewhat racy reputation. During the Warren G. Harding administration she was having an affair with General John Pershing who commanded our forces in World War I. Frequently she was the only woman in poker games at the White House, where she played with President Harding, Secretary of War John Weeks, and Pershing.

"One night I was playing poker in the White House," she told me, "when the president suddenly said, 'Louise, let's just you and me play a pat hand, winner name the stakes.' "

"All right, Mr. President," replied the desirable beauty, knowing full well what Harding had in mind as his prize. The two hands were dealt. He lost.

"Well, what do you want, Louise?" he asked her.

"A set of White House china," she replied.

The next day, the china from the Benjamin Harrison administration was delivered to her house. That is why so little of it can be found in the White House china room today.

* * *

Parties—mostly glamorous ones—have numbered, I figure, about fifteen thousand for this columnist. On rare days I might actually get to five—even during a so-called "summer slump." One mid-July day in 1954, I started with a foreign ambassador daughter's wedding at noon, and ended with an embassy supper dance at 11—after two other parties and a cabinet member's dinner cruise on the Sequoia, along with Sam Rayburn, Lyndon Johnson, and cabinet member Oveta Culp Hobby.

That was an unusually packed day even for the fifties and sixties. But it was nothing compared to Washington in earlier, more leisurely times.

In the 1850s, Mrs. C. Clement Clay, wife of the senator from

Alabama, wrote: "The Capital was synonymous with an unceasing, an augmenting round of dinners and dances, receptions and balls. A hundred hostesses renowned for their beauty and wit and vivacity vied with each other."

Mrs. Roger Pryor, a young Virginia beauty, wrote that "Washington suppers in the 1850s were superb. One wondered if we might not some day return to the feast of the Roman emperors." So many evening parties "were crowded into a season that we often attended three balls in one evening." Balls sometimes kept going all night with breakfast served at daybreak!

A note written by Secretary of State Daniel Webster (who died in 1852) illustrates the easy working pace of that era: "My dear Miss ____ : Will you breakfast with your humble servant tomorrow at 10 o'clock to meet Lady Bulwer? I expect a poet from Boston, a beauty from the west and a wit from 4½ street. These with yourself will enable us to get rid of two hours . . . Yours faithfully, Daniel Webster."

During this century, occupants of the White House and their activities have influenced but not *dictated* the party pace in Washington. Take the last days of the Nixon presidency: At necessary White House functions, the Nixons were going through the motions of hosts, dispirited and drained. But Embassy Row was rolling along as usual. The very cultured Giulia Ortona, who presided with her husband Egidio over a most popular Italian Embassy, was asked if Watergate had affected the party tempo. Surprisingly, it had not, she said. Other ambassadors' wives and my own calendar corroborated her statement.

But the power and availability of the top officials around a president always provided the impetus for both diplomatic and private dinners, and the structure of Washington society.

*   *   *

To understand Washington social life, imagine a pie of which each slice is a segment of society: the White House, the diplomatic corps, the cabinet and agency heads, the Congress, the media, the military, and the social and cultural-minded residents. In the center of the pie stands the president of the United States. No matter who he is or where he comes from, he is the leader of Washington society as well as the chief of state, head of government, commander-in-chief of the armed forces, and the single someone with the most power. His are the most sought-after invitations; he is the most prestigious guest. Now, if you were to cut out the center of this people-pie with a cookie-cutter to include the narrowed points of each slice or segment, you would have the inner circle of Capital society.

The social life of this inner circle has always been more than the frosting on the cake of power, more than the silky evening that soothes jagged business nerves, or the smug flaunting of rich friends and fashions before one's peers.

Until the mid-1980s at least, it was the very essence of Washington. Without the daily lunches, receptions, and dinners where government bigwigs exchanged notes on the hottest news of the day— or headlines-to-come—with diplomats, journalists, generals, and cultural leaders, the city would have lacked much of its heart, its motivation, its meaning, and all of its glamour. Throughout most of the twentieth century this social mingling played an important role in the upper levels of power. It provided the amalgam that smoothed the way to easy communication. It warmed relations between wary factions. It capped the day's differences with the coating of gentility so necessary in a civilized society. On top of all that, it was fun, stimulating, important fun. It kept me up to 1, 2, or 3:00 A.M. night after night.

The essence of Washington was not to be found in presidential pronouncements or congressional commitments. Instead, it was alive and thriving on the nightly social scene where the activities of the day and predictions of the morrow were reported, sorted, aborted, or distorted and promptly exported to the next pair of ears at the next party. Indeed, in the Capital the laws of physics were reversed. Sound traveled faster than light.

Consider a dinner one evening at the Moroccan Embassy where Senator Richard Stone of Florida told the other guests that his colleagues were calling him "The D.C.I." (Director of Central Intelligence) because the inside information he divulged at Foreign Relations Committee hearings frequently surprised even State Department officials. Where did he get it? On the social circuit, he informed them.

"I've gotten more information out of this dinner tonight than I get out of a congressional hearing," explained Stone. By that time he had had private words with President Carter's National Security Adviser Zbigniew Brzezinski, the Saudi and Moroccan ambassadors, Secretary General of the OAS (Organization of American States) Alejandro Orfila, and newsmen John Wallach and Martin Agronsky. By the end of the evening I, too, had elicited usable items from all of them by simply getting involved in their interesting talk.

At a party given by Democratic Congressman and Mrs. Clark Thompson for their fellow Texan, Speaker Sam Rayburn, Oklahoma Senator Mike Monroney sat down near the entrance to await then Vice President Lyndon Johnson's arrival. The minute Johnson appeared he hopped up, talked to him briefly, and came back smiling. He had just accomplished in that minute, he said, something he had been trying unsuccessfully to accomplish for days.

Such brief exchanges, helpful in both national and international affairs, took place nightly in social settings all over town. Where did the city's unofficial residents fit into such a picture? Those with money and ambition greased the party wheels to become a part of it. Behind their desire to sit around a glittering embassy table or a cozy candlelit one in Georgetown was not merely the itch to be in, or to bask in real or imagined scintillating company in sophisticated settings. It was the irresistible craving to be elbow-to-elbow with someone of power in America and thus in the world. It was the burning yearning commonly called Potomac Fever. It was, and still is, an incurable disease.

Adlai Stevenson once said, "Trying to get rid of Potomac Fever is like getting rid of malaria. Just when you think it's gone you begin to shake." Woodrow Wilson described the dangerous effect of Washington on politicians thus: "When people come to Washington they either grow or swell." Whichever they do, they rarely "go back to Pocatello," an expression applied even today and even to New York City. Hence, the Capital is full of has-beens, meaning former cabinet officers, former ambassadors, former presidential aides, etc. They outnumber the incumbents, and so they make up the bulk of residential society. Though currently removed from the center of the power pie, they are somebodies who have had power, and may have it again. It is never wise, in Washington, to snub a has-been; come-backs are far too common.

There is nothing subtle about the motivation of most Washington hosts. They function in a power-motivated society and if they want to cut any kind of social swath they must lure rank to their tables. This method is so successful that even if you have no influence, no social standing and limited funds, you can still create a smoke-and-mirrors illusion of power to inveigle a cabinet couple to be your honor guests, and you can draw important ambassadors to a party—in your house, private club, restaurant, friend's garden—almost anywhere, as long as the guest of honor has the clout to draw the other VIPs. You invite social reporters in numbers to publicize your social coup, and urge them to bring photographers. Reporters unacquainted with the social scene assume that the presence of an ambassador is clear indication of the prominence of the hosts. The result is a publicized status that in some cases has been laughable. Perle Mesta used to say all you had to do to get an ambassador to your party was hang out a lamb chop. It's not that those handsomely domiciled foreign envoys are in desperate need of a free meal—it's just that they are inclined to accept all kinds of invitations, never knowing what avenues they might open to business opportunities or to a better understanding of Americans, never suspecting they are being used to enhance the social standing of the hosts.

Top drawer residential hostesses were not above using social climbers' tricks to attain their ends, too. Patrician Mrs. Robert Woods Bliss, wife of an ambassador, chatelaine of historic Dumbarton Oaks with its spectacular gardens covering six acres in Georgetown, and leader of the cultural set—sent flowers to the White House social secretary as a gentle reminder that an invitation to the White House would be welcome. And Mrs. Truxton Beale tried more than once to get a titled diplomat whom she had not met to come to her famed house on Lafayette Square.

I learned of that when a Spanish Grandee, the Marques de Zahara, became the first secretary at the Spanish Embassy and began dating my sister Nancy. One day he called her: He had received an invitation to a luncheon from a woman he did not know, he said, so he refused it. Then, some days later the same woman called him and asked him to dinner.

"I do not know her," he reiterated, "so I refused. Tell me, who is Mrs. Buxom Veal?"

The item caused a ripple of pleasure through town when it appeared in my column, because the imperious Marie Beale was not known for warmheartedness.

Despite international hostilities in various parts of the world at any given time, the decorum of diplomatic protocol prevails at social affairs. Take the Soviet Embassy's National Day reception following the unsnarling of the Cuban missile crisis. The air of extreme diplomatic friendliness, I wrote, "cloaked an undercurrent of intrigue dense enough to cut with a knife. There was Indian Ambassador B. K. Nehru whose uncle, Prime Minister Nehru, was still hoping the Soviets would send arms to aid them in their war against Soviet ally, Red China ... There were Pakistan Ambassador and Begum Assiz Ahmed who sought no encounter with the ambassador of India whose country, until a few weeks ago, considered Pakistan, not Red China, its No. 1 enemy ... There were former American Ambassador to Russia and Mrs. Llewelyn Thompson exchanging pleasantries with Soviet Ambassador and Mrs. Dobrynin while their countries still waged cold war over Cuban inspection to test the veracity of Soviet claims ... There were British Ambassador and Lady Ormsby Gore whose nation sided with the United States over Cuba against the Soviets on whose soil they were then standing and whose aid to India is worrying British Commonwealth colleagues, the Pakistanis ... And there was West Germany's Ambassador Heinrich Knappstein whose country hated the Soviets and lived in a constant duel of wits and intrigue to get individual East Germans and/or East Germany from under Soviet rule ... All under the same Soviet roof, all jostling the same elbows, eating from the same bowls of caviar and talking sotto voce in groups of two and three. ...."

On the diplomatic circuit I learned to leave my preconceptions at home. A party at the Irish Embassy gave me an insight into the enmity between Catholic Ireland and Protestant Northern Ireland. I never expected to find the mayors of Dublin and Belfast being honored together at a small gathering. But they said they got along fine and conferred with each other from time to time. And each told me, independently of the other, that the killings in Ireland would cease if the Irish Americans would stop sending arms and money to the IRA! It is mind-boggling to realize that while Americans so fear terrorist acts by foreign extremists that they sometimes limit their own travel plans, certain Americans have been financing terrorist acts abroad.

At Secretary of State George Shultz's luncheon for the Sultan of Oman I was fascinated to learn from my luncheon partner Henry McNeil, former head of McNeil Laboratories, that the millions of dollars worth of medicines sent to Cuba as ransom for hostages taken during the Bay of Pigs attack had secret marks on them so they could be traced. They never got to Cuba; they went to the Soviet Union.

At embassy parties the guest list, who snubs whom, or who smothers whom with attention, can indicate what is cooking on the international scene.

A prime example: The Soviet Embassy's annual "October Revolution" reception in November 1951. The star guest was Iranian Prime Minister Mohammad Mossadegh. Soviet Ambassador Alexander Panyushkin greeted him as if he came bearing an oil well. Mossadegh's rise to power had caused the shah to flee from Iran. (We would later join the British in helping to overthrow Mossadegh and return the shah to power.) The Soviets, I could see as I watched them embrace Mossadegh at every turn of my head, were itching to acquire influence in Iran, lusting, as they did, for the whole country.*

Perhaps the most revealing social affair was the Lebanese reception for President Gemayel on his first visit to Washington. Although the invitations were extended in the ambassador's name the Phalangists controlled it. They did not invite the leading Lebanese-Americans in our city and they tried to strong-arm out of the party Arab League Ambassador to Washington Clovis Maksoud who had

---

* Famed black singer Paul Robeson, who had denounced America for its racism and embraced Russia, was getting a hero's welcome from the crush of left-wingers at that reception, too. In those days, recall, blacks and whites were almost never seen at the same social gatherings. A photographer asked the big, strong Robeson to pose in front of Stalin's portrait, but the singer—to his credit—refused. "I like the guy," he said, "but not that much."

been personally invited by the ambassador. That party reflected the battleground in Lebanon; I needed no clairvoyant powers to perceive that the new presidency was not about to usher in an era of peace.

But sometimes appearances can be deceiving: At Secretary of State Dean Rusk's dinner for foreign ambassadors (once JFK abolished the white tie affair, the secretary of state took it over) I wondered what Soviet Ambassador Anatoly Dobrinin, India's B.K. Nehru, and Spain's Marques de Merry del Val were up to during a lengthy huddle. Before I could unobtrusively sidle up to get a nugget for my column, the Marquesa de Merry del Val beat me to it and nearly popped when she heard what consumed their interest. The three highest representatives in Washington of their sovereign nations were talking about where in Washington one could get a stiff shirt and wing collar laundered properly! The marques said he had to send his stiff bosom shirts and collars all the way to Madrid to be done up correctly. Ambassador Nehru said after much searching he had finally located a place in Washington that did them fairly well. But the Soviet ambassador had thrown in the towel and taken a cue from Secretary Rusk and Ambassador at Large Averell Harriman. Both were wearing a stiff turned-down collar with their white tie and tails.*

*   *   *

I came to realize, early in my career, how profoundly private affairs influence public policy.

Some of the most amusing gatherings in the late 1930s were given by Danish-born Mitzi Sims, a woman who had an unsung but profound effect on America's foreign policy. The wife of Canadian Harold Sims, honorary attaché to the British Embassy, Mitzi was stunning, super chic, had an utterly captivating speaking voice and a sense of humor. She also had great success with men. She called the several diamond bracelets she wore "my service stripes, my dear."

---

* Rusk, who joined them at that point, told how the tortuous wing collar came into being. When Edward VII did away with the white ascot, only a low unbecoming collar was left. To make it look better tailors raised it, then turned down the corners to make it more comfortable. "And we have been stuck with it for fifty years," said Rusk.

She and her well-heeled but dull husband lived in the same de luxe Wardman Park Annex as Michigan Senator and Mrs. Arthur Vandenberg. When the senator got to know Mitzi, he fell madly in love with her and a hot affair ensued.

Much has been written about the bipartisan patriotism of the powerful senator who abandoned his isolationism and rallied his Republican colleagues to the aid of Britain in World War II. Vandenberg told British correspondent Henry Brandon that it was Winston Churchill's address to Congress in December 1941 after Pearl Harbor that converted him to internationalism. But his paramour had told me sometime earlier that she had convinced Arthur of the error of his isolationist opinions.

Sophisticated, cosmopolitan Mitzi, whose native land had been overrun by Hitler's forces and who, by 1939, had knitted eight woolen sweaters and ten pairs of socks for British soldiers, opened her lover's eyes to the importance of Europe. The woman he loved was European. That did it.

I was thrilled to be invited to the Sims' intimate dinners for Lady Peel—better known as British comedienne Beatrice Lillie—actress Ina Claire, filmdom's Raymond Massey, or the great Danish tenor Lauritz Melchior. The Vandenbergs were usually there and I still remember the senator's passionate, piercing gaze when he looked at Mitzi. They brazenly drove together, in public, down Connecticut Avenue in her very visible, sleek cream-colored Packard convertible. *Look* magazine boldly came out with an article about Vandenberg and headlined it, "The Senator from Mitzigan."

Prominent on the diplomatic scene then, too, were Counselor of the German Embassy and Mrs. Hans Thomsen. Even as Hitler was annexing Sudetenland and the rest of Czechoslovakia, "Baby" Thomsen was whispering to friends at embassy receptions that she did not agree with Hitler at all. As she poured tea at the Austrian Embassy one afternoon she told me that the Nazis had put her brother in jail. It is unlikely she would have been spreading that news around town unless she had been told to do so to disarm Americans into more friendliness toward Hitler's representative or, perhaps, stimulate confidences.

The last time I saw the Thomsens was the night they had invited me, my sister Nancy, and Dolly Corbin, a pretty society girl, to a supper in their house. We three were violently anti-Hitler—but accepting the invitation was a must for me, a reporter, and the other two were equally curious. At that time the horrors perpetrated by Hitler were not known. If I recall correctly the other guests were members of the embassy. But indelibly etched in my memory was what happened after supper: We Americans were given a scrapbook to peruse photographs taken during Hitler's triumphal meeting with Mussolini in Italy. The others were eagerly and happily listening to the news on the radio about Hitler's latest triumphs. We turned the pages while whispering comments of disgust to each other, then took our leave. The evening was a manifestation of the Nazis' arrogance vis-à-vis the anti-involvement mood that prevailed in the United States.

Not till some time later did we learn that the suave "Tommy" Thomsen was one of Hitler's elite Black Shirts. He and "Baby," along with other Axis diplomats, were subsequently incarcerated in the luxurious minimum security of the Greenbrier at White Sulphur Springs, one of the choice vacation spots of the east.

*   *   *

Spanish poet Aurelio Valls, who served as a diplomat in the sixties, described Washington as "the eye of the hurricane," with the tranquillity derived from its trees, gardens and beautiful buildings—coupled with the niceties of its social life—belying the electrifying power that goes out from it to create the strong winds of change around the world.

It is also the capital of contradictions.

It is the city where everybody thinks, talks, and plays politics, but the residents have fewer political rights than other Americans.

It is the city of the world's biggest spender—the United States Government with its lavish charity toward foreign nations—yet has paid the most niggardly salaries to its envoys serving abroad, let alone its highest officials, whose wives must often find paying jobs in order to make both ends meet.

It is credited with soaking up the most alcohol per capita in the country—yet probably has fewer drunks among the people who count.

It is a bureaucratic pyramid where high-salaried men from other cities frequently arrive vowing to clean up the mess and end the waste and are at once humbled by the demands of public service and the brains of the lower-echelon people long devoted to it. General Motors president Charles E. Wilson admitted this common error soon after taking over the job of President Eisenhower's secretary of defense.

It is both a citadel of lofty idealism and a factory of hard realism, and all its problems derive from trying to reconcile the two. Its leaders think they have to talk like the former and they know they have to act like the latter, which naturally produces a certain schizophrenia. As a result, Washington has been called "the only asylum in the world run by the inmates."

So how did I, a nice sane girl from a proper background, become its chronicler—and in some cases its warden?

CHAPTER 2

Off on the Right Foot

My Washington Roots

I never wanted to be a journalist. Of the careers open to women at the time I graduated from Smith College, that of a columnist never occurred to me. Writing, I always felt, was a chore to be avoided; I spent more time trying to duck writing thank-you notes to relatives or family friends for birthday or Christmas gifts than it actually took to write them. I did my best to steer clear of writing courses at Smith—after the required freshman English course whose weekly composition hung over me like a dark cloud for six days until I had to take pen in hand. So how did I happen to spend a lifetime as a writer? Let me start from the beginning.

I was conceived, born, and bred in Washington, D.C. My mother came to the Nation's Capital when her father, Thetus Wilrette Sims, became a member of the House of Representatives from the Sixth District of Tennessee in 1897. With him came my handsome grandmother, Nancy Kittrell Sims, five daughters—Edna (my mother), Tom (her real name), "Bep" (nickname for Elizabeth; I'm her namesake), Marie, and Enid—and Paul, the youngest of two sons.

About the same time my father came to the big city from the little town of Point Pleasant, W.Va., where the first battle of the American

Revolution, according to West Virginians, really took place—not at Lexington or Concord. He found both a job and mother.

Father's family prided themselves on being descendants on his father's side of Colonel Thomas Beale, a royalist, who came to America with his wife Alice from Maidstone, Kent county, England, in 1640. When I went to Richmond in 1954 to cover the arrival in the U.S. of the Queen Mother of Britain, I no sooner set foot in the capital building than I met the clerk of the House of Delegates, E. Griffith Dodson. On hearing my name he immediately said, "Beale? Beale? Any relation to Captain Thomas Beale?" I said he was my ancestor. Dodson, was also, it turned out, Keeper of the Rolls of the state. He later sent me a copy of the deed to Thomas Beale's Virginia property showing that the first American Beale's grandson, by the same name, had a land grant of 339 acres from Lord Fairfax. It was signed in 1727. The first Thomas Beale,* who died in 1688, settled on 250 acres, was sheriff of York County, justice of the county, commander of Fort York, a member of the King's Council of York County, a vestryman of the first Bruton Parish Church at Williamsburg, and recommended by King Charles II for the post of governor of the fort at Point Comfort.

I never knew my grandfather, James Madison Hite Beale. He died in 1911, before I was born. He got the "Hite" from another ancestor, Baron Jost Hite (I suspect it was originally spelled Heit), a German settler in Virginia who built a nice but unprepossessing house called Belle Grove, now a National Trust property.

My paternal grandmother was Julia Lewis, a descendant of Colonel Charles Lewis, for whom Lewis County in West Virginia was named. He was the only American-born son of John Lewis and Margaret Lynn, who grew up in Clonwall Castle in Scotland. Charles, who escaped from his Indian captors when a boy, fell in

---

* From the book *The Beall and Bell Families* ("Colonial Families of the United States Descended from the Immigrants—Who Arrived Before 1700, Mostly from England and Scotland, and Who Are Now Represented by Citizens of the Following Names   Bell, Beal, Bale, Beale Beall").

Truxtun Beale, who lived in historic Decatur House on Lafayette Square, was descended from the same Thomas Beale. Because of that and also because, I understand, of a generous gift to the church, he was allowed burial in the Bruton Parish churchyard, as was his wife Marie.

October 1774 in the Battle of Point Pleasant. His mother left a diary of her life covering the years 1730–75 during which her youngest daughter was also kidnapped by Indians and rescued by a strange white woman. I have a copy of that diary.

My mother's mother, Nancy Kittrell, was descended from the Catheral (also spelled Catterall and Cateral) family of Lancashire, England, which did quite well under the English kings until it backed two losers—Charles I, who lost his head, and his son James II, who had to flee when William of Orange became king. In the process much of the family property was lost so King James' backer, Dutton Cateral, came to America and settled in Maryland, where his name was entered in the parish register of the Eastern Shore of Maryland as "Dutton Kittrell," doubtless because of his English pronunciation.

My maternal grandfather's family came from Scotland and ended up in Tennessee, where the Civil War so depleted them that young Thetus, a teenager at war's end, would never have gone to college had it not been for a family friend who backed him. Grandfather paid back every penny.

My maternal grandparents were such products of the Victorian Age that they never kissed until they were married! My sweet, refined grandmother held herself erect, never crossed her legs when sitting, always kept her knees together, and never spoke in loud tones. How she stood her rambunctious grandchildren, I'll never know.

T. W. Sims and his wife were also products of the post-Civil War South. Money was not plentiful, so pride in family prevailed. An oft-heard expression was: "He (or she) comes from a good family." Those magic words meant instant acceptance. If there was money, all the better—unless it came from merchandising, which was frowned upon, perhaps because of the carpetbaggers who invaded the South. When my grandfather came to Washington, he was a comfortably fixed lawyer; but at his death he had very little money left. He had invested badly, in Brazilian bonds, and lent money to his eldest son Kent and other cotton farmers in Mississippi; they were subsequently impoverished by the agricultural depression of the early twenties.

Judging by a small clipping my brother has from a 1906 edition of

Washington's *Evening Star* newspaper, they lived in a nice house. It read: "Mrs. Thetus W. Sims gave her second reception of the season Tuesday afternoon at her beautiful home on Massachusetts Avenue opposite Highland Terrace. Mrs. Sims was handsome in white lace. Her assistant, Miss Elizabeth Sims, was in blue silk. Mrs. William Beale, formerly Miss Edna Sims, the married daughter of the house, was effective in white." It went on to say that "Master William Beale, age three months, . . . is a highly popular and interesting member of society." That gushing style of society writing remained virtually unchanged for forty years; I am pleased to say I had a hand in changing it.

As a result of all the above, I was raised on pedigree, pride, and southern cooking. My Uncle "Brownie"* said I started talking at the age of eight months and never stopped. Uncle Brownie himself was famous as a raconteur, and even wrote a book called *The Anatomy of the Anecdote.*

Washington was a much smaller and more southern city when I was a child. I can remember summers playing outside and hearing the singsong voice of a black driving his horse-drawn wagon full of watermelons and singing, "Watermelons, red to the rind—pluck 'em all the time." As that catchy rhythm made its way down the street people would come out of their houses to buy. The hurdy-gurdy man and the Italian organ-grinder with a uniformed monkey on his shoulder—fixtures of that era—would come up S Street, too, where we lived in a cramped apartment.

I have never met more than one person who remembers it, but in those days there was a bathing beach in Washington. Sand had been brought in to provide a beach in the Tidal Basin, a marvelous place to swim. It was open to the public—if white, that is. But before long a congressman said any public beach in the nation's Capital had to admit Negroes (the term used then) as well as whites. That was fair, of course, as they also paid taxes, but since whites would not bathe with blacks, the beach was closed. It never reopened. The Jefferson

---

* Louis Brownlow, considered the nation's foremost authority on public administration, was an adviser to all presidents from Theodore Roosevelt through Truman. He headed FDR's Committee on Administration Management, which established the Office of the President.

Monument was subsequently built on that side of the basin. Nowadays when the weather is warm people pedal two-seater boats on the cherry tree-ringed waters.

In the wintertime, we kids longed for snow; when it came we took our sleds up Dean's Hill to slide down. Partly wooded Dean's Hill rose from the northeast corner of the intersection at Connecticut and Florida Avenues up to where the Washington Hilton stands today. There's an office building there now with stores on the ground floor.

Summer and winter in good weather we jumped rope and played hopscotch and all the harmless games with which children have whiled away their time for centuries. I went to Force-Adams elementary school on Massachusetts Avenue between 16th and 17th Streets. It was all white, with pupils from varied walks of life. One of my classmates was the son of the Italian cobbler whose shop we went to on 18th Street above S. (He was not a personal friend; in those days the kids who shared similar backgrounds flocked together.)

I had my first date in my fifth grade at grammar school. A classmate took me to a matinee movie at the old Knickerbocker Theater and to the drugstore next door afterwards. His way of offering me a choice of delectables was to say, "You don't want an ice cream soda, do you?" Being a well-brought up child, I quickly agreed that I didn't want an ice cream soda (which I craved) and suggested something less expensive. To this day I have a difficult time ordering an expensive meal unless my host is a millionaire. In the eighth grade a nice boy by the name of Douglas Cordiner got a crush on me and kept a mirror propped up on his desk so he could see me. He was so short he had to sit in the front row whereas my height relegated me to the back row. The difference in our height did nothing to dampen his ardor; one day, in our living room, he suddenly jumped up and gave me a kiss on my cheek. It was my first kiss from a beau.

I also went to dancing class, to Miss Hawkes, who had the city's monopoly on teaching genteel children the steps of a waltz and foxtrot. She was a short woman with a pouter-pigeon build—slender ankles and legs, a well-corseted midsection, and ample bosom. Like all children's dance teachers, she had trouble getting the boys to dance with the girls. Not being a beauty, or a saucy turned-up-nose type—I would have sold my soul for a turned-up nose—I knew the awful misery of being a wallflower until some undashing, bespectacled boy approached. I came into my own on the dance floor in my midteens, when boys really wanted to cut a rug with a girl who could make them feel like experts. Dancing was to stand me in good stead for my entire career among the world's elite.

Among my earliest memories of Washington are the military parades of World War I veterans, marching in public-spirited demonstrations that stirred patriotic fervor in the breasts of even the very young. Such feelings were part and parcel of our lives then; we pledged allegiance to the flag every morning in school, and we meant it.

Uncle Brownie—Louis Brownlow—Bep's husband, was running the city then. President Woodrow Wilson appointed him one of the three commissioners of the District of Columbia and the chairman. As such he could provide us—my brother Bill, sister Nancy, and me—with good seats for parades and rides in his open touring car, a godsend in pre-airconditioned Washington.

I loved it when we went to see the Brownlows in their Florence Court apartment on California Street, full of mementos of his world trips for the Haskins (Press) Bureau. (That apartment building, facing Phelps Place, is still there.) We could walk through the then woodsy block to Wyoming Avenue where my grandparents, the Simses, had one of the two apartments on the second floor of 2139 Wyoming Avenue (also still there). The other apartment on that floor was occupied by Senator and Mrs. William Borah of Idaho. The senator, a great orator with a leonine haircut, would sit me on his knee and tell me how he shot the elk or deer whose antlers were on the wall. I didn't think about the suffering of the animals then; I was simply fascinated. Mrs. Borah, always elegant in a flowing housegown and long rope of pearls, kept parrots, the only ones I saw outside the zoo. Being a Republican and an isolationist, the senator was the political opposite of my grandfather, but they were friendly neighbors. With no children of their own, they welcomed our visits.

The Brownlows, who were also childless, were our wonderful second parents. They took us to Keith's Theatre where President Wilson had had a box to see the best in vaudeville and to the Belasco to see John Barrymore in *Hamlet*. They played Caruso and Galli-Curci records on their Victrola. When I was thirteen, my aunt took Nancy and me to New York to see the Ziegfeld Follies with Will Rogers, Fred and Adele Astaire, and other greats. Afraid that we would be shocked by the almost-nude women in the extravaganza scenes, the very proper and plump Bep Brownlow explained that the perfect female form was a thing of beauty and worth seeing, especially when decorated with discreetly placed strings of rhinestones. I felt quite sophisticated after that.

They took us to see Woodrow Wilson the last time he appeared at the window of his S Street residence. He was then a sick, drawn man barely able to acknowledge the waves and cheers of a group of followers on the street—far different from the vital man Brownie had seen frequently at the White House. There was mist in the Brownlows's eyes. They thought it a great tragedy that Wilson's desire that the United States join the League of Nations had been blocked in the Senate and they credited Senator Henry Cabot Lodge with the defeat. In our strongly Democratic family, where politics were discussed at every evening meal, Lodge and all his Republican colleagues were the enemy. Years later I was to become such a good friend of his son, John Davis Lodge, and his wife Francesca, that my husband and I visited them in Buenos Aires when John was ambassador to Argentina, and in Marbella, Spain, where they had a villa next to the Duchess of Alba's.

After Brownie became city manager of Petersburg, Va., we children visited them during summer vacations and they would drive us in their Model A Ford to see some of the beautiful stately homes on the James River.

When he became city manager of Knoxville, Tenn., we, and my new little sister Barbara, would go there and spend part of the time in a rustic mountain inn in Elkmont, Tenn., in the cool of the Great Smokies. That was rattlesnake country. I remember that Brownie's brother and a friend walked the mountain paths to a good fishing spot and came back with three rattlesnakes they had clobbered en route.

My father started out as a tax assessor for the District of Columbia and then joined the real estate branch of what is now the American Security Bank. Father soon acquired a reputation as Washington's most knowledgeable, if conservative, assessor of property. As such, he helped increase the fortunes of several Washington men, or so they subsequently told me. He himself did not invest in land—the biggest money-maker in our city—probably because he felt it was unethical to benefit privately from information acquired on his job.

By the time I entered Western High School in Georgetown we had moved into a comfortable house in the 1900 block of S Street. I walked part of the way to and from school; when my boyfriend, Daniel Van Voorhees, walked with me, he would carry my books. Back then females were delighted with any and all courtesies shown by males. My brother Billy had successfully prepared for Princeton at Western, but my three years there did little, I fear, to add to my knowledge. So my Aunt Marie (Mrs. Edward Riddick of Memphis) underwrote my senior year at Holton-Arms School, where my older sister Nancy had gone. I adored Holton. There I learned to study for the first time, and had the finest teacher of my life, Miss Mildred Brown. After her courses in algebra and geometry I got 98 on my College Board Entrance exam in math. I couldn't wait to go to college, although it meant I could not make my debut. After a finishing year at Holton, my sister Nancy had been given a debut by our youngest aunt, Enid, who was then married to wealthy Chester Snow. By the time Barbara entered Smith College, father, now vice president of American Security, could afford to give her a debut party too—a swinging tea dance in the Mayflower Hotel ballroom. (Because the hotel had gone into the hands of receivers—i.e., the American Security—father became president of the Mayflower Hotel.)

At Smith, I was away from my family for the first time in my life. It was a heady experience. I must have cut one hundred classes my freshman year. If you maintained an above-C average you had unlimited cuts. I adored Smith, from the gigglefests we had every night at Hubbard House, to rowing on the varsity crew on beautiful little Paradise Pond, to getting a "Cheese dream" at our favorite restaurant in Northampton. I broke enough rules to be suspended, but wasn't. As an upper classman I once smuggled two quarts of gin into my room and my group—we called ourselves the Swiss Navy—mixed some of it with lemonade from the Plymouth drugstore and had an hilarious picnic in a nearby meadow. To this day I remember running across the meadow with the speed of Mercury, the ground rushing under me as if I were not touching it. I was deliciously tiddly. When we got back to Hubbard House we all flopped in a relaxed heap on two beds pushed together in Mary Brown and Marjorie Lewis's room and, warmed by the heat of the house, were dozing off when Mrs. Gilchrist, the house mother, looked in. She was obviously suspicious, but with no evidence—we had been chewing Lifesavers like mad—she left. Mrs. Gilchrist was a woman of ample proportions, drooping jowls, and basset-hound eyes that examined you through pince-nez glasses. She was not an unpleasant woman and she did have a job to do. It included confiscating the copy of *Lady Chatterley's Lover* when she discovered that we had it, how I never knew. Pornography was not permitted even in liberal Smith College. But we didn't doubt she perused it herself— particularly the naughty pages that fell open automatically.

I smoked once or twice in my room, which also was strictly verboten. And while still underclassmen, we borrowed a car from Mary Brown's beau a couple of times, dressed another Swiss Navy- ite, Dudley Breckinridge, as an old aunt, and drove to Springfield to have cocktails. In those days you couldn't drive a car until the spring of your senior year and then only if you had a B plus average. We had to be in the house by 10 P.M. every night except Saturdays when we were allowed to stay out till midnight. We could have male visitors before bedtime but only on the first floor in full view of everybody.

Morning chapel was obligatory; it was there I learned from Presi- dent William Allan Nielsen of the dangers of Hitler's rise to power.

Upon graduating from Smith College, I returned home to the family. Nancy's husband, Billy Mann, son of I.T. Mann, one of the founders of the exclusive Burning Tree Club, died my first year back, having gambled away a fortune on the Depression-hit stock market. His father had died the year before after losing about $20 million. We moved into Nancy's house on Tracy Place because she needed help running it; it was big enough to house the six of us as well as Nancy's baby girl and nurse. In those days, servants were plentiful and affordable. Young society matrons had nannies to look after their small fry so they could shop, go to luncheons and the beauty parlor, play tennis, golf, or bridge, and help with charity functions. Very few had nannies in order to take on a job. In addition to "Fraulein" who cared for my baby niece, we had a black cook and a black houseman named Booker. He cleaned and served lunch and dinner, in a proper butler's garb, with a vest of narrow red and black horizontal stripes around his ample girth. By the time the war came they were no longer with us. Help was so hard to get that we had to make do with an old woman who couldn't do much without assistance from us girls.

Soon after my return to town I was invited to join the Junior League of Washington. I accepted with alacrity. My two youngest aunts and Nancy were already members. The Junior League, started in New York (where Eleanor Roosevelt became a member), was an organization aimed at getting debutantes and postdebutantes involved in helping the poor and disadvantaged. In Eleanor's day, few young women went to college, and even fewer took jobs. The League gave them something worthwhile to do, instilled in them a sense of civic duty, provided real services for many needy, and at the same time introduced each new member to a circle of "acceptable" friends. From New York it spread all over the country.

By the time I joined the Washington League many of its members were college graduates and some of the unmarried ones had regular jobs and had to fulfill their compulsory charity work on the side.

I was eager to become financially independent. Getting spending money from father was like pulling hen's teeth. His theory was, if you can get along without it, don't buy it. To this day I have more built-in sales resistance than I need. I wanted a full-time paying job. I quickly found out that an AB degree cum laude from Smith would get me nowhere without secretarial skills. So I went to Temple School and learned typing and shorthand—both, as it turned out, invaluable for a journalist.

In the meantime, I was having fun. Sister Nancy was my entrée into the young diplomatic and official set. I was also doing Junior League work, writing press releases and taking them to the society editors of Washington's newspapers. They must have been acceptable, because out of the blue, Hope Ridings Miller, society editor of the *Washington Post*, called to ask if I would do a weekly column for her section.

I hesitated. How could she count on me to produce them on time? She wasn't worried. She asked me to write up the party I was going to that evening as a sample. I did and I was hired—for the munificent starting salary of $5 a week. I thought I'd try it for a year; just maybe it would lead to something better. I hadn't a clue that I was being propelled into a lifetime profession.

Washington was so much smaller in those days that I could not go to a theater opening without seeing literally dozens of people I knew. Indeed, on any night of a show's run or at whatever the popular nightspot of the time I would run into friends—not officials, but real Capital residents like myself. Today, we of that ilk feel like strangers at any public gathering.

Mrs. Miller later offered me a full-time job in her section, but I declined. I was not in robust health and knew the working hours were limitless. Instead, I took a job with regular working hours which also came about through the Junior League. The president of the Security Storage Co., Clarence Aspinwall, had called the League offices to see if they had a member who would like a job greeting customers and doing some secretarial work. I took it; it paid $100 a month. At that time Security had a monopoly on the shipments of U.S. diplomats' effects overseas and it had the most social clientele in town. Among the prominent women who appeared at the front office to get access to their things in storage, the most astounding was Evalyn Walsh McLean. She invariably arrived at the offices and warehouse on 15th Street wearing the Hope Diamond!

I had written the *Post*'s "Top Hats and Tiaras" column (we didn't mess around with egalitarianism in those days) for three years when my health took a turn for the worse and I had to quit work altogether. It was one of the great disappointments of my life that I wasn't well enough during World War II to join the American Red Cross and follow colleagues and friends in uniform to England and Asia. As soon as I was a little better, I answered a public appeal from the Veterans Pension Bureau for half-day stenographic work. I simply didn't have the stamina to work a full day. I soon learned about the incredible waste caused and maintained by government bureaucrats.

The word came down from above one day that everybody, however lowly, should analyze her job and present a plan for eliminating all unnecessary steps. I presented five different plans for saving time and paper and all five were implemented. The one recommending form letters, though, infuriated the women who had been dictating the same letters, with only a different name inserted, for decades. It had given them a sense of importance to have a secretary take down every word they said.

As soon as I was completely well, as a result of embracing Christian Science, I looked for a job at the *Evening Star*—then the biggest and most important newspaper in the city, and one of the richest in the country. In December of 1945, I was hired as a daily reporter and weekly columnist in the society department. I was to write for the *Star* until its demise in August of 1981, graduating to three and eventually four columns a week written in the comfort and quiet of my own home.

When I walked into the Society Department of the staid *Evening Star* I had been given only one guideline: Always write within the bounds of good taste. Nobody had to explain what good taste was; you knew. The output of that department bore about as much resemblance to today's social reporting—or at least what's left of it—as a Viennese waltz does to hip-hop.

Besides my weekly column, which I dubbed "Exclusively Yours," I did general "women's" reporting, wrote up weddings, and typed captions for the brides' pictures daily dumped in our office. The *Sunday Star* sometimes carried six pages of veiled faces, forty-eight brides to a page! Editor-in-chief Benjamin McKelway called all those photographs of unknown girls "a friendship builder," although the families of at least half of them did not even subscribe to the *Star*. When I complained to the society editor, Margaret Canby, about filling our pages with weddings she asked, "If we didn't have them, what would we put in the paper?" "News," I replied. My comment was not well received. Mrs. Canby wanted nothing to upset the easygoing applecart she ran. She regularly came in late and frequently not at all but would phone to tell us to sign her in. She wrote virtually nothing, spent most of her days chatting in her office with family members or friends, and frequently didn't decide who was to cover a six o'clock embassy reception until three hours before it began. As all of us had been working since 9:00 A.M. that meant somebody would have to put in an eleven or twelve hour day.

The big deal in the *Star*'s society stories in those days was who "poured": Who was to pour tea or coffee at afternoon functions, private and official, was one of the first questions the women in our department asked when they phoned the hostess. Hostesses picked the most prestigious women they could ensnare to take turns pouring tea at one end of the table and coffee at the other. Of the two pouring simultaneously, where was one to put the highest-ranking? Tea outranked coffee for years, but then coffee became so popular the lower-ranking pourer got more attention than the greater VIP at the other end. That would never do. A perplexed hostess finally called the Protocol Office in the State Department to settle this world-shaking problem. Protocol pronounced no difference between the two beverages; I passed this important government ruling on to my readers, thereby settling the question and soothing the coffee pourers' egos.

The *Star*'s social writers were used to filling scads of space writing which Mrs. Justice and Mrs. Senator poured, what edibles were served, what the aforementioned and hostess were wearing, and who had been on a trip. They would get all these gripping facts over the telephone, before the party was held. The five traditional White House official dinners and five official receptions were handled the same way; the entire staff called the ranking women attending to ask if they were wearing cerise taffeta, purple velvet, black crepe, or whatever. Such information was painstakingly woven into the completed story before the affair was held. The covering reporter had only to check the galley after the event to see if anything needed to be changed.

But having written the "Top Hats and Tiaras" column, I was accustomed to getting my news in person at parties. So I would rush home every afternoon at five o'clock, change my clothes, and sally forth to one or more cocktail parties and/or dinner. In the office at 9:00 the next morning, I would correct the galley proofs of that day's paper and send them to the composing room, write up the parties I had been to the night before, telephone the hostess of any party the *Post* had covered that we had not, write a different story about it, send them all up to be put in lead type, proof the galleys, and remake the page in the composing room for the home edition, which was supposed to be completed by 12:00 or 12:30 P.M. I was as busy as the proverbial one-armed paperhanger with an itch.

As I was writing up everything of any interest I could glean, I eventually heard from the managing editor, Herbert Corn. He summoned me from the third floor—where the women covering fashion, food, women's clubs, and so on were kept at an untroubling distance from the bustling newsroom and editorial offices on the seventh floor—to tell me that my column was getting too political. "You mean," I said, "I can write what people wore and what they ate but not what they said?" Mr. Corn who, I think, secretly was on my side, simply suggested I cool it for a while. The criticism had to come from the only man above him, editor Benjamin McKelway, who had the old-fashioned idea that real news—that is, comments by politicos on topics of national or international interest—should not fall into the delicate hands of genteel ladies who wrote for the "Women's Section."

Gradually, however, I won out, and Washington social writers began to home in on political comments. In 1952 the paper even sent me to cover both national political conventions. I was admonished that I, myself, would have to decide what to file because nobody from the women's pages had ever been sent to the political conventions before! I did. And for the next twenty-four years, I went to both conventions. Politics, politicians, and presidents were to become my life.

CHAPTER 3

Capital Quickstep

The Roosevelt-Truman Years

The late thirties were exciting years to be in Washington. The governmental innovations of the Franklin Delano Roosevelt administration, the attractive new people it drew to the city, and, subsequently, the electric pulse of a capital that was an international crossroads geared to a momentous war effort, made a heady mix.

Eleanor was the most active first lady in history. She not only traveled hundreds of thousand of miles visiting everything from sharecropper camps and coal mines to our armed forces abroad as her husband's surrogate, but she was more active socially than any other first lady. She was also the author of the daily "My Day" column that appeared in scores of newspapers around the country, not only chatting of her domestic, social, and charitable life, but boosting her husband's New Deal projects and putting a feminine spin on his view of social issues and world events.

With all this, she managed to give teas, musicales, luncheons for sixty or more women, a great many unofficial dinners for seventy or eighty, the full official schedule every year of five big dinners and five huge receptions until the war began, and more unofficial dances than any first lady in the past five decades.

She gave them for sons Franklin and John who were nineteen and seventeen when they moved into the White House. She threw a debut dance for over five hundred for her niece and namesake Eleanor Roosevelt. And she gave a debut dance for Joan Morgenthau, the daughter of Secretary of the Treasury Henry Morgenthau, during Christmastime, 1940, which my debutante sister Barbara attended.

Mrs. Roosevelt's thoughtful acts were legion. When FDR's close aide Harry Hopkins was ill, she invited both him and his daughter Diana to live in the mansion, which they did for some time. Little Diana went to Potomac School where my niece, Nancy Mann, was also a pupil, and Mrs. R. would ask Nancy over to play with Diana. My niece still remembers snitching a goodie from the president's tea tray.

Born to the privileged class, Mrs. R. was unawed by the White House. After all, she had been invited there by her Uncle Theodore thirty years before she entered it as First Lady.

Once installed, she didn't hesitate to innovate. She gave a masquerade party for "Gridiron widows"—wives of the all-male Gridiron Club members who held a stag dinner and review each year—and performed in its skits herself.

She led a rollicking Virginia Reel the night my brother Billy, who was with the Associated Press, took me to the Roosevelts' black-tie beer party for the press in the midthirties. I had been to the presidential mansion once before.

In those days it was the custom of young ladies and their mothers to leave cards for the First Lady. With no expectation of being received, the two would dress as if going to a tea, drive through the open gates to the North Portico, and stop. Immediately, an impressive-looking black butler in white tie and tails would come out bearing a little silver tray. The ladies would then place the cards on the tray and drive off. Within a reasonable period, an invitation to an afternoon reception from the First Lady would arrive.

After my mother and I had left our cards an invitation came for an afternoon musicale, a formal affair at which noted pianist Jose Iturbi played. But it was at the beer party for the press that I first shook the hand of a president of the United States. I remember a handsome, powerfully built man who exuded vigor, confidence, and charm

from his wheelchair. I never guessed then that I would be hobnob-
bing with his eight—and even nine—successors.*

My forty-three years of White House coverage began at one of
Bess Truman's teas for congressional wives. Due to postwar short-
ages abroad the Trumans did not resume the traditional white-tie
dinners and receptions during the 1945–46 season. In the fall of
1946 they started the series with two diplomatic dinners.†

Other traditional White House functions, held periodically until
mid-February, were separate dinners for the cabinet, the chief justice and associate justices, the president pro-tempore of the Senate
(there was no vice president until January 20, 1949), and the
Speaker. The receptions, which I began covering, were in honor of
the whole judiciary, the upper echelon of the diplomatic corps, the
military, the Congress, and the executive departments together with
the agencies. All these were annual affairs until the jet age brought
with it an influx of foreign chiefs of state, necessitating dinners in
their honor. The old schedule gradually disappeared. Still sensitive
to hunger abroad, the Trumans threw only receptions during the
1947–48 season. It was at the last one that a strange tinkling of an
East Room chandelier heralded a collapsing ceiling. The entire
White House needed reconstruction; and the Trumans moved into
Blair House, delighted that it was too small for any big, formal
affairs.

It was at Blair House that the Trumans received the future queen
of England, on her very first visit to the United States. There were
those who wondered how the former haberdasher would get along
with the exquisitely reared Princess Elizabeth. The fact is they got
along famously. Elizabeth confided to Colonel Martin Charteris, her
personal secretary, that she was simply crazy about President Truman. She was enchanted with his naturalness and felt completely at
home with him; he seemed to understand her shyness. They hit it
off beautifully.

For the British Embassy reception for Elizabeth and Philip, we of

---

* Ten—if I count meeting Bill Clinton at a party for governors in 1982. "You can't
be a governor," I told him, "you're still damp behind the ears."
† Two, instead of one, were now necessary because America's postwar preemi-
nence had prompted more countries to open embassies here.

the social press were among the 1,500 to receive impressive, crested invitations to shake hands with the royal pair between 3:30 and 5:30 P.M. Other reporters were confined to a raised platform behind a rope. (The same system was followed at all the embassy receptions for the royal pair after she became queen.) As glamorous as that party was for all the guests, the thing I remember best was a conversation that preceded it. I did not have a car then, and my sister Nancy let me use her rather dented old blue Ford sedan on occasion.

At the time we had a houseman named Curtis, a tall, thin, black gentleman of great civility. Curtis had definite ideas about propriety. The afternoon of the party, he tactfully asked if I would like to borrow his Cadillac Fleetwood to drive to the embassy. I was touched by his thoughtfulness—and floored to learn he owned the finest car of anyone in our family! Father's was a Buick. I am afraid I did not spare his embarrassment: I took the Ford.

As a member of the American Newspaper Women's Club, I was in charge of entertainment at the club benefits to which my boss, Margaret Canby, invited President and/or Mrs. Truman. For the club's spring luncheon honoring Bess I wrote a poem about her running for president herself. It was made into a record, and presented to the First Lady to give to her husband. Mr. Truman, who doted on his wife, was tickled by it, played it for visitors, and told me he agreed with the idea and was going to wire Democratic chairman Bill Boyle at the meeting in process in Denver to that effect.

My most vivid memories of Harry Truman are of the five or six private conversations I had with him. The first was at a party the White House social aides gave in the Trumans' honor, May 1950, in ornate Anderson House.*

The president had greeted the fewer than two hundred guests when suddenly I saw him standing alone at the foot of the steps to the spacious garden. It was not considered good form in those days to crowd around a president at a party or stare at him or, if a reporter, to brandish a pen and notebook to take down everything you heard.

---

* Built by one-time ambassador to Japan Larz Anderson, it was left by his widow to the nation's oldest patriotic order, the Society of the Cincinnati, and has since been used frequently for official-filled functions.

After greeting and having a word or two with Mr. Truman, each guest had politely moved on—and there stood the head of the greatest nation in the world, with no one paying any attention to him. Manners as much as my reporter's instincts propelled me toward him.

I opened the conversation casually: "I understand you have been dieting, Mr. President," I said. He observed that he had already lost the four pounds he had gained on his last trip—with the help of his dentist, who "fixed me so I couldn't eat."

"When I succeeded President Roosevelt," he continued, "I weighed 162 pounds and in the first three months I went up to 183. My brother said I gained because I stopped worrying about becoming president."

He still didn't worry, which was why he could nap for fifteen or twenty minutes twice a day, sometimes three times, he said. He would lie down, go right to sleep, and, when awakened by his valet Prettyman, would feel completely refreshed.

How could he relax so quickly with so many world problems on his mind, I asked? He answered in picturesque style.

"The best epitaph I ever saw was on Boot Hill in Tombstone, Arizona. It said 'Here Lies Jack Williams. He Done His Damnedest.' What more can a man do?" asked Harry.

I put all that in my next day's column, sent it down to the paper, and in short order had a call from the copy desk—questioning my right to quote the president! In those days news people covering presidential press conferences were not allowed to quote the president directly. But to get direct quotes from the most important man in the country and not be able to use them? I was ready to blow my top. "Look," I said, "there are no rules about quoting a president at a social function and he didn't put anything off the record." The copy editor remained doubtful. But the quotes stayed in, and there were no repercussions.

Our next chat took place during his last months in office. It was at the June debut dance the Clark Cliffords gave for their daughter Joyce. As soon as he arrived at the Cliffords' comfortable, rambling house set in spacious grounds in Bethesda, Maryland, Truman turned dutifully to his own daughter for instructions.

"I'll do whatever you want me to," he told the apple of his eye.

Margaret wanted him to sit with her and some of her friends, but a line of would-be greeters soon formed. To avoid rising to his feet every second, he went over to the buffet table. I was standing there when he opened the conversation by observing rather sadly, "I always break up a party, so I think I'd better go home."

"Oh, no, Mr. President!" I exclaimed in sincere protest. "You ought to stay. You add glamor and interest to the party."

"It isn't I, it's the office," replied Harry truthfully. His personal popularity had been the topic of a conversation I had heard earlier that evening. I broached the subject of his running again.

"That wouldn't be right," he said. Although the new law limiting a president to two terms did not apply to Truman, who succeeded FDR only eighty-two days after the start of a new term, in a real sense it did, he said.

"Well, Mr. President," I said, inwardly thanking God that no one had come over and interrupted us, "you should have heard your courage praised tonight at the dinner party I went to. Everybody was disagreeing politically all through the meal but when the subject of your courage came up, everybody agreed immediately for the first time."

"Any man has courage when he's president," he said. "Every president makes mistakes. But what mistakes I have made were mistakes of the mind, not of the heart."

So spake the soul of Harry Truman.

Years later I heard that President Eisenhower had snubbed his predecessor during a visit to Kansas City and that Mr. Truman would include that item in the second volume of his memoirs. I called him in Independence to see if it was true. I knew there was ill feeling between the two because President-elect Eisenhower did not show retiring President Truman the traditional courtesy of going into the White House when he arrived to pick him up for their ride to the Capitol on Inauguration Day.

The rumored snub was true, confirmed Mr. Truman. President Eisenhower had been in Kansas City for three or four days in the fall of 1953. "He was stopping at the Muehlebach Hotel in the same suite I used to stay in. I called up and said I would like to call on him and pay my respects. That was what I ought to do because he was in my town. His secretary said he was too busy to see me. He said, 'His time is all taken up.' "

Mr. Truman observed, "That's something I never did to Mr. Hoover."

My story made the front page.

He talked of child-rearing during another chat in Independence, Mo., April 19, 1956, two days before Margaret's marriage to Clifton E. Daniel, Jr., which I covered for the *Star*. I asked him if he had given his daughter any advice as she embarked on marital seas.

"Margaret was raised with good advice all her life and she knows how to act," he said. "She's had good training and the reason for that is her mother. The greatest influence on a child is his mother and his Sunday school teacher and his first teachers in school." His future son-in-law didn't need any advice either. "He belongs to a good Democratic North Carolina Baptist family and, of course, that helps," he said with a twinkle in his eyes.

I had never realized before that visit what a scholar Harry Truman was. His office was lined with history books. As he walked me around the room he paused here and there before a particular volume to give me a capsule lesson. Knowledge of history was essential, he emphasized, to avoid the mistakes of the past.

* * *

A dinner cruise aboard the presidential yacht *Sequoia** was given in my honor toward the end of the Truman years, an unusual enough distinction to rate the columns of the *Miami News*. It came about because Truman's secretary of the navy Francis Matthews had been given a rough time by the press. I had always treated him kindly, and he wanted to show his gratitude.

At the end of dinner, to which some officials and personal friends had been invited, he rose and said that only the president of the

---

* The 104-foot *Sequoia* has been called the presidential yacht for decades because it was always at the disposal of the commander-in-chief. But it was actually the navy secretary's yacht from 1933 to 1977, except for the first three years of FDR's presidency and the first five months of Nixon's. Roosevelt's yacht was the 165-foot *Potomac* and modest Harry Truman's was the 244-foot *Williamsburg* that carried a crew of 125. In 1977, ex-naval officer Jimmy Carter ordered the *Sequoia* to be sold. It had been a good way to entertain visitors informally and it gave presidents a chance to get away for a few hours from their goldfish bowl without having to go all the way to Camp David.

United States could be toasted on the yacht, but he wanted to make some remarks. He made some very nice ones. Forgetting his introductory statement I promptly rose to reply and toasted him. If the others noticed my slip-up they didn't mention it.

The climax of that dinner cruise for me came as the *Sequoia* approached Mount Vernon. As George Washington's home loomed into view, the yacht's engines were silenced; as we slowly and noiselessly floated past, the boat's bell tolled in measured deliberation twenty-one times, saluting the first president of our country. Standing by the rail we were equally silent, feeling that, somehow, Washington was listening.

*   *   *

Bess Truman saw no reason to give interviews nor in any way express her opinion publicly. She would not even answer written questions. "A woman's place in public is to sit beside her husband, be silent, and be sure her hat is on straight," she once proclaimed. She let it be known at the outset that she could not possibly be like Eleanor Roosevelt. She was, in fact, a far more private person than a future First Lady who was so often described that way—Jacqueline Kennedy. For newswomen she was a letdown after Eleanor, but the average American housewife of the 1940s probably felt comfortable with Bess.

She was a no-nonsense, unemotional person who seemed brusque in the brevity of her replies. But we got along famously. She had a good sense of humor and enjoyed banter—especially about her poodle haircut. Of all the First Ladies I have known, she was the only one who really did not want to live in the White House.

Dutifully, she invited groups to tea, served as the president's hostess at official functions, and turned out for parties at the Woman's National Democratic Club or the American Newspaper Women's Club and the opening of the Washington Cathedral Mart. Her husband liked to refer to her as "the Boss" even when speaking to reporters. And he would grin when he told us—after using the word "damn"—that she would reprimand him later.

We didn't know at the time how valuable she was behind the scenes. She had helped her husband make political decisions at the

Senate where she worked in his office for an annual salary of $4,500 and earned "every cent of it," claimed Harry.

After he left the White House, Harry revealed that she had been his "chief adviser" there too.

"Why not? . . . Her judgment was always good. She never made a suggestion that wasn't for the welfare and benefit of the country and what I was trying to do. She looks at things objectively, and I can't always. . . ."

There were a limited number of places for the press in the fairly small church where Margaret and Clifton exchanged their vows in April 1956 so reporters had to draw for them. (I was told later that it had been "arranged" for me to draw an inside seat because the Trumans wanted me there.)

The day after Margaret's wedding I called on Mr. and Mrs. Truman in their home in Independence and had an enjoyable private visit. I brought up the subject of the numerous valuable gifts President Eisenhower had received at his farm in Gettysburg—gifts reported to have added up to a six-figure sum. The Trumans had been castigated by the press for what came to be known as the mink coat and deep freeze scandals.

Bess Truman said she couldn't recall the name of the woman who received the mink coat, and she hadn't known at the time where the deep freeze came from. "I didn't know until all this came out that Harry Vaughan [a major general and Truman's military aide] had gotten a deep freeze for the John Snyders [Snyder was secretary of the Treasury], the Vinsons [Chief Justice Fred Vinson] and us. I thanked someone else for it," recalled Mrs. Truman. It was an experimental model that never worked properly.

"I have a dandy one now," said Bess.

Besides, something had happened in Washington. Newer, subtler ways had been found to sway the powerful at their play.

*   *   *

After World War II America and its Capital occupied front and center on the world's stage. Up until midterm of the first administration of Ronald Reagan the party pace was a fast and furious one. During the late forties, fifties, sixties, and seventies there were several five-to-seven, later six-to-eight, embassy receptions every week. During the early decades cabinet members—even the secretary of state—and other politicos would turn up for them. Later on the wives of the secretaries of state would attend and tell the ambassador how sorry their husbands were that the pressure of business retained them at their office. Mrs. Foster Dulles, Mrs. Dean Rusk, and Mrs. William Rogers did yeoman duty taking in two or maybe three a day to keep the foreign envoys from feeling slighted. On those same days they had probably been to a "must" luncheon, possibly a meeting and/or tea, and had to rush home to change into evening dress to accompany their hard-pressed husbands to a White House, embassy, or some other official black tie dinner. The appearance of the aforementioned wives at the embassy receptions was so important to the host that when I arrived I was immediately informed with glee that she had just left or was due to arrive.

Why did secretaries of state et al push themselves to go to a dressy evening affair after such a long working day? Either because it was important not to slight the hosts, or because it offered an easy setting for a fruitful discussion, or perhaps because a good dinner, good wines, pleasant conversation, and maybe some pretty faces would help them unwind. Maybe, too, their wives wanted to go. In any case, they were simply fulfilling what, at that time, were considered the obligations of the job.

Glamorous or stiff dinners through the ages have climaxed meetings between rulers, ministers, politicians, or businessmen. Being invited to high-level dinners supplied me with gobs of material and widened my upper-level readership. I never asked if I could attend such parties. I received the customary engraved invitation because ambassadors were delighted to be seen as playing a prominent role in America's capital.

When Senator Russell Long, the impressive Democrat from Louisiana, finally retired from the Senate, he opened a law office in Washington. And framed on his wall was this sage maxim: "Entertainment is to businessmen what fertilizer is to farmers. It increases the yield." It certainly did for diplomats.

French Ambassador Herve Alphand told me some of his most important business was accomplished after six. Henri Bonnet, the first French ambassador to come to Washington after World War II, was a knowledgeable, topflight chief of mission but his super-chic Greek wife, Helle, was possibly an even better diplomat. Besides drawing the official and social cream of Washington to their receptions and dinners, she played bridge many a late afternoon with some of the powerful senators—who left their offices earlier in those days—and Chief Justice Fred Vinson, a very close friend of President Truman. Often when her husband came home from his office she could tell him more about what was happening in the U.S. government than he had learned through diplomatic channels.

Madame Bonnet played the greatest role as an ambassador's wife of any I have known. She was a lovely friend to me, enjoyed wide popularity in the city, and felt grateful to the United States for our country's tremendous help during and after the war. She held the first fundraiser for an American cause ever staged at an embassy. She and her husband gave a ball for the American Red Cross in the beautiful gray stone French residence on Kalorama Road that sits on four acres overlooking Rock Creek Park. Superbly designed for the needs of an important embassy, the thirty-four-room mansion had previously been the home of multimillionaire John Hays Hammond. The city's top drawer society eagerly paid $25 a person to attend the ball—a sum in April 1952 equivalent to at least $250 per person today for far less dazzling affairs.

Helle Bonnet never dreamed that her generous gesture would spark what has become for ambassadorial couples a burdensome epidemic of benefits for local causes that civic-minded Capitalites pressure them to stage in their mansions.

*   *   *

Early in my career I appeared on television as a guest panelist on Martha Rountree's "Leave It To The Girls," a show that began in 1945. A few years later I became a regular panelist on "The Eyes Have It," one of the earliest TV game shows. A young man with the FBI had come up with the idea of showing a fragment of a building, the full-face silhouette of a famous head, or some other clue to a famous place or person on the screen. The panel's job was to identify it. If we were stumped, more of it would be shown with some verbal clues thrown in until one of us got it. The panel consisted of former orator of the Senate Henry Ashurst of Arizona, who could quote the Bible and Shakespeare with great flair, or, occasionally, well-known economist Leon Henderson, and always anthropologist Henry Field and Betty Beale. I suppose I was included with all those wise men because I had the gift of gab. The show ran for a while during the search for a sponsor but never caught on; still, we had a ball doing it.

The pictorial quiz I remember best showed the front silhouette of a man none of us could place. Then the black of the silhouette was raised to show his chin. Senator Ashurst exclaimed triumphantly, "That's Harold Ickes! I'd know the old curmudgeon anytime." Whereupon the whole face was shown: it was Henry Ashurst. Ashurst was a master of imagery. Of the so-called mink coat scandal of the Truman administration he said, "The man in public life who accepts a gift dissolves the pearl of his independence in the vinegar of his obligation." A pity members of contemporary Congresses haven't kept that in mind!

CHAPTER 4

Grand March

Of Ike and Mamie

During the Eisenhower years, 1953–1961, Embassy Row was awash with socially active hosts who took it for granted that the best way to win the friendship of the movers and shakers in the federal government was to serve them culinary chef d'oeuvres washed down with vintage wines. Differences could more easily be ironed out in mellow surroundings and expansive moods. There, plans could be made to play golf or tennis to cultivate closer friendships, and to lobby for specific causes.

During that late postwar period, swinging dinner dances were given by Sir Roger and Lady Makins in the impressive British Embassy, by the very chic Count and Countess de Motrico at the Spanish residence, and by Peruvian Ambassador and Mrs. Fernando Berckemeyer on the twenty-five-acre, in-town estate known during the Civil War as Battery Terrill. All three had personal wealth in addition to their allowances, and all entertained elegantly. (The Berckemeyers' French meals, prepared by the former chef at Buckingham Palace, were served by footmen in gold-trimmed dark green livery.)

The formality suited the administration to a T.

Having been the wife of an army officer, and the commanding general at that, Mamie was accustomed to giving orders and having them carried out pronto. We learned through the grapevine that she, and she only—not the president—controlled everything in the mansion, down to the last detail. She had become used to running big households when Ike was head of SHAPE, and orderlies and aides were at her beck and call. They had been entertained by royalty, and she liked the royal treatment.*

The first indication of this we reporters observed was the new seating arrangement for state dinners. Instead of the first couple sitting opposite each other at the head of the U-shaped table, Mrs. Eisenhower had two throne-like chairs—distinct from all the other chairs—placed side by side at the head, with the opposite side left entirely open. It meant that all the guests could have a clear view of the regally seated couple. Having been the revered head and commander of millions, it probably seemed normal to Ike. If such a dinner plan had been proposed for the Trumans, they would have quashed it with a chuckle at its pretentiousness.

The Eisenhowers' state dinner tables were awash with the more expensive flower of the day, funereal purple orchids—of the type that adorned each ample bosom of DAR officials when those formidable women met annually in Washington—held high in vermeil epergnes spaced down the length of the tables.

Despite the formality of her entertaining style, Mamie was upbeat, even hail-fellow-well-met. She had a cheery greeting for each of the hundreds of women she received at an average afternoon reception. And she gave every indication of loving the big ladies' luncheons in her honor, where she was apt to hear saccharine songs sung to her.

Her interests were those of millions of American women of that time. She had a favorite soap opera and she loved playing bridge, mahjong, and canasta with "the girls."†

---

* "Mrs. Eisenhower was used to having soldiers jump," recalled White House seamstress Lillian Parks. "She didn't know how long it could take to fix a dress or sew drapery or anything. When she came in I made thirty-two pairs of curtains for the second floor. She thought you could do it in a few minutes. I don't think she ever did anything in her own house. But she had two sides. Every Christmas they had a party for the [domestic] staff and the president would pass out his pictures [prints of his paintings], then Mrs. Eisenhower would have a party for the women on the staff and give out personal presents. She would wrap gifts all fall and make beautiful bows. . . . She was very warm."

† They included Mary Allen, wife of Ike's intimate friend George E. (funnyman) Allen (who wrote *Presidents Who Have Known Me*), and Rosemary Silvercruys, widow of Senator Brien McMahon of Connecticut who became the wife of Belgian Ambassador Baron Silvercruys.

Mamie, of course, is best remembered for her bangs—the row of curls plastered on her forehead that fulfilled her wish to hide her high forehead but did nothing to become her face. A softer hairdo would have made her far prettier but nothing, apparently, could separate her from her idiosyncratic style, which extended to her wardrobe, too. I remember her arrival at one private party decked out in a purple dress, purple stockings, and purple shoes.

What you saw was what you got with Mamie. But Dwight D. Eisenhower's public image was very different from his private one.

If Ike had a good sense of humor it was not apparent. Yet, when he campaigned for president, most people who said they were voting for him immediately added, "I like his smile." Impressions, however flimsy, play an inordinate role in politics.

Eisenhower was often mocked by political pundits for his syntax. I went to only one of his press conferences to ask about a possible second term, and I took copious notes. But as I walked out of the Executive Office Building where they were then held, I compared notes with Count "Ziggy" de Segonzac, correspondent for *France Soir.* We discovered that neither of us had a story. It was always that way, said Ziggy. Ike had a faculty for giving logical-sounding replies, of saying a lot, but without revealing much, if anything. The columnists blamed his syntax for clouding the clarity of his statements. I think he was simply a master at camouflaging his real intentions and opinions, and used doubletalk so that the press couldn't get its teeth into any real meat.

I met the Eisenhowers right after he returned from successfully commanding the Allied Forces in Europe. I covered his and Mamie's official parties from time to time when he was army chief of staff. The invitations came from Quarters 1, Fort Myer. At the one for Field Marshal Montgomery, I met one of *my* heroes, General George C. Marshall, and was so awed by this great and humble man that for once I was tongue-tied.

I had covered John Eisenhower's marriage to Barbara Thompson in June of 1947 at Fort Monroe, Va., and I saw the general and Mamie at several of Perle Mesta's* parties. Always, I presented the

---

* Mrs. Mesta was an active Democrat then. One of the best parties of my life was the one she gave during the Democratic Convention of 1956 in Chicago. The

World War II hero and his wife to the public in the most pleasant manner, befitting well-mannered polite society at a private party dedicated to enjoyment. But of the eight presidents I wrote about fairly and factually, Eisenhower had the least warmth. He was not disdainful or rude—simply more distant and impersonal than any other president I knew, including Richard Nixon.

White House seamstress Lillian Parks, who was portrayed by actress Leslie Uggams in the NBC-TV series, "Backstairs at the White House," said President Eisenhower did not even know the names of the people who waited on him for eight whole years. "Sometimes President Eisenhower would say good night but he didn't speak much." Her recollections of his coolness and lack of personal interest confirmed my impressions. Lillian and some of the others on the staff were watching when the famed general and president-elect came to be briefed by Truman. "When he left the briefing with President Truman," said Lillian, "he was so mad his face was red."

Ike had barely learned where to hang his hat in the Casa Blanca when a story I wrote caused all hell to break loose. According to presidential custom, within a week after being inaugurated he received the chiefs of foreign missions. I was not there but my friend, the dean of the diplomatic corps, Norwegian Ambassador Wilhelm Munthe de Morgenstierne, mentioned afterwards what a pleasant surprise it was to find highballs and old-fashioneds served at an afternoon function at the White House. Former White House staffers were at a loss to remember the last occasion at which whiskey was offered in an undisguised state before eight o'clock in the evening. Until then, fruit punch with a strong bourbon base had been served; for those who pointed the finger of criticism at whiskey, of course, liquor in punch was harder to put the finger on.

No sooner had the Associated Press wired my story across the

---

glamorous dinner dance was attended by former President Truman, future Presidents Kennedy and Johnson, presidential candidate Adlai Stevenson, two vice-presidential hopefuls Senators Estes Kefauver and Hubert Humphrey, the four most famous publishers in the U.S., top columnists and the most famous commentator H.V. Kaltenborn. H.V. took off Truman taking off Kaltenborn during an impromptu show by VIPs.

country than the White House was deluged with protests. The letters that poured in for me indicated that enthusiasm for the new president had already gone down the drain. Some readers criticized me for reporting it! The upshot was that at the Eisenhowers' reception for the diplomatic corps the following November—the first white tie one in years—no liquor at all was served. Indeed, it was never served again at any Eisenhower function covered by reporters.

In March of 1953 the Post-Hall Syndicate asked me to write a weekly column which they would sell to papers around the country.*

My column grew until I had around ninety papers in the midsixties, including some of the biggest and best-known dailies. It appeared in the Sunday or Saturday editions of the out-of-town papers and, as all features for Sunday papers had to be in the Wednesday or even Tuesday before, all the news in it was anywhere from a week to two weeks old. I agonized over every one, wondering what the hinterland already knew of my choice items and what new slant to put on them so they would sound like hot scoops. I had to bolster my nerve before opening each month's financial statement that showed what papers may have dropped the column. It wasn't until Walter Lippmann told me that the addition of a new outlet or loss of one was something that happened all the time to columnists that I ceased to suffer so much.

What with all that cross-country exposure plus four columns a week in the *Star*, I gained the reputation as the authority on official doings. Heaven knows I came by it fairly! I ate out so often that my own food bill was only $15 a week.

I survived the stiff dinners either by polling the table of guests on some provocative topic or by starting a hot discussion. After all, I had a blank page waiting in my typewriter. One remark that never failed to evoke sputters in a Latin embassy was: American women

---

* Robert Hall, who headed it, soon after bought out the *New York Post* and it became the Hall Syndicate. Several years later he teamed up with Marshall Field and it became the Publishers-Hall syndicate. He eventually sold out to Field who later sold it to Rupert Murdock who later sold it to King Features. By that time, it was called North American Syndicate, the sixth name for the same syndicate.

are second class citizens. The dullest ladies' luncheon I ever attended was during a World Bank meeting when I was seated at a table with bankers' wives from countries circling the globe—from black African and European to remote Asian nations—all strangers to each other. So I asked this question of each: What one characteristic is most desirable in a husband? The conversation took wing. Whether in French, English or broken accents, their answers added up to one characteristic: Kindness.

Notwithstanding the sorry effect I had had on the new White House, when I played President Eisenhower before President Eisenhower at the Women's National Press Club's annual dinner and lampoon of Capital bigwigs, Mamie gladly cooperated in my costume needs. Unbeknownst to her husband, she lent me one of his golf jackets—a satiny, cerise job that I had to take in eight inches on both sides. The club's wire service members, eager to publicize our dinner, promptly sent out an item that I'd be wearing the real McCoy in the show, and it was carried in papers across the country.

That was in May 1953. In May 1956—the last time I impersonated him (I had been President Eisenhower just as long as he had!)—I borrowed a Burning Tree Club golf cap from a friend to wear with a sweater and the photo used by some newspapers showed him pulling my visor down to get a look at the B.T.C. insignia.

That was the last stunt dinner Ike attended. Once reelected, he didn't have to sit through any more painfully amateur press shows and pretend he loved being made fun of. So the next year I played Vice President Richard Nixon before Vice President Nixon. (It's not that I always hogged the top part. It's just that I was too tall to play the little woman, I could belt out a song, and I always generously offered to fill the most important role before anyone else could open her mouth.)

In June 1956 I met Konrad Adenauer, the man who had led a broken and defeated Germany to a respected position among civilized nations. The 80-year-old chancellor of Germany was the guest of honor at a dinner given by the first post-war German ambassador to Washington, Heinz Krekeler. After dinner I had an opportunity to have a private conversation with the big, wise leader.

What should America do to really assume the leadership of the free world, I asked?

"America is too cautious," Adenauer replied. The United States was afraid of the Soviet Union when we were so strong we had no reason to be, he said, referring to our altercations with the Russians over a divided Berlin. "You should demand something when you give money. You have given so much money to the French without asking for anything in return. That's a mistake."

"This country," I explained, "is afraid we will be accused of dictating to other sovereign nations."

"You Americans think we Europeans are always so wise and such clever people. But that is not true," he told me.

Despite his years spent in England and France, President Eisenhower was distinctly unenthusiastic about entertaining the diplomatic corps. Between November 1954 and 1958 the two dinners required for wining and dining all the chiefs of foreign missions were omitted. They were skipped in 1955 because of his heart attack. The reelection campaign was the excuse the following year. And when the traditional white tie dinners were announced in November 1957, there were none for the diplomats, only for important Americans, i.e., the vice president, the chief justice, and the Speaker.

Without naming my sources—which would have caused an ambassadorial exodus from Washington—I wrote a column expressing the ambassadors' outrage at the snub. Without that annual party they were not apt to see our chief of state during the years between their arrival when they presented their credentials and their leavetaking. In early January the diplomatic dinners were restored.

Judging by both his private and official dinners Dwight Eisenhower liked the company of big businessmen and his old army cronies. Perhaps the moneymakers had a particular glamor for him because he had lived most of his life on an army officer's pay, in days when it was far lower than it is today. The most telling example of this preference was the guest list for the Eisenhowers' state dinner in honor of Queen Elizabeth II, during her first visit as queen, and Prince Philip.

Invited to this social plum of the year were the heads of Continental Can, Coca Cola, Seagram's Whiskey, Young & Rubicam advertising, CBS, Tiffany's, and so forth. The royal pair did not meet a single celebrity in the field of literature, science, music, art, or, indeed, any of the Americans famous abroad for their cultural achievements. I wrote a column to call attention to this shocking oversight and a couple of months later, on January 19, 1958, I wrote another column to goad the White House into action.

I pointed out that in the United States, where we could not recognize our outstanding achievers by conferring knighthood as in England, we should at least invite them to our most prestigious state dinners at the nation's No. 1 residence. It would not only compliment the guest of honor, it would add immeasurable interest to the occasion.

If I were president, I wrote, I would show off to visiting heads of state such great Americans as Ernest Hemingway and William Faulkner, Helen Keller, Carl Sandburg, Aaron Copland and Leonard Bernstein, Artur Rubinstein and Isaac Stern, Robert Frost, Paul Tillich and Jacques Maritain, Edward Hopper and Mark Tobey, and Eleanor Roosevelt—to name but a few. There was an amusing offshoot to that piece. A Catholic newspaper in Missouri reprinted much of that column under a big headline: "IF BETTY BEALE WERE PRESIDENT"—causing Adlai Stevenson to remark, "You may make it before I do."

For that same dinner for Elizabeth and Philip, President Eisenhower, who loved the Waring Pennsylvanians, had them perform in the East Room after dinner. The famed choral group sang popular songs but in tribute to her majesty also sang, "God Save the Queen." Everyone stood, of course, in deference to Britain's national anthem. Then, feeling that the hostess should get equal billing, the Pennsylvanians sang to Mamie. Several people stood for that too, but sat down when they saw that others had not, just as the latter, not wishing to appear rude, popped up. This discombobulating bobbing up and down in the East Room may have been the only time such a song was accorded such reverence.

Eisenhower's cultural tastes were pedestrian—as are those of most presidents—but it was in his administration that the National Cultural Center Act came into being, the center that was named after John Kennedy following his assassination. It was also on his beat that the International Cultural Exchange, which sent our great orchestras and artists abroad, was inaugurated. Ike also called for the establishment of a federal advisory council on the arts, but the

Democratically-controlled Congress from 1955 on did nothing about it.*

On the art front, I still chuckle over the furor that erupted when Ike's cabinet members received paint-by-numbers sets at the White House. Naturally, they assumed it was Sunday-painter Ike's wish that they complete their respective pictures. I first caught wind of the grumbling at a luncheon at Secretary of the Treasury George Humphrey's house. Pamela Humphrey and a couple of other worried cabinet wives were complaining that their husbands had too much to do running their departments to spend time on those canned paintings. The upshot, they said, was that they, themselves, or their husbands' secretaries, were taking on the tasks. They couldn't understand why he would ask them to do such a thing.

To get a story on how this bizarre situation came about I called Secretary to the Cabinet Tom Stephens and discovered that the fey Irishman, himself, had handed out the sets. Inwardly tickled by his success, he obviously had let them think the capricious assignment was based on a presidential order. Six cabinet members sent their completed pictures to the White House right off. Mrs. Humphrey said she never did see the palomino's head her husband signed and returned. Stephens hung Postmaster General Arthur Summerfield's portrait of an Indian chief and Agricultural Secretary Ezra Benson's desert caravan in his office, lined the corridor with the rest of them where Ike was bound to see them, then resigned. Surrounded by that much manufactured art he probably couldn't take it any longer.

Throughout Eisenhower's two terms, I received countless phone calls from magazine writers and out-of-town reporters asking me if Mamie overindulged in the sauce. I never discovered any confirmation of that rumor, which stemmed from her occasional unsteadiness.

---

* These facts were recalled in the early sixties when all the euphoria over the Kennedys' interest in the arts got Republican Congressman Carroll Kearns' dander up. The Pennsylvania lawmaker, long promoter of national and municipal cultural projects, fired a broadside on the subject on the floor of the House and read into the *Congressional Record* my column containing material he had given me. He pointed out that President Kennedy had called for spending $10 million to rescue treasures of the Nile and had rescued Harvard Yard from development but his own artistic adviser William Walton favored the destruction of the historic buildings around Lafayette Square. In the end the Belasco Theatre was the only one destroyed.

Lillian Parks had this to say on that subject: "I'll tell you truthfully, I never knew her to drink anything. She drank Coca Colas. She'd come to the solarium to play canasta and come see me first and she never smelled of anything but perfume. She had an inner ear problem."

But she may have needed consolation of some sort. During the war, rumors were rife linking the general and his attractive British driver Kay Summersby. Mamie, three thousand miles away, unable to join her husband and probably suspecting the worst, was reported to be in very low spirits. At that time I was seeing a man who led me to think he was covertly attached to the army Counter-Intelligence Corps. One evening we were sitting in my car across from his apartment on New Hampshire Avenue when he smilingly and excitedly told me the naval officer I had just seen enter the modest apartment building was none other than the great commander-in-chief of the Allied Armies in Europe. Mamie, he said, was upstairs in his apartment waiting for a visit from her husband on this secretly arranged trip to Washington to lift her out of the depths and restore their marriage. If he had gone to their own apartment at Wardman Park he would have been recognized at once. The naval uniform was to confound anyone he might run into. The man I saw in the vestibule of the apartment perusing the mailboxes to check the name and number of the flat he was heading for had Ike's build but I never saw his face. Nor did any other occupant of the building come or go while he was in that small public passageway. If the story was true—and I had no way of checking it without breaking faith with my informer—the general was flown back to his post in London the next day.

The story that Eisenhower wanted to divorce Mamie and marry Kay Summersby was reported by Drew Pearson in his column, and over twenty-five years later confirmed by President Truman in his conversations with Merle Miller, author of *Plain Speaking*. But son John Eisenhower and others have vigorously denied it. John has quoted from his father's letters to his mother which were filled with expressions of his devotion.

But when years after the war I asked General Omar Bradley if it was true that Eisenhower had written General George Marshall asking for permission to divorce Mamie, he indicated it was.

CHAPTER 5

Camelot Conga-Line

The Kennedy Years

A month after Jack Kennedy had won the Democratic nomination for president, I went to the Capitol hideaway office of Senator Allen Ellender of Louisiana for the most power-packed small luncheon I had ever attended. There were twelve seated around the narrow rectangular table—nine men and three women. The eight male guests were the biggest wheels in the Democratic party, the sinew of the Senate. They were the future president; his vice president Lyndon Johnson, who was still the strong, perhaps the strongest ever, majority leader of the Senate; two elderly titans of the upper chamber—Richard Russell, chairman of the Armed Services Committee, and Harry Byrd, chairman of the Finance Committee; Henry ("Scoop") Jackson, chairman of the Democratic National Committee; Stuart Symington, defeated presidential candidate; George Smathers, who was to run the campaign in the South; and Frank Church, convention keynoter. The three women Ellender invited were myself, Liz Carpenter of Carpenter News Bureau, and Nancy Hanschman of NBC.

Luncheon had been cooked by the host—his specialty, shrimp gumbo. The hideaway office, with its high ceiling, chandelier, and

54

fireplace, was one of the plums of seniority. It had no number on the door, and was so well concealed that even the constantly-covered Kennedy managed to slip in unobserved. I attended several of these luncheons over the years, generally honoring a first lady or a president.

There was much political wooing of undeclared Senator Byrd, some election predictions, the usual banter enjoyed by politicians, and one comment by Jack Kennedy that encapsulated his charm. He was meeting with former President Truman the next day, he said, to seek his support. What would Truman say, someone wondered?

"I guess," said Jack quietly with a half-smile, "he will apologize for calling me an SOB, and I will apologize for being one."

The Kennedy family hit Washington like a cyclone for Jack's Inauguration. Papa Joe and Rose leased a big house at the corner of 31st and P Street in Georgetown. Youngest son Teddy and wife Joan rented a house on P Street catercornered from his parents. Jean Kennedy Smith and Stephen took a house a block away on O Street. Eunice and Pat Kennedy and their respective husbands, Sargent Shriver and Peter Lawford, rented an abode at 30th and O Streets. And the Robert Kennedys, who had their own estate across the river in McLean, Va., leased a house less than two blocks away on 30th Street for Ethel's family and their own if they should need it. The traffic in Kennedys on those two blocks resembled Washington rush hour on Friday afternoons.

By the time the Stephen Smiths threw a dinner party, three nights before the Inauguration, Washington knew that everyone who was not a Kennedy, a good friend of a Kennedy, a political asset, or a devotee of the Kennedys, would never step within the private circle. And with the Kennedys—less so with Jack and Jackie than the rest—if you were not In, you were Out.

I had known the new occupants of the White House for several years.* When Jackie returned to Washington after graduating from

---

* I had known Jackie's stepfather, Hugh D. Auchincloss, longer than she or her mother had, as he had been a close friend of my first brother-in-law Billy Mann. Hugh D.'s signature was one of those engraved on the huge sterling silver tray presented to Billy at his bachelor dinner. Hugh D.'s first wife was a Russian; his

college and became engaged to the young senator from Massachusetts, I telephoned her to get a story. I was shocked to hear
Jackie say that Jack was going to Eden Roc, Cap d'Antibes, for his
usual summer vacation. I had never before (nor have I since) known
a man who preferred to take his vacation away from the girl he had
just become engaged to. This, coupled with his reported behavior in
Cap d'Antibes, was proof to me that he was not really in love with
Jacqueline. I think his father, who had been socially rebuffed in
Boston, wanted Jack to marry a girl who would add the lustre of
class. When someone spoke of the planned marriage to Joe Kennedy, his comment was: "This is how you build a dynasty." The man
who told me that was under the impression that Joe had told Jack to
marry Jackie, but I am quite sure that Jack wanted a wife who would
grace his home, and Jackie filled the bill.

My invitation to Jack and Jackie's wedding in Newport on September 12, 1953, meant, of course, that I would cover it. The James
Van Alens of Newport then invited me and Peruvian Ambassador
and Mrs. Berckemeyer, also wedding guests, to spend that weekend
with them in their summer mansion.

At St. Mary's Church, where the marriage took place, four little
street urchins had slipped into the front pew before anyone else
arrived. No one asked them to leave although they sat with the
bride's mother and her stepfather, who gave her away. Jack Bouvier,
who was supposed to escort his daughter up the aisle, checked into a
Newport hotel but come ceremony time had had too much alcohol
to perform the task. The bride hid her disappointment.

Luckily, I was chauffeured to and from church and on to the
reception at the Auchincloss estate—luckily, because it took over
two hours for the cars bearing one thousand guests, Boston-Irish
pols to the Newport upper crust, to inch their way to the front door
of Hammersmith Farm. My story started on page 1 of the next day's

---

second wife was Nina Gore Vidal, Gore Vidal's mother, who was having an affair
with a Polish diplomat even while becoming engaged to Auchincloss; and his third
wife, Janet, had been divorced from Jack Bouvier of New York. My sister Nancy
Mann and I, who frequently encountered the Auchinclosses on the social circuit,
were invited to Lee Bouvier's marriage to her first husband, Michael Canfield, and
I had been to Lee's debut dance.

Sunday Star, and continued inside under two big pictures—one of the smiling newlyweds cutting the cake, and one of the bride dancing with former Ambassador to Great Britain Joe Kennedy.

Kennedy's inaugural festivities had barely simmered down when new press secretary Pierre Salinger announced that he would be giving out all the feminine and family news. Maybe he thought he could keep a handle on the Kennedys' image if he was the only channel. Certainly, the First Lady's press secretary, Pamela Turnure, was totally unfamiliar with the ways of the press. All such news, said Pierre, would be given out by him daily at the regular news briefings at 11:00 A.M. and 4:30 P.M. Of course, the hungry social press flocked to his first briefing, only to find that he had nothing to tell us.

Nonplussed after breaking my neck to make the downtown trek, I pressed him.

"Well," he offered limply, "the cat is arriving at five today."

"A ripple of excitement went through the room," I wrote in my next day's column, which probably did nothing to endear me to Salinger. Meaningful questions started coming fast and furiously from the alert group.

"What cat?

"Caroline's cat."

"What's its name?"

"Tom Kitten."

"What color is it?"

"I don't know."

"Is it a Maltese cat?"

"No, it's an alley cat—kitten."

"Is it a cat or a kitten?" I persevered. The nation had a right to know.

"I don't know," responded Pierre. "How can you tell?"

"If it's over forty, it's a cat," replied one woman archly.

"Which door will it use?" asked a Pulitzer prizewinner, who obviously wanted to see it come and go. (To the distress of the press, some of the new president's visitors had been slipping in and out through an unseen entrance.)

"Are they going to let it out at night? That's normal for cats, you know," I said recalling former Illinois Governor Adlai Stevenson's famous veto of the restricting "Cat Bill" because, he wrote, "It is in the nature of cats to do a certain amount of unescorted roaming."

"I don't know," responded the exasperated Salinger, fresh out of feline facts.

"How about a picture of it?"

"If you will just clear out of my office for ten minutes and let me think I'll see what I can do about it," gasped Pierre.

"This is the hottest news we've had all day," cracked a noted byline as we all trooped out of his office. A few minutes later Assistant Press Secretary Andrew Hatcher came into the press lobby to announce, "The kitten is resting. Would you mind waiting until tomorrow to see it?"

"The kitten is resting," mused a newsman. "This is the ever-living most!"

First thing the next morning the Associated Press took a picture of Pamela Turnure holding the cat, and the three-column-wide photo appeared in the *Star* beside my column. You can't say we weren't on top of the important news!

Jack Kennedy had not been president very long when the rumor was suddenly bruited about that Jackie was his second wife. An item in "The Blauvelt Family Genealogy" had been uncovered in the genealogical records of the Daughters of the American Revolution. In no time I received a copy in the mail. It stated that Durie Kerr, who took the name of her stepfather, Malcolm, first wed Firmin Desloge, IV, then F. John Bersbach, and thirdly "John F. Kennedy, son of Joseph P. Kennedy, one time Ambassador to England. There were no children of the second or third marriages." Typed beside a copy of the cover page were these comments: "It seemed that all documentary substantiation had been destroyed or suppressed. . . . Perhaps overlooked was the privately printed Blauvelt Family Genealogy."

Pierre Salinger informed all journalists that the first paper that printed the story would be slapped with $10 million libel suit. *Newsweek* subsequently came out with a long article denying the whole thing. Questioned in Palm Beach, Durie, by then married to Thomas Shevlin (ex-husband of Mrs. John Sherman Cooper), was reported as saying only, "ask the President."

It was unfortunate for me that Pierre assumed management of

press relations for both the East and West Wings of the White House. President and Mrs. Kennedy held their first diplomatic reception early in February. And I, who wrote more about diplomats both in town and across the country than any other newsperson, was not allowed to cover.

Pierre Salinger had no knowledge of Washington society and probably, at that point, had never attended an embassy function. Nor did he care how such things had been handled in the past. So instead of allowing the social press to cover this most social of all functions, he selected twelve reporters who covered hard news, six men and six women, perhaps thinking that by balancing the sexes he was being fair.

Fortunately, President Kennedy knew more about Washington, knew me, and had seen my byline four or five times a week for years. (He had been to my house as a congressman in order, believe it or not, to participate in the Pyramid Club—that money-making scheme whereby it cost you $1 to get in on the ground floor, but when your name reached the peak of the pyramid of names, others' dollars rolled in. Whether the son of the megamillionaire was in need of a few bucks or thought he might meet some young eyefuls at the gathering is anybody's guess.)

Jack also knew the value of a favorable press—which, heaven knows, I gave him.

When he came to Texas Representative and Mrs. Clark Thompson's party for Speaker Sam Rayburn to do honor to this important man whose cooperation he would need, he walked through the crowd of guests greeting familiar ones along the way. When he spoke to me I started to say something, then thought better of it.

"What were you going to say?" asked Kennedy, who had a strong streak of curiosity. At that I leaned forward and whispered in his ear, "I am not being allowed to cover your diplomatic reception."

"Why not?" he asked in surprise.

"I don't know."

I left that party with my beau, Missouri Congressman Bill Hull, to go to dinner. When I returned home to write my column about the event (I thought nothing of working till 2 or 3:00 A.M. in those days) Pierre Salinger had called five times. I telephoned him at once.

Sounding annoyed, he told me I could cover this reception this one time—meaning, obviously, that I couldn't count on covering White House functions in the future. No doubt adding fuel to his anger was this item in *Newsweek*'s "Periscope" in the February 20 issue: "Never underestimate the power of a woman reporter. On a personal appeal from *Washington Star* society columnist Betty Beale, who buttonholed him at a party, JFK overruled Press Secretary Pierre Salinger on coverage of the Kennedy's first diplomatic reception . . ." My syndicate was so delighted with the mention that it sent reprints around, including a batch to me suggesting I might have fun handing them out to press club friends. Of course, I did nothing of the kind.

From then on Salinger made difficulties for me in covering the White House for my syndicate. If I wasn't reporting for the *Star* I could not get in. It wasn't until Mrs. Kennedy made some complimentary remarks to me about seeing my column in numerous cities that I wrote to her and asked if I could be accredited to the White House on behalf of my syndicate because the whole country was so eager for news about her and the president. She gave orders that I should be allowed to cover everything from then on.

Pierre Salinger was to get his revenge later.

The Kennedys introduced a glowing new ambiance in the White House. They destarched it—beginning with their first official party on the Sunday following Inauguration Day. My *Star* column the day after tells the story:

"President and Mrs. Kennedy's first White House party was a precedent-shattering, thoroughly relaxed affair. To begin with, it was given on Sunday afternoon, and nobody seems to recall when the last Sunday party was held at 1600 Pennsylvania Avenue.

"Next, it was the first such big party for new presidential appointees that the press ever knew about or, at least, was invited to.

"Also, it was the first time that a barrage of photographers functioned in the East Room.

"It was the first time in many years that guests waiting to be received were not lined up four abreast and kept that way either in the East Room or in the corridor below.

"It was the first time that the press covering the function and the invited guests were allowed to mingle in one big cozy group before the reception began.

"It was the first time this reporter remembers seeing any ashtrays available at a reception, though I did not see anyone smoking.

"It was the first time I recall seeing anything besides cakes, cookies and party sandwiches on the buffet table. This time there were fresh shrimp, raw celery and cauliflower with a mustard dip, cocktail canapes and tiny hot cheese patties, in addition to the cakes and sandwiches.

"And it was the first time any of us had ever seen a bar in the Executive Mansion.*

"Obviously, President and Mrs. Kennedy have decided that they are going to offer the same hospitality to their guests when reporters are present as they would naturally do if they weren't, or if they were living back in their house on N Street." In addition to the buffet in the State Dining Room, I wrote, "there was a table bearing champagne [domestic] on ice, Coca Cola, tomato juice, martini glasses with olives waiting to float, and highball glasses beside bottles of scotch, bourbon and vodka.

"Naturalness was the keynote of this party. It differed in atmosphere from previous White House receptions about as much as a proper embassy party differs from a military drill."

Gone were the regimentation, rules, and ropes that had prevailed in their predecessors' eras. Alice Longworth told me that when she lit a cigarette in the East Room during the Eisenhower regime, a uniformed social aide approached and said no smoking was allowed in the East Room. To which she replied with a withering look, "Young man, I *learned* to smoke in this room."

The new presidential pair were unpredictable. He dropped in at a dinner Frank Sinatra was having for the Inaugural Gala performers before he and Jackie went to the Inaugural Balls. She, still not strong after the Caesarean birth of little John, retired after two of them but JFK went to all five, leaving the last at 1:50 A.M. and then going to

---

* No cries of outrage this time, as when Eisenhower served highballs. Either Republican voters insisted on more purity in their president than did Democrats, or the liberal press didn't spread the story around this time.

columnist Joseph Alsop's house for another party.* His intimate friends never knew when he might pop in just for the fun of it. A week after he was sworn in he walked unheralded across Lafayette Square to Decatur House, the eighteenth-century residence of Stephen Decatur now owned by the National Trust for Historic Preservation. The butler's thirteen-year-old daughter was putting out the lights when the doorbell rang at 5:00 P.M. When she opened it, there stood the president. The president of the National Trust, Bob Garvey, had invited Kennedy that day, but had been told by his staff that it was out of the question. They neglected to tell their boss.

Jackie, having leased the Middleburg estate of Mrs. Raymond Tartiere, started riding to the hounds again as soon as she felt strong enough. And she immediately dispensed with Secret Service protection when hunting. The chief of the service said the law required protection of the president and his immediate family, but "immediate family" was defined by the president.

The freedom of action coupled with the glamor of the young, rich, good-looking, and stylish couple captivated the nation. Suddenly, Washington, instead of Hollywood, was the focus of gossip columns and magazine articles from New York to the west coast.

The Kennedys' first official evening reception—a white tie affair for the Congress—was held at 10:00 P.M., April 18, 1961. My column the next day reported it thus:

"President and Mrs. Kennedy led the dancing onto the ballroom floor of the White House last night at what turned out to be the liveliest and most gracious presidential reception in fully two decades.

"The precedent-shattering pair dispensed with the receiving line and with it the hour-long wait White House guests had previously endured. As Texas Representative George Mahon's wife said, 'The last time we were here everyone stood in line, row after row after row and stood and stood.'

"Republicans as well as Democrats were lavish in their praise of the new system. When they arrived at the White House and found that they were free to go upstairs and into any room on the first floor

---

* It was rumored in Washington that Kennedy used Alsop's house as a place for assignations.

they were amazed. No doors were closed, no ropes up, no aides barred the way. No one told anyone to go in one direction and not another.

"It was the first time this reporter and her colleagues had ever seen an official white tie reception there where everyone was free to make himself at home in any room he chose on the official floor. The only time anyone was asked to stand back was when President and Mrs. Kennedy made their entrance and a path had to be cleared."

At 10:15, when all the rooms were well filled with familiar Capitol Hill figures, President Kennedy and his First Lady, her white-gloved hand resting in queenly fashion on his right forearm, descended the stairs followed by Vice President and Mrs. Lyndon Baines Johnson, Speaker Sam Rayburn, and Senate and House leaders. Jackie wore a bateau-necked, sleeveless, floor-length sheath of pink and white printed straw lace, above-elbow white kid gloves, and one piece of jewelry—a feather-shaped diamond clip in her dark bouffant locks. When the procession paused at the edge of the corridor, the nineteen-piece formal Marine Band burst into a fanfare, followed by "Hail to the Chief," at which the handsome young couple proceeded into the Blue Room.

After they had passed through the other rooms and entered the East Room, the dance Marine Band began to play "Mr. Wonderful." The Johnsons followed the Kennedys onto the dance floor and after a few steps they exchanged partners. Said Jackie with an impish look as she started twirling with the faster moving vice president, "Oh, I am getting a much better dancer." The president then "told his audience, 'Dance!' . . . they followed this order with a lot more alacrity," I wrote, "than they have passed his legislation." Kennedy, never a dancer, then stood at one end of the ballroom greeting more of his nine hundred guests while one cabinet officer after another claimed Jackie for a dance.

Not only were there ashtrays in the various rooms, but there was an innovation in the East Room: a long, flower-trimmed table bearing two bowls of punch, an orange juice punch, and a champagne punch. In the State Dining Room was the most complete and varied buffet served at any official evening reception since Woodrow Wilson's time at least. White House footman John Pye, who had joined the domestic staff in 1916, testified to that. The buffet consisted of four hot tureens of chicken à la king with rice, platters of artistically rolled slices of cold roast beef, pheasant, tongue, turkey, ham, salami, galantine of pheasant ornamented with birds in full plumage, galantine of beef, sliced pumpernickel bread, sandwiches, cookies, and cakes. Even ice water was elegantly ladled from a big gold bowl into punch glasses.

By 11:50 the Kennedys had retired to the second floor where the Johnsons joined them for a nightcap. The orchestra played until twenty minutes past midnight.

That was the routine for their official parties. Their private ones were another story. Those lasted till 3:00 or 4:00 in the morning and drew such Beautiful People as Italy's Fiat tycoon Gianni Agnelli and his wife and the John Jacob Astors of New York. The president and First Lady gave two their first year for Jackie's sister Lee Radziwill and her husband, a rich Polish prince. Washingtonians invited to these were the envy of the town—at least honorary members of the inner circle—and adopted a comical air of smugness.

It was a White House dance the following year, for Stephen and Jean Kennedy Smith, that earned me a dig in *Time* magazine.

I had learned and promptly written that Jacqueline Kennedy had danced the twist, the hip-wriggling craze of the early 1960s, with Secretary of Defense Robert McNamara. "Anyone who still has any misgivings about the current dance simply hasn't seen it done the way Mrs. Kennedy, who looked lovely in a long white satin sheath, and Secretary McNamara, frequently called 'The Brain' of the cabinet, performed it," I wrote. "It was rhythmic, fun and peppy and more restrained than the good old Charleston which doesn't seem to shock anyone." I took such care presenting it in the right light that you might have thought I was describing the minuet.

Yet, three months later *Time*'s story on the "New Frontier's New Order" reported, "The *Washington Star*'s veteran society columnist Betty Beale is in deep disfavor; she once wrote that Jackie had done the twist, and nowadays any New Frontiersman who gets over-mentioned in her column is likely to be left off the next guest list."

The statement was absurd on the face of it. Nothing had changed, either in my access to the White House or the pleasant manner of the First Couple toward me. I called *Time*'s bureau chief to ask where the magazine got such a cockeyed idea. John Steele told me that he knew it was true: it had come from the White House. Certainly not from Jackie, I told him, because the day the item came out I was at a White House military reception, and the instant Jackie saw me she said, "Betty, I saw the article in *Time* and it isn't true; it simply isn't true."

It seemed obvious: Pierre Salinger was getting his revenge—trying to cut me out in print, if not in fact. Of course, it didn't work.

Adding to the aura of a swinging, chic social life that now permeated the Capital were the Robert Kennedys' big poolside dinner dances at their McLean, Va., estate. Ethel, now the No. 1 hostess after Jackie, was famous for doing the unexpected—from pushing fully clothed people into the swimming pool to releasing a chicken on a dinner table in a darkened room. Their most famous party—which I spread around the world—took place in the summer of 1962. It was for Peter and Pat Lawford. No social press was invited, although a dozen newspeople were present. But after calling several of the three hundred guests I pieced together these facts:

"One, John Glenn bears a charmed life; two, Ethel Kennedy likes to live dangerously; and three, poolsmanship is an integral part of Hickory Hill ... Perched on the middle of a plank that stretched across the pool was a separate small table with three chairs around it—one for the hostess, one for Astronaut Glenn and one, it was said, for Justice Byron White, although he never sat there. With the chair legs about three inches from the edge of the plank it was bound to happen, but it didn't happen to our boy Glenn. He, who remained dry after orbiting through space and landing in the ocean in his capsule, had no difficulty apparently staying topside. It was his hostess who fell in, evening dress, shoes and all."

Before the evening was over Ethel had pushed Arthur Schlesinger into the drink in his impeccable light blue dinner jacket, and also her good friend Sarah Davis who endured during those years several dunkings in her beautiful evening gowns before their friendship cooled.

Though I warned the *Star* I had a scoop, and my story was headlined "Poolmanship at Hickory Hill," it wasn't even carried on the front page of my section, nor was it promoted anywhere. It ended up on page 5 of the section. But such highjinks at the attorney general's bash were instantly picked up by the wire services. They blazed next day on front pages from New York to Rome to China.

On July 6, *Time* wrote another, longer piece on me, under the title "Social Snooping." It distressed me to the point of tears and caused my father to pace the floor in shame at having his daughter so inelegantly described. It read: "The scoop was typical of a style official Washington has ruefully come to know. Betty Beale is nosy, pushy and blunt. She snoops. She pries. Society is scared stiff to be noticed in her column, because mention once too often brings prompt exclusion from the nation's most elegant salons—the White House especially. She behaves like a police reporter, thinks like an editorial writer, and, as a perfectly natural result, she is easily the best society reporter in town—and in the country." *U.S. News and World Report* devoted a page to me and my story. But I was still smarting over *Time*'s digs when some newswomen, including UPI's Helen Thomas, told me I should be thrilled by the accolade. Happily, it had no effect on the people I covered.

Two or three newsmen congratulated me on having the courage to write about "poolmanship." Bobby Kennedy, they implied, was not one to mess around with, and my article had revealed behavior ill-befitting a high government official. For my part, I was shocked to learn they thought it took courage to write something Bobby might not like.

I never knew Bobby or Ethel well. They were too involved in their own activities to frequent the party circuit, and I saw them at only a couple of private parties. One was a memorable dinner dance in honor of Prince Bernhard of the Netherlands, given on Maryland's Eastern Shore by Madelin Gilpatric and husband Roswell, deputy secretary of defense. Hawaiian musicians and dancers entertained. Not to be outdone, French Ambassador Herve Alphand, always in demand in the Capital's drawing rooms for his mimicry, did an exhibition hula with Margie McNamara, wife of the secretary of defense. At one point in the evening, Bobby was sitting on the floor next to one of the Hawaiian dancers, putting his hand up her skirt. That was the only example of tastelessness at that fun party.

In the fall of 1961, director Otto Preminger brought the filming of *Advise and Consent* into the town's new jazzed-up atmosphere. Accepting the invitation to appear in the famous party scene were such well knowns as Senator "Scoop" Jackson, Deputy UN Ambassador and Mrs. Jerry Wadsworth, the president's air aide Colonel Godfrey McHugh, the First Lady's press secretary Pamela Turnure, Gwen and Morris Cafritz, and the book's author, Allen Drury. We all showed up in our best evening attire at Tregaron, the former mansion of Marjorie Post and the late Joseph E. Davies, to be bossed around for hours by the renowned Preminger. All were happy to make their Hollywood debut and see stars Gene Tierney and Peter Lawford at work; and besides, each extra's $25 to $50 pay went to the Washington Hospital Center.

Preminger, who suffered no nonsense, made us stand, mingle, or dance for hours, repeating one scene over eighteen times! When, during a lull, I stepped off the spot assigned to me to ask Peter Lawford a question, I got a calling-down that sent me back— giggling, but pronto. (In the finished film the glimpse of me was so brief that if you blinked or sneezed you obliterated me entirely.)

At about the same time, there was much ado in Washington's exclusive clubs. Incredible as it seems, Kennedy's name was dropped from the waiting list of the high-brow Cosmos Club when he was president.*

It was George Lodge, outgoing assistant secretary of labor for international affairs and son of future Senator Henry Cabot Lodge, who precipitated the citywide club crisis. He took his designated successor at Labor, George Weaver, a black, to the exclusive, all-male Metropolitan Club for lunch. At the time, it was against the rules of the club to bring any guest who was not eligible for membership.

Weaver had warned him that it wouldn't work.

But George Lodge, the liberal member of his Republican family, was told to go ahead and do it if he wanted to test the rule. Several members came over to his table during lunch to show their support and shake hands with Weaver, but Lodge later received a reprimand from the club. (It turned out that Arthur Krock, noted *New York*

---

* In Palm Beach, the only club where Jack Kennedy was allowed to play golf was the Palm Beach Country Club where, he told me with a smile, he was the only gentile. He could play there because his father was a member; it was the only club that had invited his father to join.

Times columnist and a Jew who, himself, had difficulty joining Newport's exclusive Bailey's Beach, was the one most opposed to opening the door to blacks.)

Bobby Kennedy promptly resigned and announced why. The hornet's nest he stirred up stung the Cosmos Club* as well; it had recently turned down black columnist Carl Rowan. Prominent liberal economist and ambassador to India Kenneth Galbraith immediately resigned from the Cosmos Club. President Kennedy had been on the Cosmos waiting list for nine months and his proposer for membership was Galbraith. Privately, JFK had wondered why he had to wait that long; presidents were usually taken into clubs without any to-do.

In any event, his name was due to come up at the next meeting of the admissions board, but as soon as his proposer resigned it was removed from the list, so Kennedy never got in.

I wrote in my column that if the president, as a result of Bobby's public remarks, could not belong to a segregated club, he would have to give up his membership in the Hyannisport Club, where he played golf in the summer, and he might also feel obligated not to play at any segregated club, which would include his father's in Palm Beach.

"There is not any club on any level of society which is not segregated in one way or another," I wrote at the time. "The meaning of the word segregate is to set apart, separate, select, which is how a club is formed. The privilege of forming such groups on the basis of compatibility and mutual interests is one of the rights of free citizens."

It is my belief, though, that famed black statesman Dr. Ralph Bunche would have sailed into the Cosmos Club without any opposition at that time, even though it turned down one of every three (white) men proposed. But a columnist, such as Carl Rowan, can arouse antagonism in several quarters.

At a joint reception African chiefs of mission (excepting only South Africa's ambassador) gave for President Bourguiba of Tunisia in the spring of 1961, I asked a black African envoy what he thought

---

* Unlike the social Metropolitan Club, the Cosmos chooses its members on the basis of intellectual achievements.

of the suggestion that the Metropolitan Club take in black ambassadors. His reply: "I never thought a private club should take in anybody because of their official position. It is a question that is determined purely on a personal basis. We don't take in every official in our private clubs. Not all would want to join."

That envoy and his colleagues, incidentally, complained of being lonely in Washington.

"We expected to be welcomed with open arms by the colored population of Washington," one of them told me; no such thing had occurred, even though, he said, "We are more inclined to speak freely with the colored group than with the white."

"Some of the white people are now inviting us to their homes," he continued. "They are people who have visited our respective countries or who are interested in them. It's just beginning to be this way. Before, even if they did invite you they never had their wives and daughters around, and now they not only have their wives and daughters around, but they bring them to your home. Another thing, we are now being invited by you newspaper people," he added with a smile, mentioning the Walter Lippmann postinaugural reception which had been attended by the Weavers.

"I don't think color has anything to do with it," said a prominent Washington hostess. "The Weavers are charming people and interesting to talk to."

* * *

Until the Kennedys occupied the White House, all formal evening functions were full dress, white tie affairs. Even when Nikita Khrushchev wore a business suit to the Eisenhowers' dinner in his honor to flaunt his image as a man of the people, Ike appeared resplendent in white tie.

It was the fashion-conscious rich John Kennedy who announced that his second evening reception for the Congress on April 10, 1962, would be black tie. Most members of Congress, he knew, balked at getting into white tie and tails which they had to rent and which, heaven knows, were generally so ill-fitting they looked ludicrous. (When Lyndon Johnson became president he proscribed black tie for all such occasions, saying, "I don't want to dress like the waiters.")

The handsome, gold-crested invitations with "Black Tie" engraved in the lower lefthand corner were no sooner out than telephone wires began to burn.

Some senators' wives were upset over the informal garb which Adrian Tolley, a social office staffer from 1915 to 1960, said had never before been worn at the White House for formal parties in cool weather. When President Kennedy saw me at that party he asked me if one of the objectors was Lorraine Cooper, wife of Republican Senator John Sherman Cooper and a prominent hostess who had entertained the Kennedys at dinner. I told him truthfully, "No." But again, I was amused by his curiosity.

The Kennedys' state dinners were so stunning that friends invited to their private parties sometimes wished they were on the official list instead. In April of '62 there was one dazzling night when the shah and empress of Iran came to dinner; Farah topped her jewel-encrusted gold gown with a crown studded with emeralds the size of jumbo olives and enormous diamonds, varying in size from five to thirty carats. I asked. "Is the crown heavy, your majesty?"

"Yes," she replied, "but I have put cotton and velvet underneath it so it is comfortable."

On the heels of this royal visit came another. The duke and duchess of Windsor popped into Washington to visit her nonogenarian "Aunt Bessie" Merryman. Hostess Gwendolyn Cafritz had asked British Ambassador and Lady Ormsby-Gore sometime earlier what night she could give a dinner for them. A date was finally set, but when the time drew near Cissie Ormsby-Gore called to ask if she could bring the Windsors who, she had just learned, would be their houseguests. Gwen, who almost swooned with delight at such a windfall, promptly sent out two hundred more invitations for an after-dinner party in honor of the duke and duchess of Windsor. If a hostess is going to have that big an attraction she might as well make points with two hundred instead of just twenty. The duke, who watched some couples do the twist in the Cafritz's "nightclub" after dinner, impishly tried to do it with Wallis but she quickly stopped him. It was the commoner, not the royal, who was concerned about appearances.

Also that month was the dinner—the first of its kind in White

House history—for forty-eight Nobel Prizewinners: President Kennedy called it "the most extraordinary collection of talent, of human knowledge, that has ever been gathered together at the White House—with the possible exception of when Thomas Jefferson dined alone."

I found myself mingling with Pearl Buck, Robert Frost, Robert Oppenheimer, Reinhold Niebuhr, Linus Pauling, Alexis Leger, John Dos Passos, Katharine Ann Porter, Van Wyck Brooks, and dozens more. Film star Frederic March entertained the 175 guests with readings from Sinclair Lewis, the Marshall Plan speech, and an unpublished work of Ernest Hemingway whose widow was present. It was heady stuff—but not more so than the next dinner, a few days later, for French Minister of Culture André Malraux. This produced Tennessee Williams, Charles and Anne Morrow Lindbergh, Arthur Miller, Julie Harris, Isaac Stern, Leonard Bernstein, John Hersey, Thornton Wilder, Robert Lowell, Saul Bellow, George Balanchine, Mark Rothko, Paddy Chayefsky, Archibald MacLeish, S.N. Behrman, Geraldine Page, and Irwin Shaw.

JFK was so young that more than once at the White House, when I suddenly turned around to come face to face with him, I simply said, "Hi." I would quickly recover: "Oh excuse me, Mr. President."

Despite Jack Kennedy's shocking private life and his own limited cultural tastes, he cared deeply about appearances. He never once allowed a photograph of himself in a Texas hat or Indian headdress; it didn't conform to his presidential image. He no sooner became president than newspapers were informed that he should be referred to as John Kennedy, never Jack, even though President Eisenhower, many years his senior, was referred to as Ike.

Later, the press would refer to Nixon's imperial presidency. But except for the snappy white uniforms planned for the White House security men—which were laughed out of existence—Nixon added nothing to the pomp and ceremony of Kennedy's White House.

According to JFK's own naval aide, Rear Admiral Tazewell Shepard, the president was so impressed with the appearance of French soldiers lining both sides of the seven-mile route from Paris to Versailles when he rode with De Gaulle that he began the custom of stationing soldiers along the driveway on the White House grounds for the arrival of a chief of state. He also had them posted along the walkway from the dock at Mount Vernon to George Washington's mansion when he and Jackie gave a dinner there in honor of Pakistan's President Ayub Khan. He had the Marine Corps' crack drill team jacked up to add class. And when he and Jackie celebrated the unveiling of the Mona Lisa at the National Gallery of Art, a cordon of Marines flanked two gallery entrances and two Marine sergeants stood beside the painting that received the honors generally accorded a chief of state.

A profoundly moving event was the White House gathering on the South Lawn to honor those who had won America's highest decoration—235 men entitled to wear the light blue, star-dotted ribbons of the Congressional Medal of Honor.

They had come from as far away as Vietnam and Korea; all had won the medal for acts above and beyond the call of duty, as far back as the Philippine insurrection and World War I. The respect for their valor was so palpable that no man without the medal, not even the president or secretary of defense, could feel superior to the chief warrant officer with one on his breast.

We had new American heroes too, like Major Gordon Cooper and the Project Mercury astronauts. I went to NASA Administrator and Mrs. James Webb's cocktail party for them. "Gordo" Cooper turned out to be the most relaxed man I have ever met. He couldn't remember ever feeling tense. This prompted Walter Lippmann to ask me how I would like to have Cooper's nerves. "I would love it!" I exclaimed. "Then you couldn't write a column," said Walter, who was even loath to go up in an airplane. Cooper only laughed when rocketeer Wernher Von Braun told him the question a reporter once put to John Glenn: "How does it feel to be out there whirling around in space in a capsule?" Glenn replied, "Well, how does it feel when your life depends on 150,000 parts purchased from the lowest bidder?"

To environmentalists who cried that the billions spent on space projects should be used instead to clean up the earth, Von Braun had this reply: "If Christopher Columbus's voyage to America had been postponed until the Spanish harbor was cleaned up, America would never have been discovered."

With all the rave notices Jack and Jackie enjoyed, two announcements came as a shock in February of 1963: The first was the news that their social secretary Tish Baldrige was leaving. As most people thought supervising the glamorous events at the White House for the most glamorous couple ever to reside there was the *ne plus ultra* in jobs, it was immediately assumed Tish had been fired. And as she had always been praised to the skies for her energy, efficiency, and taste by former employers Ambassador to Italy Clare Boothe Luce and Evangeline Bruce, wife of envoy David Bruce, the guess was that her open personality had clashed with the very private person she worked for. Some years later Tish told me that she had wanted to leave a year earlier but President Kennedy had persuaded her to stay on. The fact was, she said, she was working seven days a week for $15,000 a year. She was just plain tired, and Papa Joe Kennedy had offered her a job at his Merchandise Mart in Chicago.

The other shock came from my nemesis Pierre Salinger: He announced that thenceforth, those reporting on the social functions would be allowed to remain at receptions only long enough to watch the guests arrive from a distance and witness the descent down the stairs of the presidential party. A storm of protest erupted. By the next afternoon, when the diplomatic reception took place, the ruling had been rescinded; we were allowed to mingle with the guests as usual. From the outset the Kennedys had made the social press feel welcome, inviting us to have coffee with the guests, and allowing us to enter the ballroom with them. The Eisenhowers had required us to wait in the front hall as their guests marched, two by two, from the Green Room down the corridor to the East Room; of course, when we stood in the corridor to see them go by, the ambassadors who knew us personally would stop to shake hands. This held up the entire line, including President and Mrs. Eisenhower, so we were asked to watch from the other side of the columns between the corridor and front hall which got the hackles up on some of the other reporters.

JFK was the first president to bring his guest of honor—on that occasion President Prado of Peru—over to a group of newswomen to introduce each one of us. The pro-Kennedy stories across the country soared after that. I wrote that if the Kennedys "could count on receiving from political reporters, columnists and feature writers the kind of press they have received from social reporters they would have nothing to worry about."

So why that sudden, if briefly maintained, ban? Apparently, *Star* reporter Daisy Davidson Cleveland was overheard asking Mrs. William Randolph Hearst something at the last White House affair that a staffer, or perhaps Jackie herself, thought too personal. The White House did not know that Daisy and "Bootsie" Hearst were old friends, nor that Daisy's mother, the late Betty Hanna Davidson, Cleveland heiress, had been one of the social leaders of Washington—daughter of Mark Hanna, the wealthy Ohio industrialist and a power in the Senate. She also, oddly enough, was a direct descendant of Samuel Davidson, who sold some of the White House property to the Federal City and then built the Georgetown showplace, Evermay.

Because Pierre had called the clampdown a return to the custom of the Eisenhower administration, I devoted my following Sunday column to setting the record straight. We had not only covered all of Ike and Mamie's traditional official receptions, but we had received engraved invitations to them. In fact, said longtime *Star* writer Katharine Brooks, she knew from her mother, Mrs. Hobart Brooks, who began her social reporting at the White House during William McKinley's term, that chroniclers of the official receptions were always treated as guests. When the Kennedys dispensed with the custom of sending us invitations, Evelyn Peyton Gordon, who wrote for years for the *Washington Daily News*, told me she would not go unless invited. Although she continued her daily column, she thereafter ignored the functions at 1600 Pennsylvania Avenue, devoting her prose almost entirely to diplomatic doings. I wound up my column saying, "All the worry about social coverage that seems to come up in almost every new administration is for naught. People . . . will talk about the hot topics of the day whether they are gathered for a levee of Louis XIV or an inaugural of Abraham Lincoln.

"This is what you expect in the kind of sophisticated society that surrounds a chief of government. This is what gives to history social, political and personal color. We are simply chronicling the manners, customs and personalities of our times, and it is unthinkable that this chronicling should be eliminated at our 'court,' the drawing rooms of the president of the United States."

The day after this column appeared I received a phone call from

Walter Heller, Kennedy's chief economic adviser and a warm and lovely man. He thought I would like to know, he said, that at a meeting with the president and others that morning my column was brought up and the president agreed that there should be no ban on social reporting. It was characteristic of Walter's considerate attitude toward people that he made that call when he was under no obligation to do so.

Jack Kennedy could derive some enjoyment from his own state dinners. But he had no desire to go to the visiting chief of state's customary return dinner at the country's embassy. In the crowded, sometimes hot residences of foreign ambassadors, he could not control his departure time, much of the guest list, whom he could have at his table and whom he talked to. The visiting man's wife, rarely a desirable dish, had to be seated next to him at dinner.

He established a new pattern for such visits in February of 1963, following his dinner for King Sri Savang Vathana of Laos. He streamlined his return courtesy by substituting a 6:00 P.M. reception for the usual dinner. In this manner, he could get his diplomatic duty over by 6:45 when the entire ambassadorial corps (whom chiefs of state always received in those days) was due. Other guests were received by the Laotian king and his envoy in the embassy* between seven and nine o'clock. Kennedy set a welcome precedent for his successors.

Although President Kennedy received kudos on his cultural tastes, based on the famous concert in the East Room by the world's great cellist Pablo Casals, neither he nor Jackie really cared for long-haired music. Jack preferred movies, sometimes watching two in succession.† When violinist Isaac Stern, pianist Eugene Istomin, and cellist Leonard Rose provided the entertainment for a dinner honoring French Cultural Minister André Malraux, Stern had been

---

* The house, at 2222 S St N.W., had formerly belonged to Mrs. Dwight Davis of Davis Cup fame.

† JFK was a fan of Ian Fleming's 007 books. The first question he asked the CIA was: "How real is all this?" There was plenty of substance to it, he was told. "What about SMERSH?" he asked. The answer: Something like that was the name for the Soviet murder organization whose function was to eliminate foreign spies and counterspies.

told to play only one movement of the Ravel Trio for an encore. But after one look at Kennedy's face, no encore at all was played.

The East Room, with its magnificent crystal chandeliers highlighting the jewels and gowns of the women and the starched white shirt fronts of the men's full dress attire, looked marvelously elegant on those occasions. But everything was not always as it seemed. The night of the Casals concert, composer Norman Dello Joio's wife was listening entranced to the angelic music when she glanced down and saw a large cockroach crawling across her lap. Her instinct was to brush it off with the paper program as quickly as possible but she instantly rejected that idea. She was seated directly behind President Kennedy and was afraid it would land on his coattails or on a front row gown. It would never do to have an embarrassing break in the hushed atmosphere. So, with the inner control demanded in a polished society, she watched with horror as the verminous object crawled across her lap and down the side of her dress to the floor below.

She did not know it, but the incident was immortalized by the picture carried in the White House Guide Book. It doesn't show the White House cucaracha, but plainly visible is the woman directly behind JFK. Instead of head up and eyes front, like everyone else, she is gazing fixedly down at her lap.

*   *   *

Much has been written in recent years about Jack's promiscuity. But care was taken to keep it sub rosa at the time. David Susskind told me, when I appeared on his TV show, that he knew two women in New York who had each flown to Washington for a cozy session with the president. One told him how it was arranged. She would come down two hours before the rendezvous and go to the Georgetown house of a bachelor friend of JFK, entering unseen through the garden in the rear. Knowing of the friendship, neighbors did not suspect hanky-panky when Kennedy and the Secret Service arrived. When the rendezvous was over, the New York charmer would linger for maybe another hour before slipping out.

Clare Boothe Luce told me that Jack once told her he "could not get through the day without going to bed with a woman or he went all to pieces psychologically." Clare used to refer to Camelot as came-a-lot!

And Kennedy once asked her, "Why did you become a Catholic? I have this burden on my back, but I was born into it."

People have wondered how a president can get away with extramarital exploits when the Secret Service is always with him. The answer is that they make it possible for him to have his fun and games, without his wife showing up unexpectedly. They are a cordon of protection around the room he is in, constantly in contact with all agents guarding all other members of the immediate family. The wife's agents keep his agents informed about when she is en route home and when she will arrive. That information, I discovered when visiting Counsellor to the President Bob Hartman's office during the Ford administration, is also flashed onto an electronic screen in the senior aides' offices. What other husbands have that kind of protection? The Secret Service can be trusted to keep such titillating tidbits to themselves, but they can slip out accidentally. A member of the State Department overheard one Secret Serviceman telling another that he had to go pick up a certain young woman for JFK, using the code name for the girl; she worked in the White House, but not on the president's staff.

The combination of power and glamor in the White House had so heightened interest in the social life of Washington that the *Star*'s television station, WMAL-TV, decided to do a half-hour special on me. A camera crew and director trailed me on my nightly partying for two or three weeks in June. The show ran Sunday evening, July 7. The *Star*'s TV magazine devoted a page to it under the title "Betty's Beat" with a picture of me talking to Vice President Johnson in Representative and Mrs. Homer Thornberry's garden. It was extremely flattering, but more important, it contradicted the then widespread belief that the society beat was a picnic.

"Washington viewers," it read, "will get a chance to see how the top reporter of the Nation's No. 1 society beat goes about getting stories for her widely syndicated column . . . Ron van Nostrand, the writer-director-editor of the half-hour special, says ruefully that he lost weight and sleep and has the 'makings of a beautiful ulcer' from trying to keep up with her."

Afterwards the *Star*'s Bernie Harrison praised the "caliber of the documentary," said I added sparkle, and wound up stating that it covered a "surprising slice of Washington society, and if the pace seemed hectic enough for a team of writers," it was nevertheless the picture "of a happy gal at work." That was certainly true.

*   *   *

Less than two weeks before tragedy struck the White House and the nation, the most successful benefit ball of the decade was held at the Sheraton Park. Every year, the International Ball on the night of the International Race at the Laurel, Md., track had been graced by performances of top stars. But none equaled the chic drawing power of Noel Coward. (British Ambassador and Lady Ormsby Gore sponsored the 1963 ball.) Nine hundred of the rich and the social poured into town, including eight members of the First Couple's families. Sir David Ormsby Gore, who the following year would become Lord Harlech, was such a close friend of Jack Kennedy, that the master of ceremonies that night, Under Secretary of Commerce Franklin D. Roosevelt, Jr., said, "I wonder if he doesn't spend as much time at the White House as the president."

It was late—12:30 A.M.—when Roosevelt introduced Noel as "Britain's contribution to the gaiety of the world, the humor of humanity and the art of civilization." Coward had been waiting all evening in a cold backstage room clutching his overcoat around him. He didn't take a drink because, he told me next day, "You can never drink before a performance; it puts your timing off." He had shooed his visitors out so he could think through his routine: "Mad Dogs and Englishmen Go Out in the Noonday Sun" is sung so fast, he said, that "if I had forgotten one word I would have been lost."

During the great playwright, composer, and performer's forty-five-minute repertoire, you could have heard a pin drop. Then in his sixties, his projection, timing, humor, and even his voice—not his best asset—seemed greater than ever. He added some hilarious new stanzas to "Birds Do It, Bees Do It" that included Bobby Kennedy, Charles de Gaulle, and others.

Coward was the houseguest of Grace and Neil Phillips. They invited me to come by the next day, before Noel went to the British Embassy luncheon. He had stayed up until 5:00 that morning amusing Admiral and Mrs. Phillips but he was still scintillating at noon.

Years later, I heard how, back in the 1940s Coward, who was then serving in British intelligence, was lunching at Claridge's with Sir

William Stephenson, his boss, General Bill Donovan, head of our OSS, and Ernest Cuneo, his White House liaison, when film star Adolph Menjou came up to them. "Noel, I have grave news," he said. "In the western part of England there will be four hundred children born this spring to English mothers and their fathers are black American soldiers."

"I can't believe," said Coward calmly, "that after two thousand years there are going to be some Englishmen with good teeth."

Looking back on the last five months of 1963, I am struck by the beginnings of a disastrous U.S. foreign policy, the unexpected end of the world leaders I encountered in that period, and the end of the gracious city of Washington as I had known it.

One morning, there was blood on the sidewalk in my neighborhood, where I, Secretary of Defense Robert McNamara, and such hostesses as Mrs. George Garrett, Mrs. Pete Quesada, and Mrs. W. John Kenney, all walked our dogs. The night before, a new college graduate, Newell Ellison, Jr., was walking his dog on Kalorama Road, when some young criminals drove by and shot him down just for kicks. It was the opening fusillade in the long, and terrible, war on the freedom we had always enjoyed on the streets of our beautiful city.

And, a national tragedy was in the making.

South Viet Nam, some of our Asian allies, and the U.S. press had been asking for more help from America to check the communist guerrillas, the Viet Cong.

I went to see the wife of Viet Nam Ambassador Tran Van Chuong. Her husband had just submitted his resignation, to protest the persecutions of their government in which their own daughter, Madame Ngo Dinh Nhu, was a prime force. Washington's tiniest ambassadorial spouse was also probably the most gracious, and certainly one of the most intelligent. She had commuted between Washington and New York for nine years to serve as a UN observer.

Why, I asked her, should American support a government like that?

"If you lose Viet Nam to the communists, you lose Southeast Asia," replied Madame Chuong. "I should like to urge that the American people keep Viet Nam."

"But," I objected, "we can't support a government that is oppressing its own people."

The wise woman countered, "If your house is not well built, you can change the builder, but you do not abandon the house." Some people thought we had a hand in changing "the builder" when Diem was murdered. But how prophetic she was! When we pulled out of Indo-China, the communists took over Viet Nam, Laos, and Cambodia in one of the worst genocides in history.*

The last two chiefs of state to be received by President Kennedy were, like their young host, ill-fated. In September, the last monarch of Afghanistan, King Zahir, came to America with Queen Homaira. He was so much impressed by the freedom of individual Americans that he installed a new liberal constitution in his country the following year. But in 1974, he was overthrown by his brother with the aid of the Soviets.

His Imperial Majesty Emperor Haile Selassie, Lion of Judah, arrived in time to be received at 4:15 by Jackie, who left immediately after to go on a cruise of the Mediterranean with Aristotle Onassis aboard his fabulous yacht, the *Christina*. The Ethiopian ruler presented her with a magnificent Ethiopian leopard coat and gold filigree bag. Jackie at once tried on the coat, which the laws at the time allowed her to keep.

The emperor's toast that evening foreshadowed the demise of his kingdom, also in 1974. His country, he said, "has been engaged in a never-ending struggle to maintain our freedom and independence against foreign encroachments." Nothing brought the ancient history of his land so forcefully to mind as the order his granddaughter Princess Ruth Desta was wearing. It was the Order of the Queen of Sheba!

I could not help wondering that night, as I watched the Robert Joffrey Ballet do a "Roaring Twenties" number that resembled a vaudeville or nightclub act, what this solemn, dignified little man, age seventy-two, thought. Quipped one U.S. official present, "We have just lost Ethiopia." John Kennedy expressed his displeasure later.

* The elegant, diminutive couple stayed on in Washington; twenty-three years later, they were tragically murdered here by their own son, according to the papers.

I felt one special bond with the emperor: the love we shared for chihuahuas. He always brought one or two of the tiny dogs with him when he came, I would walk my own chihuahua around the corner to his embassy in the hope that one of his entourage would be walking his dogs and I would get a human interest story. Happily, Selassie did not travel with his other pets that roamed freely with the chihuahuas in his palace courtyard—i.e., lions. They must have been well fed at all times! At the emperor's press conference his ambassador told him that I had written about his bringing chihuahuas with him in the past so perhaps this time he would bring a lion. Haile Selassie then told me, "I brought a silver lion to President Kennedy." His envoy grinned happily. "You see you predicted correctly." Eleven years later to the month the brutal, communist-supported Colonel Mengistu took over the country. The little Lion of Judah died a year later.

But his forty-six-year-old host was to last less than four months.

On November 22 I went to New York, at the request of the Hall Syndicate, to tape a televised two- or three-minute spiel it planned to use for promotion purposes. My talk, about the glamor of White House entertaining under the Kennedys, had been put onto a teleprompter. I was in the midst of describing the excitement this picturebook couple had generated everywhere when the news came over the air: The president had been shot, probably fatally. I rushed back to Washington to rewrite my entire Sunday column. I devoted it to the glamorous young woman, who had seemed to have so much, who had contributed more to White House history than most people knew or even imagined.

* * *

Three years after their marriage, Jackie regretted it. At a dinner party at the 1925 F Street Club which she attended without Jack (who was off on a cruise of the Greek Islands) Jackie was seated next to Bill Merriam, nephew of the club's founder.

At one point, by way of making pleasant conversation, Bill asked her, "How do you like being married to a senator?" Jackie replied, "It was the biggest mistake of my life."

But she would come into her own as the nation's First Lady, as my Inaugural Day story predicted.

It read:

"Jackie Bouvier Kennedy . . . enters the Executive Mansion with an open mind, a fresh approach, a refined taste and a desire to prove her mettle.

"At 31 she is the third youngest First Lady in American history, possibly the best educated, and very probably the most beautiful.

"In six months time she has emerged in the eyes of the public from a talented, fashionable young wife with a distaste for publicity and politics, to a political helpmate, capable campaigner and veteran performer before TV cameras and reporters.

"She has grown from the independent young individualist who shunned the public glare in her longing to be herself, into the courageous career woman who suddenly realized that her new job will demand the highest expression of her self.

"For Mrs. John Fitzgerald Kennedy will not only be the wife of President Kennedy, the mother of his children and the manager of his household. She will be America's most important woman, chatelaine of the most distinguished residence, hostess at the most influential parties, and for all the feminine, welfare and artistic projects in the country—the most required benefactress.

"Excitedly aware of the challenge and possibilities ahead, she has been quietly considering ways of giving her new role the greatest possible meaning. She has been planning her future with the same intelligence, creativity and thoughtful organization that have marked her steps in the past.

"For the extremely glamorous, well-dressed, soft-spoken beauty the country has come to know on television screens happens to be a highly efficient organizer.

"Though she flew to Palm Beach the same day she left George-town University Hospital after recuperating from the premature birth of her son, she left behind everything from clothes to bed-spreads carefully packed and tagged whether for the White House, for storage or for Glen-Ora, the leased Middleburg estate. She runs such a well-ordered house she could accomplish this by drawing up lists of the items destined for the two different addresses while lying in a hospital bed."

While recuperating in Palm Beach she also planned her entire wardrobe, continued her detailed study of the White House menage, embarked on exciting plans for making the White House a center for intellectual and artistic stimulation, and began filing away the names of famed Americans who would add lustre to its hallowed halls. Jackie could hold her own in any such gathering. A writer and artist, she was, and is, conversant in the fields of history and literature and could speak flawless French plus some Spanish and Italian. In addition to all that, she was a woman of sophisticated wit, impeccable taste, and fortitude.

But Jacqueline Kennedy refused to follow the pattern set by earlier First Ladies. She eschewed women's functions; she was averse to cutting ribbons to open their bazaars; she would not go to ladies luncheons.

She knew exactly what she wanted in decor, menus, fashions, art, entertainment, service—and especially in her children's upbringing. She detailed her wishes in hundreds of handwritten notes, and she was quick to pen flattering thank-you letters in her stylish script to express her appreciation.

I received one the first week after her husband's election.

Obliged to mail my column for the following Sunday on the Monday before election, I had written an open letter to the First Lady. It began "Dear Mrs. _____" and I asked the editor to fill in the name of the winning candidate. I had quizzed guests at every party the previous week about exactly what changes they wished the next First Lady would institute. By typing time, I had amassed twelve ideas. Several, of course—after fifteen years of White House coverage—were my own. The following is a condensed version of what appeared under my byline:

"Dear Mrs. Kennedy: You will soon be the First Lady of the land and today that is a job within itself. The women of America look to the wife of the chosen candidate as their personal link with what America is and should be.

"We in Washington who have observed the White House and its occupants for years hope you will take full advantage of this great opportunity. Through the years we have heard the criticisms and suggestions of dozens of Americans and foreign diplomats regarding the activities of your predecessors. Thinking you might be interested, stimulated or, at least, amused by the variety of things these people want you to do, I set them forth herewith:

"(1) They hope you will give stimulus, encouragement and prestige to the arts of the United States by attending outstanding art, musical and theatrical events—a field generally overlooked by First Ladies.

"These are the sort of ceremonial functions Queen Elizabeth has time to do and does as chief of state leaving her prime minister free to run the government. The American president has the enormous responsibility of being chief of state, chief of government and chief of party as well. You can lighten his load by filling in at such important public appearances.

"(2) They long for you to vary your guest lists so that the magnificent state dinners at the White House will always include some of the famous Americans we are most proud of, rather than only personal friends and those who contributed the most money to the campaign.

"People who accomplish the most in this country, whether in the field of science, creative arts, business or sports, generally receive no recognition from the place where it counts the most—i.e., the head of the country. In Britain and its Comonwealth such men and women are rewarded with the title of 'Sir' or 'Dame.'

"It seems to Capital observers that the least these people should receive is an invitation to an important dinner at the White House where you and your husband could proudly present them to foreign dignitaries and to American officials.

"(3) Foreign ambassadors accredited to the president hope you will persuade him to restore the diplomatic dinners so that they can at least lay eyes on him once a year. The way things are now they can go from the day they present their letters of accreditation to the day several years later when they bid farewell without so much as a glimpse of the chief executive. This sort of thing is unheard of in other civilized countries.

"(4) Washington newspaper women hope you will reorganize the East Wing, your wing of the White House, so that you will have both a social secretary and a press secretary. Heretofore the social secretary has had to do all the jobs implied in that title plus serve as liaison with the press without having had any press training.

"(5) We scribes also hope you will hold a monthly press conference—you, yourself, not your secretary. However brief it may be, why not take advantage of this available regular contact with the public to tell what you're doing and why? Even if it's only homey news about adding to the White House china collection, women are interested. You could spotlight women of accomplishment whose worthwhile projects you believe in, by bringing one to each conference.

"(6) Washingtonians hope you will restore the receptions to which some local residents were always invited. One of the charms about Washington used to be that people who belonged in society could leave their cards on the First Lady and an invitation would be forthcoming.

"(7) Everybody who has ever been to one of these receptions hopes you will reorganize the arrangements so that you do not receive in the Blue Room behind closed doors where the line of guests passing before you gets less than a 30-second look at you and the chief executive all evening, after preparing for days for the big event. The anticlimax is apt to be flatter than the White House floor.

"(8) Capital society would like to see you give some dances in the White House. That's what the ballroom (East Room) was designed for in the first place. Give them for yourselves or for other members of the family, but give them because that's been the tradition there and society longs to see 1600 Pennsylvania Avenue glisten with spirit and life. You could even have dances after state dinners where aides could twirl with the wives of men your husband wanted to talk to.

"(9) Some people think it would be wonderful, too, if there were children's parties in your future domicile, not just for your own children, but for Girl and Boy Scouts, or honor students or for the kids in local orphanages. They'd never forget it. You probably wouldn't either—you'd be so charmed.

"(10) People who do welfare work long for the First Lady to personally visit and take an interest in such places as the Receiving Home for Children and the Family and Child Services Center. Sometimes it seems as if the wives of visiting chiefs of state see more of hospitals, Red Cross facilities, etc. than their hostess.

"(11) And, yes, people here are even full of ideas, too, on how you can improve White House dinners. The lights, they say, are too bright to encourage intimacy, the table too wide to talk easily with anybody across from you and the flowers too abundant to see over, under or around. People who dine at the White House are scared to death anyhow, and when they are fenced in by a floral hedge, unable to communicate with more than two people, the situation becomes stiffer than the men's shirt fronts.

"(12) And finally, they say, make the White House a showcase for the best in American food and fashions as well as American citizens and culture. Your own clothes can give a boost to American designers, but you'll probably have to get a salary raise for the head of your cuisine. Previous White House chefs have said they couldn't afford to stay at the White House because the salary was too small. They just work for a limited period for the sake of the prestige.

"The American people want the top residence in the Nation to have top quality in everything. Sharing in that pride, I am, Respectfully yours, Betty Beale."

The same day that column appeared in the *Sunday Star*, November 13, 1960, Jackie wrote by hand the following letter:

"Dear Betty—I must say I appreciate your article in the *Star* today.

"It has saved me hours of talking to a million people and groping to find the right things to do in a rather frantic new life.

"I thought every suggestion such a good one and all in such good taste.

"Give me a little time—as I will stagger from the hospital to the White House—the move is a big one in anyone's life but with 2 young children and not terribly good health—it will be longer before I bounce back. But I will—& have every intention of really trying hard at my new job. You will see within a year I bet I will have done most of the things you suggested.

"I repeat, I am ENORMOUSLY grateful for your suggestions and they will be such a help. This letter is just for you—so please don't publish any of it. Gratefully, Jackie (Kennedy)"

It was a touching and extraordinary letter, revealing a side of Jackie so few people knew. How many persons at the highest pinnacles would be so generous in giving, even privately, an outsider credit for suggested improvements in their own bailiwick?

Jackie's staff experienced a surprising switch immediately after the first press conference on her behalf. As the person in charge of seeing that Jackie's side "all works smoothly"—with possibly a press assistant under her—the capable Tish Baldrige held that conference; it proved to be her undoing. Tish told the reporters that Mrs. Kennedy wanted to make the White House a showplace for the best in America in painting, music, ballet, etc. When someone asked where she would hang the works of contemporary artists when all the space was occupied with historic portraits, Tish said she might move some. Then, discussing the problem of entertaining club women, she used the phrase "vast hordes of women," correcting it with a grin, to: "I mean large groups of interesting ladies."

The press loved the witty, effervescent Miss Baldrige. But the ink was barely dry on the newspaper reports when her wings were clipped. She was named social secretary. Pamela Turnure was named press secretary. The choice was surprising. The twenty-three-year-old Pamela had never had any press experience. She was not—as Tish had been—a former schoolmate or particular friend of Jackie's. Strangest of all, she had been an intimate friend of Senator Kennedy. Considering his reputation as a womanizer no one could understand why Jackie would want her in that post. Mrs. Gene Markey, owner of famed Calumet Stables in Lexington, Ky., later told me that Aly Khan once brought Pamela to her Lexington, Ky., estate and she reproached him for leading such a young girl astray. The charming Aly, who was old enough then to be her father and had a worldwide reputation for womanizing, told Louise Markey he couldn't possibly lead the then twenty-year-old astray; she had already been Jack Kennedy's girl. Whether Jackie did not know about their affair or just made the best of the situation isn't known. But quiet, low-key Pamela, who withheld as much as possible from the press, apparently suited the low-key, private Jackie as well as Pierre Salinger.

At the end of the "First Lady's First Year" I got permission from Jackie to quote one paragraph from the letter she had written me right after election. I totaled up the score and she had, indeed, accomplished most of my twelve suggestions, including getting a first rate chef for the White House even though the president had to pay him out of his own pocket.

Her most brilliant accomplishments had to do with giving authenticity and artistic enrichment to the White House. To accomplish this she sought help in all directions, even mine. In fact, Jackie credited me in a letter to me dated April 12, 1962, with helping to acquire the White House portrait of Chief Justice Marshall as a permanent "resident." I had written in a January column that Mrs. Kennedy wanted the John Wesley Jarvis portrait of John Marshall. New York columnist Leonard Lyons saw it and told Mrs. Samuel Newhouse (of the noted publishing family) about it; she underwrote its purchase for the White House.

Jackie then sent me a list of other paintings she thought should be permanently hung in the White House and which I promptly described in my column. Her letter illustrates her sense of history and intellectual approach to projects. "As you can see," she wrote, "there are only eight pictures. That is because we decided the only way for our Committee to accomplish something really worthwhile, was to settle only for the best—even if it takes us much longer to raise the money to acquire them.

"All these pictures are very expensive—all have a reason for being in the White House. They are of great Americans or historical figures of interest.

"Our Committee feels that because of the limitations of hanging space we could never have a representative collection of all American paintings here. That is the task of our galleries—and heaven knows it takes them a lifetime to realize that goal. Also, many paintings of great American artists would be totally unsuitable in the dignified State Rooms where the President has his State Receptions.

"So the pictures we acquire should all have a certain reason and appropriateness for being in the White House. They can be of people or events that are a part of our history, of significant American landscapes, or historic houses. But they still can and must be great pictures—or we will defeat our own purpose of acquiring art for the White House which will augment the feeling everyone has when they come here—a feeling of pride in the Nation's most beloved house—and a feeling of pride in our country's history.

"Anything you can do to help would be so appreciated. If you feel you can do nothing, I will always be so grateful for Chief Justice Marshall. Affectionately, Jackie."

The list of paintings:

"Portrait of Lafayette presently hanging in the Toledo Museum" by Jules Heinsius, a painter of the French court who fled France for America with the advent of the French Revolution.

"Life Portrait of Thomas Jefferson painted in 1800 in Philadelphia by Rembrandt Peale"; it was not until 1959 that the editors of *The Papers of Thomas Jefferson* identified the painting owned by the Peabody Institute of Baltimore as the long-lost likeness.

"Portrait of John James Audubon painted in Edinburgh in 1826 by John Syme."

And four portraits of Indian chiefs and one of a chief's wife painted by Charles Bird King shortly after their arrival in 1821 in Washington where President James Monroe presented each with "the Monroe medal." They were: "Shaumonekusse—an Oto Half Chief; Sharitarish—Wicked Chief, Great Pawnkee Tribe; Petalesharro—Generous Chief, Pawnee Tribe; Hayn Hudjihini— The Eagle of Delight, Wife of Shaumonekusse; Monchousia— White Plume, Kanza Tribe."

All of them are wearing the Monroe medal, wrote Mrs. Kennedy. "Now we are searching for one of these medals."

All of the pictures came to the White House.*

An aftermath to the acquisition of the Lafayette portrait occurred the night the Kennedy's included the Arthur Zepfs at a state dinner to show their appreciation for his help. I was there that evening and happened to leave the East Room at the same time Arthur Zepf did. As we walked out he slyly slipped his hand in the pocket of his

---

* As soon as my article was published, Arthur L. Zepf of the Aetna Life Insurance Company, who read my column in the *Toledo Blade*, got in touch with me. He said he would get the Lafayette portrait and on June 1st I received a note from him saying: "You have the news I know. Tried to reach you yesterday by fone. Was asked to 'hush' until all was cleared. I told you it would be done!" It came but, alas, only on loan. The White House had it for a period—I forget how long—and hoped to wheedle it out of the museum permanently but was unable to do so.

The Thomas Jefferson portrait was given to the White House by Paul Mellon, son of the founder of the National Gallery of Art and a friend of Jackie's who may not have even seen my column. The portrait of Audubon was acquired by James Fosburg, a member of Mrs. K's Painting Commission, who hardly had to read the newspapers to know that she wanted it. But my story helped acquire the Indian paintings. After it came out Sears provided the money to buy all five, which now hang in the Library on the floor below the East Room.

dinner jacket and showed me the souvenir of the dinner he was taking with him. It was a gold spoon!

I just as slyly slipped over to Tish Baldrige and told her about it. Her response was, how could she do anything about it when he had gotten the Lafayette for them? People were forever lifting souvenirs from the White House, she said.

* * *

Considering Jackie's promptness in writing notes, thank-you ones or otherwise, her failure to do so on one occasion shocked me. Three-year-old Caroline was playing in the pool at the birthday party of little Ivan Steers, son of Jackie's stepsister Nini Auchincloss and Newton Steers, when Mrs. William Saltonstall, daughter-in-law of blueblooded Republican Senator Leverett Saltonstall of Massachusetts, arrived and began to get her two small fry into their bathing suits. Suddenly she heard one of the other mothers say, "Is she all right?" She looked toward the pool in time to see Caroline lose her hold on a little flutterboard and begin to sink in four feet of water. Without any thought to her own pregnant condition, Jane Saltonstall jumped into the pool with her clothes on to rescue the little girl who did not know how to swim. By the time she reached Caroline, the child had gone under. It happened so quickly the other nurses and mothers sitting around the pool had not taken in the situation. Caroline's nurse had gone into the house to change into her swimsuit. Jane Saltonstall was acutely aware of the danger because a friend of hers had seen her child fall face down into a stream not seventy-five feet away and though she ran as fast as she could to her rescue she got there too late. A child can drown in thirty-seven seconds, a prominent Washington pediatrician told me.

Although my story made the front page of the *Star* above the fold, and headlines around the world (I received clippings on it from the *China Post* in Taipeh, the *Rome Daily American*, a paper in Bologna, Italy, and the *New York Herald Tribune*'s European edition) the White House press office pooh-poohed the whole incident. And although I subsequently wrote that Mrs. Saltonstall's jump into the pool gave her such problems in her pregnancy that she was confined to her bed for a long time, she never had a note of thanks or a telephone call from Mrs. Kennedy.

Perhaps to save her own neck the nurse had told her that Caroline was never in any danger. The White House may have thought there was an element of publicity-seeking in the incident, which there was not. The Saltonstalls were low-profile people. If I had not pursued the story it never would have come out. But it was all the more surprising because Jackie, herself, was such a good mother.

* * *

A measure of Jackie's ever-growing hold on the public was the reaction of the audience in the National Theatre on April 1, 1963, when she and her dinner guests attended the opening night of *School for Scandal*. During intermission, when the lights were on, people in the orchestra, balcony, and second balcony stood against the walls, in the aisles, in the front rows, in order to stare transfixed at the First Lady, seated in the center of Row G. This had never happened when Eleanor Roosevelt, Bess Truman, or Mamie Eisenhower went to the theater. She was also the only one of those four ladies to leave her seat at intermission—as most people did—to go out front for a breath of fresh air. And the Kennedys were the only presidential pair theater manager Scott Kirkpatrick could remember who sat through the customary four curtain calls until the lights went up; their predecessors were always ushered out during the second curtain.

Eleanor Roosevelt never needed the help of Secret Service men or ushers to hold back the crowds, recalled Kirkpatrick, perhaps because she was so tall. No matter how jammed the lobby was, as soon as people saw her they stepped politely back of their own volition and cleared a path for her. Mrs. Roosevelt went to the theater without any Secret Service protection. One night she even walked back to the White House alone, declining an usher's offer to escort her. "Oh, no, thank you very much," she replied. "It's such a short distance and such a pretty night I will just walk along." It's hard to imagine a First Lady doing that today. Of course, the city was much safer then.

On the night of President Kennedy's assassination I rewrote my column for Sunday, listing Jackie's contributions to the presidential residence over thirty-four months:

She got a bill passed through Congress that gave the White House permanent museum status so that no gift made to it could be given away, sold, lost, or left uncared for.

She established a Fine Arts Committee, headed by the knowledgeable antiquarian Henry F. duPont, to advise her on what should go into the White House.

She established the post of the first White House curator for the Executive Mansion. Under her, it became a museum of beauty, antiquity, and authenticity.

She ordered the first White House Guidebook and established the White House Historical Association, chartered as a nonprofit-making organization, to publish it. And she arranged for its sale to provide a continuous source of income to be used toward purchasing more authentic antique beauty.

She ordered the first catalogue of the White House library, and established a library committee to select books for it.

She got well-to-do friends to make gifts to the White House, either of a fine piece of furniture or art or the money with which to buy an item already located. And she put out word across the country that caused contributions to pour in. To stir up this proprietary pride in the mansion, she conducted the first First Lady's televised tour of the White House.

She had a special stage built for the East Room, and established a series of firsts in the programs presented there. She brought in a whole ballet company, an opera company, the Shakespeare Stratford Festival, an act from a musical comedy, and more.

She made the White House glow with life even at the hitherto stiff state dinners. She added jubilant music from the Air Force Strings, eliminated regimentation of guests to certain rooms and the desegregation of the sexes after dinner, and she used both the Blue Room and State Dining Room for important dinners.

She introduced special concerts for children, both underprivileged as well as the children of friends and diplomats.

She invited to the White House not only statesmen but scientists, poets, playwrights, Nobel Prizewinners, and so forth.

She redecorated almost every room in the President's House except the East Room and vastly improved the appearance of each.

She added to the beauty of Washington, particularly when she stopped the destruction of the buildings around historic Lafayette Square. The needed office buildings were erected but the historic facade was preserved.

And she initiated the redecorating and beautifying program for Blair House, the presidential guest house, for visiting heads of state.

CHAPTER 6

Texas Two-Step

LBJ and Lady Bird's Era

A measure of the pace in the Johnson era is best illustrated by my syndicated column of June 1964.

"Nothing much happened last week," I wrote. "In seven whole days all I did was: Go to the White House party for Prime Minister Eshkol of Israel and dance with President Johnson to the lilting strains of 20 violins; go to a garden party in honor of the Shah and Empress of Iran; chat with former President and Mrs. Eisenhower at a pleasant Sunday afternoon reception; attend a small party for Adlai Stevenson after he spoke at a dinner for 800 given by the Women's National Democratic Club; delve into past history when Lady Bird Johnson formally received in the White House the $500,000 urn that was used there by John Adams and hear his great-great-great grandson Thomas Boylston Adams say he had been surprised to find that any of the family 'loot' was 'on the loose'; dance at the Opera Ball at the beautifully decorated French Embassy with that super-duper twirler and able wit of the Senate, Hubert Humphrey; do a mad frug at the Kuwait Embassy dinner dance where the 40 guests watched a limbo dancer go under a bar only 9 inches high without touching his hands to the floor; dine at the Italian Embassy where I had a fascinating political conversation with Walter Lippmann, Pierre-Paul Schweitzer, head of the International Monetary Fund, and Italian Ambassador Fenoaltea; and whip by the debuts of Angela Russell, granddaughter of the late Dowager Lady Ampthill who was lady-in-waiting to Queen Mary of England, and Alexandra Villard, Ambassador Henry Villard's daughter who is on the cover of this month's *Town and Country*. There was a wedding reception, too, and a couple more cocktail parties and another dinner, and I played golf twice to counteract that in-a-rut feeling—once with the Elliott Roosevelts." (The small party for Adlai I "attended" was one I gave for him in my house and the one President and Mrs. Johnson attended.)

Parties were endemic in the city's fashionable areas. One evening, Adlai Stevenson was to be the honor guest at a dinner given by the Ambassador of Iceland and Mrs. Thor Thors, who lived on the corner of Tracy Place and 23rd Street. Stevenson's taxidriver took him instead to the corner of Tracy and 24th Street. There, he was greeted at the front door by a familiar-faced butler who took his coat and hat and asked what he would like to drink. He proceeded into the drawing room, where the black tie party included such good friends of his as the Walter Lippmanns and Senator and Mrs. Mike Monroney of Oklahoma. They chatted for a while before Adlai asked, "Where's Thor?" It was then he discovered he was not in the Icelandic Embassy. He hurriedly walked down the street to arrive at the party for him only fifteen minutes late. "It's been years," observed Adlai later with a chuckle, "since I lived in a neighborhood where there was a party going on in every house."

It was the era, too, of my very best entrée into 1600 Pennsylvania Avenue.

I had known the Johnsons longer than any previous presidential pair, had been to many of their parties, had stayed overnight in their house at the LBJ Ranch, had a wonderful, warm friendship with Liz Carpenter,* who became Lady Bird's chief of staff and press secretary.

Liz had as close a personal relationship with the new presidential couple as probably any press secretary in history. When Lyndon Johnson became vice president she became his executive assistant.

---

* Ten years earlier she and her husband Les had persuaded Hall Syndicate that my column was worthy of syndication.

It was she who penned the first announcement to the world made by the new president immediately following the tragedy in Dallas.

Having been a newswoman herself, she knew what would make news and how to dispense it. If she had an item particularly suited to my column she would give it to me, even pointing out the best or most amusing angles. Of the many, many parties I had been to in their house, the most memorable was their dinner for six—Speaker Sam Rayburn, Senate Majority Leader and Mrs. Lyndon Johnson, and me—long before any of us knew that three out of the six would end up in the White House. (Besides being a wise and true patriot, Sam Rayburn viewed politics with a sense of humor. The five rules for getting elected, he maintained, were: (1) explain nothing; (2) deny everything; (3) demand proof; (4) don't listen to it; and (5) give the opposition hell.)

So it was not surprising that five days after the Johnsons had moved into the White House, the new president and First Lady included me in their first social gathering. They moved in on the 7th of December—having given Jackie all the time she wanted to make plans for the abrupt change in her life—and on the 12th they gave a very small party in the Yellow Oval Room on the second floor. It was one of two informal affairs for members of the press and White House staff and their wives. Each was small, as the nation was still in the month-long mourning period. It was the first time, I learned later, that the presidential senior staffers, with the exception of Kenneth O'Donnell, had been entertained by the president in his private apartments. The fact that McGeorge Bundy, JFK's National Security Affairs assistant, and Pierre Salinger were there for the first time was amazing to us all. How strange that Johnson, for whom the Kennedy staffers had no affection and little respect, had shown them a hospitality that their adored Jack had never done.

Lyndon Johnson, who as vice president had managed beyond anyone's expectations completely to subjugate his own opinions and powerful impulses to run things, was now as proud and happy as a boy with his first car.

He had always loved new conveniences, new gadgets. When telephones were first installed in cars, Senator Johnson had them installed in his cars on the ranch; he used the phone all the time he was driving, so the people he called would know he had one, his longtime Texas friend Dale Miller told me. He couldn't wait, of course, to call his Republican counterpart in the Senate, Everett Dirksen, on the newfangled instrument. Not to be outclassed, Dirksen immediately ordered one for his car, then he called Johnson, auto to auto. But LBJ was a master of one-upmanship: In the midst of their conversation he interrupted, "Excuse me, Ev, my other phone is ringing."

He couldn't wait to conduct a personal tour of the second floor that day. He was to show it off again and again, to each different visiting group.

But it was certainly not new to see LBJ in the role of a warm and expansive host. That was his style. As a senator he was always inviting people to dinner, and Lady Bird often had to change dinner menu plans two or three times in one afternoon with each call from her husband telling her there would be two, three, or four more guests than before. He liked company at dinnertime.

One evening in 1966, during Indian Prime Minister Indira Gandhi's state visit, he went to the Indian Embassy for the customary brief courtesy call which was scheduled prior to Mrs. Gandhi's dinner for forty. In no hurry to return home and dine alone, as Lady Bird was sick in bed, LBJ sat and talked. Finally, at nine o'clock, when all the dinner guests had assembled, they invited him to dine with them. He accepted at once.

LBJ's first Christmas in the White House prefigured the shape of parties to come. Official mourning had ended December 22. On the 23rd, at 1:30 in the afternoon, Johnson decided to give a party at five o'clock that same day for members of Congress. His personal assistants, who knew that "can't do" was not in LBJ's vocabulary, went into high-speed action, and the three hundred members of Congress who were still in town, plus a number of press, came to an outstandingly successful reception. The lawmakers were ecstatic. They loved the freedom and ease of the impromptu affair and the many opportunities to exchange banter with this convivial president. I recall Senator Jennings Randolph of West Virginia fairly bursting with enthusiasm because the new president picked up the phone and called a senator whenever he had something he wanted to talk to him about, where previous presidents would have had an aide call. Needless to say, the Johnson method was far more productive.

I learned a lesson that evening that I never forgot. When Mrs. Johnson went upstairs and Liz Carpenter left I figured it was time for the press to leave and I departed. But Mr. Johnson stayed on to chat with a group of nine remaining congressmen. The four newswomen who remained were treated to another surprise by their unpredictable host. As soon as the congressmen left, he took the women to see his offices and the swimming pool. (I never did see the pool; it was to disappear in the next administration.) That unexpected tour was a foretaste of the five years to come that would never be cut and dried, never stiff or stuffy. The Johnson era would be the swingingest of any administration of the eight I covered. The tenor of it set the whole town on its toes.

One mark of the openness of the new regime was the ease with which anyone calling the White House could get satisfaction. The southern accents on the other end of the line were unfailingly polite and easygoing. If I called Liz for some information about presidential entertaining that she did not have at her fingertips, her response would be, "Call Bess." If Social Secretary Bess Abell had the answer to a question she gave it—a delightful contrast to the usual bureaucratic division of labor. From my point of view, it was the most satisfactory arrangement of any administration.

Cultivated people were prepared to see the new Texas informality and folksiness downgrade entertainment at state dinners. Political columnists had been writing ever since Kennedy's death that Johnson did not have the Kennedy style. The Johnsons were daily subjected to printed putdowns. It was true that neither the president nor Lady Bird had the personal style of JFK and Jackie. But neither did the Eisenhowers, nor the Trumans, nor, indeed, the Abraham Lincolns. The announcement that Johnson would receive German Chancellor Erhard at Stonewall High School in Stonewall, Texas, and entertain the state visitor with a barbecue, evoked snide comments. But they died down when it was learned that the performer at the barbecue would be the famous concert pianist Van Cliburn. From then on every state visitor wanted to be received at the ranch. To be invited to the president's own private home indicated a cozy relationship with the head of the world's most powerful nation.

At Johnson's first state dinner in the White House (it was for Italy's President and Mrs. Antonio Segni), Metropolitan Opera baritone Robert Merrill sang arias from *La Traviata* and *The Barber of Seville* followed by nine young people singing American folk songs. It was quite a contrast but it presented to the foreign visitor something totally American. Perle Mesta was at that dinner, her first since Eisenhower left the presidency because she had backed Nixon instead of Kennedy.

The Johnsons were the only presidential family in four decades with four active adults living in the White House, each doing his or her own thing. On occasion all four were holding forth at the same time in different parts of the mansion. The Johnsons added more music to every function, and more liveliness. The society press had never seen the liveliest Kennedy parties—which were strictly private—and there were no really lively parties during the Truman and Eisenhower eras.*

The LBJs even introduced musical entertainment at luncheon. At the one I attended for the beautiful and witty Queen Frederika of Greece, the Metropolitan Opera's Lois Hunt and Earl Wrightson of TV-nightclub fame burst into song, first one, then the other, from their places at their respective tables, astonishing and delighting the guests. In keeping with the Kennedy innovation, Army or Air Force Strings always burst into melodies when the dining room doors opened following such state functions. And while the Marine Band's dance group played after dinners in the East Room, a calypso band sometimes filled the cleared dining room with enchanting airs.

President Johnson so loved to dance that he had dance music at nearly every state dinner. At parties for the diplomatic corps, he made a point of dancing with the wives of at least one European, one African, one Asian, and one South American ambassador so that no group felt left out. He also danced with us reporters who were covering the scene. He had a good sense of rhythm and did a smooth foxtrot. I had danced with him before. In fact, *Newsweek* magazine of August 7, 1961, carried a picture of the then vice

---

* When I told John Eisenhower in 1958 that his father's regime was the first peacetime one in this century that had not had a dance in the White House, he looked stunned. Soon after that he and Barbara gave one for their army friends, and they danced to army music. But from what I learned it was not the most animated event in town.

president dancing with me, cheek to cheek, both of us smiling broadly for the camera.

Other Johnson surprises:

He showed up unexpectedly at a women's press party of four hundred in honor of Liz Carpenter and said he loved, honored, and respected Liz second only to his wife.

He turned up for the lunch reporters Marguerite Higgins and Pete Lisagor were giving for presidential assistants Bill Moyers and Jack Valenti at Maggie's house. She was floored.

He dropped by unexpectedly at a party at the Army and Navy Club for Senator Edmund Muskie of Maine.

He went to the wedding reception Congressman and Mrs. Hale Boggs of Louisiana gave for their daughter Barbara.

He danced with nearly every senator's wife at the three informal dinners the Johnsons gave for senatorial couples.

He answered the phone in his bedroom at 8:00 A.M. while conferring with Jack Valenti and when the caller asked if it was Valenti he said, "No, this is the president. I am handling Mr. Valenti's calls this morning."

On January 10, 1964, Mrs. Johnson invited some newswomen to tea and her personally guided tour of the White House. In Luci's blue and white chintz room, where Luci's beagles had bounced in to see her when she was sick, Lady Bird recalled that when Theodore Roosevelt's children were sick he allowed their pony to be brought upstairs to cheer them up. In "our own room," as she described the presidential bedroom that faced south to the Washington Monument, we saw a plaque over the fireplace that read, "In this room President Abraham Lincoln slept during his occupancy of the White House." And in small type: "In this room lived John Fitzgerald Kennedy with his wife, Jacqueline, during the two years, ten months and two days he was president of the United States, January 20, 1961–November 22, 1963." Jackie had it placed there before she moved out. It was one of several efforts she made to hallow Jack's memory.

That the country now had an iron man in the White House in Lyndon Johnson was soon apparent. The diplomatic reception on February 11, scheduled for the first time as an informal 7:00 to 9:00 P.M. affair, was a supper dance and the president danced from the minute he finished receiving until 9:30, except for one fifteen-minute interlude. He spent that "recess" with the four new ambassadors who had presented their credentials on that occasion.

Two nights later at the state dinner for British Prime Minister Sir Alec Douglas-Home there was dancing instead of the usual musicale. Besides twirling Lady Douglas-Home, his wife, and special guests like Julie Andrews and Mrs. John Steinbeck, Johnson switched partners with other men so often he danced with about fifty women. He made a point of taking on the homely and heavy as well as the pretty and petite. He danced with me again and when I mentioned the country's concern over his pace he simply grinned and said dancing was relaxing exercise for him. That was the night he told Sir Alec that the latter had "the greatest advance party of any British prime minister in history." Sir Alec was puzzled until Johnson said, "The only thing wrong with them was they needed a haircut." Then the Britisher realized he was talking about the Beatles; Beatlemania was sweeping the country, and they had just given their first performance in Washington.

The Johnsons could not have been more open with the press—all of the press. The opinion molders who had basked in having an inside track before decided there was something highly suspicious about a president who would talk to all of them—proving once again that occupants of the Casa Blanca are damned if they do and damned if they don't.

No previous occupants, I wrote, had been so considerate of society reporters. "The first time we went there for a press conference we were served tea around an open fire. The first time we arrived, decked in our finery to cover the after-state dinner proceedings, we were served cocktails while we waited for dinner to end. The first time we had tea with the First Lady she took us on a tour of their private apartments. The first time we were invited to cover a dancing party we were provided with an escort, a newspaperman, so that he, too, could share in the experience." And, I added, the president had danced with all of us. We were grateful for such hospitable treatment.

Nobel prize-winning author Steinbeck and his wife, who were Johnson guests on more than one occasion, were the source of a grand prank that played out its finale in the White House. Eight years earlier, while on a Caribbean cruise with Broadway director John Fernley, Elaine Steinbeck had been conned into buying a ghastly purple handkerchief. She promptly disposed of it by sending it to Fernley. From that day on, whoever had it would send it to the one who didn't—in the least likely way. The challenge of ingenuity was irresistible, however costly. It might be delivered by a footman with a glass of wine during dinner, or found under a plate in a restaurant, in London, Paris, or New York.

The untoppable delivery of the pranky hanky occurred in the East Room of the White House. Mrs. Steinbeck was dancing with the president of the United States when he pulled out of his pocket and handed her—the purple handkerchief!

The smaller Blue Room became the ballroom the night the LBJs entertained twenty-eight-year-old King Hussein of Jordan and English wife Princess Muna. Royal custom required the women to ask his majesty for a dance rather than the other way around. I was one of them.

There was even dancing at the 5:30 reception for the American Society of Newspaper Editors and their wives when one after another wife cut in on the president—a not inconsiderable number as there were 1,100 guests in all. LBJ even twirled one wife around without music when she told him upon her departure that she didn't get to dance with him.

The new dance craze to rock music called the frug—pronounced "froog"—hit Washington with a bang that April of 1964. Senators Teddy Kennedy of Massachusetts, Frank Church of Idaho, and Birch Bayh of Indiana were even caught huddled on the floor of the U.S. Senate comparing notes on how well each could do it!

In May I went to another of Senator Ellender's power-packed luncheons in his U.S. Capitol "hideaway." This time the president, himself, was there and such important southern opponents to his civil rights bill as Senators Dick Russell, Harry Byrd, John Stennis, Lister Hill, and Russell Long. The others who enjoyed the host's home-made shrimp gumbo and pralines were Senate Majority Leader Mike Mansfield and Senators Stuart Symington, Maurine Neuberger, Howard Cannon, Milton Young, and Robert Byrd. I and two other newswomen loved being in that rarified company, with no newsmen present. Ellender liked women and probably thought Johnson would get better treatment from us.

Two months later, LBJ was to sign the civil rights bill into law.

LBJ's gregariousness continued to color the entertaining. Other presidents have had parties on the South Lawn, but the LBJs' for one hundred twenty-one presidential scholars was memorable for two reasons. The great black actor Sidney Poitier held everyone spellbound as he introduced Jose Ferrer to the subject of Shakespearean acting; afterward, Leonard Bernstein played the piano.

Lying on the grass in back of the rows of chairs and cloaked in the privacy of a dark starless night, I drank in the incomparable sight beyond: The lighted Jefferson Memorial shining like a jewel in the midnight blue, as Jefferson's words have shone through history; and the soaring, illuminated shaft of the Washington Monument so symbolic of his aspirations for his country. As Bernstein played a nocturne by Chopin I saw the dark forms of a man and a woman noiselessly approach and sit down on the grass twenty-five feet away. He leaned on one elbow as he watched the distant stage. She put her head next to his shoulder. Young lovers? No, the president and First Lady of the United States.

That same week the state dinner for Danish Prime Minister Jens Krag and his beauteous actress wife saw the frug uninhibitedly performed for the first time in the East Room, under the portraits of Martha and George. The Johnsons did not frug, but he foxtrotted from 10:15 P.M. to 12:45 A.M., changing from a black dinner jacket to a white one around midnight. Comedian Victor Borge decided that the vigorous husband and father of Lady Bird and Lynda Bird could no longer be called Gentleman Bird. The nation's chief dynamo must be called Thunderbird—after the Ford Motor Co.'s fast new product.

But the possessor of the now most famous dancing feet in the country did not dance even once at the White House dinner for President Tsiranana of Malagasy in July. The inventive Bess Abell had set up an enchantingly decorated cabaret on the South Lawn where Lester Lanin's society dance orchestra beat out beckoning rhythms. LBJ refrained, thought some, in self-defense. To twirl with the chief executive had become such a status symbol he couldn't take to the floor without wives of congressmen asking him to dance to increase their husbands' prestige back home.

In September, following his nomination at the Democratic Convention, the social season started when LBJ awarded the Medal of Freedom to America's foremost couple of the stage, Lynn Fontanne and Alfred Lunt; to T. S. Eliot, who received his by mail in London; to Helen Keller, whose niece came in her place; and to Walt Disney, Samuel Eliot Morison, Carl Sandburg, Edward R. Murrow, Thomas J. Watson, Jr., Walter Lippmann, Willam de Kooning, and others. Afterwards Undersecretary of State and Mrs. George Ball gave a reception for the honored. There the famous abstractionist De Kooning told me that Peter-Paul Rubens had advised his students not to paint from live models. He said instead they should study the masters until they had learned the measurements of forms; *then*, when they started to paint, they should "put in the dimples. Rubens, you know," added De Kooning, "loved dimples."

Walter Lippmann, who would later feel such hostility to LBJ because of his Viet Nam policy that he would move to New York, was an admirer in those days. When Lippmann gave himself a birthday reception the Johnsons came and brought a handsomely bound, gold-tooled guest book bearing the presidential seal. Autographed by the First Couple, it was also inscribed with an excerpt from Walter's Freedom award citation: ". . . measured reason and detached perspective . . ."

The Johnsons suffered a blow that fall—a blow that led to my getting an unusual story about J. Edgar Hoover. The president's dedicated, top assistant Walter Jenkins was arrested on a homosexual morals charge. Jenkins, highly regarded as a husband, father, friend, and probably the most overworked man in Washington, had a complete physical breakdown and was hospitalized in the depths of despair. Somebody tipped me off to the fact that among the messages and flowers that had poured into his sickroom was a bouquet from Hoover, director of the FBI, which, at the time, was investigating the case for possible security implications. The card with the flowers read: "J. Edgar Hoover and staff." In addition, there was a note from Hoover. It said, "I send these to you only with the understanding that you show this card to everyone who comes to your room."

When I telephoned the FBI director to be certain it was he who had sent the posies, he indicated that he felt Jenkins had been the victim of overzealous police action. Such support from Hoover, of course, put an end to talk of security risks. That he would openly sympathize with anyone involved in such a charge surprised me. There was a belief in some circles that J. Edgar, himself, was homosexual; certainly, he was never seen anywhere with a woman, and he lived with Associate Director Clyde Tolson.

Later, when Hoover made a rare appearance at a party given by hostess Gwen Cafritz, he told me that all he had known when he sent the flowers was that Jenkins, whom he had known for fifteen years, had been rushed to the hospital with a serious breakdown. It wasn't until that evening, he said, that the president asked him to investigate to see if there had been any breach of security. My story had brought him a lot of critical mail, he told me, but he didn't pay any attention to it. Quoting Jesus's admonition: "He that is without sin among you, let him cast the first stone," he expressed disgust that two policemen could devote their time to looking for odd behavior through a peephole in the YMCA. "There were four policemen there when Jenkins was picked up!" he exclaimed.

But what did Hoover mean when he urged Jenkins to show all visitors his card? Especially if he didn't know anything about the morals charge when he sent the flowers?

                                    *   *   *

Lady Bird Johnson was the model political wife. Her daughter Lynda once said, "Mother is like Voltaire's Candide. Whatever is going on, it's the best possible world. She always looks on the bright side."

She was also patient, understanding, cheerful, devoted, long-suffering, warmhearted, supportive, intelligent, and philosophical about her mate's vagaries, including his interest in younger charmers.

She took every demand and every blow with such serene dignity it disarmed the gossip mongers.

At least while he held office she was spared the embarrassment of publicized extramarital interests. Later, when Chuck Robb's alleged affair as governor of Virginia with shapely Tai Collins, Miss Virginia USA, was broadcast around the world, Lady Bird told her daughter how she must face the public:

"Just hold your head high," she said—an attitude she embodied and one that earned the respect of all who knew her.*

Lady Bird also knew her husband was a flirt; his august job had not changed one iota of his nature. It amused him to flatter a woman by saying, as he once did to me, "I have to use enough restraint where Viet Nam is concerned without having to use it with you." (I can't remember what prompted that but my response was, "I have known a lot of men with long lines, Mr. President, but yours is the longest.")

She also had incredible stamina.

How many women would go through grueling months to help a spouse get elected, stay up half the night waiting for the opponent to concede, and then, after only two hours sleep, give a barbecue at the ranch for hundreds in the press—because he wanted her to— and do it without a word of complaint? And we "Bird-watchers" had to have stamina too. I remember one icy raft trip in particular.

While Mrs. J. and Lynda stayed with the Laurence Rockefellers at their truly simple, rustic log cabin thirty-three miles from Jackson Hole, Wyo., we journalists were urged onto Snake River by Liz, who believed that a moment unspent was a moment lost to print. It poured during the three hours we floated toward the only possible landing, the cold rain trickling down our necks. When the ranger produced a tarpaulin we women and the only man, Art Buchwald, huddled under it.

Another "watcher" expedition took us to Big Bend National Park in west Texas. We stopped first in San Antonio, where Mrs. Johnson turned on the new "moonlighting" of the San Antonio River banks which wind through the city. It took us six or seven hours to arrive at our accommodations the next afternoon; immediately, we set out to hike the three-mile Lost Mine Trail with Mrs. J. That evening we gathered around a campfire on a hill to dine and listen to guitar

* The Robbs ended gossip about their future when they gave a 25th wedding anniversary party in their big McLean, Va. house on December 12, '92 and toasted each other with expressions of great love and respect.

music and tall tales of the West; above us, the sunset turned the Casa Grande peak into a lofty, high-walled castle bathed in gold.

"It's like the Lord was trying to make up for what he didn't give us [Texans] in lush greenery by giving us brilliant light," mused Lady Bird.

The next morning sixty-four newspeople, probably the greatest group of unfit outdoor types ever assembled, bused two hours to the Rio Grande, where we filled up most of twenty-four rafts. I shared a raft with Liz, Bill Blair of the *NY Times*, Jim Pitt of *Time-Life*, Frances Kolton of *Mademoiselle*, and two rangers. The five-and-one-half hour trip, half awe, half laughter, was broken sporadically when the raft began dragging in shallow water and the heaviest—i.e., the men and Liz—had to get out to pull and push. Slim Frances and I remained seated inside, our feet soaked in pools of water. At times the precipitous walls of stone—Mexico on one side, the U.S. on the other—towered to 1,900 feet above us and only fifty feet apart.

Johnson called his wife the best organized person he ever knew; she had surrounded herself with an equally efficient staff. The planning and preparation for her trips guaranteed her a splendid relationship with the press. For her "Flying Whistle-Stop," there were special postcards already stamped and signed by Mrs. Johnson, given to everyone who wanted to send one. There was the University of Texas professor who rode on the press bus in Texas' Big Bend Park to provide the background of that area. There were places assigned and labeled in every car in her caravans for the cabinet wives traveling with her; cards already signed by Lady Bird to be dispatched with the flowers she received at every stop to a hospital; an ever-present Western Union man to handle our copy as fast as we could give it to him.

Most trips focused on her primary interests—beautification and conservation. But Lady Bird also traveled widely to show her support for the arts.

In September of 1966, she went to New York—with us watchers in tow—for the opening of the new Metropolitan Opera House at Lincoln Center. It was the last word in resplendence. The Diamond Horseshoe boxes glittered with old money names like Governor and Mrs. Nelson Rockefeller, the John D. Rockefellers, Mrs. Vincent Astor, the Henry Fords, the Cornelius Vanderbilt Whitneys, and the

Alfred Gwynne Vanderbilts. So spectacular a display was it that film star Irene Dunne was among the sidewalk gapers.

That same month, we flew with her to California, where Governor Pat Brown was running against Ronald Reagan. (Reagan won.) We opened the San Francisco Opera season, drove down the beautiful Big Sur along California's magnificent coast, dined at the late William Randolph Hearst's San Simeon castle, and stopped in Santa Fe to visit the Institute of American Indian Arts.

We of the press admired Lady Bird. She combined some of the greatest American virtues: the adventurous spirit of Lewis and Clark; Henry Thoreau's love of nature; Daniel Boone's willingness to rough it; and Dolley Madison's political sense and ability to melt the ice at any social function.

* * *

Lyndon Johnson's Inaugural, which I covered by phone from a press table below the Capitol Plaza stand, drew a raft of celebrities. Telegrams had gone out to fifty outstanding Americans in the field of the arts—writers, poets, artists, actors, musicians—inviting them to attend the festivities. "The greatest party of the Great Society," I wrote, was the "brilliant blending of artists, writers and composers . . . with the cream of the Capital's society" at the State Department dinner after the inaugural concert. "It was a vibrant, living example of the Washington that novelist Herman Wouk described in the Inaugural Program under the title *A Sort of Overture*: 'My impression of the city is probably romantic. It strikes me as one of the nicest and most exciting places on earth to live. I have a vision of its future so brilliant that cynical oldtimers may well smile at it.' " During the course of the evening, which naturally wound up with dancing, the Johnsons greeted composer Aaron Copland, Admiral and Mrs. Samuel Eliot Morison, Marian Anderson, Mark Rothko, poets W. D. Snodgrass and Richard Wilbur, sculptor George Segal, Dr. Paul Dudley White, authors Bill Goyen, William Styron, Tom Lea, and Wouk, Van Cliburn, Freedom Medal winners, and artist Peter Hurd. Later, Hurd would paint the presidential portrait that Johnson, for reasons I never understood, rejected, calling it, "The ugliest thing I ever saw."

The thirty-three parties I managed to attend between January 12 and the 23rd were a name-dropper's paradise: Perle Mesta's apartment drew Johnson relatives and new Vice President Hubert Humphrey, Carol Channing, Eva Gabor, and congressional and Texas bigwigs—including Judge Sarah Hughes, who swore Johnson in on Air Force One that fateful night in Dallas.

At Gwen Cafritz's supper dance, elbow-rubbers included Gregory Peck, Harry Belafonte, Barbra Streisand, Rudolph Nureyev, Dame Margot Fonteyn, Woody Allen, Carol Burnett, Alfred Hitchcock, and Bobby Darin. Carol Channing was still doing fancy footwork there with Hubert Humphrey at 2:15 A.M.

By the time I had covered the biggest of the five inaugural balls— one for seven thousand at the Sheraton Hotel—and then gone on to the supper dance Scottie Fitzgerald Lanahan gave in honor of Adlai Stevenson, I had reached the celebrity saturation point.

* * *

Look magazine published a surprising article in April of 1965.

Although it emphasized the Kennedy administration's culture and style, and called Johnson an effective "country boy," it contained almost the first printed criticism of Jack Kennedy to appear since his assassination. He was aloof with Congress, it said; he rarely held a cabinet meeting; he didn't understand or care about agriculture; and he had "turned aside a good conservation idea" of Secretary of Interior Stewart Udall with the question: "Where were your Western voters last November?"

It also said—and I have no doubt that these words are truthful— that "Every passionate admirer of John Kennedy is waiting for every Lyndon Johnson fan to fall on his face—and vice versa. The Johnson people felt snubbed by the Kennedy people who made little or no effort to hide their opinions."

There was more "country boy" criticism when LBJ invited American Indians in full regalia to do their Indian dances in the East Room. They were the first Native Americans ever to perform at a state dinner. Some thought it was a patronizing performance before the president of an undeveloped country, President Yameogo of Upper Volta—not knowing that Yameogo had asked to see real American Indians. Besides, Upper Volta didn't seem so undeveloped when his wife showed up in a magnificent beaded gown from Paris topped by a gorgeous chinchilla wrap. Nor did the Indians seem the least bit primitive when the Sioux mistress of ceremonies addressed the state visitor in fluent French!

Smarting from the criticism about culture, Johnson established the National Council on the Arts; that April, he swore in twenty-four members.

In June, the Johnsons held the first-ever Festival of the American Arts in the Executive Mansion. It was the best and biggest event ever given there for the arts. The all-day affair displayed thirty-five major modern paintings including Andrew Wyeth's *Christina's World*, a Jackson Pollock, De Kooning, and Robert Motherwell, as well as fourteen fine pieces of contemporary sculpture. There were readings by poets Mark Van Doren, Phyllis McGinley, and authors Saul Bellow and John Hersey; acting by Maureen Stapleton and George Grizzard; singing by opera star Roberta Peters; narrating by Helen Hayes and Gregory Peck, and so on. It was a thrilling day.

But for the Johnsons, who were trying to show government enthusiasm for the arts, it was ruined by Robert Lowell's reaction to the invitation to attend and read his poems.

He wouldn't come, he told the world, because he disagreed with the president's Viet Nam policy.

Helen Hayes called it "shame-making"; various other artists dubbed it "rude" and "in poor judgment" to discourage government aid to the arts.

The media virtually ignored the wealth of artistic accomplishment all around them, and made headlines only of the antiwar controversy. Lowell's criticisms had overshadowed the day completely. The Johnsons were so stung that they never tried anything like it again; nor has any president since.

But that did not end LBJ's belief in the arts. When he opened the White House to concerts by Americans who had won honors in the Tchaikovsky competition in Moscow, he called the young performers "national treasures." Former winner Van Cliburn, who emceed the event, praised the Johnsons—but the greatest tribute came from Democratic Congressman Frank Thompson of New Jersey. A staunch promoter for years of government aid to the arts as well as for a cultural center in Washington, Thompson said that evening it was President Johnson's personal efforts in getting behind the arts bill that got it through.

"One of the first things he did as president was to get me on the phone and say he wanted me to get behind a national arts bill. He also called Senator [Claiborne] Pell and the majority leader and the Speaker. The bill was the president's bill, make no mistake about that," finished Thompson.

LBJ also got the 10 percent admission tax removed from all opera, theater, and ballet performances; made Chairman of the National Council on the Arts Roger Stevens his presidential assistant for the arts; and gave a grand dinner for famous names in the arts modeled on the one President and Mrs. Kennedy did for Nobel Prize-winners.

A country boy, yes. A hick, no.

* * *

The zaniest evening I have ever witnessed in officialdom took place June 17 in the State Department auditorium. Astronauts James McDivitt and Edward White narrated the film of their Gemini 4 flight in space for a crowd including the Johnsons, Vice President Humphrey, NASA Administrator James Webb, Charles Mathews, head of the Gemini program, the astronauts' wives, some diplomats, and other officials. The astronauts' children were being baby-sat by Luci Johnson at the White House, where they and their parents were to spend the night.

The minute the film was over, the president took the stage and launched his own surprise rocket. He announced that he was sending McDivitt, White, the vice president, and their wives to Paris "in the very next few hours." The NASA officials and their wives were also to go. The news hit the group like a thunderbolt. None had had any advance warning. LBJ said he wanted them to be at the Paris air show, to share with other people "the excitement and thrills you experienced." Wily Lyndon both wanted to keep the Russians from monopolizing the air show, and to pave the way to an important interview with De Gaulle. He told me the idea had been brewing in his mind for three or four days.

His announcement sent the White House and State Department

aides into a frenzy. It set off a chain of frantic preparations even while the Johnsons were greeting people at the State Department's postmovie reception. It was already 10 P.M.

Passports had to be provided for everybody who didn't have theirs in Washington; France had to be notified—and it was 3 A.M. there. Humphrey had to rush a call to Muriel in Minnesota to tell her to wing it back immediately, in time for Air Force One's 4 A.M. take-off. The young wives had to have laundry done in a hurry.

Our embassy in Paris had to pull together a reception for two thousand, two dinner parties at the embassy, and a luncheon at the air show. The small fry at the White House were to be sent back to Texas the next day. It was all done in an exciting, mad, wild rush. And it worked!

The plane took off at 4:27 A.M.—with Mrs. Humphrey aboard. Once again, LBJ had proved that nothing is impossible. I rushed home, wrote the story, sent it to the *Star*. It made the top of next day's front page.

If that evening was the wildest, the night Congress passed the "Lady Bird' beautification bill was the runner-up.

The president was due at Bethesda Naval Hospital October 7, 1965; his gall bladder was to be removed next morning. That did not keep him from holding a White House buffet supper and State Department "Salute to Congress" that evening. Half the senators and their wives were enjoying the lavish buffet and music at the White House; the wives of representatives—dressed for the party and watching from the House Gallery—were mentally egging their husbands on to a quick passage of the bill.

In the meantime, film stars Frederic March and Hugh O'Brian, opera star Robert Merrill, singers Mahalia Jackson and Anita Bryant, and others were waiting at the State Department to put on the 8:30 salute in the auditorium. We of the press waited there too, complaining of hunger and thirst until Liz Carpenter ordered a bar and buffet. In no time we had a swinging party, complete with music, when suddenly a handful of the press, I included, were pulled away and whisked over to the White House's Yellow Oval Room. There, the Johnsons were receiving the stars, to make up for their long wait.

In short order, with the help of another trio, we had a third party going.

At ten o'clock, with the bill still unpassed, everybody on the second and first floors of the Casa Blanca, using every stairway in the mansion, sped to the ground floor and into cars and buses to rush back to State's auditorium. By 10:30 the Johnsons, the Humphreys, most of the cabinet, a flock of senatorial couples, and all congressmen's wives were seated, and the show began. At 11:14 the president and Lady Bird thanked the performers and left for the hospital; everyone else went back to the White House for more fun, more food, more jazz by the Marine combo, and another great show by the cast. In the wee hours I went home and wrote it up.

*   *   *

In the fall of 1965, President and Mrs. Johnson gave possibly the gayest party ever held in the White House for a high level visitor. She was Princess Margaret of Great Britain, accompanied by her husband Anthony Armstrong-Jones, the earl of Snowdon. It was the most bejeweled gathering in years, a blinding assortment ranging from Margaret's choker of big diamonds and matching long earrings and bracelets to a king's ransom of diamonds and emeralds worn by Mrs. Nelson Rockefeller, Mrs. Henry Ford II, Mrs. John Loeb, Mrs. John Sherman Cooper, and others. Even Lady Bird sported new diamond drop earrings, a thirty-first anniversary present from her husband.

There were gorgeous "jeweled" dresses on Mrs. Kirk Douglas, Mrs. Edward Kennedy, Mrs. Lloyd Hand, and Mrs. Jack Valenti—but the most talked-of gown was Christina Ford's. Husband Henry had told the fiery Italian that her strapless white sheath was too low. Eventually—inevitably—as she waved her arms to the hot rhythms of Peter Duchin's orchestra, it slipped below one breast—thereby immortalizing the event, as only titillating trivia can.

Lynda Johnson was squired that evening by handsome actor George Hamilton, and Luci by her fiancé Pat Nugent.

Despite his recent gall bladder operation the iron president led off the dancing with the princess, danced most of the evening with such partners as Mrs. Arthur Krim and Mrs. John Connally, and had a final twirl with Margaret in the front hall before the royal pair left a little before 2 A.M. Tony Snowdon danced all evening and was just starting to do a frug with me when his wife signaled it was time to leave. I told him I had to go home and turn out a story; he'd write it for me, he said. I handed him my notebook and pen, and he jotted down the following about himself: ". . . did one waltz and then sat out for the rest of the evening." Snowdon, of course, was definitely not the waltzing type—and neither was Princess Margaret, who got a rush on the dance floor, but behaved with great decorum that evening.

That, recall, was the decade of the frug, the watusi, the jerk, and other free-wheeling gyrations to rock music in every ballroom. I labeled it the sizzling sixties, and you could not escape its beat, even on Embassy Row.

Algerian Ambassador Cherif Guellal, a handsome young bachelor, gave a very correct dinner for fifty in honor of new Chief of Protocol and Mrs. James Wadsworth Symington. Immediately after dinner the Hangmen, a band of long-haired, mustachioed "perpetrators of the palpitating pulsation," deadringers for stereotyped West Virginny hillbillies, burst into their cataclysmic electronic rock beat, and the distinguished assembly was seized with something resembling St. Vitus' dance.

Even big Indian Ambassador B.K. Nehru succumbed, while his Hungarian-born wife did a wild watusi with Leslie Carpenter.

The night before, the LBJs had given a dinner and dance for Danish Prime Minister Jens Otto Krag and his beautiful actress wife that seemed almost calm by comparison. Yet it was the most uninhibited I had witnessed at the White House. It, too, began sedately, but as soon as the orchestra switched to rock beat everybody but the hosts loosened up. Hubert Humphrey did such a spirited frug with Gregory Peck's wife Veronique that Bob Hope dubbed the vice president, "Hubert-a-gogo."

The Hopes had forgotten their entrance card that evening, and were stopped at the north gate. The W.H. cop, who obviously recognized America's best known comedian, said he would let him through if he told him a joke. Quick as a flash Hope said, "Did you hear about the president arriving in Mexico the other day and saying, 'This is a part of Texas I have never been in?' " The officer burst into laughter and let him through.

One guest, Jack Dempsey, told me that Mr. Johnson had phoned him at eight o'clock one morning and invited him to the party, right after Jack appeared on the "Today Show." An unbelieving Dempsey turned to his wife and said, "A fellow who says he's Lyndon Johnson just telephoned." Not till later was he convinced he had talked to the real LBJ.

At 1:15 A.M., the former heavyweight champion of the world and his wife were still sitting at one of the small tables that ringed the East Room. They were told they could leave if they wanted to, as the guests of honor had left. Replied Jack, "This is the first time I've ever been here and I don't want to miss anything. I'm going to stay here until the president goes."

He finally gave up at 2 A.M.

Social Secretary Bess Abell said she had the orchestra play "The Party Is Over" three times hoping Mr. Johnson would stop dancing, but every time he asked for "Hello, Dolly." Finally, at 3 A.M. he shook the hands of all thirteen members of the Lee Evans orchestra and strode out of the ballroom, still looking fresh.

In the midst of all this gaiety on the social scene I had a personal loss. Father died October 21, 1965, at age ninety minus two months. Suddenly, I was alone in our six-bedroom, memory-filled Tracy Place house. It was time to move.

I found an adorable house on the corner of 32nd Street and Reservoir Road, the only house I saw in Georgetown with bright light on three sides. I redecorated, moved in, threw a housewarming—it drew dozens of friends, including the Spanish Ambassador and Marquesa de Merry del Val, Perle Mesta, the Clark Cliffords, Kuwait Ambassador and Mrs. Al-Ghoussein, and Scottie Fitzgerald Lanahan—and buckled down to the Sizzling Sixties. It was after the Opera Ball, at the Smithsonian's Museum of American History, that the national brouhaha erupted. The catalyst: A picture of Johnson's press secretary, Bill Moyers, doing the watusi with Libby Cater, wife of Presidential Assistant Douglass Cater. Under the heading, "Look What's Going On In Washington," *U.S. News and World Report* of May 30, 1966, devoted two full pages with six pictures to parties in the Capital, quoting from my, and others', stories.

Iowa Republican Congressman H. R. Gross exclaimed on the floor of the House Chamber, "I couldn't believe my eyes seeing the Reverend Moyers [Bill was a theological seminary graduate] doing the watusi or the frug or something. And the wife of a State Department official was reported to be sent home because she didn't have on enough clothes. Apparently she was half naked." If there ever was a gross misstatement, Gross' was it.

The so-called "half naked" woman was Joy Carter, a chic, genteel Philadelphia Mainliner whose husband was in the CIA; in fact, she had on more clothes than most women at the ball. Her one-of-a-kind, long, jeweled, designer gown of white lace had a high neck and long sleeves. Under it she wore a nontransparent, neck-to-toe body stocking and pantyhose. After arriving at the museum she decided that "somebody might just feel it was wrong" for the outline of her legs to be seen through the peekaboo dress so she rushed home and added a long white slip. But word of the original eye-stopper had spread and started the rumor. As usual, it was spicier than the truth.

A reader sent me a letter-to-the-editor clipped from the *Minneapolis Star* which said my columns reminded the writer of the old saying: "Nero fiddled while Rome burned." The reader also enclosed my column about the Opera Ball, noting in the margin: "We have a war going on, you know. Our sons are being killed and wounded. How can our own national Capital have stupid parties?" And a *Charlotte* (N. C.) *Observer* reader scribbled across the top of my column which the paper had headed: "White House Shindig Swings": "This is unforgivable behavior in Washington while our boys are dying in Viet Nam."

Of course I couldn't blame readers for feeling that way. Yet again, I answered in my syndicated column:

"The President is in a predicament. As the head of the nation it is his duty and obligation to entertain other chiefs of state or heads of government. Yet because of the war in Viet Nam and its resulting horrors for the young men participating and their families back home, Johnson is being harshly criticized for the party he gave for . . . Danish Prime Minister Krag. The kind of entertainment that is served up to the visitors, after the required dinner in their honor, is based on their tastes, likes and dislikes determined by research done at the State Department or in the White House. It can be a concert, which some people adore and others find dull, or ballet and ditto, or a reading. Or there can be simply dancing in the East Room. In the case of Mr. Krag the dancing was decided upon because they are a young couple and it was thought they would have more fun at this kind of party.

"The President, who adores dancing, . . . doesn't get such an opportunity even on an average of one evening in a whole month. Yet because he kept the music going until 3, and himself participated until that hour, some parents of sons lost or serving in the war have decided that he doesn't care what happens in Viet Nam.

"The President stays up until 2 or 3 every night—requiring only 5 or 6 hours' sleep—going over a mountain of nighttime government reading that is put on his bedside table every night . . . [When he] stays up till the same hour to entertain a government visitor, the parents of soldiers are horrified.

"So what does the chief executive do—rule out dancing from now on and sit through the musicales that bore him and have bored most presidents? Doubtless if he was listening to something that bored him there would be no criticism. But as soon as he glides around on the dance floor and enjoys himself he is damned by the citizens he devotes every other waking moment to."

My own dancing in his house, I was aware, had added to the problem. The night of the dinner for the shah and empress of Iran, Johnson retired five minutes after their departure but the American Ballet Theatre performers began dancing up a storm in the front hall to the Marine Band's rock music. Les Carpenter and I, finding the beat irresistible, were wiggling our bodies and waving our arms in what we were sure was the hottest frug east of the Alleghenies when I suddenly realized we were right in front of the north portico doors which were wide open. Through the doors across the darkened front lawn I could see a whole row of people lined up, their faces glued to the picket fence, watching the brilliantly lighted antics within the dignified facade of the President's House. We were pouring fat on the fire of the anti-Johnson criticism that was sweeping the country, while he was upstairs poring over government papers. We quickly moved to the side.

The letters I received must have been a drop in the bucket to what poured into the White House.

So that was the end of dancing to rock. There was only mild Glenn Miller-type dancing at the military reception, and the Johnsons, usually so friendly with us who wrote about such evenings, had no words for us at all on that occasion.

* * *

Earlier in the year I had had an extraordinary conversation with Lyndon Johnson. I had written that Speaker John McCormack and his wife, the ranking guests at the Johnsons' supper-dance for the Congress, had cocktails with their hosts in the yellow Oval Room upstairs, then left before the party began. To avoid making them look rude, I had said, "The Speaker and his ailing wife" left one minute before the Johnsons came downstairs. I also assumed she was ailing because she walked with difficulty.

At the next state function President Johnson pulled me aside in the Blue Room to tell me that the Speaker had been very upset by my calling his wife "ailing." Supposedly tough LBJ said, "Can you please write something nice about her to make him feel better? He dotes on her."

I was touched by his concern. But my response was: "What has that woman got that makes him think she's so hot? She doesn't keep house for him. [They lived in the Washington Hotel.] She doesn't cook for him. [They ate the hotel food.] She doesn't have a good figure [she was a big, heavy woman], she's not good-looking [she wore a black hairnet that came down on her forehead and dark-rimmed glasses], and she's worn the same dress for years on end to every White House party."

"I know," replied the president, "but he adores her and I would appreciate it if you could write something nice about her."

The opportunity, though, never arose. I almost never saw either of them and when I did she never stopped to chat with or smile at anyone.

I subsequently learned from Malvina Stephenson's article in the *Washington Star* that she was arthritic and seven years older than her husband; that she had never given an interview during the four decades of her husband's public life; that the Speaker's staffers protected her from press queries; that she took daily outings in her husband's chauffered limousine (supplied by Congress); and that

John McCormack never missed having dinner with her every night, even when he had to rush away from a political banquet!

A year after their youngest daughter Luci was married to Pat Nugent* in the Catholic Shrine of the Immaculate Conception (on one of the hottest days of the year) the Johnsons announced Lynda's engagement to White House social aide, Marine Captain Charles Robb. Chuck was attractive, a he-man, and a patriot. When assigned to the White House social duty he asked to go to Viet Nam instead—and he went soon after his marriage to Lynda. He was reluctant to talk about himself but there were no fewer than twelve trophies in his Washington apartment testifying to his past excellence in football, basketball, volley ball, tennis, and golf. When he graduated from the University of Wisconsin in 1961 he was a six-striper, the top ROTC man in his class. And he was the honor man at his Quantico graduation, the only Marine presented with a sword. Lynda was radiant in her happiness. The wedding was to take place December 9 in the White House—the first there since Eleanor Wilson married William Gibbs McAdoo in 1914. I was particularly pleased because I had known Chuck's family all my life. His grandfather Robert Woolley was a good friend of my Uncle Louis Brownlow and I had been in a "strip tease" comedy skit in the Junior League Follies with his aunt "Ootey" Woolley.

The romantic pair became the lions of the social scene, sought-after for every charity event and important embassy dinner. They were at British Ambassador and Lady Dean's party for Princess Alexandra, the Queen's cousin, and her husband, tall, handsome Angus Ogilvy, younger son of the Earl of Airlie. But they were not the chief attraction, for me.

Midst the beautiful and royally correct surroundings, impish Alice Longworth started a contest in facial expressions. She showed her table companions, columnist Stewart Alsop and pretty Mrs. Desmond Fitzgerald, how she could twitch one side of her nose, and keep it up indefinitely. (When she was a child, Mrs. L. said, she once practised it in church and heard a woman nearby remark: "Poor President Roosevelt, his daughter has a twitch.") Whereupon Barbara Fitzgerald showed how she could twist her mouth so that the

---

* The marriage was to end in divorce.

upper lip went in one direction and the lower in another for a horrific look. Not to be outshone by his Cousin Alice or Barbara, Alsop began demonstrating how he could cross his eyes and wiggle his eyebrows at the same time—no mean feat. It was a rare vignette.

*   *   *

October 1967 witnessed an extraordinary counterpoint: At an antiwar demonstration outside the Pentagon, some of the crowd of 35,000—mostly white, unkempt, unbrushed, and unwashed— desecrated the walls with indecent words or actions; at the Pablo Casals United Nations Association concert, scrubbed members of the Catholic and Howard University choirs, blacks and whites together, raised their voices in a chorus, "Glory Be To God."

The demonstrators left an unholy mess at the Pentagon; Pablo Casals left beauty, and later, at dinner, uplift: "America . . . that country that I love so. . . . You're the richest and most generous of any country," he said. "You have helped the advance of every noble thing. . . . I have faith in you Americans. God bless you."

The hundreds at the dinner, including ninety foreign ambassadors—the Soviet, too—gave him a standing ovation. His words meant all the more because he was a man of unassailable moral fiber: He had not only exiled himself from Franco's Spain, but had refused to play his cello for years, in protest against fascism.

The antiwar, anti-Johnson demonstrators led to the following conversation between a "close Johnson official" and myself at a Turkish Embassy reception. I ended my column of November 5, 1967, with it, protecting the name of the official as I had agreed to do. It presaged Lyndon Johnson's withdrawal from the 1968 presidential race.

Q. Why doesn't the American public hear about the continuous atrocities of the Viet Cong and North Vietnamese? The only thing it seems to hear about is the destruction done by American forces. Why isn't a daily report put out on what real horrors the enemy has perpetrated on the South Vietnamese?

A. It should be. The Viet Cong sometimes cut off hands or cut out insides so that they die slowly. But the president does not want to spread hate.

Q. Why not? In a war there has to be an enemy, so there has to be some hate. In the absence of another enemy, America has become its own enemy. Americans are now hating America.

A. The president is afraid that if American hate is escalated there will be an overriding demand to use the A-bomb.

Q. Doesn't the president realize that by deviating the hate from the real enemy that he is becoming the enemy and may lose the election? An awful lot of misguided Americans are beginning to think that Ho Chi Minh has been grossly mistreated, is a great guy, and Lyndon Johnson is the enemy.

A. It's ironic, isn't it? But he makes the policy.

Even more ironic is the fact that both Johnson assistants, Harry McPherson and Horace Busby, said that the president was far more afraid of pressure from the extreme Right than that from the Left.

* * *

Whether as a friend of the family's or a writer of Johnson-supportive columns, I was invited to Lynda's wedding in December 1967 as a guest. I stood by the center door of the East Room to witness the ceremony at the improvised altar that centered the opposite wall— an excellent position in the room full of standing guests. And when the four o'clock wedding and reception were over I went home, took to my typewriter, and wrote over two thousand words.

It was all done, Mrs. Longworth, the last White House bride, noted, in perfect taste. Lynda, in her embroidered & seed-pearled white satin gown, with fifteen yards of silk illusion springing from a seed pearl crown on the back of her swept-back raven hair, looked ravishing; Chuck couldn't take his eyes off her.

When all the guests—who included Merle Oberon, Christina Ford, Carol Channing, and Charlotte Ford—had been received, and the cake-cutting and customary first dances had taken place, the president came over to me. "Come on, Betty, I want to show you something," he said. With the reception still going strong, he led me to the elevator and upstairs to the West Sitting Hall and invited me to sit down on the sofa. A second later he produced a letter to read aloud to me. It was from Chuck's Grandfather Woolley, written on his law office stationery June 26, 1940, to Charles S. Robb II. It said:

My precious Grandson:

On this day, the first anniversary of your birth, I salute you. Also I thank you for the pleasure you have given to all of us. Little will you ever realize how joyful a baby you were, how bountiful the love for you in all of us.

When you are old enough to read and understand this letter, either there will at last be peace on earth again or civilization will have had its Gethsemane. Today Adolf Hitler, whose name will for centuries to come be anathema to those who cherish liberty of thought and freedom to follow the dictates of their conscience, and his Huns are devastating Europe with their mechanized warfare, destroying millions of God-fearing people whose only offending was that they dared to fight for what they believed to be the right—in defense of their homes and the faith of their fathers. [Here Mr. Johnson interrupted his reading to comment, "Like Viet Nam."]

Thank God, it will all be a memory while you are still a child, but it will carry a lesson which you and your generation must heed. May love of country, love of liberty in its finest sense (in defense of both of which you must ever be ready to offer your life if necessary) always find sanctuary in your heart. May you grow to manhood the splendid fruit of a fine ancestry, a comfort to and the pride of your parents—and be a gentleman ever.

> Your devoted grandfather,
> Robert W. Woolley

I thought it was a wonderful letter; I remembered so well the man who had written it. I asked the president if I could have the letter long enough to phone it in to my paper. He said I could, and suggested that I use the phone in the second floor dining room.

Lynda had taken Chuck completely by surprise when she read the letter in her toast to him at the bridal dinner. Without telling anyone, her father said proudly, she had gone to the Library of Congress and found it in Woolley's papers which had been willed to the library.

LBJ read another letter to me while we were in the West Sitting Hall. Dosed daily with denunciations of America and himself from some quarter or other, he wanted to show what somebody out there thought of this country. It read:

Dear Mr. President:

We're a typical American family. We have a mortgage, a car, kids and debts. On Thanksgiving Day we went to church, watched football and ate turkey. We gave thanks to a generous God for our good life.

At times like this one tends to reflect on life. Has it been really good: And have we really been good to it?

It has been a good life; good wife, good kids, good country. Like any typical American I love my wife. I don't always tell her this, but she knows. I also love my children and they probably find this hard to believe, especially when they're being lambasted. I also love my country, but I haven't told her either.

The way we men are made it isn't easy to tell a wife of many years, "I love you." And it isn't easy to convince the kids of your love either. But how do you tell a country you love it. Hire a billboard?

You know what I've always wanted to do? Some year I'd love to tell the tax people to keep that two hundred dollar refund check, my compliments. I don't pay much in taxes, I never have. Too many kids, too many medical bills, and not enough money. But this would be one way of saying, 'United States, I love you!'

Well, right now the country is having a little trouble, this drain on gold. Now I have a very modest coin collection and my prize piece is a ten dollar gold piece. There's been many a Christmas I came close to cashing it in, but I never did. We don't have any money in the bank and this coin represented something—oh, I don't know. It just seemed that as long as I had it, we'd never be broke, it was something to fall back on. Some day I guess I'd give it to one of the kids. Maybe with the passage of years it would have a collection value and I could think, "I gave that child something of value."

Like the typical American, that's a typical dream, huh? Kinda silly, isn't it?

Now this isn't going to stop the gold problem. It won't scare off Charlie de Gaulle. Maybe it won't mean a thing to anyone, except me. But can I give you this gold piece, to help? And since I couldn't rent a billboard, and I need that refund check to put the car on the road, could this be my way of saying I do love my country?

Sincerely yours,
Jack Ryan
223 Village Street, Medway, Mass.

Scotch-taped to the bottom of the letter was the gold coin.
The president then read his reply:

Dear Mr. Ryan:

I was so moved by your letter that I have kept it by me for some
time now.

But this is a good day to tell you of my gratitude and admiration.
Tomorrow, my daughter Lynda will be married. I have shown your
letter to her as an example of what love can mean to a man—and his
wife—and their nation.

God bless you for the inspiration and warmth of your heart. My
family is proud to share with yours the kinship of a country and its
bright causes.

The gold coin I am returning to you with deep appreciation. I think
that it belongs more properly to your sons. Its greatest value will be in
reminding them of their father's feeling for the American family and
nation.

Mrs. Johnson joins me in wishing all of you all the happiness that
life holds for the good and wise heart.

Sincerely,
Lyndon Johnson

*   *   *

Wedding guest Merle Oberon, the famed movie star, was to become
a good friend. Later, she told me that Teddy Kennedy—still married to Joan at the time—called her for a date. How could he take
her out, she asked, when everybody recognized him? The American
people would love him whatever he did, the senator replied. "That
was a few weeks before Chappaquiddick," she said.

Less than four months later Lyndon Johnson rocked the nation
and the world with the announcement that he would not run again
because he could not unite the country.

With LBJ out of the race Hubert Humphrey immediately became
a viable candidate. His presence four days later at a Democratic
congressional fund-raising dinner at the Washington Hilton stirred
up excitement and new hopes for his party. But the adrenalin had
barely started to flow when he stood up and stilled the ballroom
with his announcement: Martin Luther King had been shot. A few

minutes later three thousand stunned subscribers had left the ball-room empty.

The shaken city watched in shame, horror, and pity while blacks devastated their own most-frequented areas, the columns of smoke rising like malignant prayers. For the next seven days the curfew imposed on the Capital kept me and everyone I knew locked in our houses from 4:00 in the afternoon on through the night. Washington had not seen anything like this since the British burned the city in 1814. It was eerie to rush home past soldiers with helmets and guns on a sunny Sunday afternoon, to lock oneself in.

With Senator Eugene McCarthy having defeated Johnson in the early New Hampshire presidential primary, and with Bobby Kennedy and Humphrey now in the running, Democratic politics took a revealing new twist: It turned out that those who played together, stayed together. Robert McNamara, who as Johnson's secretary of defense for five years had supported and carried out his policies while Bobby Kennedy had denounced them, now gave Bobby his public support in a TV film.

Of course, the McNamaras had been in the Kennedy social circle from the start, dining and skiing with them. They had entertained and been entertained by both the John Kennedys and the Robert Kennedys at intimate dinners—something not true of Secretary of State Dean Rusk, Secretary of Labor Bill Wirtz, and some others in JFK's cabinet.

Some of the columnists who had also given LBJ a hard time were members of the Bobby-and-Ethel set, and frequent guests at Hickory Hill, their McLean, Va., estate.

The Kennedys recognized that the social side of life was very important in politics. Humphrey, with his enormous happy vitality and wit, could outshine the other candidates at social affairs, but he did not have the kind of glamor that goes with wealth, or the charisma that causes crowds to grab a candidate's clothes and steal his shoes. Bobby did.

Retiring President Johnson made such a point of complimenting his vice president at his state dinner for King Olav V of Norway that all those listening thought he was about to endorse Humphrey's candidacy. But he did not. Humphrey was on his own. Of course, he made the best of it.

He made a point of telling the king that his mother had come from Norway, so he was 51 percent Norwegian.* The next day H.H., son of a small town pharmacist, hosted a luncheon at the State Department for the king. His majesty, a big, strapping-looking man with a patrician face, humorous eyes, and a balding pate, told me in the receiving line that he had liked the Joffrey Ballet performance at the White House.

"It was sexy, wasn't it?" I remarked, remembering a scantily clad duo apparently glued together on the floor.

"Isn't that the way we're supposed to be?" replied his majesty with a grin.

"Did you say 'we,' sir?" I rejoined. He chuckled.

With presidential politics heating up, Drew Pearson gave a cock-tail party "To meet Frank Sinatra and his candidate." The singer had come to town to entertain at the Big Brothers benefit dinner organized by Pearson. Drew was president of the Brothers, an orga-nization that enlisted volunteer male adults as surrogate big brothers for delinquent or neglected boys. Sinatra donated his en-tire troupe for the cause.

Wearing a diamond-studded Russian cross of St. Anne on a gold chain with his dinner jacket, he wowed his audience of one thou-sand. The diamond cross, he said, was given to him by Mrs. Leland Hayward. Producer Leland Hayward's wife at the time was Pamela Digby Churchill, the future Mrs. Averell Harriman. The beautiful Pamela reportedly had a fling with Frank.

This was Sinatra's first visit to Washington since running the Inaugural Gala for Jack Kennedy in 1961. After reports of their behaviour then, President Kennedy had deliberately distanced him-self from the Rat Pack. He was already too closely connected to one, his brother-in-law Peter Lawford. Frank took a dim view of the estrangement after all his inaugural efforts, so he came out for Humphrey. He told Hubert he would give fund-raising perfor-mances for him in six to ten cities starting later in May, and promised to organize a committee of one hundred entertainers for him. He

---

* In an election year it was smart to claim a majority kinship to a minority that numbered 3 million in the U.S. Norway itself had only 3.7 million inhabitants.

also made a generous offer to District of Columbia Mayor Walter Washington. During the upcoming poor peoples' encampment in the Capital, he said, they would have to be kept occupied: "At any time if you need me to come back and help, just give me a few days notice and I will do it," he told the mayor. It was never necessary.

There were other undercurrents. When LBJ made Sargent Shriver his ambassador to France, people speculated that it was to keep Sarge from campaigning against him, and for his brother-in-law, Bobby Kennedy. (Eunice planned to campaign for her brother, anyway.)

State Department officers seethed over the special treatment Shriver received at his Paris post: The timing was delicate: Everyone of our overseas posts around the world had recently been forced to cut its personnel by at least 10 percent to meet the president's January order to help the U.S. balance of payments. Nobody was fired, but home jobs had to be found for those in abolished posts. Two hundred senior career diplomats had to retire before the age of sixty.

It then turned out that Ambassador Shriver had asked for four new positions at his embassy. They were: (1) a personal public relations officer for himself (his predecessors used the USIA); (2) an additional personal assistant; (3) a foreign service officer to advise Eunice Shriver—a brand new post; and (4) an extra chauffeur for the ambassador. The embassy already had a motor pool with twenty-six men who did nothing but drive and twenty-five other mechanics and dispatchers who could double for drivers.

Shriver got them all. What's more, the new chauffeur, who could not speak French, got the salary of a first secretary in the diplomatic service. All except Eunice's FSO adviser were already serving Shriver before his appointment. There was no explanation of why he was given special treatment—but it was another indication that the Kennedys were, still, a law unto themselves.

At a dinner in June honoring President José Trejos of Costa Rica, LBJ toasted him in strangely prophetic words. "You have been in Washington now for ten hours," he said, "and there are not many days when this political Capital can go that long without an eruption." Before the party was over the world learned that Bobby Kennedy had been shot in California.

*   *   *

The Johnson administration ended in a glorious whirl of balls, dinners, receptions, luncheons. One party, the White House farewell reception for the National Council on the Arts, was a thank-you to the stars who had donated performances there. Isaac Stern and Justice Abe Fortas played the violin; Duke Ellington knocked out some jazz; and the Alvin Ailey dancers performed before an audience of Leontyne Price, Martha Graham, Rudolf Serkin, Marian Anderson, David Brubeck, Oliver Smith, Robert Merrill, O'Neill Ford, Edward Villella, fashion designer George Stravropoulis whose evening gowns for Lady Bird were her husband's favorites, and even make-up artist Eddie Senz who had improved her appearance.

Three vignettes from that whirl stand out in my mind: Vice President Humphrey observed, on seeing the David Lloyd Kreegers' art collection, "I *try* to understand art, but some of these modern ones really don't grab me." . . . Marjorie Post revealed that her Russian treasures cost only a song—"The Russians based their price on five cents a gram," she said—thus her beautiful lapis lazuli and gold high chest cost only $250! . . . And the president disclosed that his wife had predicted, long ago, his withdrawal from the race in 1968. In her diary on March 2, 1965, she wrote that she would count the months until March 2, 1968, when her husband would do as President Truman had done in March 1952 and tell the American people he would not run again.

CHAPTER 7

Pas de Deux

Madly for Adlai

ADLAI

March 1, 1962, was a red letter day in my life. That night there was a gala benefit aboard the longest luxury liner in the world, the SS *France*, docked in New York harbor. French Ambassador and Madame Alphand had arranged for a chartered plane to fly the Washington subscribers to La Guardia Airport. Top couturiers of Paris had each sent three dresses to parade in the on-board fashion show. French entertainers would perform; two French orchestras would play; French perfumes and other Parisian products would be given out as favors. All who chose could spend the night on the ship without charge, providing they debarked at 8:30 the next morning. But I had a better arrangement.

My close friend Scottie Fitzgerald Lanahan, the daughter of F. Scott and Zelda Fitzgerald, a talented writer and prominent young hostess, had heard me exult over Adlai Stevenson's successes, expound on his virtues, and sigh over my hopeless love for him for ten years. She decided to invite Adlai to be my date at the gala to join her and husband Jack, even though the tickets were, at $100 each—in 1962 dollars—expensive. And Adlai accepted. From then on, I was on Cloud Nine. A date with the witty and charming statesman, whom half the country loved, who was respected around

129

the world, who couldn't walk down the streets of New York without being stopped by admirers? I was beside myself!

But the day before the event Scottie called me with distressing news. Nicole Alphand had called and said she wanted Adlai, then the UN ambassador, at her table.

Scottie didn't know how to tell the gala's benefactor and ranking woman that she couldn't have him. I, though, reacted like a tigress whose cub was being snatched. "Madame Alphand can't do this to me!" I exploded to Nicole's social secretary. "Adlai is my date! It's the first I've ever had with him, and I've been in love with this man for ten years!"

If there is one thing the French understand, it's love. The beautiful Nicole, who had been in love with her husband for years before his divorce from his first wife, responded at once. She wouldn't think of taking Adlai. She had been unaware of the circumstances. *L'amour* won out.

Adlai invited me to stay in his very commodious official UN ambassadorial apartment in the elegant Waldorf Towers. The handsome abode encompassed two double guest rooms with baths at the far end of the apartment, off a hall leading from the dining room. Although I had not stayed there before, I knew the flat well. I had breakfasted there with him and five other guests—two UN ambassadors and three Washington officials—when I went to New York to cover a day in the life of Ambassador Stevenson at the UN. There was fine art in every room (except for the hotel-style guest rooms), including two Picassos and a Dufy in his bedroom and a Matisse nude over his big double bed.

"He had *Washington Crossing the Delaware* there," said Viola, his elderly, longtime housekeeper as she showed me around. "Then I came in one morning and saw that. What a switch!"

I had become a Stevenson admirer when I first met him at a party given for him in Washington by the William MacCrackens. He was governor of Illinois then; the election of 1952 was approaching and he was being mentioned prominently as the Democratic candidate. As a *Washington Star* reporter covering both the 1952 and 1956 conventions, I saw him often, got to know his sister Buffie Ives (whom I interviewed as his possible White House hostess), and ran into him throughout the fifties at Democratic or State Department functions, or at Perle Mesta or Scottie's parties. He had come to my party for Lady Astor in 1958 and to a Women's National Press Club dinner with me in 1961; and I had given a nightcap party in his honor after the Women's Press Club dinner dance on February 22, 1962. In short, I saw him every time I got a chance.

But to be alone with him at night in his apartment? Back in No. 42-A of the Waldorf Towers after the glamorous gala we sat together on a settee in his library and looked over the party favors we had brought back. I admit it—I made the first move. I kissed him. He responded and after a minute or two he said softly, "Go take off your clothes and come to my bed."

That was the beginning of our affair. It lasted until the last night he spent in Washington, May 30, 1965, six weeks before his death.

From that memorable March first night on, I was constantly anticipating our next meeting. I didn't even wait to hear from him. Two days later I wrote him that I felt like "a 16-year-old with stardust in her eyes, high on a cloud that simply won't come down." I asked: Was it possible to write a letter for his eyes only?

On March 11 he wrote to me at the *Washington Star*. Unfortunately, I had left instructions there for all mail addressed to me to be opened. (I worked at home, but occasional invitations were sent to me there.)

So society editor Lee Walsh opened the letter. She telephoned me, a little breathlessly. I raced to the *Star*. Alone I read:

"Dearest Stardust—Yes, it's possible to write for my eyes only, if addressed as above. [The Towers, Waldorf-Astoria, etc.] . . . Thank you, dear Stardust, for being so starry. I've not recovered from your astral charms and I don't want to, but I do want to rub my eyes enough to wake up and rediscover reality—or do I? I'll be down this weekend for the Gridiron, as usual, and will find you somehow, somewhere . . . Your devoted, Dust."

The Gridiron dinner was a week off but I could not wait for that day. I rushed back a response that began: "You darling! Already cloudborne I am now hopelessly in orbit!" I enclosed my private telephone number as well as our household number.

I was wildly, classically in love. Poems flew into my head and out of my pen. One began: "Lord—Please get him to phone/ Just nudge him a little and plant the seed/ Of my idea and make it his own . . ."

Adlai responded to that one on a sheet from a little Waldorf-Astoria memorandum pad: "Betty Beale—You've tied me! And I don't even struggle, like any brave free animal should. Is it age—or is it BB?"

I promptly sent him back another, entitled "What have you done?" which ended:

> . . .
> *Whatever it was, oh Adlai, my dear—*
> *You've another girl in your bumper crop*
> *Who cannot rest till once again near,*
> *Or forever go off her cotton-pickin', fat-headed,*
> *dizzy-brained top!*

We did not get together after the Gridiron Sunday afternoon reception. Sir David and Lady Ormsby-Gore took Adlai and other guests—including prominent women friends of his—to their embassy for supper. But he penned this note while flying back to New York the next morning: "Beloved BB—I couldn't call last night. First I couldn't get those girls out of the U.K. Embassy and then when I did we were followed back for more talk. To get up and leave at 12 and for another 'engagement' was obviously impossible. But it was almost more than my cotton-pickin', fat-headed, dizzy-brained top could stand. I'll be back and I'll telephone or ask you to come up when there is a break—but meanwhile you *must* go about your life and business as usual. And please don't laugh at my banalities. I don't know how else to say quickly that this can be very *good* or devastating—for what have *you* done, Betty my dear? I'm old enough to prefer a long spring to a hot summer. Thank you, oh thank you, for yesterday—and tomorrow and tomorrow. AES."

In every letter he wrote me during those three years he was honest and forthright, but did his best to spare my feelings. As soon as he realized the depth of my affection he delicately informed me he could not return it in full. "I am already committed," he told me one evening while I was driving him to Georgetown, where he stayed with the Paul Magnusons. He did not say to whom, nor did I ask. I assumed Marietta Peabody Tree was the one to whom he felt committed—the elegant, glamorous and capable blond whom he selected to be U.S. representative to the Human Rights Committee at the UN with the rank of ambassador. In that capacity he saw the wife of wealthy Ronald Tree more often than any other of his feminine devotees; she could also serve as his hostess at official functions without causing undue talk. Later I wondered if he meant his heart was committed to Alicia Patterson Guggenheim, owner of the *Long Island Newsday*. When he accepted Mrs. Eugene Meyer's invitation to go on a Mediterranean cruise on her chartered yacht, he asked her also to invite Alicia, which she did—unwillingly— because she had wanted Adlai as a single man. Alicia died in 1963; according to Porter McKeever's thorough biography, at one time she was ready to leave her husband and marry him. Drew Pearsons' wife Luvie told me that tears came to his eyes when he spoke of her afterward. From then on Marietta was probably the woman he cared most about. It was Marietta who was with him when he dropped dead on the street in London; and who tried in vain to resuscitate him. I believe she was in love with him. In fact, it was an epidemic. After Adlai's death Nan Tucker McEvoy, whose family owned the *San Francisco Chronicle*, sat in my house one evening and the two of us composed a list of ten, including ourselves, who were in love with Adlai. Years later I learned that two English women he saw regularly in London were equally stuck on him.

Looking at Stevenson's picture today, you would never suspect his great appeal. He wasn't handsome; he did not have the physique that draws feminine raves. But he had a marvelous speaking voice, great charm, elegance, kindness, and a delicious wit. He was a man of great intelligence and high standards—qualities women admire—yet always gave full attention to anyone speaking to him. As Evangeline Bruce once observed: "Men are attracted by what they see; women by what they hear." And what people heard "managed, by sheer force of [his] intelligence and moral distinction, to lift the whole level of public life and discourse," wrote historian Henry Steele Commager, "and to infuse American politics with a dignity, a vitality, an excitement it had not known since the early days of the New Deal." Indeed, he not only electrified the nation but the world, as witness the huge crowds that gathered to greet him on his world tour as the defeated candidate of 1952.

That last letter of Adlai's was another delicate effort to remind me that he did not share my ardor. But being human he could hardly help but enjoy such adoration. It was he who once said, "Do you know the difference between a beautiful woman and a charming one? A beauty is a woman you notice; a charmer is one who notices you." Heaven knows I could not have noticed him more. There was nothing reticent about this woman in love with the man Grace and David Darling* called "perhaps our most beloved statesman in this century." He was on such a pedestal I was not ashamed to be one of the worshipful ones.

In one syndicated column, I quoted two or three paragraphs of his remarks at the big dinner Interior Secretary Stewart Udall organized to honor Robert Frost on his eighty-eighth birthday; and I even had the nerve to send him my own poetic efforts after typing the lines he quoted from Frost—how, I'll never know. It was just another indication of how far gone I was.

But he was generous about my poetic offerings.

"BBB—I've read them again and again—and shivered and tingled—and wondered. What an extraordinary gifted, candid and tender person you are. Such a lady is for loving, not for harming or bruising, and for loving wisely and everlastingly.

"We must talk. But when? Everything is difficult. I don't know when I'm coming down again—probably not until the week of April 16, if then. Next week I must go to Illinois.

> Ah, when to the heart of a man
> Was it ever less than a treason
> To go with the drift of things—
> To yield with a grace to reason.

"But to yield to reason with grace I must.

"I will telephone at the first rift in the clouds. For now—tender thoughts, all good things—and a warm embrace from—??"

* In their book, *Stevenson*.

My portrait during the 1960s.

With my colleagues on the porch of Hubbard House during my senior year at Smith College.

Former President Harry Truman, with me and Florida Congressman Paul Rogers in the spring of 1961.

President Eisenhower checking the Burning Tree Club initials on the golf cap I wore, as Ike, in a Women's National Press Club show. (Copyright *Washington Post*; Reprinted by permission of D.C. Public Library.)

Dancing with Vice President
Lyndon Johnson.

With LBJ at the White House the night Carol Channing (center, in costume)
performed in a scene from "Hello Dolly."

(ABOVE LEFT) Arriving with United Nations Ambassador Adlai Stevenson at *Time* magazine's fortieth anniversary dinner for cover-of-*Time* headliners.

(ABOVE RIGHT) With King Hussein of Jordan in the Blue Room of the White House.

(BELOW LEFT) Danny Kaye is resigned as I ham it up at the Symphony Hall.

(BELOW RIGHT) With Marjorie Post in her Hillwood mansion.

Talking to Vice President Nelson
Rockefeller at a dinner at the Iranian
Embassy.

A cozy chat with Gregory Peck at a
White House dinner and dance given
by the Johnsons.

I meet the Duke of Windsor.

(ABOVE) With Perle Mesta and my fiancé, George Graeber, the night of Perle's dinner-dance in our honor.

(LEFT) The Ambassador of Kuwait Talat Al Ghoussein greets us at our wedding reception.

(BELOW) On our honeymoon in Key Biscayne, Florida.

(ABOVE) Cocktailing in our garden: Bunny Buchen, retiring Secretary of HEW Caspar Weinberger, I, President Ford and my stepson, George B. Graeber II.

(LEFT) With President and Mrs. Reagan, at our 1986 dinner.

(BELOW) President and Mrs. Bush with George and me in our front hall.

Supreme anecdotist Ronald Reagan enchants an audience in our bedroom. L to R: Arnaud de Borchgrave, I (sitting on floor), Mary Jane Wick, Jackie Bengelloun, Alexandra de Borchgrave, President Reagan and Countess Roland de Kergorlay.

President Ford confronts hamming-it-up lady guests, in our bedroom. L to R: Susan Goldwater (partially hidden), Val Cook, Betty Rhodes, Jane Weinberger, Ann Dore (later McLaughlin), Bunny Buchen, Barbara MacGregor and Eleanor Ingersoll (both partially hidden) and the hostess looking as if she's spotted a hot iron about to drop on Ford's head.

I asked him to please stop worrying about hurting me. After all, he had been honest; the decision was mine.

Whereupon I whipped off another ditty that I thought might amuse him—and a serious one two days later. Now, I wonder how I found time to write my column.

On very rare occasions—when Dr. and Mrs. Magnuson were out of town—I went with him to his permanent guest room on their third floor. The first time he warned me: The window on the second floor landing gave columnist Rowland Evans and his wife Kay next door a clear inside view of the Magnusons' stairway. But I didn't see them, and trust they didn't see me.

On June 1st I went to New York at Adlai's invitation to have an evening with him—dinner, the theater (we saw *The Night of the Iguana*), and a stroll through the theater district afterwards. We had to stop several times; strangers recognized him, and wanted to shake his hand and tell him how sorry they were that he had lost the presidential election. I was bursting with pride to be at his side.

He was scheduled to go to Europe that summer, but first he went to Oregon. In a letter postmarked June 18, 1962, he wrote from there:

"BBBB—The best place to read the poetry of Betty Beale is by the Metolious River in the Cascade Mountains of Oregon—because it tumbles merrily like the brook beneath your window, because it soars like the snowy mountains, because like nature it's uneven, full of surprises and beauty, lusty, forthright beauty.

"So I'm glad I brought a sheaf with me. It would have been nicer if I had brought *her* with me to keep my cotton-pickin head on my business! Just now my business is to visit the Corbetts—(charming family of natural, intelligent, civilized people from Portland) in this wilderness. . . . We arrived in startling hot sunlight yesterday by 'scenic' (awful word) motor road from Portland, lay in the sun, ate, drank and wandered among great trees in the dappled forest all day. How cool it is under the giants out of the mountain sun, and last night was sharp and cold in the white moonlight and dark forest all about. . . . Tomorrow the idyll ends and we take off for Seattle and the hosts of men for another damnable speech. At Boston last week I proposed a new freedom—freedom from speech. It was a welcome suggestion after a half hour of oratory, exhortation and wisdom and wit that fell somewhere short of inspiration or the target; indeed the target wasn't visible. So my commencement circuit for 1962 is done, thank God, and after Seattle the only utterance ahead of me is Geneva and then silence, that golden state of carefree being that I've hardly known for more than 20 years.

"Later—on Wednesday I go back to my beloved Libertyville for a few days. Then to N.Y. and Washington the following week for a few hours before flying to Europe you know when. I'll hope for a glimpse in Wash.—and right now I'll hope for a big rainbow trout. If it's pretty enough it will be BB.

"Later—I didn't get that lovely rainbow trout—but I hope I have BB—in spite of this disorderly, unworthy document from her—Devoted, Governor."

I was so pleased, I didn't even mind being likened to a fish!

I immediately dashed off the following: "Darling—I love your letter. It was so delightful and so flattering you deserve the enclosed rather long and narrow portrait which if it doesn't go to your head nothing ever will.

> *You're fire*
> *And champagne*
> *And gentleness*
> *Like soft rain;*
> *You're sensitivity,*
> *Creativity,*
> *And brain.*
>
> *You're wit*
> *And delight*
> *Like the spark*
> *Of sudden light;*
> *You're vitality,*
> *Actuality*
> *And might.*
>
> *You're truth*
> *In clear diction*
> *You're the courage*

Of conviction;
My fascinating,
Exasperating
Addiction.

You're soul
And great heart
You are strictly
A man apart;
Though persistible
Too resistible
From the start.

You're love
Warmly passioned,
Attentive
In your fashion;
Too exciting
And igniting
To be rationed.

You're charm
Polished fine
You're quality's
Special shine;
But captivatingly
Irritatingly
Not mine!

On an unusual balmy July 6 I wrote to him in Italy. *Time* had written a piece on me that I thought was unfair*; I waxed romantic, but ended with a grumble: "I sit here alone helplessly aware that you are with another woman. I hope her husband is along. If you must know, I hope you are surrounded by husbands! I also hope you are not having a single affectionate moment away from me. Piggish, aren't I? Also a little nutty, you might say."

His reply, mailed July 20 in Italy, began on a postcard that pictured two children and a goat on a Swiss mountain. It read: "BBB—

---

* See page 64.

Your letter enlivened a deadly day—and another and another. I was on the verge of cabling, 'Come at once. Too many husbands.' But instead I went to the mountains to cool off and improve relations with the natives, as you can see. The Palio* was a glorious mixture of carnival, medieval pageantry, excitement and terror. See it if you can—with me, of course. Buffie's houseparty† burst the bounds and was an Italian-American cocktail with a Rumanian ex-Queen thrown in. I mean the party, not the pool! Now I'm relaxing at the Plimptons‡ on Lake Como with John Fell, Natalie§, yes, and Alicia. Today we go to Lugano to see the Thyssens and their art collection; then we go on to Florence by motor, Rome, Athens and the yacht— and home Aug. 8-10 and none too soon! I dread to think what you might be doing on 'nights filled with an aura of sensual expectancy!' "

In the letter's postscript he said he had not seen the *Time* article "but I'm as angry as you are—probably more so! I hope you will show it to me and I'll give Herr Luce a piece of my mind. But I'm sure it didn't hurt you, just as most of their ugliness didn't hurt me— in the long run. As for 'balmy evenings like a lover's kiss in Washington in July'!! What the hell—as we boys say. Yes, you need a cold shower.

"My speech was a dandy, if I do say so, and stirred up a very small pool hereabouts. So I felt well content with my Geneva interlude and look forward now to a good holiday. . . .

"I wish I knew what you had done about your vacation. I wish you were right here to laugh and talk and drowse and stir up this torpid spirit. And when I get back I'll have to work like the dickens to catch up, get things started for the fall and go out to Illinois. So when, oh when, do I get a chance to test the temper of your prose!! Goodbye, BBB, I hope it won't be too long. x E x P.S. My visit with

* The famous, incredibly wild, no-holds-barred, medieval-costumed, horse race around the big piazza in mid-town Sienna, Italy.
† His sister Buffie Ives leased for several summers a beautiful villa in Florence.
‡ Francis Plimpton, Stevenson's deputy ambassador at the UN and the father of George Plimpton.
§ His youngest son and wife.

dear Queen Helen of Rumania, Carol's first wife, brought back boyhood memories of a vulgar lyric:

Said red-haired Magda Lupescu
Who came to Roumania's rescue:
Monarchy's a wonderful thing
It's so nice to be under a king.
Is democracy as good, I esk you?"

Of course, it was hard to believe that with Alicia along he really wished I were there.

He signed his next communication, a postcard from Yugoslavia, "Frank," to confuse anyone who might choose to read it en route. It said: "BBB—Anchored here last night and tonight I'm by a trout stream in the mountains of Montenegro—thanks to Drew's interesting management. Downstairs the vacationing comrades are whooping it up and you are the beneficiary of my sleeplessness! But it is a glorious journey and would be lots better if you were along. I miss you!" The picture on the card was of the beautiful little island-like town and harbor of Sveti Stefan. "Drew" was columnist Drew Pearson who, with wife Luvie, went on each of Mrs. Meyer's yachting trips.

While Adlai was gallivanting abroad, I went to Bishop's Lodge, Santa Fe, N.M., for two weeks' vacation from the *Star*.

In Santa Fe I met composer Virgil Thomson and Pulitzer Prize-winning authors Paul Horgan and Oliver La Farge. The latter, part Indian himself, told about a trip to Pierre, S.D., where he was soon surrounded by other French Indians. "There I was," said the author of *Laughing Boy*, "having to polish up my French to talk to a group of Indians in Pierre, South Dakota, with names like Rene de Montigny!"

I returned to Washington August 11, and two days later received an in-flight telegram from Adlai: "Am in Tenn. for Kefauver funeral. Return to Washington tonight. Will call you then." We only talked on the phone that week but he came back to town the following week and told me we were dining at the Arthur Schlesingers. Arthur was then married to Marian Cannon Schlesinger, the mother of his children who waited on the table that evening, charmingly. There were ten at dinner, including the indefatigable Senate Whip Hubert Humphrey—in rare form. He regaled the company the entire time. Stevenson didn't even try to get a word in edgewise and enjoyed him as much as everyone.

Humphrey told how, during the Eisenhower administration, he frequently received mail and telephone calls meant for Secretary of the Treasury George Humphrey. One day a White House staffer phoned him and said, "Mr. Secretary, we have Mr. [So-and-So] from Akron, Ohio, and he wants a job. What should we do for him?" "He's a good man," replied the Democrat, who'd never heard of him, "Give him a job." Said the staffer, "We just wanted your okay." "Well, you've got it; he's a good man," said the Minnesota liberal. He was still wondering what the fellow was like.

When we left the Schlesingers I took Adlai back to my house. My sister was away and my father was confined to his sick bed in the rear of the house. His nurse, in the adjoining room, went to bed early. Adlai spent the night in my sister's front bedroom, and early in the morning, after I checked to be sure the coast was clear, he slipped out, hailed a taxi, and went straight to the Metropolitan Club for a breakfast meeting. There he dashed off a note: "Betty dear—It's only 8:30 and they haven't arrived for breakfast so to improve each shining hour I send you this word from a full, fat, grateful heart for such a cool fresh night."

But again he worried that he was not being fair to me, because, he said, "in my way I love you so!" But, he added in a postscript, his way was not my way. Of course, that was not news; perhaps he had been frightened by our domesticity. In any case it had no effect on my devotion.

On the sixth of September, Adlai invited me to New York to have dinner with him and new Soviet Ambassador and Mrs. Anatoly Dobrynin in his Waldorf Towers apartment, and attend the opening night of the Bolshoi Ballet in the Metropolitan Opera House. I was dizzy with joy sitting beside him, exhilarated to be his date in the center box of the Diamond Horseshoe in full view of the entire audience.

En route to the ballet, Ambassador Dobrynin told us that his wife Irina constantly took pictures—all of them of sunsets. She had taken pictures of sunsets in New York, Chicago, San Francisco, and every city she had visited. Adlai observed wryly, "The picture of a dying America, I suppose."

After the ballet we all went to the St. Regis for the supper given by impresario Sol Hurok for the cast of over one hundred. When the orchestra played waltzes, hardly anyone danced except the Arthur Murrays. When it burst into twist music the whole place came alive, cast included. Prima ballerina Maya Plisetskaya and her predecessor, new choreographer Galina Ulanova, enjoyed the caviar while the aging, blind Bolshoi conductor Yuri Faier had a tearful reunion with his brother Myron whom he had not seen for forty-five years. Myron had been a precinct captain in Stevenson's presidential campaigns. I spent that night again at 42-A, returning to Washington the next day.

A week later, Adlai came to Washington for Undersecretary of State and Mrs. George Ball's reception at the State Department in honor of UN Secretary General U Thant. I covered it. Marietta Tree was there, too. I made a point of hiding my feelings toward A. and my pangs of jealousy when I looked at the beauteous Mrs. T. She was the only woman for whom I can ever remember feeling jealousy.

The white tie Symphony Ball was to be held October 19 that year, preceded by a concert conducted by filmdom's most famous comic, Danny Kaye. The benefit chairman, Anne Frailey, had asked me to be the mistress of ceremonies, with the job of introducing Danny and Washington VIPs with a quip about each. As Kaye was working for UNICEF, I figured it would seem both normal and nice for Adlai to be there too, so I invited him. He had to send his regret but managed to make it a compliment. "I find now," he wrote, "that I'm obliged to be in Chicago that night and will have to forego both Kaye and Beale. And I don't know which is the funniest so the sacrifice is distasteful and I feel grossly abused. And I am sure you will keep a transcript of your remarks, which I will doubtless find occasion to use in the General Assembly." As it turned out, the Cuban missile crisis was to occupy his attention as the dancers whirled.

On the sixth of December Adlai came to Washington to be the toastmaster at the International Awards Dinner of the Kennedy Foundation. The chief members of the Kennedy family would be present. He had agreed to do it before the publication of a magazine article by Charles Bartlett and Stewart Alsop that cast Stevenson in the role of appeaser, and the president as a hero who stood firm against the Soviets in the missile crisis and won out. The story was accepted as fact and caused worldwide reports that AES was going to be eased out. He was characterized in the article—which the authors said was based on interviews with senior administration officials—as a superdove, one who wanted to trade removal of U.S. missiles in Turkey for removal of Soviet missiles in Cuba.

Stevenson was furious. It was a lie. A transcript of the four hours of discussions at the White House meetings on October 27, 1962, released by the John Fitzgerald Kennedy Library twenty-five years later—on October 21, 1987—prove that it was the president, himself, who wanted to make that concession to the USSR in return for removing the missiles. Kennedy's advisers, who included Secretary of State Dean Rusk and Assistant Secretary of Defense Paul Nitze, had to talk him out of it. (JFK did not know that the fifteen Jupiter missiles in Turkey belonged to the Turks; only the warheads were ours.)

Kennedy told Arthur Schlesinger that he had not talked to Charlie Bartlett or any other reporter when, in fact, he had both seen the article and approved it. It was a stilleto job aimed, perhaps, at making Stevenson look less impressive to reduce his enormous constituency.

The whole affair left Adlai in no mood to be charmingly amusing about the Kennedys in his role as the foundation dinner emcee. He was also in the bind of a busy UN schedule. So, though accustomed to penning his own pearls of wit, he asked me to come up with some introductions. I promptly solicited the help of my funniest friend, Liz Carpenter, and together we turned out what we modestly thought were gems. I had to go to New York the night before the dinner to appear on CBS the next morning so I took our gems to Adlai at his apartment. I slipped them to him privately in the hall because Marietta and a couple of other people were in the drawing room.

Using our quips he introduced Sargent Shriver* as selling "instant peace"; Rose Kennedy as "head of the most successful employment

* Shriver was the first director of the Peace Corps.

agency in America"; and President Kennedy as the "author, producer, director, and star of Mr. Khrushchev's new play in Moscow— *A Funny Thing Happened to Me on My Way to Cuba.*" There were others, but it was mostly Stevenson's sense of humor, superb timing, witty additions, and magnificent voice that charmed his listeners, including the president and First Lady. As I covered the dinner for the *Star* I had the deliciously pleasurable job of writing about "his deft wit" and the great applause he received! No one else knew our secret.

Nor did anyone, other than my confidante Scotty Lanahan, ever know of my intimacy with Adlai.

A week after the dinner I flew back to New York for a star-studded party given by the Bill vanden Heuvels in honor of the cast of the British comic revue, *Beyond the Fringe*, and stayed again with my favorite host.

Adlai gave me a gold-and-black pillbox that Christmas. I had a jeweller make my gift for him. "I had it made of gold so you wouldn't throw it away," I wrote. "It's for your key ring. You said you had a hard time remembering telephone numbers and I want to make it as easy as possible for you to remember mine. The one beginning 667 is my private phone; the other the house phone. The digits are grouped in an unfamiliar pattern to disguise them for unexpected eyes. Now will you be an angel and slip it on your key ring?"

On May 5, 1963, *Time* magazine celebrated its fortieth anniversary by giving a dinner for all the people who had been featured on its cover who were still alive and ambulatory. Over 330 people— an incredible collection of names from politicians to prelates, divas to dancers, jockeys to jokesters—filled the ballroom of the Waldorf Astoria. As I stayed in 42-A in the Towers again, I had the thrill of entering that remarkable gathering with the UN ambassador. Later that night, when we were alone, we talked for hours. We talked of sports—he had broken a bone while skiing, ridden like fury on a boar hunt in Spain, "played a fair game of golf." I knew he had bagged twelve quail on a shooting weekend in South Carolina and played a good game of tennis. He might get married some day but not in the immediate future, he told me. He had been contemplating it for fourteen years.

In Porter McKeever's biography he notes that in his sixties Stevenson "was not prepared to make the personal adjustments that marriage would entail. He radiated in the company of attractive, intelligent women, and enjoyed the amenities provided by the wealth of some. But the prospect of having to deal with servants and other aspects of the deeply entrenched life-styles of women with strong personalities as well as wealth appalled him. He had always traveled light, traveled fast, pursuing his insatiable curiosity, and he was not prepared to risk losing that freedom."

I don't think he was, either.

Come July, Adlai was to visit his sister and brother-in-law, the Ernest Iveses, at the Villa Caponi in Florence again; I was to see friends in Rome, Florence, Beirut, Istanbul, and Athens. Adlai sent me his itinerary so I could plan my stay in Florence when he was there. I promptly told my close friend Frances Wilkinson Rosso and her husband, the former Italian ambassador to Washington, that I was coming. She invited me to stay with them in their handsome Villa Poggiobello. I arrived in Florence—all pepped up to be in that divine spot under such advantageous circumstances—only to get the disappointing news. On a hastily written letter on lined paper addressed to me in care of his sister Buffie, Adlai had written: "Dearest Betty—I'm heartsick and angry! Why, oh why, must it always happen this way? Another brief holiday spoiled—and this one to share in laughter and sunlight with you in my beloved Florence. The orders came suddenly—just as I arrived on Lake Como. There was nothing to do but repack and reverse and regret. And that's what I'm doing now—soaring in sunshine above the Matterhorn and Mt. Blanc—en route to Washington and trouble this very evening. Goodbye—a bientot—with sorrow, fury and prayers that you'll have a good, gay vacation in Italy—and think of me amid the pasta and the wine. Me."

I was devastated at first, but Florence was beautiful and my stay there fascinating, thanks to the Rossos and to Buffie Ives who invited the three of us to dinner where I, too, met Queen Helen of Rumania.

Rome was an enchantment; Beirut, then the Paris of the Middle East, yet dating back to fifteen centuries before Christ, was fascinating. But the most extraordinary experience of that whole tour—

which included a palace reception by King Paul and Queen Frederika in Athens and a twenty-four-hour sail on a beautiful yacht to Greek islands and a sail on the Bosphorus—was a visit to Jerusalem.

I had not been prepared for its beauty. Lovely pale golden Jerusalem looked then as if in biblical times, unspoiled by signs of modern life, with shepherds still watching their flocks near its ancient walls, people in flowing Arab robes softly treading its old stone streets. This jewel of antiquity touched me deeply. As I walked its narrow old streets I could only think I was walking where Jesus Christ had walked. Actually, I learned later that the stones I trod were layers above those Christ had trod. But no matter, the ambiance was reminiscent of 30 A.D. I was distressed to find on a return visit in 1985, during a Greek cruise, that the twentieth century had invaded that gem and even surrounded it with highrise buildings! I could have wept.

One of the most moving experiences of my life was a visit to the Garden of the Tomb. There, on the side of a hill, was a big stone slab rolled back to reveal a spacious vault. It could have been the sepulchre "hewn in stone" described in Chapter 23 of St. Luke, Verse 53, or the very same place described in Chapter 19 of St. John, Verse 41. I went inside and sat on what appeared to be an ancient sarcophagus; I thought about the three women who came into the tomb to anoint the crucified body with sweet spices, and instead saw a young man clothed in white, who told them Jesus had risen and to carry the tidings to his disciples. Pondering in solitude in that tomb, it was easy to imagine that scene narrated in the gospels.

Back in the U.S., I was plunged again among worldly things. I flew almost immediately to Newport for the brilliant debut ball of Jackie Kennedy's half-sister, Janet Auchincloss. Even before the loss of her newborn infant a week earlier, Mrs. Kennedy had not planned to attend, knowing the spotlight would have been on the First Lady rather than the young star of the evening. But social Washington was strongly represented. The ambassadors of Peru, Australia, Belgium, Greece, and Italy were there with their wives as well as our ambassador to Great Britain and Mrs. Winthrop Aldrich. Randolph Churchill and his son Winston came from London. The dance tent at the Auchinclosses' Hammersmith Farm, and all the table decor bore a Venetian motif; Meyer Davis's orchestra and society pianist George Feyer played. Half the one thousand guests were older crème-de-la-crème friends of the hosts, decked out in their better jewels. The finest gem there was the famous "Afghanistan" diamond worn by Jo Hartford Bryce, mother-in-law of Senator Claiborne Pell of Rhode Island. The blinding 75-carat stone hung from a dazzling choker of diamond solitaires. "Touch it," commanded Mrs. Bryce. "You will have good luck in a week."

It wasn't within a week, but one month later that I was out with Adlai. Justice and Mrs. Arthur Goldberg gave a dinner for the Willard Wirtzes, a year after Wirtz succeeded Goldberg as secretary of labor. Justice Goldberg told Adlai, "You are the voice of the conscience of the world." Stevenson described Bill Wirtz, his former law partner, as "younger than he looks and older than he acts." I breakfasted with Adlai the next morning, but was not to see him again until the night before fateful November 22, 1963. Ironically, I had gone to New York to tape a television show on the glamor of the Kennedys' White House entertaining.

Soon after Lyndon Johnson became president, he wrote Stevenson to tell him he wanted him to stay on as UN ambassador. The next time I saw Johnson he said, "Ask Adlai to show you the letter I wrote him." Adlai sent me a copy and urged me to be discreet. If the White House had not released it and I printed it, it would look as though he had maneuvered to get it published. Dated December 19, 1963, the letter read:

Dear Adlai:
This week—and, I should say—this past month—has impressed upon me again the good fortune of our country in having you as a spokesman for and an influence upon our relations with the other nations of the world. These are times of more profound change than many realize. With so much of the world groping to find and give meaning to independence, it is a great and reassuring asset for the United States—and the cause of freedom—to have a voice so eloquent, so respected, so unselfishly dedicated as yours to help guide a diverse planet toward unity under peace and freedom. I congratulate you—and thank you—for your service to our country. I also thank you for the generous and unstinting support and strength you have given to me. Your vision, your firmness, your confidence in the future—and the role America has to play in that future—have meant much to me

already and will, I am sure, mean much more as we continue to work together in the future.

Sincerely,
Lyndon B. Johnson

That Christmas Adlai sent me a Steuben cat with a formal card inscribed under the U. S. eagle, "With the compliments of the Representative of the United States of America to the United Nations." Scribbled across the bottom A.S. had written: "A present from a dog!"

For his birthday, February 5th, I sent him a poem.

In his long and warm response he said he thought it might be my best yet, and ended it with: "Blessings on the 'madness in your veins,' Elizabeth—love—Browning." I liked that.

Stevenson came to my nightcap party for President and Mrs. Johnson after the Women's National Press Club dinner in March. Of course I rushed him away from everybody at the dinner who wanted to greet him so we could get to my house before the Johnsons. Richard Nixon was not at the dinner but Adlai saw him in the corridor, where some admirer had slowed him down, while I waited on the stairway. When he joined me A. said Nixon had looked as though he wanted to greet him. "But I would not shake his hand." Nixon had painted Stevenson as a pinko during the presidential campaigns of the fifties, although Adlai had made it very plain that he was anticommunist. Nixon's oft-repeated accusations had been unforgivable.

My party was small. I'd invited only thirty or so guests, carefully culled with Liz Carpenter's help. I later thought it was a mistake to limit the list to people the president saw all the time, but Liz knew he would feel completely at home surrounded by top aides and intimate friends. Vice President and Mrs. Humphrey also came. As topheavy with rank as it was, I kept it secret: I was convinced the Johnsons would appreciate my not trying to capitalize on their presence. In those days, a president could go to a private house without the "news" being posted in the press room. No noisy caravan of motorcycles tipped off the neighbors at 10:30 or 11:00 that night; just a couple of quiet cars of Secret Service. As it turned out, I did myself a disservice. Another woman in the media gave a big party for them later; it was widely reported, and added much to her prestige. To hide my light under a bushel was absurd, I realized, during a time when the title "hostess" evoked a more glamorous image than "reporter" or "columnist."

I acquired a cozy efficiency apartment in Georgetown that spring, both to work in and for privacy. My sister Nancy went out nearly every night, but when she returned to the house she couldn't resist popping in to greet whatever man I might be entertaining. A natural flirt, she would immediately turn on the charm. If I was ready to throw something at that point, I was in the mood to croak her when she described the difference between us: I was the one with the brains, she always told them. She was the one who knew how to cook and keep house!

I went to New York for the opening of the fabulous Texas pavillion at the World's Fair which starred handsome Governor of Texas John Connally and his wife Nellie, and spent the night again in 42-A. A few days later I sent a passionate note to A.S., beginning:

Darling—May I tell you—before it bursts like a wellspring within me—how much I love you?

He wrote back:

Blessed B.B.—I'm off to Europe tonight—with your farewell note in my pocket.

I went to New York again on May 25 to cover the rededication of the Museum of Modern Art and its new wing by Lady Bird Johnson. Stevenson's party for her afterwards was at his ambassadorial pad— most convenient to my night's lodging. And I was with him after he addressed the Women's National Democratic Club in D.C.

"I went to church the next night," I wrote him afterward, "and not even that spiritual atmosphere could quench the flame in my brain." Our steamy correspondence continued. I was busy—covering the GOP convention in San Francisco, spending a week at La Jolla in July, a weekend at Marjorie Post's Topridge estate, covering the Democratic Convention in Atlantic City in August—but saw him when he came down for White House state dinners.

That summer I decided I must end my fixation on our UN ambassador. I was beginning to think that way when I penned and sent him a poem titled, "I Shall Not Weep," which began:

> *Would that I had not met you—then*
> *Unblinded by the dazzling sun*
> *I could have looked at other men*
> *And settled on a lesser one.*
>
> *But it is done; I shall not weep*
> *For quiet joys that might have been*
> *Nor curse the fate that would me keep*
> *From loving so again.*
>
> *For I have seen a petalled spring*
> *As few are blessed with seeing,*
> *And sensed within your magic ring*
> *The ecstasy of being.*

And it was true. Any other man seemed lesser to me until four years later, when I met and quickly came to appreciate the breadth and depth of the marvelous man I later married.

But Adlai and I entered a cool spell. A planned get-together with Elliott and Patty Roosevelt, following the Eleanor Roosevelt Foundation dinner in October, fizzled. I blamed him, and decided to put him out of my mind. I let weeks go by without a word. He finally wrote: "Dear Miss Beale—Is it the approved way to treat an old and loving friend? It would be so nice to see or hear from you now and then." He added that if I was still annoyed about the dinner incident, he thought I was being quite unreasonable. "But I shall always love you all the same. A"

I wrote that he ought to be ashamed of himself for taking an injured air with me. And why would I get in touch with him when he was in Washington frequently and knew both my telephone numbers and never used them? "But I am the warm and sweet type so I still wish you a very Merry Christmas— From—Me."

Stevenson had long made a practice of sending out New Year cards as responses to the Christmas cards he received. And always the card carried a printed message in his handwriting and some meaningful quote inside. The one I received that year also included: "And love and a kiss to you, my beloved feline! The Dog." By then, I was ready to be friends again; communication was resumed.

In March 1965 I left on a round-the-world trip that took me to Morocco, Egypt, Kuwait, India, Thailand, Hong Kong, Manila, and Tokyo. Liz Carpenter had written on White House stationery to every ambassador, charge d'affaires, or consul general where I was stopping to say I would appreciate any doors they could open for me and I was worthy of any confidence. But I was not prepared for the reception I had in Casablanca. I was truly embarrassed to find six people at the airport to meet me—everybody from our ranking diplomat Dean Brown and his wife, to the king's representative who remained at my side for three days.*

In Cairo, Ambassador and Mrs. Luke Battle had a luncheon in the oriental-rug-carpeted embassy tent close to the great pyramids; outside, I could watch a camel and its turbaned owner stride by and an Arabian horse and rider gallop across the sea of billowing sands. At every stop I was treated royally. Our Ambassador to India and Mrs. Chester Bowles offered me—all to myself—the beautiful new residence, Roosevelt House, designed by Edward Durell Stone. (They preferred the old residence, as every sound in the new one carried through its interior openwork walls.)

I had put a certain man far back in my mind. And then it was announced that he would narrate Aaron Copland's *Lincoln Portrait* on the Mall, Memorial Day evening, accompanied by the National Symphony orchestra.

I sent him a line saying I would be in the audience, adding that sister Nancy was to marry Ted Maffitt, his former assistant at the UN, the day before. Adlai called me and suggested we get together after the concert. Twelve thousand people, seated on folding chairs or sprawled on the grass, heard "his magnificent voice give flight to the words which Lincoln spoke to the people so long ago," reported the *Washington Post*. Smithsonian Secretary and Mrs. Dillon Ripley gave a reception for him afterwards. And—finally—I had him to myself in my little apartment. I hoped he would be so charmed by its privacy he would want to come there often. It was his first

---

* My audience with King Hassan in his palace in Rabat is on page 274.

opportunity to relax after a day that included a flight from Canada, tennis in the afternoon, the performance that evening, the reception and the date with me. He had a habit of overscheduling himself. I did not know until recently that for some time his doctor had warned him to slow down. We talked and talked. One subject was President Johnson's military rescue of the Dominican Republic from a communist takeover. Adlai did not call it that night "a massive blunder from beginning to end" as had been quoted. He said our country's mistake was in not waiting twenty-four hours to present our plan to the OAS.

For me, that night was wonderfully tender and enriching.

But it was the last time I ever saw him.

He went abroad in early July, giving me permission to stay in his apartment in his absence. July 8 I flew to New York to appear on Merv Griffin's show the next day. I stayed, as always, in the distant guest room, but as I had the whole apartment to myself I went into his room just because it was his. Lying on his big desk was a printed page entitled "Desiderata." It was a philosophy for living which I found to be so beautiful and so full of the kind of good advice I needed, I wanted to copy it down. I thought perhaps he planned to put it on his next New Year's cards.

While sitting at his desk, I wondered if I might find a letter-size sheet of paper on which to write it in the top drawer of the desk. So I opened it. There, on top of a pile of handwritten letters, was one with the ending in full view. I froze. I had invaded his privacy in a way not intended. And what was worse, the letter was signed, "I love you" and a woman's first name that was unknown to me. I don't know what else the letter said. Already ashamed at having opened the drawer, and stunned by my discovery that other women wrote him love letters, I couldn't bear to see more of it. I closed the drawer. I guessed from the partly visible letter underneath that it, too, was written by a woman. I had felt so special receiving letters from him it never occurred to me that he was getting affectionate letters from other women. I could only wonder how much he must have thought of them to keep their letters in a drawer beside his bed. It did not occur to me that further down in that pile might be some letters from his boys, his sister, or his lawyer, or even me. I had to copy "Desiderata" down on stationery I found in "my" room.

Before leaving the next day I wrote him an affectionate thank-you note, sealed it, and addressed it to him so no one else could read it and jump to correct conclusions. Six days later, Adlai Stevenson was dead. I poured out my feelings about him in my Sunday column. In part it read:

"His great vitality of intellect, heart, soul and wit had an electric effect on every gathering he attended. The picture of him as a lonely, frequently gloomy man, as portrayed in the Ben Shahn sketch on the cover of *Time* in December 1962 was for his intimate friends a totally false one. He was a blithe spirit who delighted in so many things—an active useful life, the beauty of art, music and poetic words, humor wherever it might be found, and the kindnesses of people, big and little, scores of whom were so deeply devoted to him he had no time for loneliness.

"He had but one manner toward all. It was the manner of grace and ease and warmth, and it came to him as naturally as breathing. He was never rude or brusque with people, never impatient with boredom, though he was frequently detained by people he would gladly have escaped. He didn't think he was so important he could offend others. It was perhaps this humility as much as anything that kept him from becoming president. . . . That is why it took a draft to get him in the race in 1952."

He told me, I wrote, that Bobby Kennedy had offered him the vice presidency in 1960 if he would nominate Jack for president, but he had given his word to Johnson that he would remain neutral.

"He once said, 'You cannot pluck out the mystery of the human heart.' But perhaps this gives more insight into the mystery of his." And here I quoted the printed piece I had found on his desk:

"Go placidly amid the noise and the haste and learn what peace there may be in silence. . . . Speak your truth quietly and clearly; and listen to others, even the dull and ignorant; they too have their story. . . . If you compare yourself with others you may become vain or bitter; for always there will be greater and lesser persons than yourself.

"Enjoy your achievements as well as your plans. Keep interested in your career, however humble; it is a real possession in the changing fortunes of time. Exercise caution in your business affairs; for the world is full of trickery. But let this not blind you to what virtue there is; many persons strive for high ideals; and everywhere life is full of heroism.

"Be yourself. Especially do not feign affection. Neither be cynical about love; for in the face of all aridity and disenchantment it is as perennial as the grass. Take kindly the counsel of the years, gracefully surrendering the things of youth. Nurture strength of spirit to shield you in sudden misfortune. But do not distress yourself with imaginings. Many fears are born of fatigue and loneliness. Beyond a wholesome discipline, be gentle with yourself. You are a child of the universe no less than the trees and the stars; you have a right to be here. And whether or not it is clear to you no doubt the universe is unfolding as it should.

"Therefore be at peace with God, whatever you conceive him to be. And whatever your labors and aspirations in the noisy confusion of life keep peace with your soul. With all its sham, drudgery and broken dreams, it is still a beautiful world."*

Senator Eugene McCarthy, whose speech nominating Stevenson in 1960 had evoked rave plaudits, was enchanted with the beautiful philosophy in "Desiderata" and Adlai's interest in it. So his office got in touch with me to verify its source and he had it reprinted and mailed out to thousands of Stevenson admirers.

I went to the memorial service at the Washington Cathedral two days after his death. As the *Star* planned to use the wire report on his interment in Bloomington, Ill., and I could not stand the thought of not being there for the last farewell, I wrote my own check for more than $300 to go on the press plane. The paper got my long and more complete story—free of charge.

President and Mrs. Johnson flew on Air Force One and brought most of the Washington contingent with them. Chief Justice and Mrs. Earl Warren went, as did Vice President and Mrs. Humphrey, Justice and Mrs. Arthur Goldberg who made room for me in their car en route to and from the church service, Secretary of Labor and Mrs. Willard Wirtz, and several members of Congress. Prominent Demo-

* Adlai had bracketed two sentences which I thought he planned to omit when he used it; the dots in two places indicate the omissions. Although on Adlai's copy was noted at the bottom, "Found in old St. Mary's Church, Baltimore," it turned out to have been written by Indiana poet Max Ehrmann in the 1920s.

crats from around the country were at the service and such good friends as Jane and Edison Dick, Bill Blair, Mrs. Marshall Field, and Marietta Tree, her head draped in a black scarf. She must have been even more miserable than I, having worked with him at the UN.

A few days later I received in the mail from Stevenson's able secretary Roxane Eberlein a letter enclosing my thank-you note I'd left for her boss. It read: "I wish there were anything I could say to comfort you—and myself." My letter had, of necessity, been opened.

Lyndon Johnson has been denounced for many things in his life, but I have always had a warm spot in my heart for him because of what he did that day. Like other members of the press, I was not invited to the luncheon Buffie Ives had afterwards in the Stevenson home. The family had no way of knowing what Adlai had meant to me. So we in the press stood on the shaded lawn in front of the house. I, wrapped in memories, was standing by myself beneath a great spreading tree when the Johnsons came out.

Without saying a word, the president, who knew that I had been in love with Adlai, came over to me, kissed me solemnly on the cheek, then got into his car with Lady Bird.

I loved him for it.

CHAPTER 8

Rock and Roll

And Riots and Romances

The Republicans had complimented themselves on their choice of Miami Beach for their convention site in 1968. They were convinced Democrats would have such problems in Chicago, where agitators had promised to disrupt the convention, it would make the GOP look good in November. They were right.

As at every convention, I had only to attend the candidates' parties to know who would be nominated. Obviously, Nelson Rockefeller knew it wouldn't be he when he was an hour late to his own reception and he and Happy stayed only a little over an hour and a half. The night of the nominating the Rockefeller box was totally empty. It took Dick and Pat Nixon four solid hours to shake all the hands proffered at his reception.

By Tuesday of the Democrats' conclave, tear gas had wafted into the posh confines of the Ambassador East's celebrated Pump Room, a stink bomb had spread its unsavory odor in the Conrad Hilton, and the demonstrators in Grant Park were getting more unruly, more vile, and more noisy as the night went on.

I was appalled by the media's treatment of the convention. I still remember sitting in the convention hall and thinking proudly, this is how democracy works. The amphitheatre was tense with antiwar dissension and seething with emotions evoked by the murder of Bobby Kennedy. Yet each speaker was heard, each delegation had

155

its say. But did television report that? Definitely not! The whole time the serious business of selecting a candidate for our highest office was proceeding in orderly fashion TV cameras were on the disturbances in Grant Park. The effect: the networks prevented the election in November of their own favorite candidate, Hubert Humphrey, and put Richard Nixon in the White House.

Some time later I accosted Walter Cronkite, a staunch Democrat, on this score, assuming he had a say about what was covered. Quite naturally that charming man didn't like it. Later, CBS TV News boss Bill Leonard told me CBS focused on Grant Park because he had given that order. Obviously, the networks, competing for ratings and advertising money, figured the antics of the hippies would draw more viewers than speechmaking.

The print media blamed Mayor Richard Daley for turning Chicago into a police state, rarely if ever mentioning the actions of ten thousand hippies who provoked retaliation. I had returned from Chicago unbloodied, unpelted, and even unbruised—thanks to the Chicago police; and it was time one member of the media gave the other side of the picture; the public had the right to know.

"Never has a law-enforcing group been more sorely tried. They received both bodily injury and unspeakably vile treatment from the Yippies in Grant Park. Yet never at any time did I see policemen show more courtesy than the police of Chicago. Courtesy, of course, is only due people who show some courtesy themselves. And despite the difficult circumstances in which they had to maintain order they managed to prevent a fatal catastrophe."

The word "overreacted" had been overused by commentators and by politicians who believed the demonstrators, but, I said, it was the media who had overreacted to every effort to stop them from flagrant civil disorders and disgusting disturbances of the peace. When a newsman was hurt the screams of protest went around the world but nothing was said about the newsmen who taunted the police or tried to get action for the TV cameras.

"A member of the Vice President's coterie heard two reporters having a great laugh in the Coffee Shop of the Conrad Hilton about how they agitated in Grant Park until the police started pushing them around.

"Wyoming Senator and Mrs. Gale McGee and their two grown

children walked over to the park to see for themselves what was
going on and they arrived when the changing of the National Guard
was taking place. Walking through a gang of hippies they saw two
girls, one playing the flute. Then they saw a TV camera team lead
the girls over to the exact place by the troops where they wanted
them to stand. And when their camera started to roll, the girls cried,
'Don't beat me! Don't beat me!' It takes no imagination to figure
how this contrived scene would look on the screens in millions of
American homes."

In the convention hall Mrs. McGee said a youth about fifteen sat
in front of them and shouted four-letter words. The police first
politely asked him to stop, but when he continued they had to take
him out. The cameras probably caught the big policeman bodily
forcing a mere teenager to leave, giving the viewers no notion of
what led to it.

"Senator Daniel Inouye of Hawaii, World War II hero and Democratic keynoter," I wrote, "said the hippies were throwing paper
bags of human excrement at the police and guards in Grant Park.
They were also throwing broken beer bottles and rubber balls stuck
with long nails aimed for the eyes. How would those commentators
who thought the police 'overreacted' have behaved if those things
had happened to them?"

As I stayed at the Conrad Hilton I heard after midnight Wednesday morning some three thousand demonstrators shouting in unison
an obscene curse at the president of the United States. I asked an
officer the next day why an electronic amplifier was allowed to
remain in the park all day and night. He said there was a city
ordnance against such use but if they arrested those using it, they
would only be fined and somebody might be killed in the process.
That was certainly underreacting!

At a women's convention luncheon, Liz Carpenter spoke of the
daily clubbing of the mayor by TV commentators. "When the mayor
fails to do what the majority of the people in Chicago want they can
at least vote him out. But no vote can stop the bossism of the
airwaves where editorializing has been substituted again and again
for straight reporting."

"In the past," I wrote, "I have been proud to be a member of the
Fourth Estate, but after this past week I feel a burning inward

shame. In my mind freedom of the press has always been necessary
to liberty. The Bible states it most beautifully: 'Ye shall know the
truth, and the truth shall make you free.' But how much truth, and
how much biased opinion are the people, and especially the youth
of America, getting?

"A clean, well-combed, pretty young girl for Senator McCarthy
was one of five of us who shared a taxi to O'Hare Airport Friday and
the conversation turned to what the hippies had done to convert the
serious business of nominating a presidential candidate into a circus
of vulgarity. Unbelievably, she stood up for the right of the Grant
Park crowd to curse the president. . . . When one of the passengers
blamed the man who was leading the crowd, she said he was a friend
of hers. Why had he come to Chicago, what did he want to do? I
asked. 'Destroy the government,' she replied calmly."

The *Star* ran letters praising my column for two days. Three
Democratic senators inserted it in the *Congressional Record*. Roscoe
Drummond agreed with me and quoted me in the *Christian Science
Monitor* and Ben Maidenburg, editor and publisher of the Akron,
Ohio, *Beacon Journal* sent me the equally critical article he had
written.

The most graphic of the scores of letters I received came from
Chicago and described the experience of Michael John Kelly, who
had National Guard duty that week. The fighting tactics of the
demonstrators, he made plain, were as dirty as their bodies and
the words painted on them. They sprayed Easy-Off oven cleaner
at the policemen's eyes; they squirted lighter fluid on the police and
then set them on fire; the girls carried razors between their fingers
and slashed at the cops and National Guard; they threw vomit and
human waste at them. Despite this, they were controlled with only
tear gas; not one shot was fired.

How my *Star* colleague, columnist Mary McGrory, a brilliant
writer, could have referred to that crowd in the park as "non-
violent" and "one or two" of "McCarthy's kids that a Boy Scout
troop could have handled," I'll never know.

The Freedom Foundation of Valley Forge, Pa., awarded me a
prize for my story, and the Association of Federal Investigators
presented me with their Special Act Award; I was the first woman
to get it.

*   *   *

The marriage of Jackie Kennedy, the almost deified widow of the idolized assassinated president, to giant shipowner Aristotle Onassis astounded the world. A short man until he stood on his money, the thick-set, coarse-looking Greek seemed the antithesis of the handsome, slender, blond Jack. How could she!—was the reaction.

The *Star* decided to send me to Athens on a little over twenty-four hours notice. In that time I had to get my hair done, go to a Kuwait Embassy dinner, write it up with a prior Turkish Embassy dinner, send the story down to the paper that night, pack the next day, get a column off to my syndicate, fly to New York, and be on the plane for Greece at the very hour I was due for dinner at the French Embassy.

To try to cover that wedding on the Onassis-owned island of Skorpios was a bigger nightmare than the Chicago convention. Arriving in Athens exhausted after my overnight flight, I learned at once that all reporters, except for Ari's particular friends, were banned from Skorpios, and members of Jackie's family—all known to me—were on Onassis' yacht and unreachable. Until Janet and Hugh D. Auchincloss came to the Hotel Grande Bretagne after the festivities I had to get my material from Olympic Airlines president John Georgakis who briefed the press at the hotel. It was the most frustrating reporting experience of my life.

On top of all that, I learned when I tried to file my story late the first night that the Athens Western Union could not send my article to Washington because the *Star* had not equipped me with a guarantee-payment card required for all overseas assignments. I had to give every story by phone to my syndicate in New York—because it had a dictation recorder—and they telexed it to the *Star*. I was livid. As far as I was concerned it seemed only natural when the Kennedy-Onassis union didn't last!

But another, more successful romance was in the wings: my own. I was ready. I can remember so clearly my feelings when I walked into my overtufted, overgilded room at the Fontainebleau Hotel in a dreary, suffocatingly hot Miami to cover the GOP convention. I said to myself, "Betty, you should be married to some nice man instead of doing this." Even to entertain such a thought on the threshold of one of the two most engrossing political events to take place in our country surprised my politics-loving self. Suddenly, for the first time in my life, I felt willing to devote myself to making a husband happy. I asked a Christian Science practioner to do some work for me in this regard. I met him three months later!

On November 15, 1968, I was at home (where the Lord obviously meant me to be, sandwiched between three parties the day before and three the next) when the telephone rang at 7:00 P.M. It was my friend Constance Dunaway, a member of the Protocol Office at the State Department, calling me from a cocktail party.

"There's a handsome new man in town, he's here at the party, he's a widower, works for Union Carbide, I've asked him for dinner tomorrow night, you've got to come," she blurted out without pausing for breath.

I couldn't, I told her. I had to go to a dinner Princess Lalla Nezha, sister of King Hassan II, was giving at her Moroccan Embassy. "Then come to cocktails," she urged. Again I couldn't; I was going to a cocktail party for the great Marc Chagall. She urged me to skip it, but that was out of the question because I was the only member of the press invited. Whereupon she said, "This is a live one."

"I'll be there between cocktails and dinner," I replied.

Fortunately, Chagall, who was visiting his good friends, the John Nefs, whose Georgetown garden he had adorned with a thirty-foot mosaic, stayed at the party for only an hour. I then whipped over in my small red Rambler to the Dunaways' little Georgetown house and met George Graeber. I immediately liked his nice manner, his cleancut handsomeness, and his knowledge of current political news. But I left in a half hour to dress for my dinner party. The next morning Connie called and outlined a method for entrapment. I had always been frank and outspoken. It had gotten me nowhere; so I decided to wise-up, become a foxy, scheming female.

For the benefit of spinsters in search of a husband, here is her method: Lose no time in getting your prey to your house. "Keep him to yourself. Don't take him around. This town is full of vultures in search of an available man. (Translated: Washington is full of rich widows in search of an escort or extra man for dinners.) Don't introduce him to them."

It was all sound advice—but impossible for a partying columnist to follow. So I took him around anyhow; I just garbled his name when I introduced him to the widows or their close friends. I experienced one misgiving. Was this beautifully built, well-dressed Graeber fellow happy to escort me to parties only because he wanted to meet the people running the country?

At that time, my everyday coverage provided an entrée to the power structure that few people outside government, except perhaps Perle Mesta, could offer. But I soon learned from an old friend of his from his Charleston, W. Va., days that there was nothing crafty about G.G. He was as straight as he seemed.

Three days after meeting him Nancy gave a small dinner—just so I could ask him to be my escort. (Sisters can be helpful when they want to be.) Afterwards, we went to the Elizabeth Firestone Willis house to hear a jam session by Lionel Hampton's musicians. G.G. turned out to be a jazz band aficionado and a terrific dancer. Although no one else was dancing and there was barely any room, when Lionel broke into a good beat George asked me to dance. We were so well matched it was as though we had danced together all our lives. If any one thing did, that clinched our relationship.

Within two more weeks I was invited to be an after-dinner guest at the White House and to bring my new man. (Thanks to Liz.) The only thing George remembers about that evening was my introducing him to LBJ who chatted for awhile and then walked away, but turned around and came back. George says he then—in a characteristic Johnson mannerism—poked him in the chest and said, "Take care of this girl. She's my favorite." "Yes sir," responded G.G. Accustomed to Johnson's flattery, I didn't give it another thought. But when we left the White House, George said, "I got my orders tonight."

"What do you mean?" I asked.

"The president told me to take care of you. What can I do? I got my orders from the commander-in-chief." That sounded like a proposal to me but I was waiting for those four definite words: Will you marry me? They came, the day after Christmas when I met his daughter and son-in-law, Gretchen and Bill Quigley, their two little children, Billy and Joanie, and his seventeen-year-old son "Bern" whose real name was George Bernhard Graeber. They were a happy, healthy, sports-loving family. All of them were skiers, even six-year-old Billy and four-year-old Joanie. I must have passed muster. A few days later

Perle Mesta said, "If you don't grab this one, you're crazy." I didn't tell her the New Yorker was already mine.

I announced our engagement in my January 1st column following my sister's announcement at 12:01 at a New Year's Eve party given by former Cuban Ambassador and Mrs. Lyn Arroyo. Everybody gasped with surprise, then fell all over us with embraces and congratulations. I had sent my column to the *Star* in a sealed envelope marked for the eyes only of our Portfolio section editor Gwen Dobson. If the news had leaked before the New Year rang in, the *Post* could have scooped me. Under the heading, GUESS WHO'S GOING TO BE MARRIED!, I began: "Washington's biggest party trotter has a prediction for 1969 that may bowl her friends over. A longtime spinster who knows the gay [that had a different meaning then] life well, a free spirit who has flitted around the town and around the globe—she has frequently expounded on the joys of the bachelor woman. Then six weeks ago she met a new man in town. He was tall, handsome, attractive and simpatico and suddenly she began to think the single state was not all that blessed. In fact, he was so wonderful she knew in three weeks' time that he was THE man." I did not identify the couple until the end of the column when I added, "Wow! Life is beautiful!"

The *N.Y. Times* and *Newsweek* picked up the item. *Editor and Publisher* reprinted my announcement in its January 18 issue. As a result of the news having spread so far and wide I heard from friends all over the globe—from Chuck Robb in Viet Nam to Evangeline Bruce in London where her husband was ambassador. Chuck had received his January 1 copy of the *Star* and a tape from Lynda with a message from me. Lady Bird had invited George and me to a cozy luncheon with her and Lynda in their private quarters. It was such a sweet thing to do. We were thrilled.

The Johnsons sent us a wedding present of two silver mint julep glasses, each engraved in old English style with a special message. One read: TO BETTY / WITH THE AFFECTION OF TWO ADMIRERS / LADY BIRD / AND / LYNDON B. JOHNSON. On the other was: TO GEORGE / THE LUCKY MAN WITH OUR BEST WISHES / LADY BIRD / AND / LYNDON B. JOHNSON. On the back of each was engraved the date of our wedding, February 15, 1969.

CHAPTER 9

A Troubled Tango

The Nixons

Richard Nixon never struck the public as a party-loving guy. So Washington wondered when he picked a high priest of the Mormon Church, Willard Marriott, founder of the Marriott motel chain, as overall chairman of the Inaugural if it would be the most strait-laced in history. Mark Evans Austed, a TV personality and one of the Mormon Seventies (who rate above the elders of the church), was chairman of the Inaugural Ball.

Marriott quickly announced that "Mormons are the greatest dancers in America. They danced all the way across the plains. When they got to Utah they put recreation halls in all their churches and had their dances there and still do," including, he said, "hot rock."

The new president would astound those of us who covered his social doings. The Nixons would entertain even more people than their predecessors, and in different ways. And as formal as he was— he restored white tie attire and tried to put Graustarkian uniforms on the White House police—he would put a one-time producer of the TV "Laugh In" show, Paul Keyes, in charge of East Room entertainment. (Keyes leaned so heavily on Las Vegas-type shows that the East Wing eventually had to take over.) But however warm the program I frequently froze in the East Room. The new occupant liked open fires blazing cheerily in the fireplaces even in summer so the airconditioning was kept blasting.

RMN, so often described as stiff, basked in his role as host to hundreds of the politically and socially elite.

Even before they moved into the best residence on Pennsylvania Avenue with all those servants and a personal entertaining allowance, they pulled out all the stops for daughter Julie and David Eisenhower's wedding on December 28. There were eight bride's attendants and ten ushers at this first marriage ever to unite two presidential families. The famed Dr. Norman Vincent Peale officiated in his Dutch Reform Church in New York City; the reception was held in the fashionable Plaza Hotel. Unable to attend were David's grandparents, Dwight and Mamie Eisenhower. The former president, who was to live only three more months, and his wife listened to it via closed circuit in Walter Reed Hospital. David proudly told me the Eisenhowers' wedding present was a big color television set. I learned years later that Ike had managed to get it free. At a small dinner one evening CBS's Bill Leonard related this tale of the general's frugality:

When Ike was hospitalized for recurring heart problems, CBS sent a color television to his suite at Walter Reed—presumably so he could enjoy the network's programs. As the Eisenhower-Nixon nuptials approached, the general asked Leonard for another set for his hospital sitting room. CBS obliged. Not until the wedding gift was publicized did Bill realize where the second set had gone. It was no secret that Ike's friends donated much that was on his Gettysburg farm.

While Julie had been preparing for her big day, older sister Tricia had been shown around her future home by Luci Johnson Nugent. As they walked down to the first floor, the ever-expressive Luci said, "If walking down these stairs behind the president of the United States when they play 'Hail to the Chief' doesn't give you chills, I don't know what else will."

I covered the Inaugural, as usual. But eclipsing it all for me were two stunning dinners in George's and my honor that week—by Spain's Ambassador and the Marquesa de Merry del Val, and by

Kuwait Ambassador and Mrs. Talat Al-Ghoussein. My betrothed and I were toasted in style; indeed, Talat's toast to me was the greatest tribute of my life. I do not know what woman or man inspired the quote originally nor do I care. He said, "I asked a distinguished lady what she used to preserve her appearance. She replied:

> I use for the lips—truth
> For the voice—prayer
> For the eyes—pity
> For the hands—charity
> For the figure—uprightness
> For the heart—love.

It flattered the socks off me, and I choked up.

The following week Perle Mesta gave a fabulous dinner dance for us in the handsome Sulgrave Club ballroom; and the next night I was partying in the Nixon's White House at their first diplomatic reception. The contrast between their style and that of the Johnsons mirrored the differences in the two men themselves.

Parties given by the flamboyant rancher from Texas had been more crowded, more informal, more unpredictable, more lavish in the buffet, and more kissingly cordial. The White House photographer, looking calm for the first time in years, said the hectic impulsiveness of the LBJ era was over. When the Nixons came down the stairs, it was immediately obvious that this would be a more formal administration. The president in white tie and tails and Pat in her yellow beaded inaugural ballgown descended alone. When the Johnsons had come down those stairs for their seven to nine o'clock informal supper for the foreign envoys, they had been trailed by the vice president, the secretary of state, the chief of protocol, the dean of the diplomatic corps, and their wives—as had the JFKs at the 5:00 to 8:00 P.M. reception for the diplomats.

The Netherlands ambassador's wife liked the Nixons' entrance. "It was very royal," said Mrs. Carl Schurmann. All the formality-loving ambassadors, who had so few chances to sport the brilliant sashes and medallions of their career successes, were delighted. After greeting the guests, a third of whom the well-traveled Nixon seemed to know personally, Nixon did not dance. Instead, he sedately made a grand circle through all the rooms, addressed the assemblage with a few appropriate remarks, and then he and Pat retired. The dance music continued, but by 11 P.M. the entire corps had departed. One other difference was the absence of bars, which Kennedy had introduced. Champagne and unspiked fruit punch were passed.

The Nixons' social secretary, pint-sized Lucy Winchester, ran the evening affair—but only after a battle with Counsel to the President John Erlichmann. He had showered the social office with instructions. Why do political advisers to every president assume they are automatically endowed with social know-how? In this case the 5'2" blond went to Mrs. Nixon threatening to resign if she had to take orders from the West Wing rather than the First Lady. Mrs. Nixon called her husband and he settled it for good. As a member of an old landed Kentucky family, Lucy had been raised with a knowledge of the proper amenities.

The only inelegant note at that soiree was the grinding out of a lighted cigarette into the polished East Room floor by an ambassador. I had seen that done once before on the rug in the State Dining Room. Oddly enough, the Israeli and Egyptian ambassadors were the guilty ones. Each time I quickly recovered the offensive weed, telling the culprit that was no way to treat a fine rug or floor. The rank of ambassador is no guarantee of correct upbringing; only an indication of his chief's confidence.

The parties for George and me continued. Laura Gross, owner of the chic 1925 F Street Club, came down from Bethlehem, Pa., with her husband to give a dinner for us in their Watergate apartment. Mrs. Clark Clifford gave a luncheon and shower for the middle-aged bride, Kennedy Center Chairman and Mrs. Roger Stevens wined and dined us, and former Democratic Vice Chairman Katie Louchheim and husband Walter did likewise, in a grand manner. F. Scott Fitzgerald's daughter Scottie Lanahan took over the F Street Club for a fabulous to-do. My niece Nancy Mann Sanson gave our bridal dinner in the same location. Her mother, my only attendant, and her husband Ted Maffitt gave the wedding reception on the second floor of the Sulgrave Club. Our most intimate friends were invited verbally to the ceremony because the Washington Cathedral's Bethlehem Chapel was too small to accommodate everyone. As a late blooming bride, I eschewed a big church wedding and a long or white gown. I wore a long-sleeved, short pink dress of alaskine fabric with a wreath of matching leaves and diaphanous brim of pink illusion. My brother Bill gave me away and my new stepson "Bern" was best man.

We honeymooned in Key Biscayne, Florida, at the invitation of an old friend, Marilyn Himes Riviere, who had a compound of four houses around an inviting garden. She stayed in one, she kept an antique, highly polished fire engine in another, and we shared a third with an eighteen-inch-long tortoise, which remained immobile in our living room. As it wouldn't even eat she finally sent it to the Washington zoo where it recuperated nicely. Marilyn had another, bigger, and more modern, fire engine that we whipped around town in one night. Besides her attachment to fire engines, she has a predilection for strange animals in and about the house—an emu, a Vietnamese pig, and, until it got too big, a tapir.

In the months to come we were honored at dinners given by Italian Ambassador and Mrs. Egidio Ortona, Oklahoma Senator and Mrs. Mike Monroney, Union Carbide Vice President and Mrs. Morse Dial, Admiral and Mrs. Tazewell Shepard, newsman Pat and Mary Munroe, former Ambassador and Mrs. Wiley Buchanan, and Chase Manhattan Bank's Russell Dorr and his wife who staged a Japanese dinner with everyone in kimonas, sitting on floor cushions, playing geisha games between courses, and loving it all. Included in the play were Turkish Ambassador Melih Esenbel, whose wife Emine told me I should always ask for the right side of lamb or cattle when buying my meat "because it is much more tender. That's because cattle and lambs always lie on their left side." I thought you'd like to know.

Washington was going strong socially. The Capital always welcomes a new administration with open arms. By the time a new president is elected, hostesses, lobbyists, diplomats, and journalists have entertained, influenced, sized up, and written about all the important faces in the previous administration; it gives them a shot in the arm to try their charm on new ones.

The Richard Nixons continued to confound their critics who figured their parties—like GOP convention parties in contrast to the Democrats'—were bound to be boring. At three receptions on three successive days Nixon gave his old Capitol Hill colleagues more freedom even than Johnson had. They could wander at will on two floors and inspect all the gifts the president had garnered on his European trip in March. They were so busy looking at everything they didn't dance much, though the East Room resounded with the right rhythms. And the president held forth to the feminine scribes with as much ease as his gregarious predecessor. He surprised us when he complimented me on the long fancy earrings I was wearing, adding, "I'm an earring man, myself."

"He never was before he was president," chuckled his friend Secretary of State Bill Rogers, within earshot. We of the press thought Rogers, who had known him since they both served in the Eisenhower administration, was a close friend. But he turned out not to be a confidante. Nixon was a loner; as his biographer Stephen E. Ambrose wrote, he had no real friends except for Bebe Rebozo.

Black tie was stipulated for those receptions. One woman, Joan Kennedy, came in a mini-dress, the new thigh-high style, and captured the headlines in the next day's papers, though I doubt Joan did it for that reason.

Only domestic champagne and fruit punch were passed. French champagne, we were told, would be served at state dinners and diplomatic functions. When Republican veteran Senate leader Everett Dirksen drawled in his basso profundo to a uniformed aide, "I'd feel better if I had some sipping whiskey," a glass of Jack Daniels and soda was brought to him pronto.

The heads of nations from around the world came to former President Eisenhower's funeral at the end of March and were received at the White House afterwards. Mrs. Nixon was still in black, but two Asiatic beauties who had time to change after the service came to the reception in dazzling full-length gowns. Imelda Marcos wore a pink silk terno glistening with sequins and jewels; Madame Nguyen Cao Ky, wife of the vice president of war-torn South Vietnam—which only survived with the help of American dollars and American lives—came in a lavender silk dress and coat heavily jeweled in shades of violet that could only have come from Paris or Milan. The former airline hostess, decked in diamonds and pearls and a designer dress, displayed even greater insensitivity at Mrs.

Claire Chennault's tea. There, she remarked, "I'm so surprised to see you Americans thinking so much about how to be happy and what you can get. We in Viet Nam are always thinking of the suffering in our country."

The biggest social astonishment in this new conservative era was the state-size dinner honoring Duke Ellington. No Democrat had ever put on such a big shebang there for a prominent black. Besides being smart politically, piano-playing Richard Nixon may have appreciated Ellington's compositions—but the third reason is perhaps most charming: The Duke's father, Edward Kennedy Ellington, had been a butler in the White House for most of his life. As he was always called Kennedy, the Duke liked to crack that his father "was the first Kennedy in the White House."

Fifteen great jazz artists performed, including pianists Dave Brubeck, Earl "Fatha" Hines, Billy Taylor; saxophonists Paul Desmond, Gerry Mulligan; drummer Louis Bellson; and singer Joe Williams. They put on an all-Ellington show after dinner before an audience dotted with the likes of Benny Goodman, Cab Calloway, Mahalia Jackson, and Otto Preminger. As usual, the president and First Lady retired when the performance was over, but invited everyone else to stay and enjoy themselves. That's when the White House became unglued with a fabulous jam session. Even high-toned National Gallery director John Walker and his proper British wife, Lady Margaret Drummond Walker, hung on every note from Dizzy Gillespie's trumpet et al until it ended at 2:00 A.M. One usually dignified White House waiter sashayed and shook his head to the beat while collecting champagne glasses on his tray. "The White House ain't never been so cool," he said.

Nixon was the first president to go to the Kentucky Derby; I believe he enjoyed the stir and excitement when a president shows up in public places. George and I were there, too, as guests of *Louisville Courier Journal* Editor and Publisher Barry Bingham and his wife. The weekend had started with a pre-Derby dinner dance, given by the Cornelius Vanderbilt Whitneys at their horse farm in Lexington, that drew two future presidents, Ronald Reagan and Gerald Ford. Pat Nixon told me at the races they had a party coming up for all the aides and press who went to Moscow with them in 1959, the time of his famous kitchen debate with Khrushchev.

Another Nixon original was the White House dinner for top U.S. diplomats—perhaps the first white tie dinner ever at the Casa Blanca where every man felt completely at home in those six-piece outfits. The honorees, all career ambassadors and mostly, if not all, Democrats, were David Bruce, Robert Murphy, Llewellyn Thompson, and "Chip" Bohlen. Averell Harriman regretted.

With the new splash at 1600 Pennsylvania Avenue, embassies were vying to get Vice President Agnew to dinner. As vice president, Nixon had tried to attend dinners at all 119 embassies in his eight-year term. The Agnews went to two dinners at the Iranian Embassy in the first six months. "The first gesture of friendship extended to my wife was a visit from Mrs. [Hushang] Ansary," he explained. The fact that Mariam Ansary was a real beauty and dinners there were glamorous may have influenced him, too. The shah's comely twin, Princess Ashraf—in the U.S. to receive an honorary degree from Brandeis University for promoting women's rights—came to one wearing a crown of diamonds and pink rubies and a matching three-tiered necklace above a pink Dior gown studded with crystals and pearls. The former $15,000-a-year governor hadn't seen many visions like that.

The Nixons staged another presidential innovation with their big banquet in Los Angeles for America's new heroes—all the astronauts—to celebrate the landing on the moon. "There never will be a dinner to match it until they have the first one on the moon," I wrote. For sheer number of celebrities, the closest thing to it I had witnessed in a quarter century was the dazzling dinner *Time* magazine gave in 1963 for every person who had appeared on its cover. The L.A. gala was so packed with the famous and able a newsman remarked, "I have never felt so small in my life."

I stayed with a longtime friend in Los Angeles, Carroll Righter, the country's best-known astrologer. (Nancy Reagan mentioned him in her book, *My Turn.*) He was known as a trusted, kind gentleman. I have never believed in astrology, but Carroll really did and he saw no conflict with his Christian religion. The advisory board of his astrological foundation was interesting—Marlene Dietrich, Mrs. Francis V. duPont, Mary Pickford, Mrs. Clint W. Murchison, Jr., Danny Kaye's wife Sylvia, Robert Cummings, Trenton, N.J., bank president Mary Roebling, and other well-knowns.

While on the west coast, several of us women of the press were invited by Mrs. Nixon to their house in San Clemente. I called it "a dream" in my column. The wide horizon of the Pacific Ocean stretched out before it, fresh coastal breezes swept it, lush tropical foliage beautified it, and the scent of honeysuckle hung in the air. And everywhere Pat, who was obviously so happy there, had dipped into the palette of a Van Gogh painting to brighten it with a sunny yellow. (Pat also had the walls of the big second floor hall in the White House painted yellow; she was the only first lady to invite all the press women upstairs to see it.)

President Nixon, known to the rock generation as the nation's No. 1 square, had a rock band, the 5th Dimension, enliven his party in December for the country's governors. When all five Dimensions belted out "Let the Sunshine In" from the musical *Hair*, two of the singers snared New Jersey's Governor Richard Hughes and Virginia's Governor Linwood Holton for a dance. The president tried to get Tricia to join them, in vain; so he simply clapped his hands to the beat, along with crusty scholarly economist Arthur Burns. New Orleans jazz virtuoso Al Hirt made his trumpet do everything but talk to Martha and George on the East Room wall. Oddly, the most liberal politician in the White House, Presidential Assistant Daniel Moynihan, was the picture of square contentment, puffing his cigar by the open fire in the Green Room.

Ten days later, RMN and Pat gave a Christmas party for Bob Hope and his troupe. After dinner, with the vice president gazing at him from the front row, Hope said, "During the campaign the Democrats were saying Spiro Agnew's library burned down and destroyed both books. And one he hadn't even colored yet!"

Representative George Bush and Secretary of State Bill Rogers stopped in their tracks on the way out that night to watch the sexy gyrations of Hope's dancer Suzanne Charny, boogalooing with a White House aide. She was wearing a mini with a jacket over it that cloaked some of her movements. Rogers turned to me and said, "See if you can get her to take off her jacket." I offered to hold it for her, as she "must be getting warm." Nothing now hid her uninhibited wiggles; the men remained riveted until she left the floor.

The first anniversary of every president's Inauguration calls forth comparisons with predecessors. A 1970 newspaper article stated,

"Nixon men do not live in the fashionable neighborhoods where ranking White House and cabinet figures did before." The Kennedy people, it said, "tended to buy houses in such fashionable regions in the city as Georgetown and Cleveland Park."

I had been a lifelong Democrat but when the biased press, in an attempt to belittle the Republicans, wrote absolute bunk I had to refute it. The press who lived in Georgetown and loved it (I was one of them) liked to call it a status symbol and link it to the Kennedys. Actually, as I wrote, only one member of JFK's cabinet—Abe Ribicoff—lived in Georgetown, and he wasn't in the cabinet long. Not a single one lived in Cleveland Park. Bobby Kennedy lived in McLean, Va., and the other two most socially *in* cabinet members— Douglas Dillon and Robert McNamara—lived in the richer Kalorama section. Not even McGeorge Bundy, Ted Sorenson, Kenny O'Donnell, or Kennedy's social intimate Charles Bartlett lived in Georgetown. The article also said Nixon people favored the Watergate apartments where Kennedy people didn't consider living. That was absurd! It wasn't built in the Kennedy years. The truth is, it matters not where you live in Washington, nor where you sit in a restaurant. It's how much influence you have that counts.

A dinner to discuss Nixon's first year was staged by the British Broadcasting Company at Perle Mesta's. Designed for disagreement, it brought a strange group together: moderate Republican Senator Howard Baker, middle-of-the-road Congresswoman Margaret Heckler, ultra-liberal Senator Charles Goodell, former aide to Bobby Kennedy Peter Edelman, black militant Chuck Stone (who wore a silver clenched fist on his lapel), *Chicago Daily News* bureau chief Peter Lisagor, and historian and statistician Richard Scammon. I guess I was invited to toss in personal criticisms. Said Lisagor later, "I was utterly surprised we got through the evening with no blood spilled and no wine thrown." In an after-dinner exchange I took on the complaining militant Stone. I told him I couldn't care less about the discrimination in our country against black men, who were a minority, as long as the majority of the population, women, were discriminated against in laws, in the upper levels of government, in corporations, you name it. The ones I really felt sorry for, I told him, were black women. They got the worst of everything, and they were the backbone of their race. He was surprised into silence.

*   *   *

By the end of the first Nixon year, the cabinet celebrity was Martha Mitchell, wife of the attorney general. Bubbling with warmth, she couldn't walk into a room without drawing attention. She was getting more publicity than the First Lady. Her mail box bulged with fan mail and requests for interviews and speeches. Before Martha, cabinet wives were seen but not heard. Martha voiced her opinion on everything that riled her. For example, after the Supreme Court's decision forcing the busing of schoolchildren to attain racial balance, the attorney general's wife told me, "The Supreme Court should be abolished! . . . Things like this should be put to a vote of the American people," a statement that earned me front page stories across the country.

Time magazine had her portrait painted in oils for its cover and she starred in a *Newsweek* feature—and ultimately acquired such a following that the GOP was torn between worrying what she would say next, and conceding that she was the Republican party's biggest drawing card. Eventually, she would become so carried away with making headlines that calling a member of the press became a compulsion. She sometimes called a reporter five times in one day. Her increasing agitation heralded the mental problems to come.

My sympathies were with John Mitchell. More and more, when he came home from a hard day's work, he found no peace. Martha would be on a rampage, or sounding off on the phone to a newswoman. "Through it all [daughter] Marty and I were together every available moment," he told me later. I never heard him cross his wife, although we saw them often. We were housed together at a Williamsburg houseparty, where I watched him turn her extreme comments into humorous asides—as usual.

John took his Watergate medicine without pointing the finger at anyone. Out of prison temporarily in 1978, he gave me his only interview. He said he and Nixon were still friends. How could he feel that way, I asked, when he was the scapegoat? "If you were up on all the technicalities on those things and the nuances involving the people around him you would understand," he said. He devoted his time in prison to giving legal advice to inmates and got quite a few out. "The poor people were lost," he said.

It was at Williamsburg, in the renovated antique house where we stayed, that we sat up late one night listening to John reminisce about his days in a PT boat in the navy. Some of the zany antics in the TV series "McHale's Navy" were supplied by John and his comrades. He chuckled when he recalled the number of times his group ran the admiral's jeep "accidentally" over the dock into the water.*

Guests Galore

The number of White House guests soared. Now, after dinner 140 were invited for the entertainment. In addition to dozens of dinners for chiefs of state from around the world, there were evenings at the White House with comedian Red Skelton, Sammy Davis, Jr., Beverly Sills, etc., a dancing evening after the screening of *Topaz* (we were invited), a dinner for ambassadors to the OAS, a dinner for Nathan Wyeth with an exhibition of his paintings on the main floor, religious services on Sundays, the presentation of the inspiring one-act musical *1776* about the founding of our republic, and the upper crust-packed dinner for the duke and duchess of Windsor when the comments of my colleagues forced aged Fred Astaire into a short—alas—dull dance with me. I told him he did not have to do it but he led me perfunctorily around the floor. "I never liked ballroom dancing," said the world's greatest ballroom dancer afterwards. "I don't dance even for benefits." Years later, his daughter told me the same thing.

Whereas during the Johnson administration Lady Bird always stepped up to the microphone to introduce the after-dinner program, President Nixon did it now with grace, and a touch of humor, right up until the end. Perhaps this was proof of what biographer Ambrose described as "his genuine if too often unappreciated acting ability. . . . He could pretend to an innocence that was not there, to a curiosity that he did not have, to an ignorance that hid a perfect knowledge, in a manner that was entirely convincing. . . . He dissembled even with Haldeman, leaving his chief of staff thoroughly confused."

---

* It wasn't until I heard the eulogy at John Mitchell's funeral service that I learned he had won the navy's Silver Star and two Purple Hearts.

The night of the Red Skelton party, I drove to the White House with HEW Secretary and Mrs. Bob Finch and Postmaster General and Mrs. "Red" Blount. As we passed the tennis court they remarked how nice it would be if it had a bubble over it so they could play in winter. An hour later Tex McCrary introduced me to multimillionaire Bill Levitt; I casually mentioned the tennis buffs' wish. Just as casually Tex, a TV and public relations success, said, "Why don't you donate a bubble, Bill?" Levitt, who had not even met the two cabinet members, said, "I will." A few days later he confirmed his offer in a letter to me. I passed it on to the White House. It was ruled out—supposedly for appearance's sake—but I suspect it was because Nixon wasn't a tennis player.

Amid all the entertainment, the event that caused the most excitement was Tricia and Julie's dinner and dance for the prince of Wales and his sister Princess Anne. The press had a field day, suggesting that Tricia had designs on Prince Charles. It told her in print that he couldn't marry a commoner, and certainly not an American. The party was Tricia's way to return the hospitality she had been shown at Charles' investiture as the prince of Wales. Of course she did not expect to launch a royal romance; she already had a steady beau—the man she would marry.

Five hundred and fifty of the offspring of governors, Washington officials, and foreign ambassadors were invited to the outdoor affair, which lasted till the wee hours. Although the royals were unaccustomed to cutting-in on a dancing couple, they were used to rock music. The month before a rock band had held forth for the Queen Mother's seventieth birthday dance and that party was still going strong at 4:00 A.M.!

* * *

Prince Juan Carlos, now officially declared the next ruler of Spain, and Princess Sophia came to Washington in January 1971. They received the A-1 treatment accorded chiefs of state—i.e., a big luncheon given by the secretary of state, the president's formal dinner that evening, and a party the following day at the visitor's embassy. Juan Carlos had called his ambassador in advance to ask him to include his karate teacher at the embassy dinner in his honor. Colonel Allan Bell, who lived in Washington, told me the prince had such talent for karate that he could break a brick with the side of his hand, one of the tests for a black belt degree—at his first session. At Secretary of State and Mrs. Rogers' luncheon, the tall, handsome king-to-be told me he could no longer flatten out his fingers properly because of karate.

"So karate broke the royal fingers," I observed.

"The fingers are not royal," was Juan Carlos' smiling response. "They are just fingers."

At the White House that evening while he was dancing with Adele Rogers, he called out to me, "I have someone for you to meet—Allan Bell." His future queen, Sophia, was equally friendly. A caring mother, she drove her children to school when they were small. When told that a quail shoot in Texas could not be worked into their schedule, she said, "I don't shoot. I can't stand to kill anything."

The wildest dance performed that night was the one to rock music by the voluptuous Charro, fourth wife of noted dance band maestro Xavier Cugat. The rest of the guests cleared the floor to watch. The royal pair missed it having been reluctantly, I thought, escorted out by the Nixons after the entertainment so the Nixons could retire as usual. The thrice-divorced, aging Cugat wore a gold cross Pope John had given him. How come?

"He didn't know," replied the mischievous Cugat, smiling broadly.

President and Mrs. Nixon announced Tricia's engagement to good-looking, blond Edward Cox of New York at a dinner in honor of the prime minister of Ireland and Mrs. John Lynch, on the eve of St. Patrick's Day 1971. My story announcing it two months earlier had made the front pages across America. Though denied at the time by Pat's staff director, Connie Stuart, it must have pleased Tricia's parents because George and I were invited to the White House that evening.

March 1971 was also the month the hit musical *Hair* came to town. It introduced frontal male nudity to the Kennedy Center, some of the best rock music of the time, and confirmed lots of hair and sloppy looks as the hip style among the young. In stunning contrast, George and I took a break in Aiken, S.C.—*the* winter resort for the elite horses of the East. In this peaceful world of old money, the beautifully cared-for, sleek polo ponies, racehorses, show horses, steeplechase horses, and hunters paraded every morning from their spotless stables past the "cottages" (mansions) to their training grounds. It was not uncommon in this elegant world of the rich society sportsman to have a groom for every horse.

Among their beautifully cared-for owners was the only child of the woman President Franklin Delano Roosevelt had loved—Lucy Mercer Rutherford. Tall, dark-haired, fine-featured Barbara Knowles, wife of Robert Knowles, who described her mother as "a wonderful and exquisite woman," had a treasured possession. It was a small duplicate of the big, unfinished portrait of FDR which Madame Elizabeth Shoumatoff was painting at the time of his death. President Roosevelt, himself, had given Mrs. Knowles the painting, and it usually hung in her bedroom. But after the disclosure of his devotion to her mother, the very discreet Barbara Knowles would remove it when she entertained.

* * *

Washington, on September 8, 1971, changed forever, with the formal inauguration of the John F. Kennedy Center for the Performing Arts. Thenceforth the great European opera and ballet companies would come to Washington even before New York, predicted Chairman Roger Stevens, correctly.

Leonard Bernstein's *Mass* made its debut that night in the monumental, multi-auditoria building by architect Edward Durell Stone. As the center was also a memorial to her husband, Jackie Kennedy was expected at the brilliant gala opening. But she was unwilling to face the crowds. Other Kennedys occupied the presidential box. President and Mrs. Nixon, feeling the opening belonged to the Kennedys, went the next night.

A year later Jackie came to Washington to attend a graveside memorial mass for Bobby Kennedy. Her mother suggested she go to the opening night of the return of Bernstein's *Mass*. She agreed— but the news broke, and it was just as Jackie had feared. Frenzy seemed to grip the city. The Opera House sold out. Press and photographers' requests for tickets or access badges flooded in. A special meeting was held with the Capital Park Police on how to handle the rubbernecking crowds. The Roger Stevenses, who were in London, quickly lopped four days off their vacation to arrive in town an hour before the dinner Mr. and Mrs. Hugh D. Auchincloss were giving prior to the concert. Kennedy Center Director Bill Blair offered Jackie and her mother the center's private entrance and the president's elevator to avoid the crowds. But Janet Auchincloss declined the offer.

"I think she should walk right into the Hall of Nations," she said. "She isn't the president and I think she should go in the front door." When reminded that her daughter was the most glamorous woman in the world, her mother was not so sure.

"I think she is one of the brightest and she's certainly original," she observed. But "Jackie isn't doing anything now except bringing up her children and being a wife."

Others at the dinner were Leonard Bernstein, who came to be Mrs. Onassis' escort; World Bank President and Mrs. Robert McNamara; the Blairs and their guests; and French Ambassador and Madame Jacques Kosciusko-Morizet. At table Bernstein, who was proud that his wife had spent a night in jail as a war protestor, raised his glass in a toast to Angela Davis, the self-avowed communist. A dead silence followed.

Before dinner, at her mother's suggestion, Jackie called me. It was her first on-the-record interview since she became First Lady, and probably my least productive one. Changing her name had not changed her. She had the same mystique, the same very soft voice, the same unhurried poise, and the same delicious sense of humor. Would she ever write her memoirs? I asked her.

"No, I hope not," she said, as if never planning to go that far off her rocker.

How did her life with Onassis compare to her life with Jack Kennedy?

"That's all private to me," she whispered.

The public's need to know about her apparently baffled her.

"There was a point to it when I was in public life," she said. But people devour everything they can about you, I rejoined. Look at all the pictures in magazines.

"I don't understand it," she remarked.

"Movie magazines," I pointed out, "can't guarantee their circulation without something about you on their covers."

"Who cares about magazines?" she asked. Perhaps if she gave firsthand some of her own thoughts and actual facts it might put an end to the ridiculous stuff written about her, I suggested.

"I don't care about it because it's going to be there whatever I do." One had to be oneself regardless, she added.

I asked if she still did sketches and made up little booklets with pictures and poems such as she had given her mother and children in the past.

"No, but the children do. Mother always made those drawings sound like a collection of Rembrandts." She sounded tickled.

What did she want most in life? The reply came quickly. "The happiness of my children." There was no way of knowing if this very private woman was concerned about her own happiness four years into her marriage to Onassis; reputedly, it wasn't doing so well.

Jackie walked up the Hall of Nations as her mother wanted. It wasn't roped off, and there was a crowd on either side of her closing in to get a good look; a host of photographers in a semicircle in front of her simply backed up as she walked forward with Stevens. All she saw were the chandeliers. Despite all the gems Onassis had showered on her, her green Valentino dress was unadorned. Her only jewelry were earrings virtually hidden under a long, full hairdo.

As a national memorial, the Kennedy Center had to be open to the public from 10:00 to 5:00 seven days a week. It rapidly became a happy hunting ground for souvenir collectors. In one month's time, everything one could lift, pull, or twist off was pilfered. Thousands of silver-plated knives, forks, spoons, salts, and peppers had been taken from the "buffeteria." Crystal drops from the beautiful Waterford wall brackets in an Opera House lounge—part of the jewel-like set presented by the government of Ireland—were removed. Even the pink marble faucet handles in the ladies' room were wrenched off, though how that was possible without a tool box, I wouldn't know.

*   *   *

My life as a society columnist among smiling, well-groomed party-goers, bejeweled and besatined groups in elegant settings, was an ironic counterpoint to the national news of the early 1970s. The antiwar demonstrators, the bloodshed, bombs, and banner-carriers were headlined day in and day out, but such sights seemed far removed from the drawing rooms of Washington hosts or the White House—at least until the Nixons' dinner for the De Witt Wallaces. The founders and owners of the *Reader's Digest*, whose magazine claimed 100 million readers, were getting the Freedom Award, America's highest civil award, for their contribution to the "wonder of common life and the scope of man's potential."

It's a proven fact that the quickest way to get instant nationwide publicity is to accuse a president of the United States of something. The Secret Service tries to screen out such types. But it had no way of guessing that a troublemaker lurked among Ray Conniff's sixteen singers who performed after that dinner. The young woman had never been part of a rally or marched on the Pentagon. But in the middle of the program of popular songs she pulled a banner out of her bosom and held it up. In big letters it read: STOP THE KILL-ING. Everybody froze. If she could hide a banner on her person on the stage in the East Room in those pre-metal-detector days, could she have hidden a weapon or even a small bomb?

Millionaire New York realtor Jack Mulcahy, shouted, as if he were at a baseball game rather than in the crystal-lit East Room, "Throw the bum out!" But President Nixon said, "No, let her stay." He assumed she was just another rebellious teenager. She wasn't. She was thirty years old, had no one close to her in the Viet Nam War, and admitted she did it for publicity. As a result, she got very little.

The general who had commanded our forces in Viet Nam under President Johnson, "Westy" Westmoreland, was host at one of my more memorable parties. Now the army's chief of staff and living in Quarters I at Fort Myer, he and his attractive wife Kitsy gave an off-the-record dinner attended by Bob and Dolores Hope. The company of twenty-four was awash with rank, starting with Vice President Agnew, Chief Justice Warren Burger, Ambassador Cabot Lodge, Senator Stuart Symington, UN Ambassador Jerry Wadsworth, and their wives. As always with government officials at meals, there was serious talk interspersed with banter. At the end of dinner, Hope stood and tried to give a toast; he was outranked by another guest every time, and had to sit again. When he finally began to speak the Westmorelands' dog threw back his head and gave full voice to his canine tenor. The comedian couldn't have had a better stooge. Dolores Hope sang love songs looking at Bob; Cabot

Lodge sang, so did Jerry Wadsworth; Bob did a soft shoe number. It was social Washington at its best.

In the spring of 1972, Washington's noted Gridiron Club, which was composed of fifty reporters of dailies, invited fifteen prominent women to their star-studded annual dinner. They were the first females ever to attend—and only included because some newswomen had picketed the dinner the year before. At the time I wrote: "I'm for equal rights for women, and I sent in my check along with hundreds of others to the National Women's Political Caucus. But sign a petition to keep 50 men from having their one big night a year together? Not on your life!"

One reason given for the petition was that women should belong to the Gridiron Club because it represented "itself as an organization of the most distinguished journalists in Washington." Yet, I wrote, it did not take in any of the most influential, opinion-making columnists or big name commentators. The Gridiron president, Edgar Allan Poe of the *New Orleans Times Picayune*, said, "We have never represented ourselves that way." The other reason the petitioners gave "was that they should not be denied access to all the important people invited to the dinner." But, I wrote, the daily reporters in the club membership had few chances to rub elbows with the Capital's mighty compared to the protesting women who covered the Nixons, their official family, and the big name guests at their social functions as often as two to five times a week. "By contrast, the poor males are only asking for one night of glamor."

Cathy Douglas, wife of the very liberal Supreme Court Justice Bill Douglas, said she had been on the side of the picketers until her husband explained it was simply a question of having the right to associate with whom you please. Senator Barry Goldwater said, "It's the first amendment—the right to peaceably assemble." Liberal Justice Harry Blackmun dittoed their stand.

My coming to the defense of the male scribes did not affect my friendship with the women petitioners; later, at any rate, the club took in the most qualified.

*   *   *

Republicans were wishing they could skip a convention in the summer of 1972; it would, after all, be cut-and-dried with the guaranteed renomination of Dick Nixon. But Democrats were jittery, and for good reason. Maryland's biggest fund raiser, Esther Coopersmith, told me that 80 percent of the delegates to the Democratic Convention had never been to one before. Senator George McGovern had succeeded in getting the delegate-selection system changed. Instead of experienced politicians like governors, senators, and representatives gathering to choose a qualified candidate with a chance of winning the election, delegates were being elected in their own bailiwicks; now, the only way the governors and members of Congress could get on the floor of the convention hall was to get a VIP badge. This time, agitators who had demonstrated outside the turbulent convention of 1968 would be inside.

All six of the Democratic delegates from affluent Montgomery County, Md., were for McGovern. One was his eighteen-year-old nephew, who threatened to walk out of the convention if his uncle wasn't nominated. Another was nineteen-year-old Cathy Toland, whose foul talk had shocked listeners at precinct meetings. Yet another was former clergyman Tom Allen, a man who had divorced his wife and mother of his four children, shed his clerical garb, married a rich divorcee, and also used four-letter words at precinct meetings.

The new politics of the Democratic party would cause thousands of registered Democrats, myself included, to vote Republican for the first time and weaken Democratic chances at gaining the presidency for years to come.

Their convention was the most unorthodox of my life. Before the vote on which Illinois delegation would be seated, former FCC Chairman Newton Minow put it in a nutshell: "One side looks like the cast of *Hair*; the other side looks like the cast of *Guys and Dolls*; and I'm in the middle." A Swedish reporter sent back this description to his country: "If I tried to paint a clear picture it would only confuse you." On the third day Mrs. Drew Pearson, who had been going to conventions of both parties since 1936, complained, "There hasn't been a laugh so far."

Foreign ambassadors who wanted to observe our interesting way of selecting a possible president were flown down for a couple of days and entertained by the Democratic fat cats of the "72 Sponsors

Club" at the Playboy Plaza. Said an observer later, "Nobody enjoyed the overdeveloped bunnies more than the ambassadors from the underdeveloped countries."

A topic detrimental to Republicans had emerged in Capital drawing rooms before the Democratic convention. But no one was taking the bumbling bugging of the Democrats' national headquarters in the Watergate office building very seriously. It evoked humorous comment but no real concern; Washingtonians are too steeped in politics and the shenanigans that often accompany them. Not even Republican insiders were worried. When I asked the new director of the campaign to reelect Nixon, former congressman and presidential assistant Clark MacGregor, about it at a dinner party, he dismissed it. "You don't have to bug the Democrats," he said. "They blow their guts every day." He figured it was just another one of those stunts pranksters in both parties pull off in an election year.

MacGregor, who couldn't imagine what the GOP stood to gain by such a stupid act, subsequently ran into Democratic National Chairman Larry O'Brien, who had slapped a $1 million suit on the Republican National Committee for allegedly breaking into his office. "Are you planning your strategy about Watergate? You know that's a Jack Anderson operation," said Clark smiling broadly. "It may be," replied Larry. "One of his recent articles printed material that could only have come from my secret files." (I doubt that Jack had to break the law to get material.)

The month before the GOP convention, Washington was humming socially; that's always the case during presidential campaigns, scorching heat or no. So many bigwigs have to remain on the scene it's the easiest time to corral a distinguished group at mealtime. George and I gave a dinner in our garden for Barbara and Clark MacGregor and invited Henry Kissinger, telling him to bring Nancy Maginnes, his favorite lady friend. Also among the twenty were British Ambassador Lord Cromer (Esme Cromer was away) and ABC commentator Howard K. Smith and his wife. Henry, as national security adviser to Nixon, had overshadowed Secretary of State Bill Rogers and everybody else in the White House (including the president) by his witty banter with the press, by dating the most glamorous women he knew, and by knowing whereof he spoke. He was always a sparkling guest.

His rating as the second most powerful man in the world had once led him to quip that he had just had a call on the hot line from Brezhnev complaining that Henry had replaced him. As any comment of Kissinger's was column material, I used the story. But as soon as the item appeared it was sent posthaste to the Kremlin. There, they had never heard of chitchat columns. Promptly a query came back to Soviet Ambassador Dobrynin—who burst out laughing when he saw it. The query did not concern Brezhnev being demoted to third place by Kissinger. The Kremlin was simply perplexed. They couldn't, for the life of them, remember when they had used the hot line!

One of the most moving experiences of my life occurred after midnight December 7, 1972. It was the night launching at the Kennedy Space Center in Florida of Apollo 17.

We flew down with the president's Chief of Staff Bob Haldeman and Jo, the Donald Nixons, several foreign ambassadors, and members of Congress and their wives, King Hussein of Jordan's soon-to-be ex-wife Princess Muna (with four security men), and other prominent figures. We were treated to a fascinating movie briefing on arrival, a tour of Cape Kennedy facilities, and a meal. Sitting in the stands next to ours, facing a corps of gapers, were Frank Sinatra, Jonathan Winters, and Hugh O'Brian.

The launch was even more awesome at night, I am sure, than it would have been in daylight. In the blackness, the fire underneath the spacecraft was a torch of unearthly dimensions. As the rocket's thrust slowly wrenched the craft from the powerful jaws of gravity and set it free into the boundless beyond, man's daring invasion into the cosmos became, for me, a religious experience. Man, as the image of God, knew no limitations; he included infinity.

*   *   *

The second Nixon administration had not even begun when once again a stupid ruling regarding social coverage erupted from the West Wing. Apparently the decision was based on an unfavorable article in the *Washington Post*. Again I took issue in print.

"No more asinine policy toward the White House social press

could be pursued than that which has now been adopted by the Nixon administration," I wrote. "To exclude women with long experience in covering White House parties—especially those from the two Washington papers that have reported on White House parties for over one hundred years—in favor of political reporters from scattered papers, makes as much sense as prohibiting Pete Lisagor of the *Chicago Daily News* or Garnett Horner of the *Washington Star-News* from attending the President's press conferences and inviting this columnist instead.

"How absurd can the West Wing get? For it is apparent that this new ruling is the brainchild of some supermind on the President's, not the First Lady's, staff.*

"After almost three decades of reporting on the newsmakers within the polished confines of the nation's No. 1 mansion, this columnist has no more desire to cover a jammed presidential press conference than the reluctant political reporters had to cover the Nixons' recent party for new members of Congress. Their tongue-in-cheek articles or their failure to write anything could hardly have done the Nixons any good.

"To blame the latest antisocial Nixon policy on the failure of a newspaper to support the President in his campaign simply won't wash. The *Washington Star-News* supported Nixon and was barred from last weekend's reception, and this syndicated columnist showed no preferential treatment for McGovern—indeed was accused of the opposite—yet has been barred from the last three receptions.

"The astounding thing is—just two weeks ago someone in the West Wing was complaining because Pat Nixon does many things that could improve her public image but we don't write about them. How, I asked the complainant, are we supposed to know about these things, by clairvoyance? Another Washington newswoman recently observed that 'Pat Nixon doesn't deserve such a puny press. She could be made to come alive. She's a warm person.'

"Yet a few months ago the *Washington Star* heard that Mrs. Nixon

---

* East Wing staffers had no doubt that the "supermind" was Chief of Staff Bob Haldeman whose aim appeared to be the isolation of the president, but he took his orders from RMN.

had an herb garden in a glassed-in section of the White House roof
and the President had a strawberry barrel and Pat's press secretary,
Connie Stuart, was asked if the *Star* could get a photograph of either
or both of them with their gardening projects. What a good human
interest story that would have made. But Mrs. Stuart said she
wouldn't think of intruding on them in that manner.

"If the President and his wife want to lose friends and alienate
people among their most favorable press to date—they couldn't
have picked a better way than to ostracize the social reporters."

Just before this got into print I ran into senior Nixon staffer John
Ehrlichman at some function and asked him why I had been barred.
He was amazed. He not only was unaware of my exclusion, but he
knew I had been fair and the president needed more such objective
social reporting, not less. His efforts, reinforced by my column, got
the policy reversed.

*   *   *

The month of Richard Nixon's second Inaugural witnessed two
other presidential milestones: The memorial service to Harry Truman, and the death of Lyndon Johnson. In the death of Johnson I
felt, as did other social reporters, as though I had lost a personal
friend. He had teased me, flattered me, lectured me, made me
laugh, kept me guessing, greeted me with a kiss, and danced with
me. After his retirement, he had sent me jars of peach preserves
labeled "From the LBJ Ranch," a color photo of him and Lady Bird
in Western dress at Christmastime 1972, and two or three dozen
peaches from the Johnson orchards. I have no doubt other reporters
received similar tokens of remembrance. There were some misty
eyes at his memorial service in the National City Christian Church,
but I remember only the tears on one face—the face of the black
uniformed pallbearer. The man who did the most for equality for
blacks would, I believe, have considered that his greatest tribute.

The inaugural festivities spread out over three days, and produced some surprises:

At the Salute to the States gala in the Opera House it was not the
First Lady, nor Bob Hope, nor Frank Sinatra who got the lion's share
of attention. Every time the lights went up Henry Kissinger was
besieged by at least fifteen autograph seekers . . . At the Inaugural

Concert a few hours before the curtain, temperamental Frank Sinatra withdrew from his emcee role although his good friend Ted Agnew attended. (Later he told a *Post* reporter off in vulgar terms. If he planned to make Agnew president as he had boasted, he was going about it in a strange way.). . . . At the Inaugural Ball in the Smithsonian's Museum of History and Technology, there were some chickens in a barnyard display that periodically scrambled over their fence to get out among the ballgoers. They belonged to two strains existing in the 18th century that get drowsy if an arm is waved in front of them, so somebody had to keep waving. . . . Outside the 1925 F Street Club about one hundred bystanders, mostly G. W. students, kibitzed for more than four hours during Henry and Christina Ford's party. Egged on by Senator Chuck Percy, Ambassador Henry Cabot Lodge delivered a political speech from the front stoop. At one point Philippine First Lady Imelda Marcos swept in with seven bodyguards, which seemed a bit much.

Philippine Foreign Minister Carlos Romulo, incidentally, had been a good friend of mine since his ambassadorial days in the Eisenhower era, when the Philippine Embassy cut a bigger swath politically and socially than at any time since. The able little man also had wit. Once, at a dinner in Houston, a Texan asked him: "How do you feel among all these tall Texans?"

"Just like a dime among nickels," was his fast response.

It was at his suggestion that Imelda gave me an interview. She came to my house, looking at forty-three like some Asian goddess untouched by time. There was nary a line or blemish on her flawless face, and not even a scar to show where a would-be assassin had almost severed three fingers when he slashed at her. Only the healed gashes on her right arm were visible. Her seven protectors waited outside.

Sitting more erect than any queen on the soft sofa in our library, she defended her husband's policy:

"We copied you for many, many years. What happened to our country? We had corruption, confusion, a high rate of criminality and anarchy. . . . It's like a suit. The American suit is good; it keeps you warm. But you are bigger than the average Filipino, so it does not fit and we have to make an adjustment. You claim you are liberals but you force your way on us. We ended up with twenty people, or a little more, practically controlling 90 or 95 percent of the country." I did not ask if two people, with martial law, weren't now controlling the country. She was telling me that our kind of democracy was an unaffordable luxury, whereas with their town assemblies they had a powerful kind of democracy. I printed her argument, but I didn't buy it.

As to North Vietnam dragging out the war so long when we had offered them aid, she said, "You don't understand the Asian. When you have nothing and when you are naked, the only thing you have is your pride."

*   *   *

The highest-ranking seated embassy party I ever attended was Lord and Lady Cromer's luncheon for Prime Minister Edward Heath. President and Mrs. Nixon were there along with Henry Kissinger, Secretary of State and Mrs. Rogers, Secretary of the Treasury and Mrs. George Shultz, Secretary of Defense and Mrs. Elliot Richardson, CIA Director and Mrs. James Schlesinger, future President and Mrs. Gerald Ford, Ambassador to Great Britain and Mrs. Walter Annenberg, and so on through the highest hierarchy. The place designated for new HEW Secretary Casper Weinberger was empty because he was testifying before the Senate Labor Committee. I asked Jane Weinberger what connection Cap had with labor. She replied—on the record—"None. It's a TV spectacular for Teddy."

I asked Pat Nixon at that affair if she wasn't exhausted after Inauguration Day. She said, "Not at all. When we got home after seven balls we went out into the kitchen and cooked some breakfast and didn't get to bed until 3:30 in the morning!"

I was the only member of the press who was a guest at this "summit" luncheon. The *Washington Post*'s ladylike Dorothy McArdle had to stand with the other reporters assigned to cover the event behind a rope during the cocktail period and leave before the luncheon began. The reason the *Post*'s reporter was banned dated back to the report of Lady Cromer's press conference soon after she became the chatelaine of the British Embassy. Many requests had come in for an interview with the aristocratic English beauty; after all, her father was the noted press magnate Lord Rothermere, and her husband, the third earl of Cromer, had been governor of the Bank of England. Finally, Lady Cromer decided she would answer their questions at a joint tea for the newswomen. When asked about our war in Viet Nam, her ladyship, unused to press conferences, ventured where angels feared to tread. She expressed the hope that the U.S. would persevere because "saving face means so much more to the Asians than life. Life means nothing to them." The subsequent *Post* story was so critical it sounded as if she thought Asian lives were valueless. Thereafter the *Post* was not invited to any social function given by the Cromers.

That elegant Rowley Cromer and his countess were a real love match was obvious when they gave the first private dance at the British Embassy in sixteen years to celebrate their thirtieth wedding anniversary. When he stood to welcome "only personal friends" at the end of dinner we were suddenly transported back to war-torn London in 1942. He recalled the church in the old mile-square City of London where they were married. The church was so accustomed to funerals that year that at the end of his talk with the parson about arrangements, the latter automatically asked, "Now when will the coffin arrive?" Cromer was in uniform then and "London . . . was very gray," but Esme, he said, looking across the room to where she was sitting, "brought the sunshine." For a second the memory so moved him he couldn't continue. Then he said, "I am going to ask her to dance with me and hope everyone will join us." But for a magical few moments everyone watched the romantic pair as thirty eventful years simply dropped away.

Five months later they treated 120 Washingtonians to a rollicking "Old Style Music Hall" against backdrops from Queen Victoria's diamond jubilee year. From the opening request that everyone hold their noses and gently pound their necks with the sides of their hands to give an imitation of bagpipes, to a dance with a wand by a middle-aged mustachioed man wearing a pink satin tulle ballet costume over a misplaced bosom and singing "Nobody loves a fairy when she's forty," guests laughed till they cried through the three-hour supper-show. Even sober-looking George Shultz sang along with the chorus, "Daddy wouldn't buy me a bow wow, wow wow."

Lord Cromer, the godson of King George V, once borrowed $3 billion to avert a devaluation of the pound sterling. He divulged this tale at French Ambassador Kosciusko-Morizet's dinner in his honor: When war broke out between France and England in 1802, France was too hard up to wage it "because of its largesse to the United States (during our revolution); so it sold Louisiana. But the U.S. had no money to pay for it. So it sent an American to Paris to discuss it with a Frenchman." Both went to London to get the project financed.

"I am happy to say," said Cromer, "there was a very successful bond flotation and the Americans got Louisiana, France got their money, and Britain got the commission. I know, because my great-great-grandfather was the banker."

*   *   *

Bill Rogers, who may not have seen the handwriting on the wall that March, gave his last dinner for the chiefs of foreign mission—the most resplendent event of the year. Rogers, who would lose the top post in the cabinet to Kissinger in a matter of months, had hired Meyer Davis and his top society band in the East to play after dinner for dancing—something that had never happened before at this annual event. He also invited Pearl Bailey to sing following the secretary's customary speech and the dean of the diplomatic corps' answer. Pearl so wowed the ribboned crowd that the dancing didn't begin till almost midnight. Her song, that should have struck home in that international group, was: "Let there be peace on earth and let it begin with me/ Let there be peace on earth, the peace that was meant to be/ With God as our father, brothers all are we/ So let me walk with my brother in perfect harmony." She got an ovation. Soviet Ambassador Dobrynin invited her to Russia. Rogers gave her a plaque that read: Diplomat of Love.

That spring two events took place that would have an important impact on the city. The political one was the arrival of ten Chinese who came to set up the first communist Chinese Embassy. The second was the return of the shah of Iran's Ambassador Ardeshir Zahedi, who would stimulate the social activity for the next six years as no previous envoy had. He entertained lavishly and constantly. In his first seven months he served, it was rumored, $38,000 worth of caviar. At one dinner for one hundred guests two pounds of the Caspian pearls centered every table. When games were played the winners received gold coin charms or gold cufflinks. He imported celebrities and rounded up glamor girls to perk up political bigwigs. He had a dance orchestra play continuous music or a classical artist perform in the mirrored mosaic Persian room. His goal was political but he made warm lifetime friends while fostering the closest relations ever between oil-rich Iran and the U.S. Although divorced from the shah's daughter, he was the father of the shah's granddaughter—and had the total confidence of the monarch to whom he had introduced the beauteous Empress Farah. His thoughtfulness as friend, employer, or diplomat was unmatched.

As April brightened the city with its blossoms, the Watergate scandal darkened the faces inside the White House. Nixon, who had fired his counsel, John Dean, asked his top staffers Haldeman and Ehrlichman and Attorney General Richard Kleindienst to resign.

On the social circuit one encountered foreign envoys who were cheerful about the scandal, sometimes exclaiming enthusiastically, "I love this country." Only in America, they said, would there be a public investigation of a scandal involving the head of the country.

But they laughed at the reaction to Kissinger's wiretapping of key people to locate security leaks.

"When I served in Sweden during the war," said Spain's Angel Sagaz, "everybody in every embassy was bugged, although Sweden was neutral."

"When I was in the White House," said President Kennedy's Air Aide Brig. Gen. Godfrey McHugh, "my phone was bugged all the time. Everybody's was. FBI men would even come to my office and play back something I said over the phone and ask if it wasn't classified. I would tell them, 'no.' I was discussing something that had already appeared in the *Chicago Tribune*."

Little red bug pins began sprouting around town. I asked John Ehrlichman a year later if it was possible to plant a bug on someone and be able to hear conversations some distance away. He said, apparently, yes; once, when he was in Paris with the president, he had found such a bug pinned to the inside of his coat. Who put it there he never knew.

But Watergate took a back seat on May 24, 1973. That night the beleaguered Nixons gave the most thrilling party I had ever attended at the White House. The war was over, our men had come home; it was for the over six hundred who had endured the horrors and torture of North Vietnamese prisons and were still full of love for country and gratitude for their release. Each had the same wonderful expression in his eyes—a great kindness, and a quiet self-confidence that had been tested to the extreme and never found wanting. None of the entertainers—Bob Hope, Jimmy Stewart, John Wayne, Edgar Bergen, Sammy Davis, Jr., Vic Damone, Phyllis Diller, Ricardo Montalban, Dolores Hope, Irving Berlin, Joey Heatherton, etc.—could measure up to the presence of those men.

There was Rear Admiral (later Senator) Jeremiah Denton who spent seven-and-one-half years in prison and, like the rest, suffered torture when he refused to meet with Jane Fonda during her friendly visit to North Vietnam, because he wouldn't be used for anti-U.S. propaganda. There was Lt. Comdr. (later Senator) John S. McCain III, who broke both arms and fractured one leg when he crashed landed in North Vietnam. When his captors found him they broke his shoulder and bayoneted one foot and left him in a prison cell without medical attention for days. During his six years in prison he was beaten, sometimes three or four times a day, yet he too refused to see Jane Fonda. They then put him in a 5-by-2 foot cubicle and kept him there for four summer months. "There was no air except what came under the door," McCain told me.

To this day, I will not buy a Fonda exercise video or go to her movies.

The dinner for the 1,300 guests had to be held under a huge marquee off the South Portico. Heavy rains had soaked the ground, and evening slippers and hems of gown became wet with mud—but there wasn't a disgruntled guest in the group. Never had the White House been filled with people so humbly proud to be there. One POW was so grateful for Kissinger's efforts, he said, "Do you mind if I kiss you?" Cracked Henry, "I hoped you would ask."

For the Nixons, the night was a magical elixir. Gone was the recently noted presidential stoop, and Pat's stricken mask. Elsewhere in Washington, talk was of impeachment. This group gave him a wooden shield inscribed: "Our Leader, Our Comrade, Richard the Lionhearted." After everybody sang "God Bless America" at midnight, the president and his family retired; the POWs stayed on and danced until 3:30 in the morning.

The antithesis of America's heroes was the next honoree—the USSR's General Secretary Leonid Ilyich Brezhnev. Not until fourteen years later did I learn the slick little trick Brezhnev had pulled on the U.S. All that June evening, the Russian politician was Laughing Leonid, upstaging Reserved Richard at every opportunity. No wonder he was laughing!"

Prior to Brezhnev's visit, Soviet Ambassador Anatoliy Dobrynin went to see Acting Chief of Protocol Marion Smoak, with a brochure in his hand. He opened it to the picture of a Lincoln town car. That, he said, was what the chairman would like to have as a state gift. Smoak blinked.* But the Ford Motor Company generously came across with the desired gift; the Soviets flew it back in the big cargo plane that had come over with sixty tons of communications equipment to set up on the roof of the Washington Hilton during the visit.

Two months later, Dobrynin called: Their mechanics needed extra tires, he said—as well as bumpers, driving rod, driving shaft, radio, heater, windshield, and so on through a six-page list of parts. Supposedly the fine new Lincoln had utterly gone to pieces in sixty days! But detente being detente, the higher-ups approved everything the gold-digging communists asked for, well aware that the Russians wanted to copy the parts without having to dismantle Brezhnev's pride and joy. They did not have to pay a cent!

* * *

That summer of 1973 marked the end of the era of great residential hostesses. Famed Marjorie Merriwether Post died; Perle Mesta failed to recover from a broken hip. Laura Gross, founder of the F Street Club, died, and so did Washington's most famous doorman, Thomas Cole, a black gentleman who could welcome by name every arrival at the most prestigious parties.

---

* Meanwhile, our president, like all American officials, was barred by law from accepting any gift worth more than $180.

A pall had fallen over the administration, too, with Watergate and the Senate hearings.

And yet, the social pace did not slacken. Embassy Row set the tempo.

The superb Italian ambassador, Egidio Ortona, and his elegant, rapid-speaking, arts enthusiast wife Giulia told me they were giving three dinners a week, and going to a party every other night.

One diplomat, Spanish Ambassador Sagaz, discovered a Watergate actor on his own premises: Mrs. E. Howard Hunt, wife of the ex-CIA man involved in the break-in, had been working at his embassy for eleven years when he arrived in 1972.

"She was a speechwriter," he said, "but when I gave her my first speech in Spanish she said she was sorry she couldn't translate; she could only improve English. I really didn't understand why she had been hired." He called her a distinguished lady who owned three or four horses and liked to ride. He let her go. A few months later she was killed in a plane crash with $10,000 in cash on her, presumably for defendants' fees.

*   *   *

The curtain was dropping on the Nixon administration in the spring of 1974 but no one would have guessed it by the performance on the East Room stage of the president and Pearl Bailey. Pearl, one of the great showmen of all times, wowed the nation's governors for fifty minutes then cajoled RMN into sitting at the piano and playing a song for her. When he played "Home on the Range" she said, "Mr. President, I want to sing a song, not ride a horse." Their hilarious attempts to get together on a tune and key cracked up their audience.

His impending resignation was forgotten—but only for an evening.

*   *   *

Like Lady Bird, Pat Nixon was the perfect political wife. No matter how much she might wish to be doing something else or how tired she might be, if Dick Nixon wanted her to shake five thousand hands at a reception she would do it graciously. She too believed in her husband's greatness.

She was so efficient that she could pack and go on an unexpected trip in a couple of hours. She told me, when he was vice president in 1960, that she would never hang a garment in the closet that needed fixing—a spot removed, a seam sewn, or whatever—without taking care of it first. I asked her then if it were true that she pressed the vice president's pants when she had two servants in the house. She said it was; she did it herself because she could do it better and faster. Years later, she told me how amazed the Russians were when they learned—during the Nixons' trip to Moscow in 1959—that she had brought a traveling iron with her and that she was washing out her own lingerie. The people of the so-called classless society could not understand why the wife of a dignitary should have to do such menial things.

The slender, finely-boned woman with the fragile good looks was far better than her husband at personal contacts. She and her daughters campaigned for Nixon's second term in thirty-seven states, touching base in their gruelling schedule in seventy-seven cities. It's small wonder that the effort to look interested and smiling—when all you really wanted to do was relax at home with your family—caused the press to denigrate her "mask."

In November 1968, when as usual I had to write my out-of-town column before the election, I again wrote an open letter to the wife of the winner, asking the editors to fill in the right name.

This time I urged her to stand up for her rights. First Ladies filled the most demanding, unpaid job in the United States. Their time was never their own. They were constantly serving the public yet they didn't even get travel expenses. Although President Johnson had put at the disposal of the Kennedy family four government planes at the request of Pierre Salinger when Robert Kennedy met his sudden tragic end, he never permitted his own family to use them. Mrs. Johnson had to travel on commercial lines; when Speaker Rayburn died, she had to sit in the Dallas Airport until three in the morning to wait for a connecting flight to attend the funeral of the man who was like a father to her husband. So if Congress wouldn't give the new First Lady a salary the least they could do, I said, was to supply her with a mode of travel.

I also wrote that people wished she would bring the White House into the electronic age, that television should be used to bring more to the public than just the president's speeches to the nation. It could show such performances in the East Room as those of the winners of the Moscow Music Festival. (TV stations were subsequently invited to cover such performances.)

Foreign ambassadors wished, I continued, there could be more formality when they presented their credentials. There was in all other capitals in the world. Sometimes the new ambassador shook hands with the president and that was all. Sometimes four of them were received at one time. For the top representative of a sovereign nation to be received so casually when for everywhere else a special ceremony, an honor guard, and so on, marked the occasion was quite a blow. (Nixon upgraded the envoys reception with an honor guard and trumpeteers to herald their arrival.

Newswomen hoped she would continue the kind of press relations that were installed when Elizabeth Carpenter was there. (We were delighted when champagne was served to us while waiting in the theater for dinner toasts to be piped in but relations were not satisfactory until she put Helen Smith in charge.)

As for the president's attitude toward the press—any newsman would tell her that no matter what the president might do for the country, unless he held reporters at a respectful arm's length they would criticize him. Lyndon Johnson learned that after opening his heart and his hearth to the men who covered him. Women of the social press were exceptions.

There were ten suggestions in all. As before, the column elicited a response from the soon-to-be First Lady. In a typewritten letter dated November 29, Mrs. Nixon wrote:

"Dear Betty: I do hope it is in order to reply personally to an 'open letter.' In any event, I wanted you to know how much I enjoyed your article in the November 10 *Sunday Star.*

"As you intuitively surmised, ever since the election I have been giving a great deal of thought to how as a family we can best meet the challenges of our new role in the Nation. I am delighted to have the benefit of your thinking and most grateful for your interest in using your reporting talents to set out so clearly some of your observations.

"All of us deeply appreciate the warm good wishes of your closing paragraph, and we are looking forward to seeing you upon our return to Washington. With kind regards, Sincerely, Pat Nixon."

My closing paragraph had said that everyone hoped they would use "the White House as your own vibrant, warm, music-filled home and not as a cold, public building temporarily occupied by yourselves. People like glitter, excitement, liveliness and joy which we wish you a lot of."

Did they ever fill it with music! I did not know at the time that Richard Nixon had classical music played all the time—so loud, said his wife, "you can hear every note. It practically shakes the walls down, but he loves it." As for the liveliness, their variety and number of parties testified to that although they, themselves, never indulged in even a short dance, and always left the scene before the liveliest part of the evening.

In some ways Pat Nixon was a contradiction. She showed friendliness in the way she would put her arm around a woman's waist while chatting with her; in the way she had a reception for all the newswomen who could wander at will on the main and private floors; and in giving the first all-feminine "Gridiron widows" dinner since Eleanor Roosevelt's time. And she was warm and friendly in her greetings to thousands of strangers, frequently having a personal word for so many of them.

On the other hand Pat Nixon, like her husband, had only one good friend—Californian Helene Drown. Helene, Jack, and their daughter had taken trips with the Nixon family. It was Helene that she confided in, that she periodically telephoned from Washington, that she spent three weeks with in California the summer of 1967 when she reluctantly faced another political race. Pat had no confidante on the east coast. Her neighbors during Nixon's senatorial days found her warm, friendly, and helpful where kids and schools were concerned, but none became an intimate friend. Perhaps Pat's early hard life, having to help her family when merely a child, having to work to gain an education all the way up through college and get a job to support herself, gave her little time for friends and less need of them. In any case, the Nixons seemed wary of people who would be friends once he was in a position of influence. Naturally, that made them suspicious of just about everybody in

Washington. I thought Pat looked so crushed when they left Washington after his defeat in 1960, so sad and friendless, that I tried to show my admiration for her in a friendly letter. Perhaps she thought I would use any response for column material. That was not my intention, but I never heard from her.

Just before the Republican convention in 1972 she gave me an interview. I thought she never had looked handsomer, more beautifully turned out, or more fulfilled than she did that day. Chic in a long-sleeved print dress, she was punctual to a second when she greeted me on the second floor of the mansion.

"Let's be elegant and go in here," she said, leading the way to the beautiful yellow Oval Room. She offered me a place on the sofa and sat in an adjacent overstuffed chair. When a noiseless black footman appeared she suggested iced tea and cookies for the guest. Then she settled back.

Though I now know how she treasured her privacy, she answered all my questions like the pro she was. The past four years had been glorious . . . She enjoyed being able to support the programs she believed in—education, environment, Summer in the Parks, etc. . . . She believed in day care centers for mothers who had to work but "a homemaker should never be downgraded." . . . She liked making the Sequoia available to the Future Farmers of America, to Scouts who earned their way to come to Washington, to clean-up groups and the elderly . . . She spent four hours a day on correspondence, writing in longhand or on her own typewriter what she wanted said, and penning some personally.

Were there any occasions when she had to steel herself to hide her real feelings? "Not really," she said. "I have been in this field for so long it isn't difficult for me at all." She had, of course, no idea how difficult it would become as the heavy curtain of Watergate began to lower.

What had been the most memorable incident in the White House? The evening of Inauguration Day, when the family gathered to rehash the excitement.

" 'Dick,' I said, 'Let's turn on all the lights in the White House.' He rang a bell and there was a blaze of light for everyone to see."

This was such a change from the light-saving economies of LBJ, the electricians told her later how happy they were: "The White

House is a national monument and should be lighted as a national monument, and now I am going to light the garden in a very soft light."*

The most fascinating person she had met, she said without hesitation, was Chou En Lai. "He's a world traveler, speaks several languages, and with all his power retains a graciousness that is characteristic of the Chinese people, and he has a marvelous sense of humor."

In her free time she loved to be out of doors to walk or swim. Evenings she preferred to read an historical novel or see a good movie.

Had she realized her greatest sense of fulfillment? "Yes, I think so. I think being a partner to a great man is about the top experience."

That interview offered some insight into the First Lady. But perhaps the one she gave me a week later to tell the world what the real Dick Nixon was like told as much about her. She called him "the warmest person I have ever known . . . not the back-slapping or gushing type but he is constantly concerned about others."

Was he a handy-man around the house? "He is not a fixer. Dick pretends he can't hang a picture but when I get in a pickle I call on him. . . . He loves his home. He loves the gardens. He cares enough about having some beautiful roses in the house to go out after dark and clip them [in San Clemente, not the W.H.!]."

He had never sat down to dinner without a jacket on except for one very hot night. "He thinks dinner is special."

Did he have any pet economies? "No, he doesn't, but generally we have always had to be economical. If he has a pet extravagance I think it's gifts for the girls and me." But not clothes. As for his own, Pat loves "to help him choose things. I was a merchandising major and I love fabrics. I was assistant buyer at Bullocks-Wilshire. He isn't a vain person. He dresses in a few minutes. He wants to be neat and well dressed."

---

* Later she would get the Lincoln Memorial lighted but, unfortunately, the National Park Service, which did it, lacked the expertise to give it the bathed-in-moonlight look. It is still too garish with the source lights too visible—but better than it was in complete darkness.

How strong a disciplinarian was he with the girls? "He always wanted a very happy home life so he never said a cross word to the girls. I had to do it."

Did he have special likes or dislikes? "No, he is a very easy person. He is considerate, kind and gentle. He isn't one to be critical or annoyed. He judges people as they are." (If Pat really meant that, some of his comments on the Watergate tapes must have floored her.) For the sake of credibility I was hoping she would find some fault with him. The picture she drew of her husband was in striking contrast to his public image.

When I asked her what traits of character did he most prize, her immediate reply was, "Honesty. I can remember him lecturing the girls about that a long time ago. . . . They were telling him about how some people cheated in exams and he was so shocked he told them it was important to be honest—honest in every way—to speak their minds and be straightforward."

Two years later she would learn—when the world did—that he had lied to her, to his daughters, and to the nation. Those on her staff are still certain she believed in him until the end—until the June 23rd tape revealed all. During those harrowing days, when the scandal was closing in and when for one occasion or another she had to come face to face with newswomen who invariably asked her about Watergate, she would say, with a drained look but holding her head high, "I know the truth and the truth has sustained me."

But she could not have known the truth when she was busy at the time making long-range plans for both Christmas 1974 in the White House and spring 1975. She was even picking out the Nixon china* only six weeks before her husband resigned.

It wasn't until the House Judiciary Committee voted to impeach the president, a fortnight before Nixon resigned, that Pat said it wasn't a good time to raise money for china. It was only then that she stopped working on new ways to improve the quality of the furnishings in the mansion. And Julie, whose sincerity in proclaiming her Dad's innocence shone like a beacon light from her face, was telling

* Not every administration had its own china. It was only selected when the need arose and when the selectee expected to be around to use it, especially as it had to be bought with privately raised funds.

someone the weekend before the Monday on which the tape was made public, "Everything is going to be all right." Then pausing, she added, "Unless you know something I don't know."

No three women had had more faith in, and given more support to, one man. How painful it was for them to stand behind him during the most excruciating seventeen minutes in presidential history, when he said goodbye to his staff and praised the character of his parents in that strange interjection, without mentioning the three women on the platform still backing him up.

But they stood there in silent dignity, with only the tragedy on their faces and the tears in their eyes to speak for them.

CHAPTER 10

Belles
of the Ball

Wonderful Women . . .

When I began my career, working women were rarer than they are today. That isn't to say that *women* weren't interesting. They were. And, as it happened, both my job and my inclination led me into contact with some of the most fascinating and original (and incidentally richest) women of this century. Some became my friends.

I always think fondly, for example, of Lady Astor, the former Nancy Langhorne of Virginia. I first met the wife of Lord Waldorf Astor, and the first woman member of the United Kingdom's Parliament, when she came to Washington for a visit with National Gallery Director and Mrs. David Finley. The Finleys' servants wore perpetual smiles while her ladyship was in residence. An unfettered spirit, she had matched wits with George Bernard Shaw and Winston Churchill. (Churchill got the better of her in their most famous exchange. That was when she said, "If I were your wife I would put poison in your brandy." And he replied, "If I were your husband I would drink it.") Once, when campaigning for the House of Commons, a farmer who doubted that Lady Astor could represent a rural district, shouted, "Can the lady tell us how many toes a pig has?" She snapped back, "Why don't you take your shoes and socks off and count for yourself." The uproarious laughter, of course, heralded her victory.

I went over to the Finleys' handsome Georgetown house on cobblestoned O Street to interview the wealthy British-American newsmaker. Keeping up with her crisp comments was like watching an expert marksman at a skeet shoot knock off one target after another:

"The only thing I like about the rich is their money. . . . My vigor, vitality, and cheek repel me. I am the kind of woman I would run from. . . . Anybody can die for his country; people should live for their country. . . . Men are a necessary evil. . . . The enemies of a country are the people who don't think big."

As for the days when Britain led the nations of the world, she said, "I don't think anyone need ever apologize for Great Britain." She recalled asking Mahatma Gandhi just before Indian independence, "Aren't you frightened there will be chaos?"

"No," he replied, "we have had 200 years of British rule."

When she learned on that occasion that I was a Christian Scientist, as she was, it gave our relationship special meaning. From then on, while she was in Washington, I took her to my church in Georgetown on Sundays, thus solving a problem for the Finleys and giving me hours of sheer delight.

I next saw her in London, my last stop on a European tour in the fall of 1957. After Rome, Capri, and then Paris—where I dined at Maxim's with Henri and Helle Bonnet whose other guests were Kentucky Senator and Mrs. John Sherman Cooper, and where I had dinner with the Art Buchwalds—I went to London in time for the Inter-Parliamentary Union Conference.

It was held in Westminster Hall where I watched Queen Elizabeth open it with the centuries-old pomp of British royal pageantry—trumpeters in sixteenth-century gold uniforms, elderly, spear-carrying Gentlemen-At-Arms in their brilliant red coats, knee breeches, and black velvet hats, and finally the government VIPs with the two parliamentary leaders in "full-bottomed" (chest-length) wigs, black robes, and trains carried by footmen.

Unbelievable as it sounds, just before the procession entered, when the dressy assemblage was already seated, three charwomen in green smocks appeared, removed the temporary covering that had kept the carpeted stairs clean, and began cleaning like mad. Kneeling on the steps and leaning over, with their broad rumps to the audience, they worked from the top step down, then began to carpetsweep the center aisle. I asked the British newsmen beside me how come. They grinned. "This is the way it's always done. It could easily have been cleaned earlier. It's simply British."

Lady Astor took me to lunch at the Connaught Hotel with her Christian Science practitioner, a charming woman. She also invited me to lunch at her house on Berkeley Square where both her butler and her chauffeur seemed constantly amused; they said they hadn't had a dull moment in all their years with her ladyship.

After lunch she took me in her brown and tan Rolls Royce to Hampton Court to call on the Grand Duchess Xenia, sister of the last czar of Russia. The elegant little woman, who'd had such a tragic life, lived in one of the "grace and favour houses" at Hampton Court provided by her cousins, the British royal family.

Much to my disappointment I did not meet her. While she and her visitor remained secluded in another room I stayed with the mother superior who attended to her needs. But Lady Astor reported to me afterwards that the grand duchess picked up a picture of Nicholas II with his wife and children and her eyes became misty. "They were all killed at the same time," she said, "but perhaps it was better that way." Was there then no possible truth to the story of Anastasia? "None," she had replied firmly. "My sister Olga saw her and she said she was definitely not our niece."

When leaving Lady Astor pressed a wad of bills into the companion's hand for the impoverished Russian royal. She gave her money regularly.

Nancy Astor paid her last visit to Washington at age seventy-eight in 1958 and I gave a small cocktail party for her. She wanted to meet U.S. senators so I asked the most attractive ones I knew. I also invited her longtime friend Adlai Stevenson who loved to match wits with her. It was then she told him, "You should marry me. I'm a rich widow." And he fired back, "I want somebody more mature."

At the luncheon in the Senate Dining Room given by Oklahoma Senator Mike Monroney's wife, she punctuated the conversation with these remarks: "The first John Jacob Astor who made a fortune told his family, 'Never charge over 5 percent,' and they never

have. . . . The British are the most courageous people in the world.
They face disaster better than anyone. They never whimper. . . .
Anyone who's a snob is an ass." Pausing in the Senate wives' ladies
room afterwards, the former Virginian said to the smartly uniformed
black maid who was in attendance, "My dear, I'm so glad you're not
Irish."

*   *   *

Clare Boothe Luce was the most brilliant, most multitalented, and
wittiest of all women friends in my lifetime. When we visited her at
her showplace in Honolulu I would place my small tape recorder on
the luncheon table and turn it on when she began recounting one
amusing story after another. It was a personal, inside chronicle of the
celebrated people she had known, punctuated with a humor that
was at once pithy and impish. If she wanted no record of certain
comments, she would say, "Turn that thing off." And I would.

Everyone knows that Clare Boothe Luce was the youngest editor
of the top, sophisticated magazine of that day, *Vanity Fair;* a successful playwright—*The Women* has been translated into many languages
and performed in as many countries; a World War II correspondent;
a congresswoman from Connecticut; a most successful ambassador
to Italy; a member of the President's Foreign Intelligence Advisery
Board under Nixon, Ford, and Reagan; and a sought-after lecturer.
She also, Clare told me, played golf so well she had to give it up to
preserve her marriage; she reached Olympic tryouts in fencing; took
four-foot jumps riding a horse bareback; and once swam across Long
Island Sound and competed for an Olympic swimming team. A
shooting companion told me she was an expert shot. I saw for myself
she was an artist in oils and mosaics, and a beauty right up until she
was eighty. She was the most exceptional woman I have ever
known. But she was best known for her pithy remarks. Among my
favorite are:

No good deed goes unpunished.

Never mean well—it's fatal.

Money doesn't bring happiness but it's a pleasant way to be
miserable.

The definition of an honest politician is a politician who honestly
doesn't know what his campaign manager did to get him elected.

She was the fastest "gun" with a bull's-eye comeback I have ever known. Once, when addressing a class at Hawaii University about the need for a strong defense, a black student asked her, "What is morally, psychologically, and spiritually wrong with the U.S. being a second-class nation?"

Mrs. Luce's rejoinder was, "What is morally, psychologically, and spiritually wrong with your being a second-class citizen?" That ended that subject.

Although she and her accomplishments were known around the world, when she wanted to buy an apartment at the Watergate she had to have references just like anyone else. And certainly no one ever had a reference like the one written by Charles Murphy, author of books about the duke and duchess of Windsor. Charles let his wit soar when describing his friend, whose mastery of the cutting remark hardly qualified her for sainthood. But this letter is a fair clue to the qualities that explain Clare's glamor:

"I could hardly feel more comfortable had I been called upon to vouch for the piety of the recently sainted Sister Elizabeth Seton; for the courage of a Molly Pitcher; for the zeal of a Susan B. Anthony; for the rectitude of a Carry Nation; for the rural grace of an Emily Dickinson; or for the acumen of a Hetty Green . . . you and Watergate East will become the gathering place of sages. It will acquire the healing powers of Lourdes. Vestal virgins will descend on the north bank of the Potomac to kindle the sacred fire on the hearth which Major L'Enfant in his disillusionment left cold. And the District of Columbia itself, once so gracious, will abandon its simple-minded craving to become just another state. It will declare itself a heavenly body."

Clare and I became warm friends. She invited us back to Honolulu for a Christmas visit when the highlight was two dinners with author-philosopher-historian Mortimer Adler and his young wife. The brainy Adler was one of those people Clare was willing to listen to. Others were people of political power. Her quietest evening at one of our dinner parties was when she sat at the same table with President Reagan. Otherwise her teeming, analytical mind preferred holding forth to a spellbound audience. She did not suffer gladly observations from people of lesser intelligence. On the other hand, her comments and recollections were so fascinating she could and did hold a whole dinner table mute in rapt attention.

Mortimer Adler was a spellbinder at the dinner Clare gave in Honolulu to celebrate his seventy-fifth birthday. He told about the time he went to see Dallas billionaire H. L. Hunt "who had the whole top floor of the First National Bank building. In his office was a dirty desk, a dirty carpet on the floor, a whiskey bottle on the desk, and some newspapers. We sat and talked, then he rang for his secretary and said we wanted to have lunch in the office. He asked, 'Would you like a barbecued beef sandwich?' I said, 'Yes, sir.' 'And a glass of milk?' I said yes. The secretary went out. Hunt then opened a drawer and took out of the drawer some little parafin bundles, one of which had some cut up carrots that he brought from home. And one apple. He took a dirty pen knife out and cut the apple and gave me half, then some celery stalks. Then he took a dirty newspaper off the floor and placed it on his desk and we had lunch on that newspaper. He was working on his 'Facts Forum' and he wanted my help, and as long as I was trying to give him help he listened to me but as soon as I had finished . . . he looked down my list of 'Great Books' [of the Western World] and saw Karl Marx and he thought I was a communist and that was it."

One day during a visit to Washington, Clare told me a story bearing on President Kennedy's assassination that had never been printed before.

Before the Bay of Pigs, Mrs. Luce had financed a fact-finding mission for three Cubans. They secretly visited Cuba by boat to get accurate information, which was then fed to Senator Kenneth Keating* of New York and to the White House. After the Cuban missile showdown all such efforts were halted. The FBI even told Miami Cubans to end resistance.

Two years later, the night of Kennedy's assassination, she was

---

* Keating liked to take a walk in his Georgetown neighborhood before going to bed. When I asked him in the late sixties—when he was then a judge—if he wasn't afraid of being mugged, he said, "No, I carry a shotgun." Wasn't that against the law? "Not if the gun isn't concealed," he replied smiling broadly. Suffice it to say, he was never bothered.

called by one of the Cubans. He told her that he and the other two
crew members had moved to New Orleans and started another Free
Cuba group. About eighteen months later Lee Harvey Oswald
contacted them, bragged about having been in Russia, and said he
could shoot Castro. He had no money and seemed to be offering
himself as a hired gun. The Cubans took him for a kook and tailed
him to a communist cell. Suddenly he had money and began making
trips to Mexico. The Cubans made tape recordings of some of
Oswald's meetings and photographed him distributing handbills for
the communist cell. Then President Kennedy was shot.

The young Cuban told Mrs. Luce that there was a Cuban communist assassination team and that Oswald was their hired gun. He
said Oswald had tried to report the communist plans to the FBI
sometime before the assassination, but because he was out for the
dough, the FBI didn't believe him. At Mrs. Luce's advice, the crew
members turned over their tapes and photos to the FBI and "I put
the whole thing out of my mind," said Clare.

When, contrary to the Warren Commission findings, the charge of
an assassination conspiracy hit the public in 1967, Mrs. Luce located
one crewman in Miami and asked him what happened when they
went to the FBI. "We were told to keep our traps shut and that we
would be deported if we said anything publicly," he told her. One
crew member had been deported to Guatemala and one was
stabbed to death in front of a store. The young man said he was now
married and didn't want to get involved again. A lot of people
working for a free Cuba had already been killed.

In 1975 Senator Richard Schweiker of Pennsylvania, who was
investigating the Warren Commission Report, asked Clare to persuade the Cuban crewman to testify behind closed doors. But the
Cuban friend she called to locate him said that testimony behind
closed doors would still become public, that Americans didn't understand that "there are trained communist terrorists . . . teams all
over the country. . . ." The day after that conversation bombs went
off at the State Department, the U.S.-UN mission, four banks in
New York, and three places in Chicago. And within hours of our
conversation, a Cuban anticommunist leader was exploded into bits
in his car in Miami.

*   *   *

As a hostess, Marjorie Merriweather Post was a brilliant perfectionist. Perhaps her managerial capabilities derived from running her
father's business, the Post Cereal Company, for six years following
his death in 1914.

I met the famed multimillionaire hostess, philanthropist, and by
then director emeritus of General Foods Corporation after her marriage to her third husband, Joseph E. Davies, who served as ambassador to both the USSR and Belgium. Between then and her death
in 1973 I frequently attended parties at her Washington mansion,
Hillwood; I twice stayed at her equally grand Palm Beach palace,
Mar-A-Lago, and experienced the joy of several weekends at her
unbelievable Camp Topridge in the Adirondacks. I boarded her
magnificent, 316-foot, square-rigged yacht, the *Sea Cloud*—the largest privately owned sailing vessel in the world—only once, when it
was docked at Annapolis. It was the epitome of luxury, even reflect-
ing the owner's taste for fine porcelain. At one end of a passageway
in the gorgeous vessel was a glass china cabinet and in her own
luxurious stateroom porcelain figurine lamps. I tested them. They
were bolted down. There was no way they would topple over in
rough ocean seas.

Only a part of her seventy-two-man crew was on board, but I
noticed when I passed the galley that they were getting double
lamb chops for lunch. Small wonder that keeping it afloat in the
thirties and forties cost $1 million a year, and that Queen Maud of
Norway exclaimed when she was shown around it, "Why Mrs.
Hutton, you live like a queen, don't you!"

Topridge was like no other camp you've seen. It was a whole
village on a pine-carpeted ridge that spilled down to lakes on either
side. Built of bark-covered slabs of native white birch and red pine,
its forty-two buildings, including individual housing for twenty-five
guests, blended into the Adirondack slopes with more subtlety than
a wisp of cloud blends into a blue sky. No automobile could approach it. No roads or bridal paths led into it. Except for a winding
footpath that a trained woodsman might follow, the only way to
approach either side of the ridge was by one of Mrs. Post's "fleet" of

thirty boats—five inboard motor launches and speedboats, ten canoes, rowboats, sailboats, barge, and kayak.

It took sixty-five servants in all—including the boatmen, guides, security men, electricians, carpenters, gardeners, and so on, plus her masseur and team of domestic servants—to run Topridge in the flawless way Marjorie demanded. "The foresight in this planning is comparable to the successful management of a huge corporation," observed President Kennedy's air aide and a frequent Topridge guest, General Godfrey McHugh. A whole building with cold storage rooms, dry goods rooms, and deep freezers held the food brought in by barge to keep such great numbers fed in style all summer.

As always Marjorie had us flown up to Saranac Lake in the solid comfort of her blue decorated Viscount plane with its three uniformed pilots and a steward. We were met by whatever number of limousines was needed to transport us to Upper St. Regis Landing where she maintained a five-car garage. Two matching blue motor launches, one for guests and one for luggage, driven by blue uniformed boatmen, carried us across the lake to Marjorie's private dock, where she and her chief steward Frank Moffat and a corps of footmen were waiting to greet us. It was a lark to ride up the hill in an awninged funicular to the top of the ridge to be escorted to one's cabin. At once a maid or valet—or both for married couples—appeared and noiselessly unpacked everything, leaving with the dress or suit to be pressed for that evening.

Topridge must have been the only camp in America where the butler and footmen wore different livery when serving lunch than they wore at breakfast, and different livery again at dinner!

The beautiful and always exquisitely groomed hostess, who maintained her superbly correct carriage until the end, did not make an appearance each day until lunchtime which, like the dinner hour, was announced fifteen minutes ahead of time by a warning bell; it was served in a separate big lodge. Flanked always by different partners at every meal, we lunched and dined at one long table, charmingly adorned each time with centerpieces and china that were not repeated during our Thursday-to-Monday stay.

Besides expecting her guests to appear for luncheon and dinner Marjorie had only one other rule: "Do whatever you want to do regardless of the planned activities offered, and if there is anything you want and don't ask for, it's your own fault."

What she provided in this free paradise (though we did tip for personal service) was tennis on two courts, fishing, boating, swimming, water-skiing, putting on a nine-hole green, hiking, croquet, shuffleboard, and portage trips from lake to lake. A-1 equipment and experts at each were supplied. For portage trips seven guides carried the canoes and other heavy stuff overland and, at a pine needle-carpeted spot, would spread out a tablecloth and whip up charcoaled steaks, potatoes, peas, and Adirondacks pie—a stack of flapjacks dripping in melted butter and maple syrup. I reveled in "roughing" it like that in the rustic wilds. Evenings were alternately devoted to movies or dancing, both ballroom and square dancing, with the necessary musicians brought in as well as Arthur Murray dancers to twirl expertly with the women and men guests. When not engaged, herself, in dancing—her favorite form of exercise—she wore a look of amused delight when watching the fun her guests were having. She derived real fulfillment from using her money that way.

My favorite recollection of all those weekends was the time I went to Mrs. Post's personal lodge where, attended by several private maids and two or three secretaries, she ran her private paradise and empire. Her servants were so highly trained that orders were rarely heard. She kept the same ones for years, because they were well housed, paid, and eventually pensioned. To see her privately a guest had to make an appointment.

Whatever the cause of my visit to her lodge, our talk turned to such feminine things as a one-piece, form-fitting garment to wear under strapless evening gowns. As Mrs. Post, even in her senior years, had almost the same measurements as I, including a twenty-six-inch waist, she suggested I try on the lace and elastic pink job she had made for her. So I put on the beautiful, sexy garment and also began trying on her fabulous jewels that she brought out for the fun of it. In no time I had wreathed my neck and wrists in diamonds and other precious stones and pinned to every inch of the front of the pink and lace job a fortune in jewels. To Marjorie's amusement I viewed myself in a full-length mirror with pleasure from every angle before returning the gems and the strapless unmentionable. Alas, I have no picture of me scantily clad but dazzling in more jewels than any woman has ever been seen wearing.

As one of the richest women in America, Mrs. Post could afford to surround herself with things she liked, and price was no object. When she and her fourth and last husband, Herbert A. May, sailed on the *Gripsholm* on their honeymoon, their staterooms had been redecorated to her tastes. Fine blond paneling and her own French furniture had replaced the modern furnishings of the ocean liner!

What eventually happened to her Topridge estate after Mrs. Post left it to New York State seems appalling. Governor Hugh Carey had a helicopter pad put in and used it as a vacation retreat. When Mario Cuomo became governor he put it up for sale. It was advertised with "an old black and white photo that looked like an ink blob" and suggested a minimum acceptable bid of $900,000, said well-known publicist Bob Gray who wanted to buy it. He thought it would go for millions, so he didn't put in a bid; then he found that no offers had come in. At that point he bid $800,000, but a man named Roger Jakubowski, who made a fortune selling wienies in Atlantic City, got it for $901,000—the whole four hundred acres with all the houses and all the staff apartments fully furnished, and all the kitchen equipment plus fourteen sets of china, and quantities of linen and table decorations. It was an incredible "steal."

*   *   *

The world's most famous arbiter of manners, the only American author of her time whose book outsold all but the Bible, was my first celebrity. She was tall, handsome, elegant Emily Post. I met her in Edgartown on Martha's Vineyard in the late thirties. My family had taken a house at West Chop on the island. Sharing, as she did, the anti-Roosevelt views of New York's upper crust, she was amused to find a young Washingtonian who thought FDR was great and told her why. Her sense of humor was such that when I bit into a little sandwich at tea in her house and jelly squirted out on my fingers, I didn't hesitate to lick my fingers in front of her. I wouldn't have to do this, I told her, if I had been given a napkin. "Oh, dear," she chuckled, then recalled her own etiquette errors—like the time she was so engrossed in conversation she used the wrong butter plate.

All etiquette, said Mrs. Post, was based on consideration of others so it was really a philosophy of living. But manners had to be taught; otherwise children would be little savages. She called charm "the greatest asset" a man, woman, or child could have. But without good manners, charm was nonexistent.

*   *   *

Alice Roosevelt Longworth, daughter of President Theodore Roosevelt, remained an *enfant terrible* her entire ninety-six years. She was impish, aristocratic, an irreverent wit, a commanding presence, a sought-after guest, and the fastest fun in town. She made fun of herself, called herself a crone, and after two mastectomies—the second at age eighty-six—referred to herself as the only topless octogenarian on Massachusetts Avenue. She never spoke of ailing. She described herself as the combination of Scarlett O'Hara and Whistler's mother. She may have lived among the latter's colors— "pale mauve and dim grays"—but she was rebellious and untameable like Scarlett. She started smoking when she was fourteen, in 1898, when it was unheard of for young women. When the shocking new musical *Hair* came to town in the 1970s she saw it more than once. It was "pure rapture," she said—probably because it threw off conventions, as she did. Although she had read the Old Testament through three times by age sixteen, she was an avowed atheist, even in her final years. She would not discuss religion at all and, at her request, no service followed her death.

She gave herself a birthday party every year; the most smashing was her ninetieth. "Everybody" came that February 12, 1974, from Watergate-beleaguered President and Mrs. Nixon and Tricia and Julie, Secretary of State Kissinger, the John Sherman Coopers, and Senator and Mrs. "Chuck" Percy to such prominent Democrats as the Averell Harrimans, the Sargent Shrivers, Joan Kennedy, and Clifton and Margaret Truman Daniel. Seeing columnists there who had been cutting the president to ribbons, I mumbled to her, "You have all the president's enemies." "I know," said Mrs. L., loving every minute of it. "He was amused." Nevertheless, the Nixons stayed a long time. After they left someone gave the hostess a poster of a smiling Nixon looking as if he had just stepped out of the bath and clutching a towel marked "Watergate Hotel." She would not have shown it to him at the party, she said, but she might do so privately.

Slender as a rail, she always looked smart in the same style straight-lined dress and broad-brimmed hat. And her dresses were always made of rich Chinese brocade she was given on her trip to China when a young woman. The Dowager Manchu Empress Tzu Hsi gave her so many bolts of fine material she was still having dresses made from it when of venerable age. I love the picture of her in her customary outfit taken at my wedding reception, and I treasure the little gold clock she sent us.

She had total recall, could quote pages of poetry verbatim, and had an insatiable thirst for knowledge. Except for two months at school she was educated by a governess, and by reading. Up until her last years she was buying four or five books at a time—rarely fiction—to read every night until 1:00 A.M. "I am full of curiosity and overexuberance," she said, "and overexuberance is something I hate in the aged."

No other offspring of an American president maintained her dominant position in society. No other person's recollections covered close to a century of political figures. No other had her vantage point, her penetrating eye, or her irrepressible ability to mimic— especially her first cousin Eleanor Roosevelt. Her last act was to stick her tongue out at her bedside watcher. She still had a sense of fun six hours before she died.

* * *

My friendship with Rosa Ponselle was the musical treat of my life. Perle Mesta, who had thrown parties for the Metropolitan Opera greats in New York long before I met her, invited Rosa to her Washington parties beginning in 1945. When I met her she was divorced from the former mayor of Baltimore and living in her Villa Pace in the beautiful Green Spring Valley in Maryland. After several years the unparalleled dramatic soprano developed a quirk about Washington and no attraction could induce her to come to the Capital again. But the warm-hearted, rounded Italian-American invited her Washington friends to Villa Pace on numerous occasions, and I went when I could.

Ponselle had retired from the stage while her voice was still magnificent because of the nervous strain of performing. Rosa told me that the great Enrico Caruso, who discovered her and sang with her in her Metropolitan debut at the Met, retched before every performance from stage fright. She, herself, never suffered from stage fright until the morning of her debut when she read what the critics said about the evening before. From then on she went through agonies, Caruso boosting her, then she him, during their duets. Finally, she decided it wasn't worth it. But her glorious tones enriched private parties. She was considered by many to be the greatest of all opera stars.

On one particular night the party at Villa Pace was for Miss Ida Cook, English authoress and member of the Ponselle fan club in London that once a year put in a trans-Atlantic call to hear Rosa sing their favorite arias over the telephone. The king of England's nephew, the earl of Harewood, was a member of the club. For Miss Cook's sake Rosa sang Vidor's "Contemplation," "None But the Lonely Heart," Strauss' "Morgan," and Beethoven's "In Questa Tomba." The rich, low tones of the latter were so stirring I can hear them today. Then she and opera's Paul Kelly sang every duet from the second and last acts of *Carmen*. An opera student sang "Un Bel Die," Russian pianist Chichagoff played Chopin's "Polanaise," and Rosa joined his wife Baclanova in the card song from *Carmen*. All for an audience of about twenty!

. . . and a Few Good Men

Salvador Dali was an extraordinary combination of artistic talent, bald showmanship, and deadpan humor. I met him at the National Gallery at David Finley's dinner for America's greatest collectors—Paul Mellon and his sister Ailsa Bruce, the George Wideners, Mr. and Mrs. Rush Kress, Mr. and Mrs. Chester Dale, and the Lessing Rosenwalds. When Mr. Dale introduced me I said in very clear English, "How do you do."

Dali's reply was, "Bonjour, do you speak English?"

I let that pass and proceeded with my questions. I started with the most noticeable thing about him—his mustache, which branched out horizontally under his nose then turned at opposite right angles to form spears that went straight up to just below his eyes.

How did he keep it that way, I asked?

"French wax."

Wasn't he afraid it would poke his eyes?

"No," he replied very seriously. "I'll clip it first." The wax came out before he went to bed and then it drooped. "During the night I look like a mongol."

Why did he paint pictures that shocked the sensibilities?

"I paint my dreams."

But why put telephones in such odd places?

"I hate telephones unless they are disconnected and in trees, then I like them."

What should a painting convey to the viewer?

"Anguish."

Why not soul?

"Anguish is the most important thing."

Did he feel the anguish?

"Oh, no, I just paint it for others."

At that point he asked Mrs. Walter Lippmann who was standing there, "Don't you love the fly?"

Mrs. Lippmann responded like a lover of DDT.

"Why not?" he asked claiming they were beautiful and clean; anyhow, ants from olive trees were clean. His dining room table, he told her, faced a glass wall crawling with ants. They couldn't get out of the wall and he kept them fed so he could eat while watching the underbellies of thousands of ants!

On another occasion I asked him why he gave the Christ such a feminine face in his painting, *The Last Supper*, which hangs in the National Gallery. He said he wanted to make him beautiful.

Several years later he came back with his pet ocelot (and a man to take care of it) and stayed at the Spanish Embassy for several days. He brought with him his sketches of Spain's future King Juan Carlos to begin work on his portrait. While painting he had Wagnerian music played as loud as rock is played in discotheques. Fortunately, his hostess, the Marquesa de Merry del Val, one of the funniest women I've ever known, took it all in her stride, even though the ocelot dispensed with all the foliage in the inner fountain court.

*   *   *

Buckminster Fuller, whom I met when he came to Washington for a
rally of Scientists and Engineers for the Johnson-Humphrey ticket,
was so stimulating during our brief encounter I have never forgotten
what he told me. Already famous as the inventor of the geodesic
dome and the Dymaxion map, he was later to be cited when receiving the 1970 Gold Medal Award from the American Institute of
Architects as "engineer, inventor, mathematician, educator, cartog-
rapher, philosopher, poet, author cosmogonist, industrial designer,
and architect." But it was the educator who opened my mind.

The delightful, baldheaded, bespectacled Fuller said he had
dedicated his life to helping man by improving his environment.
But it was far more difficult to alter man himself, he said, because
man, who starts at birth with 100 percent potential, is altered from
then on in only one way—negatively. He has the mental capabilities
to develop fully, but is blocked, frightened, or warped all along the
way. Scientific studies had proved, he said, that 50 percent of man's
negative changes occur between birth and four years of age.

"If the trust of a child is betrayed before he is four, that child is
almost certain to be a school dropout or have a low I.Q.," said the
scientist. By the time a person is seventeen, he went on, alterability
is only 2 percent. Yet, he said then, "95 percent of our educational
funds are devoted to the over-seventeen group."

In trying to improve people's environment, Dr. Fuller hoped to
keep mothers from giving negative answers to children that could
permanently block their mental capacities. In the twenty-seven
years since that day there hasn't been much progress made along
these lines.

*   *   *

William Faulkner, the literary giant of the South, was almost as
famous for not giving interviews as he was for his novels about his
home town, Oxford, Miss. But I didn't know that when I met him
in the summer of 1954 at a garden supper party for his daughter Jill
and her fiance, Paul Summers. He was in a good mood when I sat
down to chat with him. One of the Nobel Prizewinner's comments
was: "Nobody should be afraid to say what he thinks." In Washing-

ton, of course, that would spell nothing short of a politician or diplomat's demise. He also observed—rather perceptively, I thought—that Republicans were more reserved than Democrats because "to Republicans, politics is a mode of behavior instead of an activity."

The most he ever wrote in one day, he mused, was when he climbed up to the crib of his barn in Oxford one morning with his papers, pencils, and a quart of whiskey and pulled the ladder up behind him. By the time daylight fell he had torn off five thousand words.

After that meeting, I was surprised and very pleased to receive a letter out of the blue from pretty little Mrs. Faulkner, who must have received a copy of my column. She congratulated me on getting her husband to talk to the press. It was something, she said, he never did.

Three years later at another party for Jill and Paul in the garden of her in-laws' Rockville, Md., home, Faulkner was in an awful mood. The press, he stated, had no integrity (though my report of our first meeting proved the contrary), didn't write the truth, and only refrained from writing bad things out of fear of libel.

He never read criticism of his books, he said, and never read the books of his contemporaries. Then, in apparent contradiction, he added that Thomas Wolfe bored him. When I reminded him he had gone on record in praise of Wolfe, he said he had read some of his works but never finished them.

I took all those comments with a grain of salt because he was obviously putting on a cantankerous show for the sheer enjoyment of it. Besides, one minute he said he would not return to the University of Virginia for another semester as visiting professor because all the questions the students asked him could be answered by either a priest or a veterinarian. The next minute he indicated to another guest that he would return to U.Va. Why the contradiction, I asked him? "I never tell the truth to reporters," was his ornery reply. Then fifty-seven years old, William Faulkner died five years later.

CHAPTER 11

Foxtrot to Normalcy

The Ford Years

A fresh new breeze swept through town when Gerald Rudolph Ford and his wife Betty Bloomer Ford moved into 1600 Pennsylvania Avenue. They were as all-American as apple pie, more so than any previous occupants in the twentieth century. He had been a football hero who worked his way through law school. She had been a model in a department store who had started earning money as a dance teacher when she was only fourteen. They both believed in God. Church was a normal part of their family life. When they arrived in Washington in January 1949 they were a clean-cut, good-looking, mid-Western couple who might have stepped out of a Norman Rockwell painting.

Twenty-five years later they hadn't changed. When the Senate held hearings before nominating him vice president they heard the FBI findings. Four hundred and fifty agents throughout the country couldn't be wrong: He was squeaky clean.

Jerry Ford knew the night he and Betty came to our house for dinner (August 1) that he would be president in a matter of days. He had been told that day that the smoking gun, the June 23, 1972, tapes, had come to light and that Nixon would have to resign or be impeached. Nixon's chief of staff, General Alexander Haig, advised him to get ready, but he had not had time to tell Betty. They had even gone that day to the newly designated vice presidential residence—which Ford now knew they would never live in—to check on needed changes. As our dinner date approached George and I wondered if our honor guest would be the president instead of the vice president. When my husband observed that he seemed rather quiet that evening, Jerry manufactured the excuse of an oncoming cold.

Our twenty other guests could not but feel the air of suspense that cloaked the city and our garden that night, especially the officials present—Senators Lloyd Bentsen and John Sherman Cooper, Congressman Tom Railsback, and Egyptian Ambassador Ashraf Ghorbal. I had placed Barbara Walters next to Ghorbal—whom she had never met before—and she arranged then and there for her first meeting with Egyptian President Anwar Sadat.

As the Fords took their leave, I asked if he would give me an interview the coming week; without giving the slightest intimation of the pressure he would be under he replied, "Yes." He told me whom to call to set up the appointment, and when I phoned the next day it was obvious he had remembered. The appointment was for Tuesday, August 6, at four o'clock, two days before Nixon resigned.

When I saw him that afternoon there was nothing about his posture to suggest he now had the worries of the world on his shoulders. He was graceful and confident, with the smiling ease of a man in command of himself. I went home and wrote my story—four-and-one-half legal-size, typewritten pages—for the *Star*'s Thursday edition. It was exclusive, and the only interview with the incoming president of the United States that week or for some time preceding. Yet the *Star* cut a whole page out of it, one of prime interest in a president. Ford had been taking a beating from the press on the question of his mental qualifications for the presidency. So I asked him the following: In view of the fact that he graduated in the top third of the famous class of 1941 at Yale Law School that produced Supreme Court Justice Potter Stewart, Pennsylvania Governors Bill Scranton and Ray Shafer, New Jersey Congressman Peter Frelinghuysen, Sargent Shriver, and other political successes, not to mention corporation presidents—where did some of the news columnists get the idea that he was not so bright?

"I wish I knew," he replied with the calmness of a man undisturbed by such reports. "That statistic of the upper third came from Professor Myres McDougell who interviewed me when I applied at Yale Law."

In a speech at a Yale Law School luncheon that summer the professor had said he intended to "right some ancient wrongs. There have been suggestions about the quality of the vice president's scholarship," McDougell told the alumni. "I even had a reporter call me up when the hearings were being held to find out. He said, 'We understand that you're a former teacher of the nominee for the vice presidency. What kind of student was he?' I said, 'He was a good student, not only with me but in the law school more generally.' The fellow replied, 'I can't believe it. Wasn't he a bad student?' I said, 'No. He was a good student.' The fellow just hung up on me. He obviously didn't get the answer he wanted." McDougell added that Ford's highest grade was in legal ethics—a fact of some importance in the wake of Watergate. Furious that it had been cut out of my *Star* story, I led with the segment in my syndicated Sunday column.

I asked him how he succeeded in politics without compromising his integrity. "I think it was the basic principles I grew up with, that I live by and were taught to me by my parents . . . you darn well better tell the truth and live an honest life if you don't want to pay a penalty down the road." He thought that any qualified person, male or female, young or old, should serve in high government posts. "My principal political adviser is Mrs. Gwen Anderson," former GOP National Committeewoman.

He told me he had married Betty at thirty-five because she was attractive, they were compatible, and he thought they could make a career together. So much for the decision of the head; I asked him, what about the heart?

"Sure, I fell in love with her. But I don't wear my emotions on my sleeve very well. I was in love with her and vice versa. Twenty-six years—you'd better be! And with the minimal amount of disagreement." He consulted her, he said, on any major decision. "Often when I don't I make a mistake. She's a sounding board for most major speeches."

How could parents attain the kind of excellent rapport they had with their four children?

"I think you have to do more than just tell them what they should do. You have to make them understand why they should do it. That's the way I was brought up. There was a firmness but there was an explanation of why firmness was necessary. . . . And they must be taught that they have a responsibility not only to themselves but to their parents and to the family."

I ended my article with a quote from John Steinbeck that Ford had used in a speech in June at his alma mater, Michigan University: "Unlike any other thing in the universe, man goes beyond his work, walks up the stairs of his concepts, and emerges ahead of his accomplishments."

Jerry Ford was a man with no hang-ups. Lots of men—probably a majority on this globe—think performing a domestic chore, even carrying a package for a woman, is demeaning. Jerry always gave his wife a hand if she needed it.

"The photographers from *Paris Match* [magazine] practically flinched when I said he helped me do the dishes," said Betty, describing one of the forty interviews she had given after Jerry's selection as the new vice president. She was told that photographs of Ford helping his wife do the dishes "will just kill him in Europe. The men in Europe just don't do dishes."

Her reply: "He worked his way through college washing dishes at a sorority house. As an outstanding football player, he had a busy schedule between school, practice, and earning his way. That was during the Depression. A man like that knows where he wants to go and he's going to get there. Young people today have so much provided for them they don't know what the world is all about. We all have to work—unless one is born with millions. I don't think it hurts you any even then."

Paris Match followed Ford to the supermarket, where he marketed for the family, a chore he frequently did. (Apparently, buying ingredients for food is quite acceptable in France.) Betty drew the line when they wanted to photograph them at church. In addition to not wanting to infringe on the privacy of other parishioners, she didn't want to exploit their faith.

It took no time for social Washington to see what assets the Fords were. The night before he was sworn in as vice president, having been confirmed already, the new V.P. and Betty attended the Symphony Ball and earned the gratitude of everyone at the big fund raiser. They behaved like any other guests, stopping at tables between dances to greet friends. They were easy, normal, warm, and low-key—quite a contrast to Ted Agnew, who had always seemed socially stiff and cold. They danced nearly every dance. Ford liked to dance as much as Lyndon Johnson did—and in fact was a better dancer, doing everything from his preferred foxtrot to a dignified frug.

The following weekend, that December in 1973, the Fords went to Colonial Williamsburg for the enchanting annual houseparty given by C. W. president, Carlisle Humelsine, and his wife Mary. There was no other party like it in America—a Christmas gathering of notables to wine, dine, and dance in the same eighteenth-century manner and ambiance of George Washington and Thomas Jefferson. Tourists to Williamsburg can only imagine the elegant liveliness of its social life two hundred years ago. But living it for twenty-four hours, along with the Fords, were the Soviet and French ambassadors, cabinet members George Shultz, Rogers Morton, and Elliot Richardson; Justice Lewis Powell, Senators Harry Byrd, "Mac" Mathias, and Birch Bayh; the governor of Virginia and honor guest Linwood Holton; Walter Cronkite and David Brinkley President of Time, Inc. Jim Shepley, the wives of all the above, and Penny Tweedy, owner of America's most famous racehorse, Secretariat. Some Williamsburg residents and other out-of-towners were also included.

While assembled in the music room of the Governor's Palace for an eighteenth-century concert by costumed musicians, Humelsine told them about Williamsburg's "only one other association with a vice president, Mr. Tyler. He figured he didn't have anything to do as vice president so he came to Williamsburg and bought a house on Market Square. Then Mr. Harrison died and a post rider came . . . to tell Mr. Tyler he had become president of the United States. He found him playing marbles in the front yard with his grandchildren. You see," he said looking at Ford, "you are welcome to come down here and live."

The superb dinner was served by peruked and knee-breeched waiters, in the candlelit mansion of Carter's Grove Plantation which boasted a Christmas tree entirely decorated with lighted candles. (I don't know how they avoided fires in the past; this tree was flame-proof.) After dinner we went back to the colonial village to the Governor's Palace for dancing. Vice President Ford hardly left the dance floor, but during one pause a feminine guest lifted the white wig from the music master and placed it on Jerry's head. The unflappable Ford adjusted it, then swung his partner into another foxtrot, amid comments on how rapidly he had aged in office. Some politicians would have whipped off the wig for fear of ridicule; Gerald Ford's fearless inner dignity, without an ounce of pomposity, triumphed.

He and Betty enlivened several private parties. At Barbara and Clark McGregor's informal supper, the only diplomat there, Italian Ambassador Ortona, marveled, "No other capital in the world is as fertile for ambassadors as this one! Nowhere else would an ambassador find at one [private] party the vice president of the country, members of the cabinet [Treasury's Shultz and Commerce's Fred Dent], the president's closest adviser [Haig], the oil czar [Bill Simon], the publishers of the city's rival newspapers [the *Post*'s Kay Graham and the *Star*'s Jack Kauffmann], senators [Peter Dominick and Abe Ribicoff], noted political columnists [Joe Alsop, Rowland Evans, and Charles Bartlett], and the president of a corporation [Harry Gray of United Aircraft]. It's really incredible."

The parties that brought such combinations together night after night formed the very essence of Washington in the 1970s. Argentine Ambassador Alejandro Orfila, who was second only to Zahedi as a superb host, scored a coup when he gave a tango party and the Fords came. The media went wild. Argentina sent a TV crew and top commentator; *People* magazine carried a picture of Alex Orfila, a superb dancer, doing the tango with me. He phoned me with the news: "It's a full-length picture, the whole page," he reported delightedly. Since the tango is correctly performed with bodies glued together, I knew that only one face, his, could be seen. I mentioned that. "Yes," he said, "but your foot is in exactly the right position." There's a perfectionist for you.

Two years later, when Orfila's successor asked him how to succeed in Washington, Alex told him that decisions here were not made only in offices. "They are also made after pillow talk. Therefore, women exercise, with the equality they have with their husbands, a substantial influence on the decisions of men. If you have a man to dinner here without his wife," Orfila told Rafael Vazquez, "you have only 40 percent of the man. If you have his wife, too, and she tells her husband later what a simpatico man the ambassador was, you have 50 percent of the man plus 50 percent of the wife, which is 100 percent. Gear your parties to women and they will be a success. Have the things they like—beautiful flowers, soft lights, music for dancing, and formal dress so they can look beautiful. I never talk business at my parties unless a guest brings it up. Flowers are important. Men seldom look at flowers, but women always do, and the arrangements at the Argentine Embassy were always commented upon."

If the wife liked the flowers, food, and service she would urge her husband to come back. He would then "have a powerful ally for my ideas," finished the woman-wise, then single, envoy.

*　*　*

When straightforward Gerald Ford became our thirty-eighth chief executive, August 9, 1974, Washington, and the whole United States, felt a wave of relief.

Should he have pardoned Richard Nixon? Hubert Humphrey, who almost won the presidency instead of Nixon, told me that he believed Ford did the right thing. Even special Watergate prosecutor Leon Jaworski predicted that putting Nixon on trial could have immersed the country in Watergate for two or more years. I thought then, and still believe, that for the good of the country, Ford had no choice. With that out of the way and Nelson Rockefeller installed as the new vice president, things began to hum in the city again.

Jerry and Betty's new lofty position didn't change them. The atmosphere in their acquired grand domicile was somewhere between the John Kennedy's and the Lyndon Johnson's. The Fords were warmer, more gregarious and open than the Kennedys, but far

less harried and hurried than the Johnsons—or rather than LBJ.
Adding interest to the Casa Blanca menage were three handsome,
strong-looking sons—Mike, twenty-four, Jack twenty-two, and
Steve, eighteen, and one pretty, blond, healthy-looking daughter—
Susan, seventeen. They were so normal and natural—if better
looking and more polite than most of the young—that *Women's Wear
Daily* called them "Model Americans." They led their own lives,
held their own opinions, and didn't let the new spotlight interfere
with their peace of mind. They were proud of their parents, though,
and well brought up, and adult enough to put no unnecessary strain
on them.

First Lady Betty Ford stated at the outset that there would be a
change from the Nixon White House: "There will be dancing after
dinner. We will make an announcement that if anyone wants to go
home they can feel free to do so—because *we* want to dance."

Before August was up they gave two dinners. The first, a formal
one for Jordan's King Hussein and Queen Alia, had been arranged
many months earlier. Its ambiance was as natural and destarched as
in the Johnson era. Betty Ford retired sometime past midnight,
while noted commentator of CBS Eric Sevareid was doing the
Mexican hat dance: The tone had been set for the new administration's entertaining.

The second dinner, informal and small, was for Vice President-
designate Nelson Rockefeller and his wife Happy. It was one of the
best White House parties I've ever been to. For one thing, only the
president's official family was invited—forty-eight people in all.
They dined at six tables for eight in the Blue Room and danced in
the front hall where more tables were set up big enough to hold
drinks, ashtrays, and evening bags and surrounded by four or five
gilt chairs. "There hasn't been a party here like this in eight years,"
commented a grinning waiter. It had the cozy, charming feel of a
private party in an elegant mansion with the relaxed and smiling
hosts—as well as the honorees—doing as much dancing, chatting,
and mingling as anyone. The president danced with me. I had
danced with Jerry Ford two or three times before, but this time was
different: The Marine dance orchestra was playing "Proud Mary"
and we were dancing a frug—but his motions were so restrained
that even Martha Washington would have approved.

"Oh, come on, Mr. President," I said, raring to move to the exciting beat, "let's wiggle."

"You know I'm not going to do that, Betty," said Ford. Of course he was absolutely right. However innocent the gyrations to a frug generally were, the newspapers would have ripped into him. But contrary to the reports that Jerry Ford was clumsy (once one columnist writes a criticism, all the rest pick it up without any substantiation), I can testify: Anybody that graceful on the dance floor is definitely not clumsy.

Betty Ford told me that evening that "Jerry has so much energy, when we go on a vacation we have to go where there are about five golf courses, like out at Palm Springs or Monterey." She loved to go to the beach, "but for him, it's about a five-minute sit then he's up and off. He thinks even when you are sleeping you are wasting time. He thinks there is so much to do." Even so, refreshed from ballroom dancing, he retired at eleven o'clock to their private quarters.

George and I were invited to the Fords' state dinner for Italian Prime Minister Giovanni Leone and his beautiful wife in September, and my husband had a willing partner after dinner in Betty Ford who already knew he was a terrific twirler.

For their first diplomatic reception, President and Mrs. Ford gave a white tie supper dance, and hired fashionable Meyer Davis to provide his topnotch beat for their excellencies. Some eighty of the envoys and wives had never been to a White House party; none had ever danced there to Meyer Davis. The Swedish and British ambassadors' wives, Countess Wachtmeister and Lady Ramsbotham, wore their diamond tiaras. (The British Embassy, I learned, had lost its butler during the summer and Lady Ramsbotham had to go back to England to search for another who could head a staff of twelve live-in servants and six "dailies." That's what it took to run the most prestigious embassy in Washington.)

One Asian ambassador had obviously never seen a white tie and tails outfit before. He wore the white vest backwards and upside down, with the points of the vest pointing to the ceiling!

Later, for the Fords' first ball for nine hundred members of Congress, Mike Carney's superorchestra was imported from New York and noted feminist Bella Abzug (N.Y.), her ample figure

encased in a tight sequinned gown, wiggled in Democratic abandon
with Representative Dante Fascell (Fla.) who wore the flashiest
multicolored shirt ever sported with black tie.

Beginning with the dinner in February 1975 for Britain's Prime
Minister and Mrs. Harold Wilson, the Fords began to jazz up their
formal parties with celebrities. Present that night were Cary Grant,
Danny Kaye, Kirk Douglas, Warren Beatty, Beverly Sills, Van
Cliburn, Saul Bellow, Olympic skier Billy Kidd, Margaret Truman,
and Bill Paley with their spouses of course—a mix that plainly
delighted their honor guest, while recognizing the contributions of
America's famous.

That new year not only ushered in a new vice president so rich
that when he was a kid, said a wit, he had a lemonade stand listed on
the stock exchange; it brought to Congress the largest number of
new members in more than a quarter of a century—ninety-two
freshmen in the House and eleven in the Senate.

Nelson Rockefeller had been told at the outset by President Ford
that he would have to live in the former chief of naval operations'
house on Observatory Hill, even though Rockefeller already had a
bigger house on eleven acres off Foxhall Road.

The old Victorian-style house, with its chopped-up first floor full
of odd-shaped rooms, had a front entrance with no cloak rooms, a
back entrance with no porte-cochere, and a kitchen the size of a
pantry. The bathrooms on the second floor were anything but commodious and there were no dressing rooms. If they wanted to dine
outdoors on the twenty-foot terrace they would be in full view of
Massachusetts Avenue. Why not build a new mansion, with built-in
security and air-conditioning? To save money, was the excuse. As
always, Congress took the much more costly route.

As for the Congress, I decided to print some more tips about life
in our international metropolis for all those new members. Take
dance lessons if you don't know how, I told them. If you dance well
enough to cut in on Betty Ford she will remember you and it will
enhance your prestige back home even if you're a Democrat ...
Don't corner the sauce unless you're with your hometown buddies.
Few here are amused by the overboozed . . . If you are single, don't
show up at a private dinner with a date. You were invited to sit
between two other women . . . Don't wear your politics on your

sleeve. The three acknowledged parties are Democratic, Republican, and Social—and each has its place.

* * *

"Few people realize it," I wrote in my farewell column about the caring and popular Casper Weinbergers, who were returning to San Francisco after his spell as secretary of health, education and welfare, "but Cap Weinberger is the first HEW secretary to take any steps to correct America's greatest cruelty—child abuse. Because of him, HEW has done all the federal government can do in providing for research in causes and treatment, for training personnel in handling such cases, for aiding Parents Anonymous to prevent abuse, and for developing a model Child Protective Services Act for states to pass, which could greatly alleviate the problem." Two days after my column appeared I received a letter from Cap. It read: "Your reference this morning to my work in connection with child abuse was very generous and gratifying to read. There was only one thing left out of it, and that was the fact that you started me on the whole venture."

That was true, but I did not know he would remember. It came about when I was seated next to him at a benefit ball at the Washington Hilton; I asked him if there wasn't something he could do to correct this horror, which I couldn't get out of my mind. I remember Cap's astonishment. He simply was not aware that children across the country were often cruelly abused by their parents, and that if the case was brought to court, they were generally given right back to their parents to face more torture. He not only remembered our conversation but he did something about it.

Another member of a cabinet I asked to do something was Agriculture Secretary Earl Butz. The problem was the soring of show horses' feet to make them lift their hooves high in the Tennessee walker's gait. Both Butz and Assistant Secretary Clayton Yeutter took steps to remedy the cruel practise, though they were unable to stop it entirely.*

---

* Butz, who received no public thanks for that, is probably best remembered for rather earthy jokes, including his comment when Pope John Paul II forbade Catholics to use contraceptives as well as abortions: "He no playa da game, he no maka da rules."

At last, thanks to the Nelson Rockefellers, the vice presidential residence was entirely renovated, furnished, and ready for occupancy. They would never move into it from their more comfortable and spacious house nearby. But to show it off, they gave nine receptions, taking in all the Congress and top federal officials. The first, on Sunday, September 7, was a smasheroo. President and Mrs. Ford and Susan Ford were there, Secretary of State and Mrs. Kissinger, Ford's Chief of Staff Don Rumsfeld and his wife Joyce, and so on through a list of bigwigs.

"Isn't it ironic," said Rumsfeld, "that the first vice president to get a residence doesn't need it? He could be the only vice president for whom it's an actual comedown."

"You know you have no intention of moving into this house," I said to the vice president when going through the receiving line. "You understand very well," confirmed the V.P., with a wide grin. In fact, Happy would not really move to Washington at all. She would show up at required official functions in Washington, but otherwise ricochet between their five different addresses, exactly as she did when he was in Albany.

Rocky, himself, picked up the tab for the other eight parties. At all nine, everybody made a beeline for the second floor to inspect the famous $35,000 double bed designed by artist Max Ernst. It had been toned down for its new location. The mirror at the foot of the bed was covered; the headboard had been turned around so that its mirror faced the wall. An abstract painting now faced the mattress. Rocky had donated the bed to the house and I was not surprised. I thought it was ugly, and although the mirrors when facing each other as designed might be sexually interesting, they would also evoke hackneyed comments from everyone who saw them.

A more acceptable style of titillation was the elegant sensuality of entertainments at the Iranian Embassy. Ambassador Zahedi often had a belly dancer perform in his silken, seductive Persian room. One evening, actor James Mason, Clare Boothe Luce, and the Swiss and Finnish ambassadors were all so intrigued they each tried to emulate her subtle movements. (They didn't know that the belly dancer had a B.S. degree in mathematics from Maryland University—not that math helped her dancing—and formerly taught it. Three hours a day practise before the arrival of her nine-pound baby was "an excellent way to have a natural birth.")

Zahedi gave a particularly brilliant dinner following a gala performance by the American Ballet Theater. Elizabeth Taylor came to town for it, paying her first visit since she was very young. It is hard to imagine a more glamorous sight than Elizabeth, in an orange-red gown and necklace and eardrops of big emeralds and diamonds, on a divan in the oriental splendor of the Persian room with stunning Polly Bergen in sapphire satin, big-orbed pixie Liza Minelli, Washington glamor girl Page Lee Hufty, and two men of considerable note—Secretary of State Henry Kissinger (Nancy was out of town), and TV's most prestigious commentator Eric Sevareid. The photographers had a field day. That was only the beginning. Dinner was served to 180 people at fifteen tables in the embassy ballroom where Rudolf Nureyev was a sartorial standout in the black tie company. Rudi wore a black satin shirtwaist and matching trousers with a black belt and large silver buckle. When mountains of caviar were passed for the first course, former chief of protocol, New Yorker Angier Biddle Duke, gazed around at the scene and exclaimed, "It's great to be back in Washington. This is the exciting place to be!"

As the ranking person present, Kissinger, with his marked German accent, responded to the host's toast. "Ardeshir is the one man in Washington who is slightly more incomprehensible than I am. In fact," he quipped, he had been "trying hard to break the code that was coming out of the embassy until I realized that it was Ardeshir reporting in English."

That was also the night when Zahedi and the gorgeous Elizabeth, in her sexy decolletage, danced together with both arms around each other, the start, perhaps, of her infatuation with the vibrant, dark-eyed diplomat. Liz later did the new hustle dance with Massachusetts Senator Edward Brooke and the photo of them in this harmless pursuit appeared in the Boston papers. Having a good time with a movie star probably looked frivolous to his constituency; he was defeated in the next election. In the meantime Liza, or pussycat, as Liz called her, had already danced more than once with Mikhail Baryshnikov but she came up to me and said, "Ask him to dance with me." I said, "Is he such a good ballroom dancer?" "I don't care about the dancing," replied Pussycat. That was clear when, at my suggestion, Baryshnikov danced with her again, their bodies were glued together as they barely moved around.

* * *

In September 1975, leaving dancing Washington behind, George and I embarked on a round-the-world tour. I'll just mention a few highlights:

Hearing Prime Minister Harold Wilson and Pearl Bailey sing a duet from *Hello Dolly* in the U.S. ambassador's residence in London; interviewing King Hussein in Ammon and Empress Farah in Teheran; and, most delightful, staying with George and Barbara Bush at the American Embassy in Peking.

Can an ambassador give an impression of friendship in a country where no contact with the population is allowed? The Bushes proved he can. They traveled daily on their bicycles; they learned to speak Chinese; they steeped themselves in Chinese history and culture and food—an important part of their culture—and they smiled and spoke to people on the street. (The people were not allowed to speak back, but their government couldn't keep them from smiling.) Barbara even took up t'ai chi chu'an, the graceful group exercise the Chinese practise in public places. And she was seen by thousands of Chinese tourists when she took American friends sightseeing. She was so thorough, one guest who heard her say there were nine thousand rooms in the Forbidden City, cracked, "And I bet we'll have to see every damned one of them."

Said George Bush, "You can't see this country without realizing that this society is to be reckoned with in the future. . . . Dealing with China is a fundamental part of our foreign policy." As president, he would make this an important plank in his platform.

* * *

A group of British dukes, earls, and knights invaded Washington and Williamsburg in May of 1976, presumably to wish the United States a happy two hundredth birthday.

"Don't let anyone fool you," said the earl of Dunmore. "We are here to promote tourism." All were polished, charming, and blessed with a sense of humor.

Best known to Americans was the eleventh duke of Marl-borough—"Sunny" Spencer-Churchill—whose Blenheim Palace has three hundred rooms.

"I've seen most of them," he said. But he and his duchess were living in only seven. Next in rank was Ian Campbell, eleventh duke of Argyll, Keeper of the Great Seal of Scotland, head of the Clan Campbell, and lord of Iveraray Castle in Scotland. He had brought a lock of George Washington's hair—powdered auburn*—and told me that argyle socks were an American invention.

The ninth earl of Dunmore, the only one without a stately home, was the honor guest at the dinner in the Governor's Palace in Williamsburg because he was a direct descendant of the fourth earl, the last royal governor of Virginia. The others were the duke of Bedford's heir, the marquess of Tavistock, who managed Woburn Abbey, the family seat famed for its wild animals; Lord Montagu, third baron of Beaulieu (which the British, naturally, pronounced Bewly), which packs in the tourists because of his antique car collection, and Sir Hugo Boothby, the premier baronet of Wales and owner of the oldest abode, Fonmon Castle.

We were invited to the dinner where host Carl Humelsine told the earl of Dunmore, "201 years ago your ancestor departed here rather abruptly on a warship. There never was a friendlier beginning to a revolution." The last royal governor was so popular, said Humelsine, "he could have been 'Man of the Year' on the cover of *Time*." Where-upon he presented the honor guest with a facsimile of a cover page with the earl's portrait on it, as painted by Sir Joshua Reynolds.

*   *   *

If any proof was needed that Washington officialdom loved to step out and cut a rug it was the response to invitations we and the Morse Dials sent out for a springtime dinner dance at the Chevy Chase Club. And if any proof were needed that before she married John Warner Elizabeth Taylor had flipped for the Iranian ambassador, that evening provided it.

Of the 236 seated at tables for eight there were eight senior White

---

* Which, alas, was lost before it could be presented to his American hosts.

House staffers, nine members of the cabinet and little cabinet, two
Supreme Court justices, sixteen ambassadors, seven U.S. senators,
and seven congressmen. The rest were residential friends, all happy
to dance to Mike Carney's jazz beat.

I had asked Zahedi to bring Elizabeth. He did; I seated them at
my table, facing each other across the center of a narrow rectangular
table. If she hadn't already fallen, she fell for him like a ton of bricks
that night: The sparks that flew between them almost ignited the
centerpiece. But Ardeshir was not about to consider marriage to an
already much-married Hollywood superstar. He had introduced her
a few days earlier to John Warner. At our party, John asked her for a
dance the first chance he got. The rest is history.

In the parade of festivities for bicentennial state visitors—King
Juan Carlos and Queen Sophia of Spain, President of France and
Madame Giscard d'Estaing, and Queen Elizabeth II with Prince
Philip—none was more elaborate than the French Embassy dinner
for President and Mrs. Ford. French experts traveled back and forth
across the Atlantic for a year to prepare for it—to polish every single
facet in the main crystal chandelier; to replate everything gold-
plated; to cover the walls of the grand salon with new silk and
reupholster all the furniture; and to erect a tent like none we had
ever seen before. Built to accommodate 150 at dinner, it had a
wooden floor covered with a Savonnerie rug. Walls of ruby silk were
hung with Gobelin tapestries and paintings from the Louvre; six
gold and crystal chandeliers hung from the ceiling, and the tables
were covered with 130 yards of expensive Porthault cloth with a
bicentennial design. Beige silk curtains hung from the ceiling at
intervals to indicate invisible French windows. Between them hung
three Beauvais tapestries from Versailles and the Louis XV period.
Spaced along the semicircular wall were portraits of George Washington, Lafayette, Rochambeau, and De Grasse. The only evidence
that the tent was outdoors was the huge trunk of a tree that came
through the floor on one side and disappeared into the ceiling. It was
magnificent. George and I were among the fortunate at the white tie
dinner, along with the very top U.S. official echelon and such orna-
mental out-of-town personnel as beautiful young Margaux Hemingway and handsome Gregory Peck, sporting his Medal of Freedom.

The curator of Versailles, Gerald Van der Kemp, wore the richly embroidered full-dress uniform of the Academie Française. Most Americans believe, Van der Kemp remarked, that it was the marquis de Lafayette who had come to their rescue during the American Revolution. But French and Spanish archives reveal that his twenty-four-year-old king had aided our struggle against the British, to the tune of two billion pounds.

"This liquidated the equilibrium of the French budget and led to the French Revolution," said Van der Kemp. "One can consider that Louis XVI died for American independence."

* * *

Queen Elizabeth and the duke of Edinburgh arrived for their bicentennial visit on July 7, 1976. The media's demand for coverage was overwhelming, so we were granted only a brief look at the tented, outdoor dinner at the White House; then, the regulars were allowed to cover the rest of the evening, which took place indoors. Next night, at the after-dinner reception on the broad sweep of the British Embassy lawn, I chatted on an upper terrace with such dinner guests as British-born Bob Hope and Dolores, and British-born Lynn Fontanne, still lovely looking as she sat and surveyed the scene with husband Alfred Lunt. She was then, according to Celebrity Register ninety years old.

Queen Elizabeth came down one side of the lawn path with her ambassador, Sir Peter Ramsbotham, and up the hill on the other, pausing to be introduced to Sir Peter's choices. Happily I was one of them, but I guess I goofed. After she spoke first I recalled meeting her during the Eisenhower era and observed that there had been a lot of changes since. She laughed and quickly said with a smile, "You mean I've changed a lot." Alas and alack! I was thinking of the difference nineteen years had made on Washington and the United States.

* * *

A month after Jerry Ford's defeat by Jimmy Carter, Alex Orfila, now secretary general of the Organization of American States, gave a party for me and George. At his request I supplied him with a list of friends to choose from and the acceptances had come in before it occurred to me that President and Mrs. Ford might enjoy it. (Orfila could not invite them without sharing them with the OAS but I could, and did.) They accepted. There were three tables for ten. I sat at the table with President Ford and Saudi Arabian Ambassador Ali Alireza who explained to Ford why Moslems worship at the holy shrine that Abraham, the prophet of Judaism, built in Mecca. The Saudi told him, "We are not anti-Jew or anti-Judaism. We are anti-Zionism. Moslems consider Abraham to be the first of the three great prophets who brought the three religions of God—Judaism, Christianity, and Islam."

Chief of Protocol Shirley Temple Black, one-time child star and still the most famous in history, was the only American at that table who had read the Koran. She read an English translation before going to Egypt, she said. Liz Carpenter, "the only Democrat leaving town," gave a charming toast to the Fords—maybe her first ever to Republicans, and Shirley sang some funny lyrics she had composed to George and me, accompanied by husband Charles on the guitar. After Charles had sung a Spanish solo, Alabama dinner comedian Shearen Elebash did a takeoff on political speakers of different nationalities. He was a riot; the party was another Orfila smash, and left a strong impression on Maribel Pedroso, the elegant wife of Spain's OAS ambassador. Old friends of mine from earlier days at the regular Spanish Embassy, the Pedrosos, had come from a post in Africa, and couldn't get over how unceremonious the evening was.

"It's because you are such a big and powerful country you can afford to be normal and natural and not pompous," she wrote. "In small countries they are so pompous they don't even see you [ambassadors]; they almost walk over you. It sometimes takes a month just to get an appointment with a member of the cabinet. The less secure the country, the more seriously they take themselves—just like people. It was an unforgettable evening."

*   *   *

In two years, Betty Ford gained unprecedented affection and respect for her honesty and independence. Most presidential wives have been afraid to speak up on serious subjects; they fear making their husbands mad, and politically damaging him or the party.

Betty Ford told the truth when asked about abortion (she agreed with the *Roe* vs. *Wade* decision), about an Equal Rights Amendment (her husband had not come out for it and did not until she persuaded him), about her reaction if Susan had an affair (she didn't), about her own breast cancer, and, indeed, about everything. I believe Americans yearn for independent truth, and that's why Betty Ford was so loved.

She had set the social tone of the White House two days before Richard Nixon resigned.

"I have never had any desire to live there," she told me. "But if I have to go there, I'm going to make it fun. I couldn't stand to live there unless it could be happy and free and open." And that's what it was in those two years and five months.

The month after she became First Lady, I telephoned the White House to speak to Betty's personal assistant, Nancy Howe. The woman answering said, "This is Mrs. Howe's secretary. Mrs. Howe is busy." The voice sounded more than vaguely familiar. "I hope she is paying you well," I said. "No, I haven't gotten any remuneration yet," was the reply. It was Betty Ford.

Nancy Howe, a pretty blond dynamo, had become Betty's right hand ever since the nomination of Gerald Ford as vice president; a White House volunteer, she had rushed over to help with the flood of phone calls. She was so efficient that Mrs. Ford promptly hired her and, months later, took her to the White House. They hit it off so well attractive Mrs. Howe became her closest assistant. It was she who persuaded Mrs. Ford to have the mammogram at the Naval Medical Center in Bethesda which probably saved her life.

Nancy Howe's own life was a perfect Washington example of the meteoric rise of anyone suddenly found next to the power center and the precipitous crash that can follow. As Margie McNamara observed, when her husband was no longer secretary of defense and the flood of invitations had slowed to a dribble, "It's the job that's invited, not the person." She was so right.

Nancy's fall came about through her own and her husband's innocence. As soon as it was known she was with the First Lady every day for long hours, frequently remaining to have a before-dinner cocktail with both Fords—although this was probably a mistake on her part—the vivacious Nancy became one of the more sought-after people in town. Her husband James W. Howe, a professor of Spanish at Trenton State College in New Jersey, was away during the week, so invitations to glittering affairs were all the more welcome. Life was suddenly glamorous beyond her wildest dreams.

Then in stepped rich, Korean, influence-arranger Tongsun Park. In years past the quickest way to make a big name for oneself in Washington was to become well known as a hostess or host. And no one succeeded in doing that more smoothly than Park. He founded and owned the George Town Club on Wisconsin Avenue and began giving dinners there. He became one of the best known hosts in town. Ford went to one of those dinners when he was vice president. House Majority Leader Tip O'Neill was treated to a birthday dinner for two hundred in December 1974. The mystery man of the East spent money like it was going out of style, packing his parties with members of the Congress and other influential types. Park insisted he just liked to make people happy.

But suspicions rose when it was learned that he had paid for a trip to the Dominican Republic for the Howes. What, the media immediately asked, was he after? Maxine Cheshire wrote in the *Post* that the Howes had violated the federal code of ethics and conflict of interest laws. Jim, a West Point graduate who prized his honor, felt he had been disgraced. He committed suicide, leaving a letter (which I read) that blamed his death on that story. Later it came out that he had a drinking problem and had been seeing a psychologist. Tongsun Park remained in town until the following year when news stories linked him with substantial payments and gifts of jewelry, oriental antiques, and trips for U.S. congressmen to create a favorable image for the South Korean government.

Betty Ford immediately said, "There's no question about" Nancy continuing at the White House; of course she would. But four days later, Nancy was fired, at the insistence of the Secret Service—largely because she, too, had been seeing a psychologist. It was a terrible blow, both to her and to Betty, who visited her in her trouble; but the First Lady was not given any choice. From a thrilling, happy life Nancy suddenly fell to widowhood and obscurity. I liked her, and was sorry.

Betty Ford graced the White House with poise and dignity but also enormous fun. At their state dinners, she danced with her husband, with guests, and sometimes with an entertainer; she created an atmosphere—as did the Lyndon Johnsons—that could prompt the East Room performers to put on another show in the front hall.

The following year I asked Betty what she thought of the impact their parties were having. "I am not particularly impressed with the social impact," she replied. "The only thing I am pleased with is that frankly the White House has become more relaxed and less formal. It used to be—rather restrained. I was very pleased with the reaction of Margaret Truman. She said things were much more sparkling, and she said, 'You make it sparkle.' I was very complimented.

"You have to have the right people, the right entertainment, the right mixture. It's just like putting a cake together." Both she and the president had "a strong input on the guest list" and when it was finally drawn up went over the whole list. Jerry Ford's input was along critical lines but not all that limited. "I don't know anyone who enjoys a pretty girl more than he does. When you stop enjoying that it's time to fold your tent," said his confident wife.

Mrs. Ford's daytime pursuits covered several causes. Besides working for equal rights for women—"equal social security, equal opportunities for education, an equal chance to establish credit," and equal pay—she urged the president to appoint women to important posts, and he did: He sent Anne Armstrong as ambassador to Great Britain and named Carla Hills secretary of HUD.

She helped retarded and abused children at Children's Hospital, attending to them personally and getting others interested, even getting two new rooms donated. She also worked for the No Greater Love organization and helped several others. She is a woman full of human sympathy; that's why she believed in government funding for abortions for poor women who already had several children and could not support another, and for pregnant teenage girls who had no money and no one to turn to. I couldn't agree with her more. Unwanted children are often condemned to live a life of misery, sometimes torture.

When Betty Ford was in the hospital recuperating from her mastectomy she said to her husband, "If you had lived your life and you felt that you had saved just one person's life, wouldn't you feel that you had served God's purpose?" "Yes," replied the president.

"Well," she said, "I feel that I have saved many." And it's certain she did. She was referring to the thousands of women who had lined up at cancer clinics for checkups because her experience had shown the need for early detection.

She revealed in her first interview after the operation the rare kind of wife she was. She hadn't wanted her family to know of her cancer ahead of time, not even the president. "I was kind of foolish, wasn't I? But why should I bring up something unpleasant like that?"

"I have a very strong feeling for my family," she said. "Maybe it's too strong. I honestly believe that God lends these children to us for a certain length of time and it is up to us to do the best we can. If we haven't by the time they've gone to college, then we have lost our opportunity. So I've always been concerned about their welfare and well-being, and didn't want them to fall all apart. I figured I could take it."

As for adjusting after the operation: "I could see how a young girl who may not be married would have a big adjustment to make. But for me—I am fifty-six and I have my children and I thought my husband was adult enough to understand. I have lived a full life, and I have the most wonderful husband and the most wonderful four children, so everything from here on in is a plus. Lots of people are dead by this age."

That talk with Betty Ford made me think that she had gained, rather than lost, something by the experience. She had. "I am a religious person," she said, "and I had a real awakening. I thought that I had been searching for something in the Bible and in my religion during my whole life, but I never reached it. But when I came through this I thought that I really was a child of Christ. To experience such a beautiful thing was to me almost worth what I had to go through. Sometimes I think you have to go through those things to find yourself."

She said she planned to do whatever the doctors recommended in the future. "Because I want to live to be as old as Alice Longworth. Then I can look back and make all those funny remarks that she makes. After all, she's topless, you know."

When she was still new in the White House, Betty was asked how she liked having a domestic staff of over forty? "It's great when you can't cook," replied Betty. She said she had taught all her children how to cook so she wouldn't have to.

Although her national approval rating soared above 70 percent, it wasn't all smooth sailing. When she announced that she would economize by not "buying expensive designer clothes," our big name designers reacted like stuck pigs. From the cries of outrage on Seventh Avenue you would have thought she was planning to undermine the country instead of doing her share to whip inflation. At 110 pounds, with her model's figure, she could look chic in a $200 costume. (She bought from the less expensive designers like Albert Capraro. Later, probably because they gave her a special rate, she would buy from the more expensive designers.)

Her economies did not stop at clothes. She cut down on the lighting in the White House, and even on the wattage. She closed down the fountains on the north and south lawns and she avoided the redecorating that each of her predecessors had done.

"If Jerry gives instructions to save, save, save, and I go through the White House and say spend, spend, spend, what would people think?" asked Mrs. Ford. She also asked all her assistants to drive their own cars to work rather than be picked up by a driver and limousine, as in past administrations.

How Betty Ford could do as much as she did with a smile, while never free from pain, I don't know. When a pinched nerve in her neck, coupled with spinal arthritis, first hit her in 1964 she had to be treated at the National Orthopedic Hospital in Arlington for weeks to get her posture erect and her arm working again. She didn't complain but when asked said she had to take valium or some other painkiller every day. Despite the stress of meeting so many First Lady obligations as well as the pain, she always appeared relaxed and smiling at White House parties.

Some time after the Fords left the White House, a story appeared about her drinking while in the White House. I was indignant. I had seen her dozens of times, thrice in my own house, and I had not seen any signs of inebriation. I proceeded to call every woman in the Ford circle of close friends to determine if any had an inkling of something to corroborate the story. None had seen her take more than two cocktails before dinner, and they knew I could be trusted with the truth. Everyone knew she spoke slowly, and sometimes more slowly than others. We assumed that was because of the amount of painkillers she had taken. When she and the president dined with us in 1975 she spoke more slowly than ever, but her speech was not sloppy nor were her movements.

So I wrote a column questioning the veracity of the drinking story. But I had not seen her after they left the White House and I was not aware that even one drink combined with painkillers and/or tranquilizers could produce a "sleepy-tongued" effect. Her family intervened when, after leaving the White House, she increased the drinking and still took the medications prescribed by doctors for pain. After her treatment for chemical dependency I talked to her on the phone. The difference, I told her, was marvelous. Her speech was no longer slow; she sounded happy and alert. She had overcome her problem, and once again, Betty Bloomer Ford had gone public—and in so doing had helped thousands—no, millions—of other Americans to overcome theirs.

CHAPTER 12

Clogging to the Classics

The Carter Years

Jimmy Carter was the first president since Woodrow Wilson not to
have held a post in the federal government before moving into the
White House. The former governor of Georgia could truthfully run
against a Washington which he did not know, which did not know
him, and which I am not sure he really ever understood. And it
worked both ways. That he and his supporters thought that we in
Washington did not understand the rest of America became plain to
me soon after his election.

In late November, I went to a ladies' luncheon at the German
Embassy; I brought up the subject of the president-elect carrying
his own garment bag. None of the guests thought it looked right, but
none would speak for attribution. An American woman said, "I
think you can do one menial thing a day to keep your feet on the
ground, but it doesn't have to be done in public. I think it's showing off."

In my next column I asked, "If Mr. Average Joe can step out of a
car at the Shoreham or Carlton Hotels and have his baggage swept
up by porters hired for that purpose, why should any guest at the
No. 1 guest house in the country—Blair House—have to carry his
own bags inside?" The answer, of course, is that he did not have to
carry his bags up the Blair House steps himself. This superbly run
residence for state visitors had a domestic staff of ten, six of

whom could have come out to assist with the baggage. At least two expected to perform that duty, but were advised that they were not to come out and get this visitor's bags; the president-elect preferred to carry his own.

"Why," I wrote, "does the man who will occupy the highest office in our land want the American public to see him as a baggage carrier? If the American people had wanted their next president to be a bellhop they could have found one without all that concern about issues, debates, etc. They picked Jimmy Carter because, presumably, what's above his neck and between his ears will be able to cope with national and world problems. Millions of people can carry luggage but only one is chosen to run the country, so such conduct demeans the office."

In question No. 3 I asked, "Isn't it dangerous for him to be burdened with luggage when there is always the possibility that some kook may aim a gun and Secret Service men will have to push him out of range and sight suddenly?" In that case if he wasn't shattered by a shot he might be battered by a bag.

Lastly, I wondered, "If he thinks the President of the United States rates no service, what is he going to do in the White House, where a staff of 36 look after the house and family? Will he insist on carrying the dishes off the table himself? Will he insist that Rosalynn do all the cooking? Will he fire all those people who now do those jobs or let them stand around and watch the Carters usurp their duties?" I might have added, as he did at Blair House. But I didn't; I had said enough.

The responses to that column almost burned up my mailman. A writer in Havelock, N.C., wrote: "I start my day with the laughs I get from reading the comments being made by so-called society in the Capital." Said "an interested reader": "I can't begin to tell you how much it pleases many of us (good long-time Republicans) that you have painted yourself into a corner with the Carters." A woman in Dysart, Iowa, advised: "Come out of your ivory tower and live with the rest of we [sic] 95 percent of the population. We have always been disgusted with the accounts of the ridiculous Romanistic orgies of the affluent lifestyle of the upper crust Washingtonians." Across the top of one clipping was written: "This article shows how far afield the Washington people are from the average citizen."

Across the top of another was scribbled: "Is this Beale woman foreign born? Many out here [the Northwest] are fed up to the ears with imperial Presidents holding forth as a Royal Court on Taxpayers money and would be glad to have these social climbing snobs off our backs."

The letters came in by the dozens, and letters-to-the-editor were printed in Washington and everywhere my column was carried. The *Star* printed twelve denouncing me. Unlike the first time it happened early in my career, I was delighted. The more response to a column, the more evidence there is of widespread readership, and that's good. Moreover, the denunciations were based on a difference of opinion, not on a factual error. (I prided myself on my accuracy.) On top of all that, I had no doubt whatsoever that my criticisms were fair. Regardless how much the people of our hinterland wanted Jimmy Carter to have the same burdens as they had, to dress as they did, to look as poor as many were, to do for himself as they had to do—in short, to be like the common man—he could no longer even pretend he was like them. Not counting the fact that he was well-to-do when he came to Washington, how much of an ordinary man can a fellow be when he has three huge specially equipped airplanes, several helicopters, a yacht, a swimming pool, a tennis court, a bowling alley, the most expensive and specially designed limousine in the country, thousands of guards, more than one chef, a mansion full of priceless antiques worth multimillions, a staff of seventy-six, and the most sought-after house in America sitting on eighteen fenced-in acres protected from the public by a high iron picket fence and guards who will let no ordinary guy in without permission plus identification? With all that, to try to act like a common man in the most uncommon job in the United States if not the world would only suggest a sham, phoney posturing to curry support. Whereas he would not be the first or the last president to posture, Jimmy Carter was the only one, I believe, in this century to go to such lengths.

To indicate further his intention to eliminate trappings of richness around the chief executive, the incoming president had talked of reducing the numbers who would serve him. But head usher Rex Scouten, who had been at the White House since Truman's era, said only the barest few served the presidential family. The rest were necessary to keep America's showcase residence, which six thousand or more tourists passed through daily, in apple-pie order. Of the seventy-six total, forty were electricians, plumbers, engineers, painters, carpenters, gardeners, etc.—all employed full-time to maintain the mansion, offices, and grounds. It took four full-time people just to arrange the flowers. On a normal day they arranged a minimum of thirty-six bouquets, which were distributed on three floors of the mansion and in the most important offices of the two wings. You could tell who had status by taking a posy-check of the rooms. When there was a reception, sixty bouquets were turned out. And for a state dinner, add fourteen or so centerpieces.

The domestic staff of thirty-six—the president's valet (you can't have Mr. Big running around screaming, "Where are my socks?" when affairs of the world await his decisions), the First Lady's personal maid, the five butlers, the doormen, and all the people who cook, clean, and straighten—worked in two shifts, so there were not so many as it seemed. Twenty-five or more extra waiters had to be hired when there was a state dinner. In addition to the head usher who, with a staff of three, managed comings and goings and preparations, there was also a hotel-trained housekeeper. She was a woman with foresight. When the Carters arrived she told her husband, the pastry chef, he had better have a batch of peanut butter cookies ready for the new president's first parties.

And what a marathon of parties they gave the first two days after the Inaugural! It was a testament to their endurance and buoyancy. After walking from Capitol Hill to the White House and attending seven balls that night, President and Mrs. Carter stood at four parties January 21 starting at 10:00 A.M. and continuing until 5:30 P.M. At those four they received: (1) state representatives on the Inaugural House Committee and all the people who took in Carter family members as houseguests during the campaign; (2) state governors; (3) members of the Democratic National Committee and business and labor leaders; and (4) members of the Peanut Brigade—the Georgians who traveled at their own expense to campaign for Carter.

The next day they started again at 10:00 in the morning to receive members of Congress; then from 2:00 until 3:30 the ambassadors of foreign countries; and from 4:30 to 6:00 P.M. representatives of the

Armed Forces. It is not surprising that Rosalynn, who couldn't get into her shoes her first morning in the White House, had to slip her pumps off during the partying and receive in her stocking feet.

Jimmy Carter was an enigma to Washingtonians. A self-proclaimed candidate from a tiny town in Georgia, with no political clout, no power base, no national reputation, no following, had made it to the big top. It was as if he had used some kind of magic. Maybe it was because he was up and at 'em before anyone else.

"He wakes up wide awake. He sits right up and is ready to go," Rosalynn Carter told me. "This morning he got up at 6:00 A.M. and went fishing." Carter had plenty of determination, she said. "When Jimmy makes up his mind to do something, he does it. To a certain extent he's a perfectionist." His disposition? "Very even. He isn't easily angered. I get mad and loud and he just gets quiet. . . . He's certainly courageous. . . . He's always looking for a challenge . . . always thinking of something to do to make the business better. . . . He never cared if he got credit for something." And, of course, he wanted to be president. She couldn't even think about that for a whole year when he broke the news to her.

Asked if she had ever been jealous, Mrs. Carter said she had been in the past but not since he had been governor or running for president.

It's doubtful that the following incident ever reached her ears. Senator and Mrs. Howard Baker checked into the Sheraton Palace Hotel in San Francisco the night President Ford and Jimmy Carter were in that city to telecast their debate. Ford stayed in a private house on Nob Hill but Carter was in the Sheraton Palace so the Bakers were surprised when they were offered the presidential suite. They were told the Secret Service ruled out that suite for Carter because the bedroom windows were much too close to the windows of an office building. Back in their suite later that evening the Bakers kept receiving phone calls for one person or another in the Carter contingent. At 3:00 A.M. they were awakened by another call. Joy Baker answered it and "a nice, deep, male voice with a southern accent said, 'Rosalynn, honey, may I speak to Jimmy?' " In the wake of Carter's *Playboy* interview in which he said he had "committed adultery in my heart many times," this was too good an opportunity to miss. The daughter of noted Republican Senator

Everett Dirksen drawled back, "Darlin', this isn't Rosalynn." The caller's voice, now sounding like a lust-rejecting Baptist, demanded, "Who is this?" "This is Joy Baker," she drawled seductively and hung up. "That was mean," observed the senator sleepily.

Jimmy Carter, his wife revealed, also helped her around the house; he'd "clear the table, do the dishes, and make the beds." And he taught her how to cook. "He can cook anything. He has a wonderful recipe for cooking fish. He cuts up catfish in bite-size pieces, puts some kind of steak sauce on them, lets them soak overnight, puts them in a pancake mix in a bag, shakes them up, and fries them in deep fat. They are really good!" (You could tell the Carters had no cholesterol or weight problems.)

It was almost a toss-up in January of 1977 as to which caused the biggest stir in Washington—the installation of Jimmy Carter or the retirement of Henry Kissinger. Jerry Ford's farewells seemed almost solemn compared to his secretary of state's festive reentry into private life. Wreathed in smiles and full of witticisms, he greeted friends who came thousands of miles for parties in his honor. International socialites Gloria and Loel Guinness flew up from Acapulco and the Gregory Pecks and Kirk Douglases came all the way from the west coast for the dinner and dance for 120 of Henry's chums tossed by Ambassador Ardeshir Zahedi. From New York came CBS President and Mrs. Bill Paley, the Walter Cronkites, NBC chairman and president respectively, Julian Goodman and Herbert Schlosser, and their wives; Kitty Carlisle, Polly Bergen, and so forth. That Kissinger was enamoured of society had long been apparent. He peppered his official luncheons at the State Department with unofficial upper crust names; at his luncheon for Egyptian President Sadat were Mrs. Vincent Astor, David Rockefeller, Pamela Harriman, the Louis Auchinclosses, the Henry Fords, Clare Luce, Mrs. Douglas Fairbanks, Jr., and the Oscar de la Rentas. No wonder he and Nancy would become the darlings of New York society.

With the beginning of a brand-new administration, the question was always posed: Will there be a big change in the Washington social scene now? My answer had always been no. Presidents come and go, but official Washington goes on forever. A new administration had about the same social effect, I wrote, as a change of the leading actors in a play. The plot was the same, the setting was the same, even the cast of characters was virtually the same. Only the people playing the star roles were different. State entertaining at the White House was so tailored to protocol that the president and First Lady get locked into a social form. Jackie Kennedy's French menus were not replaced at state affairs by the LBJs with Texas barbeques, as reporters predicted. Nor would the White House chef now serve grits and chitlins in place of his fancy French dishes.

I was right about the food, but not about the rest. The Carter regime did have an effect on Capital entertaining. President Carter told the people around him that he didn't want them going to Washington parties and so most didn't go. As getting next to the power in the executive branch was the main impetus for diplomatic entertaining, embassy functions began to decrease. The biggest changes came in the manner of entertaining. We in the press were even provided with a list of the changes at the outset. Before the first state dinner—in honor of Mexico's President and Mrs. Lopez Portillo—the First Lady's press office included in the usual list of proceedings the following: "Only American food will be served . . . The menu will be printed in English instead of French. . . . Wine will be served both prior to and during dinner . . . Dinner will begin at 7:30, a half hour earlier than usual . . . The Color Guard—four uniformed men bearing the American and the President's flags as a symbol of the high office—will no longer precede the President and Mrs. Carter when they descend the staircase to receive their guests, nor will the herald trumpets be played.* The Honor Corps will no longer line the north driveway—for the arrival of the visiting president. The Social Aides have been reduced from 24 to 18 . . . At the conclusion of the entertainment and after President and Mrs. Lopez Portillo leave the North Portico, President and Mrs. Carter will go directly to the residence. The guests will then depart."†

So there we had it. The Carters had eliminated all dancing, and a lot of the trimmings that made a White House dinner so special,

---

* (The Fords had also done without indoor trumpeters.)

† Dinner guests continued to receive personalized programs that included the menu, as well as escort cards. And after-dinner guests also received personalized programs for the entertainment.

both for the state visitor and the other guests. They did keep "Hail To The Chief" and four ruffles to announce their arrival in the East Room. Having the menu in English was a plus for most guests, and so was having the great pianist Rudolf Serkin play after dinner.

But the guest list clearly reflected Jimmy Carter's intention of inviting average Americans to his parties. Some on the staff called the mansion a "People People" White House.

Their social secretary Gretchen Poston recalled years later that she didn't "know how many other First Ladies entertained people who wrote in and asked if they could come to a state dinner. Rosalynn asked that that be done and it was done." With no glamorous celebrities to dance with the president, or give an enchanting impromptu performance, or wiggle on the dance floor, there was some moaning and groaning from the press. The Kennedys had given White House parties for foreign heads of government a reputation for glitter; a lot of fun had been added since; now it was gone.

Quite a few people preferred the change. Of course many would have enjoyed rubbing elbows with famous Americans, from scientists to screen stars, but gradually an appreciation grew for the sort of dignified quiet and sweet ease that prevailed at Carter soirees. President Carter loved classical music, and had it played in his office ten to twelve hours every day; so gone now were the jazzy performers whose voices were not good enough to sing without mikes despite the East Room's superb acoustics. To be truthful, the very elegant, crystal-lit East Room had never seemed the proper setting for some of the hot groups: That had been apparent during the previous summer's visit of Queen Elizabeth, when the love-making of a muskrat was graphically described in a song by Captain and Tennille. Toni Tennille had a bright, fresh charm about her but it came across as tasteless.

Hence when opera singers performed for Prime Minister James Callaghan in the Carter White House in March of 1977, British Ambassador Sir Peter Ramsbotham beamed and remarked, "*Such good taste.*"

But there was much criticism of the Carters for including their nine-year-old daughter Amy at state dinners. To make matters worse, Amy was seated at the most important table, along with her parents and the guests of honor. And to top that off she took a book with her to the table, and read it during most of the meal. Amy must have thought it was okay; after all, back in Plains her father read at every meal.

But Washington was shocked. "I have never had a child of mine at a formal dinner," said the wife of a U.S. official who was present. "This administration isn't like anything we have ever had before. When my kids got to be fourteen and could carry on a fairly intelligent conversation, I would incorporate them." Another official dinner guest said, "I was surprised when Amy came in, and I was particularly surprised when she sat at the president's table. Of course, the reading should not have been allowed. But this is a new ball game. We have to get used to it." It was the talk of the Mexican Embassy reception the next day. Carter supporters looked pained when the subject came up. "I wouldn't allow my children to stay up. They need their sleep," was the most one of them would say. When I subsequently asked Rosalynn Carter if Amy would be attending other dinners, she replied, "If she wants to." No one found out what Mrs. Santiago Roel, wife of Mexico's foreign minister, thought when she discovered her dinner partner was a kid with a book who read most of the time. This rudeness could be laughed off by Mexicans; two other breaches of conduct could not.

The Mexicans in Acapulco, where George and I went two days later, felt their country had been insulted, first when President and Mrs. Carter decided not to attend the Mexican Embassy reception in their honor; and again, when Speaker Tip O'Neill stated, even as President Lopez Portillo was addressing Congress, that such addresses were a waste of legislators' time. The Speaker's remarks were characterized as impudent and rude, both privately and in the Mexican press.

March witnessed another extraordinary happening in the Capital—the holding of 134 Jewish hostages in a Washington building by a group called the Hanafi Muslims. No progress was made toward their release until help came from three Moslem ambassadors—Iran's Zahedi, Pakistan's Yaqub Khan, and Egypt's Ashraf Ghorbal. Ardeshir Zahedi went without sleep for sixty hours during negotiations, and, over the objections and fears of the authorities, insisted on meeting the Hanafi leader face to face. By his sympathetic understanding of the leader's problems, Zahedi won the release of all 134. In so doing he won the instant respect and gratitude of the Carter administration which, up until then, thought of him as only a giver of glamorous parties. (Many people think big party-givers, as well as party-trotters, are superficial and flighty—perhaps forgetting the intense daily pressures on the powerful of the earth, and the importance, after each long day's journey, of congenial recreation.) At a dinner at the Iranian Embassy for all who had worked to end the hostage siege—from Mayor Walter Washington and police chief Maurice Cullinane to Attorney General Griffin Bell—the latter called the diplomats "the three brave ambassadors."

Of the key figures of the Carter administration, two were most popular and most often seen at social affairs: National Security Chairman Zbigniew Brzezinski, a warm and outspoken conversationalist who was at ease socially and loved to dance, and Attorney General Griffin Bell, a man of wisdom and high principle. Bell and Presidential Press Secretary Jody Powell were the wits of the new regime. Jody liked to tell the story of a cabinet meeting when a suggestion from the former Atlanta judge sent two other cabinet members "up the wall" for five minutes. The attorney general then told the president, "It's clear to me that I have offered one of those suggestions that works well in practice but not in theory." "It collapsed the whole cabinet," said Jody. Bell called Powell "a sort of grasshopper philosopher."

Perhaps the most colorful Carterite was Presidential Assistant Midge Constanza, liaison to the public and the sole woman, Catholic, and ethnic among the senior staffers. The Sicilian-American was a free-talking, friendly, hard-working comedian who wore blue jeans in the White House and was even said to go barefoot at times. There was no formality about Midge. At the 51.3 Per Cent reception (celebrating the feminine majority's campaign efforts) during inaugural festivities, Midge, running her eyes up and down over good-looking Senator Birch Bayh, said over the microphone to the assemblage, "I'm so used to looking at men for their brain power that this is the first time I have looked at a man for his looks." "And this is the first time I have ever seen a presidential assistant with a peekaboo down to the waist," observed a guest. Dressed for the Inaugural Gala, Miss Constanza was in a sleeveless black sheath with rhinestones bordering the neck and a deep, laddered decolletage. Midge's heyday would last only until May 1978, when she lost most of her staff and responsibilities and was moved to a tiny office in the basement. Her downfall probably stemmed from protesting the president's opposition to government funding for abortion, and from her remark that a Jimmy Carter favorite, Budget Director Bert Lance, should resign. (He finally did, in September 1977.)

The most invisible and most powerful of President Carter's assistants, Hamilton Jordan, was undoubtedly the most informal and most unorthodox of all presidential chiefs of staff. Having designed the operation that landed Jimmy Carter in the White House, Ham was untouchable. He not only wore jeans and short-sleeved sports shirts with a comb sticking up in the pocket in the White House, but he had his picture taken that way for *Esquire* magazine—with his hand up as though he had his finger up his nose. Besides being totally devoid of taste, that picture made it look as though a bunch of ill-mannered Georgia crackers was running the country. Ham Jordan showed other errors in judgment: he refused phone calls from the Speaker, the third-ranking man in the U.S. government. At an off-the-record dinner Barbara Walters and Roone Arledge gave for the Egyptian and Israeli ambassadors, Jordan, seated beside the Egyptian ambassador's wife, looked down her front and remarked that he had now seen the pyramids of Egypt. The Ghorbals, regretting the remark had been overheard, were deeply offended. On another occasion the youthful Jordan walked in on Brzezinski's background press briefing in the White House. Wearing a shiny green coat, sport shirt, no tie, and big scruffy boots, he lay down on the floor in front of Zbig, and remained stretched out there throughout the briefing. NSC member Paul Henze told me the story. Did he see anything about it in the papers afterwards?

"Not a word."

If the president's staff had civilized Washingtonians confounded, Carter, himself, kept them guessing. Here was a man with fine taste in music, who loved opera, and publicly admitted that some of the great arias brought tears to his eyes, who went to the Kennedy Center more often in a month than other presidents went in a whole term, who visited the National Gallery of Art twice in a month, the first time to see the King Tut show, the second time, a small

Japanese exhibit.* And yet, for his culture-appreciation forays to the gallery, he wore a cardigan sweater instead of a jacket. I believe his informal air did him no good. Others agree.

When a picture appeared in the *Star* in May 1978 showing Jimmy Carter, fresh off a helicopter from Camp David, wearing a lounge jacket over a T-shirt and carrying a briefcase and books in his left hand with his right hanging onto a Val-Pak over his shoulder, a congressman told me that clinging to the common image was doing the president harm. There he was surrounded by guards and aides and it looked as though none of them had enough respect for him to lend him a hand. But more important, said the congressman, the president "has stripped from his high office the aura of power and prestige that former presidents have used to advantage. As a result, when he calls on members of Congress for support the pressure of the presidential mystique is lacking and they feel no compulsion to go along."

It wasn't until Gerald Rafshoon, who had given P.R. assistance during the campaign, was taken on as a presidential assistant, two years into his term, that J.C. began to improve his image.

*   *   *

Another surprise to Washington was the revelation that Carter billed his own cabinet members and staffers whenever they lunched with him. To break that story I called both Secretary of State Cyrus Vance and Zbig Brzezinski who lunched with him in his office once a week. Each confirmed it with a smile. Secretary of Commerce Juanita Kreps said how surprised she was when she got a bill for her sandwich or salad. Inasmuch as government food is always cheaper than that in restaurants, because it is not prepared for a profit, it may have cost as much or more than each lunch for a clerk to keep the records, draw up the bills, and send it to the luncheon "guest." Louisiana Representative John Breaux, who had breakfast on Air Force One, said that he received a bill for less than two dollars.

Checking this until-now-unheard-of procedure, I called J.B West, former head usher and author of *Upstairs at the White House*. J. B. said

---

* He was the first U.S. president to go there since Jack Kennedy went for the unveiling of the Mona Lisa—and JFK went only that once.

when a predecessor of President Carter "had his staff to lunch it was official and the government would pay for it. The only time the president paid for food was for his family or for private entertaining. He didn't have to pay for his own food if he had an official guest.

"We had money for entertaining and it would come out of that," West told me. "Actually, it was a travel fund, but when the president started using Air Force One he didn't have to pay so that money was used for official entertaining—except for state visits, which come out of a special State Department fund. The travel allowance was then listed at $40,000 a year, tax free. The president also gets an expense account [$50,000]. It was granted when Truman was there because he didn't have any money and he could not benefit by a raise.* It was given directly to the president and he kept whatever was left over and he paid income tax on it. It was a way of enlarging his salary."

"FDR always had guests in the office but it was wheeled over from the mansion and served by White House butlers," added J. B. All other presidents he worked for, right up to Nixon, had their business meals in the downstairs or upstairs family dining rooms in the mansion. But when "the food comes from the navy [White House] mess then they all pay for it, even the president. But I didn't know of any president who had lunch from the navy mess," West stated.

Before the Carter administration ended Congress would vote that whatever was left of the president's personal allowance of $50,000 could not be retained by him but must be returned to the government.

President Carter was responsible for all the economies that were quickly put into effect—staff reductions, reduced use of electricity, smaller cars in place of more comfortable ones, and more. But the press corps blamed Jimmy Carter's cousin Hugh Carter, whom he put in charge of running the White House. Cousin Cheap, as the press sometimes referred to him, became renowned for his glue with a sou. He was blamed for cutting down on the cleaning crews, who had cleaned the offices nightly before the Carters moved there.

---

* The presidential salary, now $200,000, was only $75,000 when Truman became president.

"If you called and complained," a staffer told me, "they would finally send someone to vacuum, but generally we had to dust the furniture, wipe the windows, and clean our offices ourselves." (When the Reagan people came in, no one could go near a certain place in the Executive Office Building because of the horrible smell; finally a policeman found some Brie cheese and old shrimp behind a radiator.)

The president's staff reduction resulted in his own secretary, Susan Clough, doing the work of three people. Her predecessors had two secretaries but she had none. Pretty, blond Susan, the first in her job to be so warm and sparkling, worked in a small office, the only one between the Oval Office and the president's private study. Such immediate access to the president spells glamor in Washington—but she didn't think of her job as glamorous; and she could spot the people who cozied up because of her connections. Thirty-two years old, and with a son fifteen and a daughter fourteen, Susan was a remarkable woman. Besides being responsible for every letter that went out over the president's signature, drafting most of them herself, she loved classical music, played classical guitar, and had played the piano since she was five. She was a Mensa member who played chess, bridge, and backgammon, was a good enough tennis player to be the president's partner in a doubles match, was a member of the Atlanta Ski Club, was a good swimmer, and had reached Class 5 in white water classes (really rough) on the Chatooga River in north Georgia. The sport appealed to her because it was thrilling and a challenge. Of Rosalynn Carter, she said, "I really love that woman." When her adored brother was fatally shot by gunmen and her alcoholic fiance jilted her, it was the Carters "who sort of watched me for two or three months" and "helped me build up confidence in myself again."

The Carters were the only presidential pair I have known who gave members of their own family precedence over their most important guests at state dinners. One example was the seating—arranged by Rosalynn Carter—at their head table for the ill-fated shah of Iran and his empress, during their last visit to an American president in late 1977. Both Carters sat at the same table with the shah between them; Mrs. Hugh Carter, Sr., sat on Rosalynn's right, and Hugh Carter, Sr., next to his wife. Next to him was Mrs. Lew

Wasserman, then her husband (the chairman of the Music Corp. of America), then the empress.

To have half the table family at a formal dinner honoring their imperial majesties was a shocker to the protocol experts, whose rules were devised to prevent international problems. And, of course, seating husbands and wives next to each other was considered unacceptable everywhere on the social scene in Washington, New York, or any "social" city, except perhaps at occasional fundraiser dinners.

In spite of my criticism of the Carters' informality, George and I were invited to that dinner because Ambassador Zahedi asked to have us there. The hosts could have crossed us off the list; either they did not choose to, or did not catch our names. In any case, we were delighted to be there.

There was one other occasion when an act of friendship was extended.

It was at one of the state functions. I was standing in the Blue Room; the only other person there, a Secret Service man, seemed surprised to see me, and asked why I was there. I told him I was a member of the press and present to cover the occasion. He next wanted to know why I wasn't wearing a press badge. I told him I never wore mine because it ruined the looks of my evening dress. He said I had to wear it.

I told him that I had been covering since Truman's time and had never been required to wear it, that he must be new to this detail. He said I had to put it on now. I was prepared to tough it out.

Just then the president walked into the Blue Room. Seeing a familiar face, he shook hands with me—before, maybe, realizing I was that Beale woman who had been telling him and Rosalynn how to behave in the Casa Blanca.

In any case, the smile and handshake did the trick. The Secret Service man faded from sight, and no one ever bothered me about the missing badge again.

Despite that little vanity, I have always considered myself a feminist.

But there are times when the best known feminists make asses of themselves. For sheer absurd knee-jerkism, there has been nothing to equal the outrage of Gloria Steinem and NOW when the Carters

deplaned and went through a receiving line during a state visit to
Saudi Arabia, with Rosalynn Carter walking a few feet behind her
husband. There are plenty of customs in Saudi Arabia that feminists
can fault, but in that case there were absolutely no grounds for
protest.

At every state dinner in our own White House, our president and
all male visiting chiefs of state precede their wives down the stairs.
Only when the chief of state or head of government is a woman, as in
the case of Queen Elizabeth or Margaret Thatcher, does the man
follow a few steps behind. Every guest at the White House or any
government reception is asked to pass through the receiving line
man before woman. This is done because in most cases it is the male
who has the title "secretary," "director," or whatever, and if that is
announced first it explains the presence both of the man and his
wife behind him.

Every president or king or queen of every country walks in front
of his or her spouse—yet NOW was so incensed that it even staged a
protest rally in front of the U.S.-Arab Chamber of Commerce in Los
Angeles over this nonexistent cause. Where, I wondered, was NOW
when Israeli Prime Minister and Mrs. Rabin came to Washington
the previous March, and only the prime minister was invited to the
president's dinner? Mrs. Carter, also excluded, took Mrs. Rabin to a
show and a restaurant dinner instead. The same thing happened
when Prime Minister and Mrs. Begin visited. Without any of these
so-called thinking women checking the facts, they started screaming as soon as the Office of Jewish Information sent out a release
quoting everybody from NOW's president to Bella Abzug saying
Mrs. Carter had been insulted.

Ignorance, sisters, will get us nowhere. In reality, perhaps more
than any other president, Jimmy Carter heeded Abigail Adams' plea
to "remember the ladies."

He appointed three women to the cabinet; together with Rosalynn, he worked hard to get the Equal Rights Amendment rat-
ified, missing it by only thirteen votes. He put several women in the
"little cabinet," he appointed forty-one women to serve as federal
judges—only five had attained that position before Jimmy Carter
came along—and he picked sixteen women as ambassadors. Married to Rosalynn, he knew how able women could be.

*   *   *

"Rosalynn is the president's No. 1 adviser," confided Zbigniew Brzezinski at a Georgetown party one evening. It was a simple statement of fact; and that fact would become the talk of the town. It was acknowledged when Mrs. Carter told one thousand Democratic women at a White House tea, "Jimmy and I need your help." Previous first ladies, when calling upon people on behalf of their husbands, had always said, "The president needs your help."

Rosalynn had every right to feel like a full-fledged partner of the chief executive. The president had been quoted as saying she "is a perfect extension of myself . . . a very equal partner." Brzezinski said that he regularly briefed Rosalynn on international affairs. She was the first First Lady to attend cabinet meetings and take notes. On Carter's official calendar each week was a luncheon with Rosalynn. Never before had a meal with his own wife been considered a part of a president's working engagements—but Rosalynn went to each luncheon armed with a folder of papers and prepared to cover any number of subjects.

One critic said the Carters' peanut business had been a Ma and Pa operation and now the White House was too. The fact that she could always get in the last word must have been frustrating for his other advisers who lacked her emotional weight—plus pillow talk.

Mrs. Carter's influence on her husband should not have surprised political observers. During the campaign she said, "I have always helped him on everything he did. When he came home from the navy I started helping him with the books [she took the children to the office with her] and I would advise him about the business—the way this part is making money, this isn't. . . . We just kind of worked together. I think he respects my opinions. He always listens to me. He doesn't always react. We talk everything over together. I have different opinions."

I sounded disapproving when I put these thoughts and comments in a column, but I confess that I did not really disapprove. If the person closest to a man cannot give her opinions to him, who can? I believe that the difference between men and women is from the neck down, not the neck up. But Rosalynn's participation in the high levels of government was a topic that wouldn't go away. It consumed a supper party one night: One guest in a position to know said Mrs. Carter had "sat in with the president at a breakfast with other summit leaders when they met in Japan, and Margaret Thatcher was fit to be tied! Mr. Thatcher wasn't there, nor were any other spouses. The breakfast was not part of the official agenda but an informal background occasion when the heads of government got together."

A prominent career woman said Mrs. Carter was doing her husband "a disservice. Last week the *Boston Globe* called her 'Mrs. President.' When you have that sort of thing outside of Washington you are in trouble." A high administration staff appointee disagreed. "Jimmy Carter is essentially a body with two brains, and one of those brains is Rosalynn Carter's. When we elected him we elected Rosalynn Carter, too, and if she doesn't continue in that role we won't get the Jimmy Carter we elected. If she's going to be in on the decisions, she ought to be in on the deliberations so she can make informed decisions." And so the argument raged.

One former official said that her objection to the First Lady participating in policy-making deliberations was based on her "non-accountability. Hers is a purely invisible, covert portfolio.

"I didn't dream of having my husband take part in any substantive official deliberations. For a wife to be in on a briefing is okay, but a briefing is not a policy-making deliberation."

The only male comment at that supper was, "By having her present doesn't he create an image of his own inadequacy?"

No one, I noticed, questioned Rosalynn Carter's mental capabilities. From the first she came across as a no-nonsense woman. Two months before entering the White House she sought ideas on ways she could focus on problems of the aging and mental health. And even before becoming the mistress of the historic mansion, she arranged for an innovation the day after her husband was sworn in. Instead of the Marine Band—or indeed any of the military bands—that customarily supplied background music for White House receptions, Mrs. Carter invited the Cleveland String Quartet (which later moved to Rochester, N.Y.) to play. They came highly recommended by Robert Shaw of the Robert Shaw Chorale, then conductor of the Atlanta Symphony. "I love Robert Shaw," said the new First Lady who, from plain Plains, Ga., or no, had shown the confidence to do something new.

"Rosalynn Carter is an absolute pro in her working relationships," said Mary Hoyt, her press secretary. "She's always punctual. She's very disciplined about her time. She has a strong sense of identity. She knows who she is. It's a pleasure because when you are working with someone like that you know where you stand."

Mrs. Hoyt also said her boss had "flashes of spontaneity." Seven months later Mrs. Carter was to prove it. She had been playing tennis with her husband. (Jimmy had been so eager for her to take up the sport that he had given her a racquet and a tennis dress for a wedding anniversary present July 7. In order to give her husband a better game, Mrs. Carter was taking lessons at Camp David from champion Billie Jean King's pro, Frank Brennan.) They had been playing hard and long on a hot July afternoon. Instead of going into the mansion, Rosalynn headed straight from court to pool—and jumped in with all her clothes on.

Jimmy Carter obviously loved sharing activities with his wife. They bowled together three times a week, and watched movies three times a week.

She also took up the violin to keep her daughter company. Amy was learning to play by the remarkably quick Suzuki teaching method which required parental collaboration. "We practice from 8:00 to 8:30 in the morning and sometimes in the afternoon, and you should hear us!" said the First Lady. "Caron [Carter] brings the baby [grandson James, one year old] and she's taught him to clap when he hears music, and the baby claps and the cat sings and it's bedlam!"

Of all the First Ladies I have covered, Rosalynn Carter did the most on the international scene. Her husband had such confidence in her ability he sent her on a tour of seven countries in Latin America to talk to their heads of government about human rights, economic progress for the people, reduction in arms sales, non-proliferation of nuclear weapons, and other substantive issues. As usual, there were eyebrows raised and expressions of dismay that a woman was being sent on a serious mission to macho Latin countries. Horrors! But she must have earned respect by her questions and background knowledge, for even today, long after any claim to influence, she still hears from some of the leaders she met.

Jimmy Carter also sent his wife to Thailand to call attention to the incredible suffering of the Cambodians in Thai refugee camps—the result of Pol Pot's genocide campaign. As a result of her trip, UN Secretary General Kurt Waldheim appointed a relief coordinator, U.S. volunteer agencies formed a crisis committee, and people throughout the U.S. began to help. Undoubtedly, many Cambodians survived because Rosalynn cared enough to go to bat for them, plugging their dire need both on television and from the speaker's podium. The First Lady also highlighted problems of the aged and made strides in the treatment of the mentally ill, resulting in the passage of the Mental Health Systems Act. In all Mrs. Carter went to twenty-nine foreign countries on thirty-six different trips, all but two states in the U.S., and made 430 speeches. But, alas, the words "mental health" are not glamorous to read about. If Rosalynn could have somehow changed the title of the project to Sex Habits of the Unbalanced, it might have received front page publicity.

With all her influence on her husband, Mrs. Carter could not at first prevail upon him even to raise the White House thermostat to 68 degrees. Because of the oil shortage he had asked Americans to lower their thermostats to 65 degrees and so insisted it not go above that in the White House. Rosalynn complained to him that her staffers were so cold they had to type with their gloves on. And all, including the First Lady, had to wear long warm underwear to work. "I have never been so miserable in my life," recalls Mary Hoyt. Happily, "after a couple of months the president decided it was counter-productive."

Like most, if not all, First Ladies, Rosalynn's appearance improved enormously in the White House. She began wearing designer clothes and, though in general she preferred simple styles, style, quality, and line gave her a new chic. She also lightened her hair and had it done for every occasion.

*   *   *

The Carters began to blossom in 1978. Music-loving Jimmy, who even had fifteen minutes of chamber music played at the end of every working dinner, not only had the world's greatest pianist perform at the White House on a Sunday afternoon in February and invited other celebrated musicians to hear him, but he danced at one of his parties two days later. Billed as "A Concert at the White House," Vladimir Horowitz demonstrated his brilliant technique in a mostly Chopin program. Transported by it were violinist Isaac Stern, the world's greatest cellist, maestro "Slava" Rostropovich, composer Samuel Barber, pianists Byron Janis and Constance Keene, and three famous jazz musicians—Dave Brubeck, Billy Taylor, and Teddy Wilson. The electricity that charges a gathering of idolaters with their idols permeated the main floor of the mansion. The world's greatest guitarist, Andres Segovia, enhanced the roster when he arrived late; it was clearly a thrill for the artists to meet the first American president who so loved their music that he couldn't stand running the country without it.

That same week, the Carters gave a ball for the nation's governors, at which silver-throated Beverly Sills and baritone Alan Titus sang arias from *The Merry Widow* operetta. Just before the last chorus of the famous waltz, they stepped down from the stage. Beverly, in an ivory satin portrait gown, held out her arms to the president, and Titus his to the First Lady, and each couple began waltzing, Sills singing, as she looked into Jimmy's eyes, "—for I love you." Titus finished the song, gazing at the comely Rosalynn's eyes. After that all the guests danced at the Carters' first ball, after which they partook of a bountiful buffet. It was charming.

And so was their Christmas ball for the Congress in December 1978—their first swinging dance. Peter Duchin and his orchestra played everything, even rock, and the president danced a lot. "If we had only done this two years ago!" exclaimed a White House staffer. "They've come a long way," said a congressman's wife.

But if the president and First Lady were learning to use the warm personal contact of entertainment to their advantage, they had not changed the social rules for little Amy. On a soft summer's eve—a moonlight-and-roses night—they gave a dinner for the heads of fifteen NATO countries in the south garden. It was an impressive gathering, a truly prestigious affair, until ten-year-old Amy, in a long print pinafore and bandanna, joined the formal dinner party and stood for awhile between her mother and German Chancellor Helmut Schmidt. She would leave, and return, and get a drink of water from her mother while her father was speaking to the assemblage; finally, she sat on the lap of her indulgent mother. Her disruptive activity must have shocked the Europeans, who are far less permissive with their young children.

Meanwhile, diplomats assigned to Washington were not happy either. Netherlands Ambassador Tammenoms Bakker, Pakistan Ambassador Yaqub Khan, and Saudi Arabian Ambassador Ali Alireza each spoke to me at dinner parties about the decline of American influence in the world. During the Carter administration, Soviet communism had taken over Nicaragua, Grenada, Ethiopia, and Mozambique, and spread its influence in Afghanistan and Angola. The USSR was also aiding Cuba and goading Castro to stir up trouble in El Salvador and other Latin American countries. Pakistan was moving Yaqub Khan, its top diplomat, from Washington to Moscow because, he told me, of the "indifference" of the U.S. toward that region and the rise of Soviet influence.

Everywhere on the international front there was a swelling undercurrent of concern over America's abdication of leadership. The Carter administration had failed to help the shah when threatened by Khomeini's forces and, in fact, urged the Iranian military not to resist. And while our government kept emphasizing human rights, Khomeini had killed, in his first eighteen months, an estimated five thousand in Teheran alone, brutalizing women into submission and eliminating all the rights they had gained under the shah and empress Farah. This time, it seemed, we were not screaming out against Khomeini's endless executions and other acts of unspeakable terror.

Ali Tabatabai, former press attaché of the Iranian Embassy, begged me to put in my column a notice of the anti-Khomeini demonstration that would take place in Washington five days from then. Threats would not stop it, he said. (He had founded the Iran Freedom Foundation and had lined up ten professional men and women who volunteered their services to speak to their people on the Voice of America. But the White House and the State Department turned a deaf ear to his inside information.)

Two hours after our talk, he went to the door to get his mail from the postman. It was one of Khomeini's men in a postman's uniform; he shot Ali dead.

Under those circumstances, it was a particularly sad day when Ardeshir Zahedi quietly left Washington. He had not only given all who crossed his path a lift in making diplomacy work, in making the U.S. and Iran closer than ever before, he had been generous not only to the powerful, but to Washington charities, and, very quietly, he had given money even to strangers in need whom he read about in the newspapers. He had braved angry American campuses to tell students "not how great his country was, but how great our country is," said Ronald Reagan at a dinner Zahedi gave for the Reagans. "I have known no one in his position who at the same time has proven his loyalty to his own country and had so much love for our country." Ardeshir had worked his way through college in the U.S. by washing dishes in a restaurant in Phoenix. Reagan had "topped him there." He worked his way through college by washing dishes in a girls' dormitory.

The Carter administration pressed the shah to make concessions to the anti-shah forces in Iran, then tried to placate Khomeini by refusing to give asylum to the man who had favored America above all his neighbors. As the *Wall Street Journal* pointed out, when we let the shah, who was dying of cancer, in for medical treatment, the new terrorists of Iran showed their mettle by taking American hostages right out of our embassy in Teheran. We rushed the shah off to Panama as soon as possible but all we got for our betrayal of friendship was "a reputation for impotence and unreliability," stated the *Journal*, "and the continuing spectacle of both is having no small effect on world politics."

President Carter's snub of foreign ambassadors only emphasized his indifference to our standing abroad. He was the first president of the United States to give no yearly reception, dinner, or whatever for the envoys accredited to him. They had not seen him in two-and-a-half years, not since the brief reception two days after his Inauguration. Only the representatives of Egypt and Israel, and those included with their bosses during a state visit, had been invited to the White House. "A diplomatic reception is useful," stated an ambassador. "It gives us an opportunity to see the president and members of all his staff, to talk to them and have an exchange of viewpoints. When we read in the newspaper that the White House had a reception to hear a musician or see a dancer, and members of Congress and the cabinet were invited to the performance, we ask why couldn't some of us be invited to each reception. Don't they believe that the diplomatic corps is part of Washington?"

"If an ambassador can have the ear of the president . . . Carter would get information about these countries that he isn't getting through bureaucratic channels. A social occasion paves the way for such contacts," said another envoy. The chief of state in every other country entertained the corps royally at least once a year. Carter had spoken of "the isolated world of Washington," but in the nation's Capital, where the pulse of the country and every part of the globe is taken every second, the only isolated island was the "Georgia mafia's" preserve.

*   *   *

Ambassadors, of course, are the reason for protocol rules. The tale is often told in Washington of the ambassador attending a dinner in a private home. His hostess decided not to seat him according to protocol, because he would end up with his back to the choice view. She placed him instead where he would face her pretty garden.

"I thought you would enjoy the view," she explained, as they sat down for dinner.

"Madame," the ambassador replied stiffly, "my country did not send me here to enjoy myself."

At least one envoy has sat stonily through dinner without touching his food to indicate his displeasure with his place.

I was present at the dinner Scottie Fitzgerald Lanahan gave in honor of UN Ambassador Adlai Stevenson, whom she correctly seated in the place of honor—on her right. On his right she put the ranking woman, Nicole Alphand, and she seated French Ambassador Alphand as host at another table—all strictly according to protocol. But when Alphand saw where he was placed, he said he would have to leave immediately if he was not given the top spot. As President de Gaulle's representative, he could not sit in a lesser spot without degrading de Gaulle. Scottie, on the verge of tears, had to delay dinner until she could reseat her guests. The only way to find out who gets top billing at a Washington event is by using The Table of Precedence in the Social List of Washington, better known as the *Green Book*. The protocol office at the State Department, if asked, always goes into its spiel: No president of the United States had ever approved a list of precedence for Washington officialdom, so the office has not had the authority to tell any other department or person what to do. Everyone is master of his own dwelling, and can do as desired. Then it tells you how your guests rate.

Everybody on the "precedence list" is numbered. Of course, the president is number one. Back when Harry Truman became president, ambassadors were listed right after No. 1, but they've been going downhill ever since. The entire group falls in the No. 8 slot today; what's more, each envoy has a separate number under category 8. If you think Germany, France, or Great Britain should get a better seat than little Mauritius, for instance, you may as well go back to using your celery as a chute for your peas. The Indian Ocean island's charming envoy has been ambassador here eleven years so he outranks those other big boys. And don't think they wouldn't object if the Congress of Vienna hadn't decided in 1815 that all nations would abide by the rule: First to arrive gets first place—just like the early bird and worm theory.

The 1948 *Green Book* listed only twenty-seven precedence categories, with the chiefs of staff of the armed forces ranked right after U.S. senators and three places ahead of members of the House. The congressmen didn't put up with that for long. Today they are twelve places above the armed chiefs.

Everybody in Washington is so crazy for rank that there are sixty-one categories listed today. People who get a presidential appointment to a commission that meets only three or four times a year are entitled to an "Honorable" in front of their names in the *Green Book*; many want it there. (Every member of Congress is called "Honorable"; in government the word has nothing to do with character.)

I'll never forget a dinner at Assistant Secretary of State for Inter-American Affairs and Mrs. Henry Holland's house, back in Ike's regime, when the women, separated from the men temporarily, sat down in the living room to chat. I took a vacant seat at the right end of the sofa and tried to engage the Latin ladies in cheery conversation. As experienced as I was on the cosmopolitan party circuit, I had no idea that I had usurped the place always reserved in Latino quarters for the ranking lady. When my hostess discreetly whispered the facts of life, I shot up from the hotspot to release it for the bigshot.

I learned about automobile protocol the same way. When Perle

Mesta or any limousine owner picked me up I wondered why she always sat on the far right leaving me to scramble over her limbs, hopefully failing to step on her toes. Being ever so alert and bright it wasn't too many years before I caught on. Of course, if the car had been empty I would have had to enter first. The owner sits in the back, right-hand seat. In most cars, too, the woman with the most rank or the eldest gets in last. That goes for airplanes, too: The last person you see before Air Force One takes off is the president.

It's just the opposite when getting in an elevator or going through a door. The most elevated lady enters the elevator first (ditto a door). But by the time she urges the eldest to go before her and the eldest coyly remonstrates, the elevator's gone.

If you're a man you've got to remember that a king of Saudi Arabia is insulted if he sees the soles of your shoes—never mind that you have on a brand new pair. Secretary of State Foster Dulles's aides sweated it out every time he changed his position in the presence of a Saudi monarch lest he indulge in the American habit of resting one ankle on a knee. Similarly, you must never show your sole to Thai royalty. It's just another example of having, when you're in government, to keep your foot firmly on the ground if you don't want it to end up in your mouth.

* * *

The Carters gave a jazz concert, another of country music, and a Broadway musical hit to entertain the 96th Congress. The president was at his best around music and religion. The most unusual program presented in the East Room in decades, perhaps in the twentieth century, was the two-hour recital of the Gospel according to St. Mark by English actor Alec McCowen. It was a tour de force as well as an unequaled feat of memory. It portrayed Christ as a vigorous, fast-talking, authoritative man, an account made all the more exciting by the beautiful language of the King James version of the Bible spoken in clear accents. The president's mother, "Miz Lillian," who had produced evangelist Ruth Carter Stapleton as well as born-again Jimmy, was among the audience of three hundred. She wasn't very religious herself, she said; and the performance "was two hours too long!"

There was nothing ostentatious about Miz Lillian: When Luxembourg Ambassador Adrien Meisch—who had met Billy Carter somewhere—was invited to Plains, Ga., by Billy, he accepted with pleasure. A foreign diplomat does not pass up an opportunity to get closer to a presidential family. Meisch always served his own guests gourmet meals cooked by his French chef, in the stately Luxembourg Embassy on Massachusetts Avenue. He was not prepared for the lunch Miz Lillian gave him and Billy: A peanut butter sandwich. The ambassador did not like peanut butter, a fact that must have been reflected in his expression. Miz Lillian hastily took it back, added jelly, and returned it to him. The jelly additive, in his opinion, had not enhanced its gustatorial appeal; but, he was an ambassador: He ate it, with style.

The informality and simplicity of Jimmy Carter's upbringing was apparent on more than one occasion to highly placed foreigners. When receiving Egyptian President and Mrs. Anwar Sadat, he kissed Jehan Sadat, a disgraceful act in the eyes of the Egyptian people. Arab men greet males with a kiss on both cheeks but to greet a woman in the same way suggested too great an intimacy.

President Carter's greatest breach of etiquette was in kissing the Queen Mother of England on the lips. British newspapers considered the unheard-of-discourtesy to royalty outrageous and the Queen Mother, herself, was plainly horrified. "Not since the death of my dear husband," she said, leaving the public to finish the sentence—had any man kissed her.

* * *

The 1979 Christmas season was clouded with concern over our hostages in Iran. Members of Congress went to parties with beepers in their pockets, to keep in constant touch with their offices; Christmas holidays were canceled by such members of the diplomatic corps as the French and the British, because of the crisis in Iran. But diplomatic entertaining went on as always. I went to British Ambassador and Lady Henderson's informal dinner for Lord and Lady Butler where I sat next to retired "Rab" Butler, who had held at least six top posts in the government, and was a Knight of the Garter. He told me that he had sold his Gloucestershire estate to the queen, who wanted it for Princess Anne and her husband. "Anne won't suit you. Anne is rude," the queen had told him. Butler also told about the British spy, Anthony Blunt, whom he had known for years but never liked. The queen, he said, had known since 1964 that Blunt was spying for the Soviets, but from that date on he had worked for the British.

While consuming the entree, a delectable George V (meat) pie, the plump-jowled baron related his experience in Johannesburg, where he had lectured on liberty at the university. He got the students so excited, he said, that they paraded in the streets and were promptly arrested. Butler protested to South Africa's home secretary that he, not the students, should be arrested, only to be told, "We don't arrest important people." He continued to protest until the three hundred students were freed, but each was fined one hundred dollars.

Lady Butler, a stately woman with a sense of humor, recalled that the last time she had sat on the sofa in the drawing room—in February 1964—Rose Kennedy, sitting next to her, had said, "The next president of the United States will be my son Bobby." Lady Butler was still surprised that Mrs. Kennedy was thinking that way only three months after the assassination of her son Jack.

International lawyer John J. McCloy, former high commissioner of Germany, told me at that dinner of his recent trip as the president's unofficial emissary to see the dying shah in his New York hospital room. The government didn't want to "participate," said McCloy—although it had participated from the beginning. The shah told him he was distressed by the embarrassment he was causing the United States. (At that point thirteen hostages had been freed, leaving forty-nine still captive.) "I am a prideful man and I don't want to be in a country where I'm causing embarrassment," the former ruler told him.

It was the beginning of the end for Jimmy Carter. Overcome by his failure to end the crisis over the hostages, he lost no opportunity to emphasize their plight, and said he wouldn't campaign till they were free—thus aiding in his defeat in November 1980.* Carter's last year in office saw an inflation rate of 18 percent and a prime rate of 19.5 percent. There's no question that Jimmy Carter, as a caring

* Eventually, he campaigned a little.

Christian, did his best as he saw it but the "malaise" that he announced was gripping the country was partly due to his own emphasis on the hostages' predicament.

Three years after Carter left Washington, I was at a luncheon with Chief of Naval Operations James Watkins, who had been a submariner for sixteen years. Did he know Jimmy Carter?

"He was a first classman when I went to the Academy," he replied. "At that time he hadn't been born again. He wasn't a humanitarian then," said the admiral, smiling.

Did the famous human rights spokesman indulge in hazing? The answer was yes.

"One of the hazing things was to make a plebe sit at lunch without a chair, holding that position and singing 'Chiquita Banana.' " If he didn't sing loud enough, platoon leader Carter would make him hold that position longer, and he wasn't remiss about using the paddle, mused the CNO.

Thank heaven Jimmy was born again!

CHAPTER 13

Royal Rigadoon

Tête-à-têtes with Kings and Things

Sooner or later, the mighty of the earth come to Washington. It was only natural that I would meet a lot of them during my career. Some impressed me deeply—the delightful young Queen Elizabeth II and the haughty Charles de Gaulle. One disgusted me. I shall not soon forget the night the Dominican ambassador invited me to a party aboard General Rafael Trujillo's yacht, moored in Washington; as the merengue band struck up, the dictator asked me to dance. Fortunately, the loathesome experience was short.

Most of my experiences with kings and things have been far more enjoyable.

When King Hussein of Jordan married Lisa Halaby, the daughter of Najeeb Halaby, former president of Pan American World Airways, Halaby said he asked someone in the king's office, "What will I be called now that I am the father of the queen?" "Your irrelevance," was the reply.

I first met Hussein at a private party given by Jordanian-born Joseph Howar, in 1959. At twenty-four, he had already been king for six years, and had been smart and courageous enough to hold onto his shaky throne. I interviewed him when he came to Washington seeking help following the 1967 war that left 200,000 Jordanians living in tents with a severe winter approaching. The pain in his face was not an act. With all his dignity, he is probably the least pompous royal to visit our shores. In an elevator in the Washington Hilton someone whispered, "There's the king." "King who?" asked the companion. "Not King Who; King Hussein," answered his majesty.

When I interviewed him in his palace in Ammon in 1975 he had on a short-sleeved, tan sport shirt though his palace guards were stunning in their cossack-type uniforms and his tall, handsome chief of protocol was the picture of sartorial perfection.

Once in San Francisco, when he wanted a hot dog for lunch and the Mark Hopkins Hotel had nothing so plebian, he went to a drug store instead. But it was so full there was no place to sit. Having told his aides they were not to divulge his identity, he stood in line waiting his turn. When he finally got a seat nobody served him for five minutes. An embarrassed U.S. protocol officer finally confided in a waitress.

"Are you a real king?" she asked in surprise when she took his order. "Yes," replied his majesty. "That's marvelous," said the girl. "The only king I ever knew was Martin Luther."

* * *

I feel as though I've watched King Juan Carlos and Queen Sophia of Spain grow up. I talked to him at parties during his every official visit to Washington, from the first, at age twenty, to the one he and Sophia made in October 1981. At one, Spain's Ambassador Alfonso de Merry del Val arranged for me to have a private word with the then prince, in a closed-off drawing room of the embassy, where I posed the question: "Are you going to be king?"

"I hope so," he replied; for the very first time, he did not defer to his father's prior claim to the throne. So I asked, "What about your father?"

"I hope he becomes king, too. As his son, I think he should be king, but I also want what is best for Spain." At last, it was apparent, he had agreed to Franco's plans for him. (My report of our talk was the first public indication, the Marques de Merry del Val later told me, that he was ready to sit on the throne.)

By 1981, he felt he knew me well enough to kiss me on the cheek and—at his own reception at the Corcoran Gallery of Art—he actually kissed my hand! I can state unequivocally that having my hand kissed by a reigning king gave me a bigger lift than Playtex. To my undying irritation not a single photographer there, including my own, snapped that unique display of kingly gallantry!

*　*　*

I interviewed the beautiful empress Farah of Iran during her visits to Washington and in the summer palace in Teheran, and again in Williamsburg during their last official visit in the days of the Carter administration. She was immensely proud of the progress in women's rights. By the midseventies women in Iran had many equal rights with men, including the right to vote and the right to divorce. And they could get bank loans as easily as men. She had traveled over thirty thousand miles in her country to check on the needs of the people. She got the pill distributed free; abortion for women for health reasons; and enriched milk for pregnant mothers and little children to ensure their brain development; she was known for visiting—and embracing—the nation's lepers. The shah so respected her opinion that he had her crowned—the first Persian queen in two thousand years to wear a crown. And he made her regent for the crown prince should something happen to him. Certain cabinet members consulted her regularly. Education was one of her main interests and she proudly told me about the service required of their young people. At a certain age they had to serve either in the military or in rural areas to help the poor.

When I told her I thought prostitution should be legalized to protect women from punishment from the law or pimps, she agreed wholeheartedly. I told the shah that later during cocktails before dinner in the Governor's Palace in Williamsburg. He said, surprised, "Did she say that?"

*　*　*

In June 1978, at a dinner at the French Embassy, Ardeshir invited George and me to take a flying, cross-country trip with three of the Shah and Empress Farah's children who were coming to the U.S. for a see-America tour. He invited us as friends. He never asked me to write about it but, if I wanted to, he insisted I wait till the trip was over for their safety's sake. (A *Life* photographer joined our party at the second stop.)

Ardeshir had been a good friend of mine since his first tour as ambassador to Washington. He had arrived in March 1960 with his wife, Her Imperial Highness Princess Shahnaz, who was just twenty years old. To have to participate in the official life of formal dinners of middle-aged people when she was a young girl longing for some informal fun was difficult for Shahnaz. I suggested they give some dances and hire an orchestra that could play some hot twist numbers. They did and the princess looked happier, but they stayed only two years. The shah resented the fact that they were not accorded the attention due a king's daughter by the young Kennedy couple in the White House.

The children came over on an Iranian Air Force 707 which, I must say, accommodated thirty-five of us comfortably. We flew first to Disney World in Florida, then to Yellowstone Park, San Francisco, Honolulu, Los Angeles, Acapulco, and back home, spending three nights in every place except for the four in Los Angeles where Crown Prince Reza, eighteen, who has since proclaimed himself shah, joined us. The three children were Princess Farahnaz, fifteen, Prince Alireza, twelve, and Princess Leila, eight. Each was accompanied by a uniformed military aide, and every time we landed the aides lined up at the foot of the ramp and kissed the hand of every child when they got off. It was an incongruous picture—these normal-looking kids wearing American jeans, T-shirts, cowboy hats, or other headgear they bought en route getting this imperial treatment.

The thirty-five passengers included Madame Diba, the empress's mother, one colonel and three majors of the Imperial Guard, five sergeants, four Iranian diplomats, four friends of the children, two personal maids, Leila's nurse, a U.S. protocol officer, and eight American guards. So the children didn't always have to have us along; and to thwart Zahedi's efforts to pay for our shelter, we accepted an invitation to stay with Cap and Jane Weinberger in San Francisco, Clare Luce in Honolulu, and Delores Hope in Los Angeles. (Bob was putting on a show somewhere. Delores said she only saw him on an average of one night a week. When she knew she was going to see him several days in a row her eyes crinkled with the excitement of a young girl planning a tryst with her lover—and Bob was then seventy-five years old!)

The trip was wonderful, from the caviar for lunch on the plane to the afternoon at the Gregory Pecks' house in Beverly Hills with the Kirk Douglases and Michael Yorks. The most fun of all was when Delores Hope took us to Hollywood Park race track where our hostess Florence Hamilton, a director of the track, had a table in the Turf Club smack next to that of another director, Cary Grant. Cary had as his guests Greg and Vernonique Peck, Zahedi, the crown prince, and his two sisters. Tips, talk, and laughter were shared between the two tables as we all tried to chalk up some wins. It was one glamorous day.

Ambassador Zahedi wanted the royal children to see how many hours it took to cross the United States and how many nationalities lived peacefully together under one flag. But he little dreamed that in six more months he would lose his country and his home and his servants, whose children were even shot. When he left Washington in January 1979 a lot of joy and kindness went with him.

* * *

I interviewed King Hassan of Morocco in his palace in Rabat during my first trip around the world; and I was allowed to watch a throne room ceremony from behind a latticed screen. It was the first and only time I saw a ruling king standing before a golden throne on a raised dais, holding out his hand to be kissed by his subjects, who on that day were all Moroccan ambassadors being sent to foreign lands. The king's political strength is due to the fact that he—as a direct descendant of Mohammed—is the spiritual leader of his country as well as the temporal. New to me was the practice of those closest to him of first kissing the outside of his hand, then turning it over to kiss the palm.

* * *

Prince Louis Napoleon Bonaparte of France looked, when we met in 1977, nothing like his illustrious ancestor. The handsome, charming gray-haired prince is 6′5″. "I get my height from the maternal side," he said with a grin.

I had met his attractive wife Alix at a party in Houston given by Joanne and Bob Herring. The princess, a tall good-looking brunette, was fun to talk to; she invited me to call her when I went to France, and gave me their Paris and Riviera phone numbers. In 1977 when we went to France to spend a week in Grimaud, a picturesque old town up the hill from St. Tropez, the Napoleons were at their gray stone villa at Cap Camarat. When I called she invited us over for lunch although they had let all their servants off for a holiday. I was delighted because the prince—clad in a navy blue knit sport shirt over swim trunks—did the cooking and even served me like a proper waiter. I told him I couldn't wait to tell my friends back home that Napoleon had waited on me! He was amused. Alix was wearing a long cotton skirt wrapped around her turquoise bathing suit. Later, when we relaxed on their terrace, some strangers appeared down below us walking along the rocky coastline. The prince explained: Napoleon I had enacted a law that made the entire coastal edge of France public property.

He was also amused at what interests Americans when I asked him if women curtsied to him. "Some do," he replied, obviously unimpressed by it. I knew that the only two titles in the French Republic recognized at the Elysee Palace were those of Prince Napoleon and the Count of Paris who was descended from the royal Kings Louis of France. In the two hundred years since Bonaparte, Louis, the great, great grandson of Emperor Napoleon's youngest brother Jerome, had acquired gallons of royal blood. After Napoleon refused to recognize Jerome's marriage to Elizabeth Patterson of Baltimore, he married Jerome off to Catherine, daughter of the king of Wurttemberg. Jerome became king of Westphalia and their son married the daughter of King Victor Emmanuel of Italy who was therefore Louis' great-grandfather. Louis' grandfather was King Leopold II of Belgium. In spite of all that, the prince was quite a guy. Because his ancestors had ruled France, he was exiled from the country until 1950 and he wasn't allowed to join either the French or British armies in World War II. Determined to fight for France, he joined the French Foreign Legion and later became an underground commando.

Back in Paris a few days later, Princess Alix invited us to lunch in their apartment on the Boulevard Suchet. Her husband was back at his banking business in Switzerland where they had another villa. The apartment was filled with Emperor Napoleon's belongings.*

---

* Having been a history major at Smith College and having taken a postgraduate course on Napoleon at the University of Chicago—and also being in the business

The first gold and enamel collar (or necklace) of the Legion of Honor, which he founded, reposed on a red velvet pillow displayed in an exquisite gold box. All his swords were spread out, fan-shape, in a corner alcove, paste "diamonds" having replaced the real ones in his coronation sword. In the bookshelves in the same living room were all the books he read in his last days on St. Helena—each stamped with the crude imperial bookmark his valet had carved from wood. A silver eagle on a stand was the only piece left of the emperor's silver. The rest had been sold to buy the necessities of his last barren days. On the wall was Jacques Louis David's famous portrait of Napoleon, the duplicate of which is in the National Gallery in Washington. All the chairs and settees were inherited from Tuileries Palace and covered with the original Beauvais tapestry, and on the wall in the dining room was a striking David portrait of the handsome Jerome.

*   *   *

Queen Helen of Romania was probably the most royal person in the world when I met her in Florence, Italy, in 1963 at the dinner given by Adlai's sister Buffie. She was so royal that I am sure if she had cut herself she would have bled purple.

The queen, a slender, beautifully groomed, warm woman, was the daughter of King Constantine of Greece, the granddaughter of Emperor Frederick III of Germany and George I of Greece, the great-granddaughter of Queen Victoria, Emperor Wilhelm of Germany, and King Christian IX of Denmark, a descendant of Catherine the Great of Russia and James I of England, the wife of King Carol of Romania, the mother of King Michael, the sister of three kings of Greece—George II, Alexander, and the then King Paul—and a cousin of the kings of Denmark, Norway, and Sweden and Queen Elizabeth of Britain. Not even the latter was kin to that many kings!

With all that privileged birth, her life had been anything but jolly. Her husband left her for his mistress, Madame Lupescu. Son

---

of chronicling the social history of Washington—I was overwhelmed by the sense of personal history that flooded that apartment.

Michael's reign was brief because the communists took over in 1945 and she lived under the hated Soviet rule before she and Michael escaped. "Romania," she said, "is the jewel box of Europe. Put anything down there and it grows." But the Russians took the farms away and tried to starve the people into submission. "Given their freedom, in five years they would have Romania blooming again." Many of the royal court, even servants, were still languishing in prison, if not dead. The powerful Anna Pauker, the Communist foreign minister of Romania, she said, would come to dinner and spend her time talking about how she trained mice and rats to do tricks during her prison years.*

Before the evening was over the queen, who had heard about America's dance rage, asked me to demonstrate the twist. I did: Next day she sent me an inscribed copy of her autobiography.

---

* Anna Pauker occupied the house in Bucharest that is now the residence of the American ambassador. She installed the indoor swimming pool.

CHAPTER 14

Golden Gavotte

The Reagan Era

Introducing Ronald Reagan at a dinner during his second term, Clare Boothe Luce said, "Woodrow Wilson called the presidency 'no bath of rosewater.' " She quoted George Washington at the outset of his second term, saying he "felt like a culprit going to the place of his execution"; John Adams had observed that "no man who ever held the office would congratulate a friend on obtaining it"; and Grover Cleveland called his second term "a self-inflicted penance for the good of the country." Warren Harding described the presidency as "a hell of a job" that gave him no trouble with his enemies, only with his "damn friends"; and James Buchanan said, "The presidency is a distinction far more glorious than the crown of any hereditary monarch in Christendom, but, yet, it is a crown of thorns." Then Mrs. Luce added, "Ronald Reagan, beloved at home and feared and respected abroad, also wears a crown of thorns, but Ronald Reagan wears it jauntily, cocked over one ear. He wears it smiling."

Indeed, Reagan was the most relaxed, most easygoing, most likeable president of the nine I have known. Even political enemies who tore him apart every chance they got, or who violently disagreed with him on all the issues, found it virtually impossible not to like him face to face. That was because he liked you, from the start. Nancy Reynolds, his assistant during his governorship, told me early on that when Ronald Reagan walked into a room he felt that everybody liked him because he liked everybody. Later, he told me that his mother always told him there was some good in everybody, and he grew up believing it.

It's a most disarming approach. If you think of people that way, you greet them with a sense of pleasant anticipation and a smile, and they respond by feeling good about you. Witness the first president in thirty years to serve two terms.

I voted for Ronald Reagan because he understood the dangers of communism, which was still expanding, and because his view of America lifted my spirits, and those of the majority of the country. But I disagreed strongly with his abortion stand; I told Nancy Reynolds so before the convention, adding that I thought it would turn off a lot of women. Later that day, I received a call from California. It was Ronald Reagan. He wanted to explain why he thought abortion was wrong. Amazed to hear his voice on the other end of the line, I listened; then I explained why I thought choice was right. In fact, I said vehemently, if [pro-lifer] Phyllis Schlafly was hanging from the nearest tree I wouldn't cut her down. Neither convinced the other, but pleasantness prevailed; *Roe* vs. *Wade* was still the law of the land, and he got my vote.

As a journalist, I had become acquainted with the Reagans at GOP conventions; but I got to know them on a friendlier basis during a governors' convention at White Sulphur Springs. There I interviewed Nancy for the first time. Then in May of 1980, in the thick of their campaign for the presidency, I received a call from Nancy's press aide at the time, Carol McCain, inviting me to the International Club for a luncheon-interview, the first with a Washington paper. The following September, I was invited to the supper party the Reagans gave at the Middleburg estate they leased from the Will Clements.* It was for members of the press who had traveled with Reagan and their spouses or dates. I didn't belong in either category, but it didn't matter. It could have been a gathering any couple might have for friends. No one took out a pen or notebook or tape recorder and tried to interview the pair who were less than five weeks from the election that would put them in the White

* It was Wexford, the modest house Jackie Kennedy had built on forty-six acres, and later sold.

House. Reagan's low-key manner, punctuated with humor that sent his eyebrows into an arch and deepened the laughter-lines around his eyes, set the tempo.

Come time for the fried chicken dinner at tables under a yellow and white striped marquee, I managed to sit at Reagan's table. During dinner he talked about Nancy's father, Dr. Loyal Davis, inventor of the aviator's flak helmet, who went with a delegation of doctors to Moscow during World War II. When it was time to pack up and leave, their medical instruments were missing, and it was Davis who had the gumption to confront the Russians with the robbery. Whereupon, various Russians pulled the articles out of their pockets and returned them. Reagan made the point that the Russians weren't the slightest bit embarrassed by being caught stealing; anything done for the state was considered okay. I think Dr. Davis' experience with the Soviet code of conduct made an early impression on Reagan, and probably influenced the formulation of his successful policy toward the USSR.

Less than a month after he was elected, Ronald Reagan set a completely new tone in presidential politics and confounded his most virulent critics: He and Nancy came to Washington and gave a private dinner at the 1925 F Street Club for the civic leaders of Washington, Democrats as well as Republicans. No president-elect had ever done that before. None had offered the hand of friendship to the residents, telling them, "I want this Capital to be a shining city on a hill." This man was 180 degrees removed from the shoot-from-the-hip, speak-before-you-think preconception that Democrats had accepted as gospel. The guest list included everyone from sports owner to music director, from businessmen to both white and black civic leaders. Marveled one guest, Austin Kiplinger of the *Kiplinger Newsletter*, "There is no organization in town that brings this varied a group together. He was demonstrating linkage between government and the capital city."

The difference between the Inaugurals of 1977 and 1981 was as night is to day. Two days before Jimmy Carter's Inauguration, the pickings were pathetically meager for reporters and Washington residents eager to meet "the new people." The calendar for January 18, 1977, shows two receptions—given by the *New Republic* and *Playboy* magazines and both sadly lacking in style and sustenance.

The weekend before the Reagan Inaugural, sixteen charming parties—not counting official inaugural functions—took place in three days, and drew hordes of the new people. Most were for incoming cabinet members or White House staffers, or the president's close friends, who had poured in from California to celebrate. Except for the eight inaugural balls that were the usual stand-and-stare crushes, the quadrennial celebrations were the most glamorous I have witnessed. The apres-ball seated dinner at the Jockey Club, given by the Guilford Dudleys of Nashville, was a dazzler from the black velvet and ivory taffeta gown worn by Mrs. Charles Price, whose husband would become ambassador to Great Britain, to the people there like actor Jimmy Stewart, the William Buckleys, and the Henry Kissingers—all the men in white tie and tails. The "new people" were well heeled and used to socializing in fashionable circles. Washington was suddenly awash with social excitement—and glamor. Suddenly, uncombed hairdos, messy beards, and raggedy jeans were a thing of the past.

The euphoria was heightened by the release of our hostages in Iran, whom the president greeted at the White House the morning of January 27. That evening, he and Nancy received the diplomatic corps at a reception. White tie and decorations were specified, to the delight of the diplomatic corps. Surprisingly, eighty or more of the 137 representatives of foreign nations had never set foot in the mansion before. President Reagan learned that evening for the first time the location of his ancestral home. Irish Ambassador Sean Donlon told him that Ballyporeen, the village of his great grandfather, had celebrated his Inaugural. Reagan, who had not seen it in the papers, told Donlon he had never known his heritage; his grandfather had died when his father was three and there were no family records. The ambassador promised to have his family tree drawn up to present to him on St. Patrick's Day.

The Reagans' first state dinner, on February 26, was for British Prime Minister Margaret Thatcher, and I was invited as a guest. As is customary, a uniformed aide checked my coat, another escorted me up the steps, another gave me my dinner table number, and still another called out my name over a microphone as I entered the East Room. From that point on, it differed in several ways from the Carters' state dinner I attended. Waiters circulated with trays of various spirits as well as wine and orange juice. Guests were not told where to stand until the last moment, when those with rank were lined up unobtrusively in front. Everyone looked toward the corridor when "Hail to the Chief" was played, and an aide announced, "The President of the United States and Mrs. Reagan and Prime Minister Thatcher of Great Britain and Mr. Thatcher." Entering before them, for the first time in four years, was the uniformed color guard of four, who split and flanked the doorway with the American and presidential flags.

Perhaps the most noticeable difference was in the socially sophisticated guest list. There were Mrs. Vincent Astor, former Ambassador to Britain Anne Armstrong and her husband Tobin, Mrs. David Bruce, widow of another ambassador to Britain, with CBS chairman Bill Paley, the David Rockefellers, Gloria Vanderbilt, the Averell Harrimans, and so forth. I wanted to be the last to go through the receiving line; I long ago discovered that it affords an unhurried chance for a word or two with the principals; but former Ambassador to Britain Walter Annenberg said he had been told by his wife to go to the end of the line. Noted hostess Lenore Annenberg, as the new chief of protocol, was introducing each guest for the first time. He now walked three paces behind her, said Annenberg, chuckling. Invited into the state dining room, guests found twelve tables for eight—ninety-six diners instead of 140; waiters no longer brushed against chairs or the heads of the guests. Gone, too, was the noise and bustle of forty or more cameramen, television technicians, and reporters maneuvering to cover the toasts; the toasts were given at the end of dinner instead of before, as in the Carter White House. Now, the photographers wore black tie, instead of rumpled shirts or jeans. There was no long queue of one hundred after dinner guests filling the main corridor. Only about twenty were invited and they simply joined the other guests for coffee, which, during the Reagan era, was minus caffeine.

After the show—a segment of the hit musical, *Chorus Line*—the Reagans bade their honorees goodnight, and the Marine Orchestra broke into the foxtrot, "Shall We Dance." The handsome hosts started the dancing in the front hall—the first to follow a state dinner since the Ford era. By 10:50 the Reagans had slipped away— an early departure considering that at no time was there a sense of haste. For every state dinner thereafter Ronald and Nancy Reagan would swing into a foxtrot at the musical cue, "Shall We Dance." They were both handsome and slender, and danced beautifully together, which added immeasurably to the scene, just as the buoyant beat and activity added to the party fun. But they never had rock music played at state dinners—even when they had finished dancing or retired from the scene—so that the floor was never crowded, and never as lively as it would otherwise have been.* During the Reagan era, too, the uniformed social aides never danced with feminine guests, a long tradition until Jimmy Carter cancelled the dancing altogether; they just held up the woodwork.

During the cocktail period I chatted with film star Charlton Heston, who couldn't remember the name of a familiar face he glimpsed across the room. Immediately, that reminded him of a story he once heard about columnist Walter Lippmann, who had the same problem. Some fifty years earlier, Lippmann was traveling in a Pullman car across the aisle from a nice-looking old lady. She seemed to know him, and looked familiar, but he couldn't place her. They struck up a conversation and she asked him if he had seen her son lately.

"Not recently," replied Lippmann. Hoping for a clue to her identity, he asked, "What's he doing these days?"

"He's president of the United States," she replied. Heston did not say if the columnist fell through the floor right onto the tracks, but he did say the elderly lady was Herbert Hoover's mother. And I printed it exactly as he told it. Later I received a letter from an out-of-town reader saying it must have been a remarkable conversation because Hoover's mother had died in 1884!†

The Washington scene never moved at a faster pace than during the first years of the Reagan administration. My calendar shows twelve parties one week, up to nineteen the next. It slackened for a week following the assassination attempt on Reagan. But only five weeks after he nearly died, Iron Man Reagan danced with his wife

---

* It was only at their evening bash for the lawmakers that Lester Lanin's orchestra burst into some wild and woolly rock after the Reagans retired.
† Elliott Roosevelt subsequently told me that the elderly lady was his grandmother, Sara Delano Roosevelt.

after their dinner for Japanese Prime Minister Suzuki. And, I thought, he danced longer than usual to signal to a worried world that he was in good condition.

At U.S. Information Director Charles and Mary Jane Wick's reception for Protocol Chief Lee Annenberg, seven members of the cabinet came with their spouses, and ten senior presidential staffers. On the heels of the huge private party given by close Reagan friends Jack and "Bunny" Wrather—who took over the Eisenhower Theater and the Kennedy Center Atrium to feed and amuse the cabinet, all the president's assistants, the entire Senate, about sixty Reagan friends, and one hundred others—young Ron Reagan appeared on a Washington stage. He danced in the Washington premiere of the Joffrey II dancers, and did very well as his parents watched approvingly.

The much reported "malaise" was long forgotten—at least in Washington, where the gaiety raised spirits, the entertaining did wonders for the local economy, and the new money in town gave a generous boost to cultural and charitable projects. And there was a new sparkle at the White House.

To add eclat to state dinners, President and Mrs. Reagan over the years sprinkled them with stars: Gregory Peck, Margot Fonteyn, Kirk Douglas, Carol Burnett, Helen Hayes, Jaclyn Smith, Dinah Shore, Burt Reynolds, Brooke Shields, Jessica Tandy and Hume Cronym, Joan Collins, and muscular Sylvester Stallone. (Sly was shorter than I had expected. He told me that they photograph him upwards from the floor to make him look taller.) At one state dinner, Gina Lollabrigida, former hottest star of filmdom, was surrounded by no fewer than twelve men! Actors, authors, musicians—all added to the glamor of the parties. When the after-dinner dancing began, Secretary of State George Shultz invariably took to the floor with a charmer.

"George always dances with the most glamorous woman," I observed to his wife "Obie."

"But," she said, smiling, "he sleeps with me."

At one dinner Mary Martin told Mrs. Dillon Ripley that "French Chef" Julia Child said she should always say "souffle" when being photographed, never "cheese." Whereupon the very proper Mary Ripley replied that the duchess of Northumberland once told her always to say "bitch" instead of cheese. The duchess was right. You get a better and less toothy expression that way.

The Reagans varied the guests at their tables, too. RR's could hardly have been more diversified than when he honored King Fahd of Saudi Arabia, who sat on Reagan's right. Then came Mrs. William Farish, occasional hostess to Queen Elizabeth at her horse farm in Lexington, Ky., Yogi Berra, manager of the New York Yankees; Mrs. John Connally, artificial heart surgeon Dr. William DeVries, religious leader Dr. Norman Vincent Peale, and Mrs. Clarence Pendleton, wife of the outspoken African-American chairman of the Civil Rights Commission. Representatives of society, sports, Texas, medicine, religion, and civil rights: Fahd could talk to Americans of six different sectors of the United States.

* * *

In mid-June George and I went to New York for the opening of the Royal Ballet and gala at Lincoln Center. The prince of Wales, rather than the ballet, was the star attraction. Conversations with H.R.H. were possible during the preperformance reception for those who paid an extra $1,000 per person. That was pennies in that world of the up-front social rich who support art and human services and have a ball doing it, and out they swarmed—four Rockefellers, Mrs. Astor, the Gordon Gettys, the Angier Dukes, and so forth. It's always nice, as a columnist, to sashay among the billionaires at the most desirable social functions without paying a nickel; even nicer, this time, was Lee Annenberg's act in seeking us out to introduce us to the prince, whose marriage to Diana would take place July 29.

Charles, I discovered—unlike his father, who is apt to be impatient or indifferent with strangers—looks straight at you during a conversation, responds, and never looks bored. That evening, he told me about his wedding plans. "I am going to have two full orchestras and Kiri" (Kiri Te Kanawa, the famous Maori-Australian soprano who sang at Covent Garden and the Met). He would be married in St. Paul's Cathedral because, he said, Westminster Abbey was too small to accommodate two full orchestras. The prince was a genuine music lover. When Armand Hammer introduced him to noted glass sculptress Pascal Regan, he was at once entranced with the sculptured glass Indian chief in gold headdress set with

emeralds, diamonds, rubies, and sapphires that she was wearing at
her neck. "That's one of the most beautiful things I have ever seen,"
he told her. Hammer promptly asked Pascal to design a wedding gift
for the royal pair. It would be a horse's head with flowing flexible
gold mane. Megamillionaire Hammer, who was born, he wrote, near
the heart of the Jewish ghetto in New York's Lower East Side,
delighted in every possible association with Prince Charles; he
immediately agreed to build a United World College, at the prince's
suggestion. The colleges, sponsored by Lord Mountbatten, brought
top students from many lands together as an instrument of future
world peace. Charles came to the dedication of Hammer's UWC at
Montezuma, New Mexico, where I had another opportunity to talk
to him. It was then fifteen months after his marriage, and he told me
that newspaper stories about him and Diana having a tiff were
fabrications.

"None of it is true," he insisted; and he wasn't reading the
newspapers any more because "it upsets me." I told him that all
America thought Diana was divine and approved his choice. He did
not accept the compliment as merely his royal due but replied
warmly, "I hope you will meet her sometime." He beamed when I
told him Merv Griffin called him "the greatest guest he's ever had
on his show." The prince surprised me with his next comment
because you would think that everyone would give the future ruler
of Great Britain his or her rapt attention: "He [Merv] listened to my
answers and looked me straight in the eye."

"So do you, Your Royal Highness," I told him, and I meant it.

Cary Grant and wife Barbara were at the dedication but it wasn't
till months later in Washington that Cary added a footnote. Cary
related how he was once shaking hands with President Nixon at a
White House function, when Nixon said how very much Pat had
liked one of his movies, but the name of it escaped him. One year
later, he was going through the line again: the instant Nixon saw
him, he said, *Houseboat*! The prince of Wales, said Grant, had the
same kind of memory.

Reagan had been president for only eight months when Dan
Rather did a segment on him in his evening newscast, mystifying
the White House by calling both the East and West Wings ahead of
time to alert them to watch.

The segment opened with a picture of President Carter in shirt sleeves at his White House party for country music singers. It could have switched to President Reagan in the turtleneck, sports jacket, and Western boots he had worn to his barbecue for Texas and California members of Congress that same week. But it did not. Instead, in order to illustrate "the riches and opulence of the Reagan administration," someone had to dig back into CBS files to find pictures of Reagan in white tie and tails which he had worn on the three occasions when the dressiest garb was called for: the Inaugural Ball, the newsmen's Gridiron Club annual dinner (when it is required) and his evening reception for ambassadors, who can't wear their decorations with any other attire. The segment wound up with pictures of the Reagans stopping by briefly at two fundraisers—a Phillips Gallery dinner with Bill Blass fashion show to raise money for the superb and financially troubled gallery, and the Ambassadors Ball at the Washington Hilton, a benefit for multiple sclerosis research. Naturally, the people at the gallery looked as rich as cream; the price was $250 a person. (The president was the only guest in a business suit.) The ball, at $300 a couple, was almost as dressy and it netted $200,000, its largest profit, because of White House participation. But the commentator didn't mention that each affair was a fundraiser and that the president had been boosting support for worthy causes. The socialites who attended either benefit thought it ill became the $2-million-a-year Rather to point a finger at anybody's riches; the president's salary was $200,000. Nonetheless, the criticism had an effect. The Reagans substituted black tie at their next two annual parties for diplomats, and in 1984 invited them to their most informal affair—a barbecue on the south lawn that was decorated with bales of hay, saddles on barrels, butter churners, little buggies, and wagon wheels. But rain was predicted so the whole thing was moved indoors where the ambassadors took their paper plates to the chow line and ate their big Western barbecued meal in the elegant East Room. And it never rained!

In midsummer of 1982 Washington witnessed something it had never seen before or since—a vigil in front of the White House by the wives of foreign ambassadors. Among the 125 women in black and holding candles, standing silently night after night, were the chatelaines of the embassies of Lebanon, Saudi Arabia, Syria, Qatar,

Tunisia, Sudan, and Oman as well as the wives of the chargés d'affaires of Jordan, Kuwait, and the Arab Emirates. They were silently demonstrating against Israel's invasion of Lebanon, and the leaflets they handed out listed the numbers killed, wounded, captured, and made homeless. They felt it was time women tried to stop, in the name of humanity, what men had wrought. The wives of former American ambassadors to Saudi Arabia and Qatar—Mrs. Jim Akins and Mrs. Andrew Kilgore—and former Peace Corps workers joined them. The most popular and prominent hostess among them was the beauteous and chic Nuha Alhegelan, who was born in Damascus, had a law degree, and was married to the Saudi Arabian ambassador. She was received by Nancy Reagan at the White House, and Nancy was moved to tears during their two-hour talk. It was already known that the president's top assistants, Ed Meese, Jim Baker, and Mike Deaver, had been opposed to Reagan receiving Israeli Prime Minister Begin after the invasion. Was the talk with Nancy the final straw that led to the resignation of Secretary of State Al Haig, who had pushed the Begin visit? Washington wondered.

* * *

Of all the First Ladies I have known, none has been so cruelly criticized by the press as Nancy Reagan. The vitriol had started well before the election. A writer on the *Evening Star* wrote a whole column attacking Nancy for offering chocolate candy to members of the press on the campaign plane. She made it look as if Mrs. Reagan forced the candy on them when they really didn't want the gooey stuff. It was a bewildering criticism of thoughtfulness. Nancy told me she was given a box of candy at every landing of the plane and the newspeople "looked tired and I thought it would give them a lift. I'll never offer any candy again," she said. Less than a week after Ronald Reagan was elected the fortieth president of the United States a two-part series about Nancy, written by a Los Angeles reporter, ran in the *Washington Post*. That the writer loathed Nancy was apparent right off; what had led to that enmity I would not know. I do know that a writer, with sarcasm, can produce any effect he or she desires.

One early detraction that was not true, yet would surface as fact from time to time during the entire eight years, was that it was Nancy's staff that came up with her antidrug project, the insinuation being that they had cooked it up to make her look good, because her own interests were so superficial. I had the first interview with Nancy after the election—on November 19—right after they arrived from California. At that time, she waxed eloquent about her most serious aim after January 20: to see what she could do about the widespread use of hard drugs by the young. Not only did she not have a staff at the time, but she had already visited a drug treatment center.

"I was so impressed with Daytop Village in New York City," she said, "I went twice. They do a fabulous job. These kids come voluntarily. They can leave any time they want to leave. They have something like 90 percent recovery. The ones there are so anxious to tell you how they got started, what made them finally change. I asked them, 'How do you feel about legalizing marijuana?' and all without exception said, 'No, it shouldn't be.' "

She stressed the same planned project in the *Washington Post* interview the next day. During Reagan's governorship they had tried to educate the schoolchildren about drugs. One Washington detractor, who asked later why it took her so long to get the drug project started, did not know that three weeks after moving into the White House she met with a group of medical professionals brought in to brief her on their evaluation of drug and alcohol abuse among the young. That was in February. In March the president was shot and that, understandably, delayed her project.

Mrs. Reagan also talked to me that day about her longtime interest in the Foster Grandparents Program, which she planned to maintain. One of the most touching events I ever attended was her luncheon in October 1982 to honor foster grandparents, each seated beside a little, handicapped "grandchild." When I walked among the tables under a big marquee on the south lawn and saw the love expressed by, and for, those little children, there was a lump in my throat. Frank Sinatra was there to sing the appealing song, "To Love A Child" which, embarrassingly, he hadn't really learned.

Nancy was made fun of for keeping her eyes on her husband the entire time he was making a speech. I asked her early on, why didn't she occasionally look at the audience? She smiled. "You mean to take a count? First of all, I think it's rude not to look at someone

when they're speaking. And, secondly, I can't listen without looking. I can't digest what someone is saying without looking at them. I
would do it if you were making a speech." As for her husband's
abortion stand, Mrs. R., who, according to some reports was anti-
abortion herself, said, "It shouldn't even be a political issue." That
is certainly what we prochoicers believe.

When Nancy visited the children's ward at Howard University
Hospital—the first First Lady since Eleanor Roosevelt to do so—
Washington Post columnist Judy Mann called it a "cheap publicity
stunt" for Nancy to embrace the little kids. Had Mann taken the
trouble, she could have learned that Nancy had been visiting hospital patients, particularly children, since long before she became a
governor's wife. She was good with kids, and frequently went out to
the Rock Creek Riding Center to observe the riding program for
handicapped children.

When Jackie Kennedy got millions of dollars in donations of
money and furnishings to bring beauty, taste, and authenticity to the
White House, she was praised and most deservedly so. When Nancy
Reagan got a little under $1.2 million donated to pay for a much-
needed redoing of the second floor and painting of the first floor, she
was castigated—although she hadn't spent a nickel of the taxpayers' money. The same goes for the beautiful china Mrs. R.
ordered. That was paid for by Ann Vojvoda, president of the Knapp
Foundation. And it was certainly needed. Mrs. Lewis Powell told
me that when coffee was poured into her cup at the White House
luncheon for new Supreme Court Justice Sandra O'Connor, it ran
out of the cracks into her saucer and had to be whisked away by a
waiter. When the man next to her turned his coffee cup upside
down to indicate he didn't want any, there were six nicks in the
bottom of it. The Johnson china may not have been used for that
luncheon, but there was not enough of the LBJ china* to serve a
state dinner without substituting other patterns for some courses.
Regardless of the supply, I can see no objection to acquiring even an
extra set of beautiful china for the White House if it is not charged to
U.S. citizens.

---

* Even Clement Couger, whom Nancy had dismissed as White House curator,
reported this.

By her second year Mrs. Reagan thought media criticisms of her were lessening. Still, some in the press couldn't resist the opportunity to cast her in the role of a big spender. She was attacked for using a helicopter to get to Camp David "at the taxpayers' expense." The writer should have done her homework, said Mrs. R. "I go the way the Secret Service tells me to go. They don't like you to go in a car beyond—I think it's 45 miles."

One reason the criticism may have been on the wane was the awards Nancy received in the first year and a half for her charitable work. In November 1982 the Salvation Army presented her with its Distinguished Service Award—the first First Lady to win it entirely on her own. It was "for her abiding concern for the most vulnerable in our society," which included her efforts in the Foster Grandparents program and in heightening "national awareness of drug abuse and its destructive consequences."

After ten months of the carping Nancy's able press secretary, Sheila Tate, exclaimed in frustration over the press blackout of Mrs. R's substantial efforts in the extremely serious drug abuse problem while writing about the new china or "silly things like the postcards of Mrs. Reagan as queen." On the one hand, they criticize her for not doing enough; on the other, they ignore her real contributions, said Sheila.* But the same could be said of media treatment of every First Lady: The public prefers colorful fluff—and it's far more fun to read about the faults of the people on top of the heap than their virtues.

At some point during the loudest carping, close Reagan friend and USIA chief Charles Wick asked me if I would jot down some notes on how to improve Nancy's press. I dashed off some informal suggestions and mailed them to him, feeling certain that they probably wouldn't be followed; some of them opposed her husband's policies. Among other things I said she could gain instant popularity among the press if she came out for ERA and abortion rights. The fact that she could have an independent view from the president's would win her widespread admiration. Betty Ford was proof of that.

* Lloyd Kaiser, president of the TV station that produced the antidrug program, "The Chemical People," told me he learned how the parents of addicted children felt about her: "She's St. Nancy of the parent groups."

(I doubt that Wick ever showed Nancy my notes because no great fondness existed between Mrs. R. and Mrs. Ford.) I also thought it would help her to be more forthcoming with the press; to have press conferences or invite them to something. Jackie Kennedy had treated a huge group of newswomen to a luncheon in the East Room. Lady Bird had welcomed us on several occasions. Pat invited us all up to the second floor to see the new decorations. I thought it would have helped Nancy to show off the beautiful results of her redo of the second floor.*

But Nancy was afraid to open up to the press at that point because she had been so badly burned. Her most successful experience with the press was her annual welcome to men and women of the media to show off the Christmas decorations. On those occasions, there were questions that had nothing to do with Christmas that Nancy answered with giggles and banter; the results were always good-natured. She had a different special person each time disguised as Santa Claus and had the White House photographer take a picture of each newsperson seated on Santa Claus's lap. (The one of me sitting on the lap of Mr. T. of "The A-Team" with all that gold jewelry around his neck is a scream.)

Like her predecessors, Mrs. R. was well organized. (I doubt if a candidate with a disorganized wife could get elected.) She worked with a list and took care of everything on it. According to Elaine Crispen, her assistant and, later, press secretary, she sent boxes of candy and gifts to the stenographers and telephone operators and never forgot a birthday, anniversary, or special occasion. "After every state dinner she will get a stack of the pictures that were taken and write notes and send them to friends." I was the pleased recipient of some.

Judging by her mail (450 to eight hundred letters a week for Nancy Reagan in the first half of 1981, to increase to one thousand in 1982), Americans feel a personal bond with—if not a claim on—every First Lady. One writer wanted to spend a relaxing weekend at the White House; another, an American, came from a coal mining family in Wales, and wanted to go to the wedding of Prince Charles

* She invited only *Architectural Digest* magazine to photograph it. She also gave a British photographer, young Lord Derry Moore, permission to take pictures of it.

and Diana with her. (Her boss at her Las Vegas bank had told her she "could have the time off only if I go with Mrs. Reagan.") Wrote a third, "My daughter and her husband are having trouble making ends meet. Please send them some money. Between $50,000 and $100,000 would take care of their problems."

After the president's reelection, while they were still in California, I interviewed Nancy via telephone, taping the whole conversation. I began by asking her what had angered her the most during the hard-hitting campaign.

NANCY REAGAN: "That he was uncaring; not compassionate; didn't care for people who were elderly or poor; that he is cruel. That angered me the most. They did that in California when he was running for governor. It's always been the same theme they have consistently done. How can you be accused of being cruel and uncaring when you have brought inflation down and unemployment down? That benefits everybody. It doesn't just benefit one section. He has created 6 million new jobs. I think a lot of people don't understand, really. They think when a man is president he can do everything he wants to do. They don't really understand how it works. A Congress can stop you cold."

B.B.: "Recently three journalists said on TV that the president works only four hours a day. What is the truth about his average work day and week?"

N.R.: "I heard that, too. All you have to do is get his schedule. It's out every day for them to see. That's another one I'm getting a little tired of. He is at his office at quarter of nine every morning. He gets home around 5:30 or 6:00 and works after dinner. He never comes over to the mansion for lunch. Four hours a day! You couldn't get anything done in four hours a day! And when you have a schedule that's distributed every day to the press—come on, let's be a little fair about this."*

B.B.: "President Truman told me he took two and sometimes three catnaps a day and awakened refreshed. Both Jack Kennedy and Lyndon Johnson went to bed after lunch and napped before returning to the Oval Office. Does President Reagan take any naps?"

* (Members of her staff I talked to confirmed those hours.)

N.R.: "No, never, never."

B.B.: "Except when he dozes in cabinet meetings?"

N.R.: "I don't know what Mike [Deaver] was talking about. I have never been in a cabinet meeting and Mike has not been in all the cabinet meetings. I've had people call me who have been in all the cabinet meetings who say it's not true. I know Mike was upset about that."

B.B.: "Maybe he was being funny."

N.R.: "Maybe."

B.B.: "A lot of people worry about your being so thin and think you need building up. I know you keep the president on a well-balanced diet that will also keep him trim, but shouldn't you be on a different and more fattening diet?"

N.R.: "I eat! I am now eating what he doesn't like, so I'm giving him something else. I eat calves' liver, spinach, all those things to build up your blood. I am well. I am fine. I burn it up. I'm like Pat Nixon, I guess. Pat ate but it never stayed with her. We have for dinner, every night, meat or chicken or whatever; potatoes or starch of some kind; we have vegetables, salad, and we have dessert. I don't eat as much as Ronnie does, but then he's bigger than I am. [At 5′ 4″ she wore a size 4 dress!] The doctor wanted me to get my red count up. The red count was down. You know it takes awhile to build your red count up. It really takes almost a year. It's not going to happen overnight. It's up from what it was."

B.B.: "One hears that Patti wishes her father was not president, instead of being proud that the country has chosen him to lead the nation. Can you explain her feelings?"

N.R.: "Her feelings? No—no."

B.B.: "Some of the other presidential children haven't cared for the spotlight, the Secret Service always in attendance, and the fawning of people, but as Patti is an actress, shouldn't the publicity be the best thing in the world for her?"

N.R.: "Patti is a grown woman, married, and has her own life, and I can't worry about that anymore. I wrote an article for Mother's Day for my mother [*Family Weekly*, May 13, 1984]. I hope for Patti's sake—as I said in the article, the saddest thing is to be an 'if only' child. When it's too late to say, 'If only I had done this. If only I had done that.' I hope for her sake she will not be. But there's nothing I can do. That's a problem Patti's going to have to face and Patti's going to have to solve."

B.B.: "She doesn't realize what she's missing?"

N.R.: "No, she doesn't. I have a wonderful son. I really do. Did you read his article in the new *Playboy* magazine? It's very, very good. He has a good style; his vocabulary's good. He has a great sense of humor that runs all through it. He's a darling boy who more than makes up for everything. And Maureen, who now calls me mother."

B.B.: "Maureen seems to be the president's only child who has inherited his love of politics and ability to speak forcefully."

N.R.: "Yes, but you know that's really not a negative for the others. Everybody has their own particular interests and abilities. Ron likes writing. He is also doing a daily radio show. He reviews movies. Doria is writing also. Doria is a very good cook and she does some food and recipe columns for a magazine."

B.B.: "Do you know what Maureen's plans are?"

N.R.: "No, I don't. I said to her the other night [in California], 'Am I going to lose my star boarder now?' And she said, 'Oh, no. I'll be back. I won't be there as much, but I'll still be there.' "

B.B.: "The president and Michael don't seem to be very close. Is that because he lived with his mother after they were divorced?"

N.R.: "So did Maureen live with her mother. [Pause] There is an estrangement and has been for three years. And I think really we should now say this and get it all done with so we can put these questions behind us. There *is* an estrangement. We are sorry about it. We hope that someday it will be solved. We do not believe and have never believed in discussing family problems in public. And that's it."

B.B.: "Have you another project up your sleeve for the next four years?"

N.R.: "I will stay with the drug thing and Foster Grandparents. I think you can spread yourself too thin and not do anything well. The whole drug problem is such a tremendous, tremendous problem and it takes an awful lot of time, effort and work. The Chemical People project took months of work. No, I will stay with that."

She answered my remaining questions as follows: Two of the most exciting times of the first four years were spending their wedding anniversary on the *Britannia*, the Queen of England's yacht, and going to China. She could see the changes happening there. She gave her clothes when she was through with them to a lot of cousins (in Atlanta who are also wee sizes). And to a lot of friends, friends people don't know anything about because they are names they don't recognize. She didn't read "Doonesbury," whose strip frequently attacked the president; she liked it better when comics were for kids, in the days of "Orphan Annie" and "Maggie & Jiggs." She didn't think they should be political commentary.

What legacy did she want to leave behind?

"Hopefully, that I cared about people—and—helped with the drug problem."

* * *

When I talked to Mrs. Reagan on the phone that day, my column for the following weekend had already been mailed. So I wrote it for the weekend after that. It appeared in the *Washington Times* on Monday, November 26, but it wasn't promoted, nor even put on the front page of the "Life" section. Helen Thomas of the UP told me she did not see my scoop until Wednesday when she called Michael Reagan to get his reaction. She promptly sent out a big story on the UP wire which the *Washington Post* played up on the front page of its "Style" section the next day, which happened to be Thanksgiving. As Helen, using direct quotes, had given me full credit throughout her story, there I was being played up prominently in the *Post*. Of course, the *Times* looked ridiculous. In fact, an embarrassed *Times* reporter called me to ask for a follow-up of some kind. Michael's reaction had been so vehement that every TV news show had gotten into the act. My harmless, delicately put question to Mrs. Reagan and her caring, concerned reply produced headlines for seven days. The sad part was Michael's violent reaction to Nancy's mild remark, which he referred to as her "holiday greeting." "Making a statement like that the day before Thanksgiving," he said, "was unthinkable." He did not know that she had made it ten days or so earlier.

Nancy's recollection of our conversation in her book, *My Turn*, is totally different. She has the unnamed *Times* interviewer pressing her with question after question about Michael until "finally, frustrated and at the end of my rope," she answered. As I only referred to Michael once—exactly as stated above—I think subsequent stories built up a sense of pressure in her that made her recollection of it different. I had based my questions on Michael's own several public statements critical of his father. Indeed, in the follow-up the *Times* requested, I wrote, "It is hard to see how such public attempts to embarrass his father would make him more desirable to have around." And in my column the following week I pointed out that Michael (who felt neglected) had not even bothered to answer the first or the second invitation to half-sister Patti's wedding, and had not accepted invitations to appear beside his father during the campaign and on election night. Since then, much misunderstanding on both sides has been cleared up.

I took Nancy's side again when her role in the departure of Don Regan from the president's chief of staff job evoked an outcry. Any number of people had come to her to use her influence with her husband to get Regan to retire because they thought he was not helping the president. When Nancy did just that, columnist Bill Safire criticized her sharply, calling her "unelected and unaccountable." I pointed out that nobody on the president's staff had been elected; as for accountability, if a woman has no responsibility for her man, who does? And "news columnists are neither elected nor accountable, yet they tell officials often and vehemently what to do, stimulating public demand for action." I ended up saying, "The country owes Nancy Reagan gratitude, not censure."

* * *

I had my last interview with Nancy one month before the Reagans bid goodbye to Washington. We talked about how much work the wife of a president must do.

"There are not enough hours in the day," she said. "I never envisaged it that way." When she and the president had a quiet evening in the mansion they both did some work after dinner. But, unlike Rosalynn and Betty Ford, she did not recommend a salary for First Ladies. A high point of their eight years was, she said, "The IMF Treaty—the trip to Russia which was part of that. Going to the Bolshoi that night and standing, the four of us [with Mikhail and Raisa Gorbachev], there in that box in that beautiful theater which I had never seen before, and having our flag on one side and their flag on the other and having their orchestra play our national anthem.

The people of Russia, who were so friendly and warm, cheered. When we were driving we had no idea how we would be treated by the people, and they were lining the streets."

I asked her how she would describe Barbara Bush to someone who did not know her. Said Nancy, "She's very capable, strong, friendly, and warm, and certainly knows her way around Washington."

In addition to her campaign to wake up parents to the problems of their drug-addicted children, Nancy Reagan, like Jackie and Pat, added to the beauty of the mansion. She renovated the upstairs from floors to furniture. The beautiful antiques she rescued from the government warehouse made the once uninteresting, long, second floor hall a place of charm and warmth. "I read a couple of stories that called it Hollywood glitz," said Nancy. Instead, it was a testament to her taste. That very week the American Museum Association awarded the whole mansion—the second and third floors included—museum status.

Nancy Reagan was the most controversial First Lady of my time. Perhaps the more strident approach of a younger press was one reason. Some reporters continually identified her with a rich lifestyle; yet the only thing richer about her lifestyle than those of her immediate four predecessors were her clothes and her friends, and neither were any richer than Jackie Kennedy's. But Nancy had been an actress—always fair game for the media—and remained a strong woman who felt things deeply, a perfectionist, a worrier. My enormous clipping file on Nancy shows that, more than any other First Lady, she caused women reporters to get out their knives. Why? She had had a career, was goodlooking and extremely chic, had divine clothes, entertained well, and on top of that was married to a handsome, macho man who was mad about her and just happened to be the president of the United States. Was it too much to take?

*   *   *

Let me take you, now, along to some of the glamorous places George and I visited during that extravagant Reagan era.

In January 1983, we reveled in a weekend stay in the house Queen Elizabeth would visit a month later. For beauty with every glance and luxurious comfort at every move, the Walter Annenbergs' Palm Springs (Calif.) estate, Sunnylands, has few equals in the world. We stepped inside the one-story house onto a coral-tinged marble floor in a 50′ by 50′ atrium where flowers and palms grew along the base of two lava rock walls. On the wall facing the door hung one of Renoir's finest works, *The Daughters of Catulle Mendes*. In the far corner, a towering skylight beamed on an indoor garden of hundreds of pink bromeliads centered by a pool, from which rose the original bronze cast of Rodin's *Eve*.*

The adjoining 60′ by 40′ drawing room combined comfort and beauty with such magnificent paintings on the walls that one felt enriched in their presence: Van Gogh's *Vase of White Flowers*, Monet's spectacular big canvas, *Iris*, and his *Water Lilies*, Gauguins, Cezannes, Seurats, Bonnards, Manets, Picassos, along with exquisite Chinese porcelain and contemporary sculpture, all in a setting so masterfully decorated by Ted Graber (who did the second floor of the White House in 1981) that the huge room did not appear oversized.

As we had been friends of the Gerald Fords, Lee (who had resigned her protocol job) invited the former president and Betty to dinner our first night along with Mary Martin, Ambassador and Mrs. Leonard Firestone, Barbara Sinatra (Frank was performing somewhere), and the Edward Hudsons of Houston. The evening was delightful, but a unique delight awaited us the next day. After golfing on Walter's two hundred-acre velvety green course dotted by trees and man-made mirror-lakes (Firestone said almost anywhere in the desert if you dig down six hundred feet you hit water) we and our hosts were served lunch by footmen in the middle of the course in a picture-perfect pink pagoda gazebo! Walter said he would not let Lee Trevino play on his course because Trevino took "over-sized divots." Guests were asked not to replace any divots (leaving a brown dead spot) because a groundskeeper would follow with fresh soil and seed to restore the damaged spot. There were no traps or

---

* That was only a small part of the art in the atrium that had accommodated eighty people for dinner and dancing, including President and Mrs. Reagan, on the just-past New Year's Eve. That was where Bob Hope and Gloria Stewart did a soft shoe, Dolores Hope and stage star Connie Tower (beautiful actress wife of ambassador to Mexico Jack Gavin) sang, and Jimmy Stewart warbled his one and only ditty, "Ragtime Cowboy Joe."

rough on the course; Walter was more affected by the serene perfection around him than by the challenge of golf.

We stayed in the first suite in the guest wing, which the Reagans had occupied. It overlooked the natural-looking pond that was the outdoor swimming pool. The indoor pool was in the Annenbergs' wing, along with the Memory Room, full of such memorabilia as handwritten notes from Queen Elizabeth and Walter's certificate of knighthood. (He was the only U.S. ambassador to the Court of St. James to be knighted.)

We narrowly missed another member of the royal family of Britain—Prince Andrew—when we visited close Washington friends, Betty Lou and Mandy Ourisman, at Tryall, Jamaica, in March. Their house was the showplace on the island, beautifully decorated and ideally served by a staff of thirteen.

During our visit, we had cocktails at jewel merchant Douglas Cooper's house and our host told of the time he had taken $15 million worth of gems to Saudi Arabia, at the request of a Saudi prince. Late one evening, the prince let all the women in his family pass the stones around for inspection, each in its own bag. When he gathered up the bags afterward, one was empty. Immediately, the prince said he would pay for the missing gem, whatever its worth, $25,000 or $750,000. The next day, Cooper discovered two stones in one bag; he informed the prince that all was well. It wasn't until a friend asked him, "How did they test you?" that he realized his honesty had been on the line.

Kentucky Derby weekend, we and the Henry Kissingers and Beverly Sills, with her husband Peter Greenough, were houseguests of the Cornelius Vanderbilt Whitneys at their horse farm in Lexington, Ky. It was a happy taste of the easy life. Our busy hostess provided for every possible need from a list of servants to send for, to advice on clothes suitable for an occasion, to comfortable transportation. Kissinger and Sills were not the only celebrities at the Derby. Jerry and Betty Ford were at the Churchill Downs track, but weren't even glimpsed till they cashed in their winning tickets, while Jimmy and Rosalynn Carter were being photographed at every turn. They had some competition from the Whitneys' box where Kissinger bantered with Beverly, and attracted a stream of autograph seekers throughout the afternoon. One man got his on a $100 bill.

The most glamorous experience of our lives took place in Venice, a city of visual poetry, in August of 1983. The remarkable Mariapia Fanfani, whose husband a month prior had been prime minister of Italy, invited us, had Gregory Peck round up a galaxy of film stars, and housed us all in either the Danielli or the Gritti Palace—both to pay a four-day memorial tribute to Ingrid Bergman, and to benefit the Italian Red Cross.

The tributes were in the enchanting eighteenth-century Fenice Theatre, with its four tiers of boxes framed in the firefly glow of hundreds of little lamps. Afterward, the dressy *haut monde* assemblage walked the dimly lit ancient streets to the nearby Gritti. There they supped on the hotel's terrace by the moonlit Grand Canal, the soft light of Venetian lanterns falling on the beautifully dressed counts and countesses of Venetian society, on Gregory and Veronique Peck, Charlton and Lydia Heston, the Roger Moores, elegant Audrey Hepburn with Robert Wolpers, Liza Minelli and husband Mark Gero, Dudley Moore and Susan Anton, Walter and Carol Matthau, Claudette Colbert, Olivia de Havilland, Maximilian Schell, Prince Albert of Monaco, the strikingly handsome young Roberto Rossellini and his half-sister Pia Lindstrom, Italian Ambassador to Washington and Mrs. Rinaldo Petrignani, our Ambassador to the Vatican and Mrs. Bill Wilson, and Rome's leading political hostess, the always dazzlingly gowned Countess Donatella Zegna, and her fiance Count Dino Pecci Blunt, the great-great-nephew of Pope Leo XIII. Every night we, with the rich, creative, and Beautiful People, boarded motor launches to dine at another palazzo, where we might run into designers Karl Lagerfeld, Laura Biagiotti, Balestra, Mila Schoen, and Krizia. Every day we cruised to another island for lunch—Hemingway's favorite place, or the fabulous gardens of the Cipriani Hotel. We took gondola rides on smaller canals, or walks over their decorative bridges and visits to the wonderful center of everything, St. Mark's Square. Glamor, elegance, and antiquity in that romantic setting made for pure enchantment.

Two years later we would soak up the splendor at a three-day, four-party housewarming at Albemarle Farms, the nine thousand-acre estate near Charlottesville, Va., of billionaire John Kluge and his British wife Pat. It's not every day you run into a fellow who will take over half a hostelry for his 120 guests (at Boar's Head Inn) and then indulge them in one treat after another. Their new Georgian mansion looked two hundred years old, tastefully decorated as it was with the finest antiques, objects of art, and French silk taffeta curtains. The domestic staff of fourteen included a butler and foot-man elegantly garbed in striped-pants-and-cutaway livery.

"Patricia calls it Albemarle House," said John Kluge. "I call it out of control." Of hand-made brick, the mansion was said to have cost $20 million, with the furnishings probably adding another $10 million. It boasted an eighteen-hole golf course, a private shoot, a swimming pool, tennis court, unbelievably handsome stables, a marvelous collection of fine coaches, several natural ponds stocked with bass, and nine hundred head of cattle.*

Into such sumptuous surroundings came ex-King Constantine of Greece, the guest of honor; Lord and Lady Romsey and Lady Carina Fitzalan-Howard, daughter of the premier peer of Britain, and her husband David Frost, and a slew of notables from all points of the compass in America. We dined formally the first night, pic-nicked at lunchtime the next day, when press lord Rupert Murdoch joined the group, and whooped it up in Western dress that evening in Kluge's cattle auction house. That was when octogenarian Mrs. Douglas MacArthur danced on the stage with country-Western star Mel Tillis. Cocktails before dinner were served between two rows of stalls in the odorless and pristine-clean cattle barn. There, the beige Simmental cows had tails fancily groomed and the little top-nots of hair brushed up into a point and fixed with hairspray. All stood on absolutely spotless blond wood shavings; not a single one had dirtied her flooring. Do billionaires have the secret to house-breaking cattle, I wondered? They do. They had been fed dry hay for two days, said the foreman!

The prince of Wales came back to America in the fall of 1985. This time, he brought Diana to attend a fundraising ball in Palm Beach for the benefit of the Armand Hammer United World College.

Any couple who wanted could attend the before-dinner reception

---

* When the Kluge marriage broke up in less than five years, rumor blamed Patricia's extracurricular flirtations; still, she got her "English country house," nine acres around it, and a rumored $1 million a year alimony.

for the royal couple and have a picture taken with the glamorous pair—for $50,000! The cash appeal of the Waleses was probably greater than any other living couple. Those only attending the dinner and dance paid a mere $10,000 a couple. Billionaire Ross Perot brought his wife and several others in his family to the dinner-dance to pay back a favor Hammer had done him. When I greeted Perot, I mentioned his newest fame—being listed by *Forbes* magazine as the second richest man in America. "It's bad being second best at anything," said the Texan with a grin. "I got a wire from the governor saying, 'Get to work. You have disgraced our state.' "

Some newspapers panned the party and made fun of the amount of money Americans will pay to mingle with royalty; Charles was not amused. After dinner and a bit of dancing with Diana, he stepped up to the mike to thank those present for contributing to a worthwhile cause. Then, to the surprise of everyone so accustomed to seeing royalty go through the required forms with calm compliance, he lashed into the critics. Where else, he asked in obvious anger, could you get financial support except from people who could afford to give? The students at United World Colleges "learn about service to others, about compassion and understanding the other man's religion and customs and history. There's so much to be done in this world; so much disease, poverty, bigotry, and prejudice, and so many people crying out for their dreams to come true." The graduates "leave with a new outlook about their fellow men and I want to put them to work." His audience broke into applause.

After a long day that included a polo match for the prince he was tired and ready for sleep in their assigned house at the Palm Beach Polo and Country Club, but a nightcap party ensued in the adjoining house for all his staffers who had worked so hard. "So there I was sitting up in bed eating cereal and ice cream and listening to everyone having a good time," confided Diana the next day.

In August George and I went to Saratoga Springs for another horsey weekend with Sonny and Marylou Whitney; other guests were Walter Cronkite and wife Betsy, Ginger Rogers, Texas centimillionaire Bob Mosbacher and his beautiful Georgette, and Manhattan bachelor Budd Calisch. All the newspapers in the area featured photos of the celebrated Cronkite whose book on sailing, *North By Northeast*, was just out. And every paper picked up this quote: "When I go," said Walter, "I would like to go like Errol Flynn—on the deck of my seventy-foot yacht with a sixteen-year-old mistress." Countered Betsy, "No, you're going to go on a sixteen-foot boat with your seventy-year-old mistress." Cronkite had arrived at the Whitneys' plush Cady Hill estate without a stitch of underwear so Betsy had to rush out and buy him some. In his new skivvies and dinner clothes he danced up a storm that night. He's a very good dancer. Ginger Rogers got the rush you would expect Fred Astaire's most famous partner to get, but, with a game leg, wasn't her usual graceful self. The local paper took a picture of her when my superdancer George was twirling her around and ran it side by side with one of Ginger and Fred. I surprised my husband with a framed copy at Christmastime.

* * *

The Symphony Ball in December of 1986 was my last opportunity to have a word with CIA Director Bill Casey. He knew he could trust me. He and Secretary of State George Shultz were often not in agreement, and when Bill expressed the opinion at a small private dinner one night that "Shultz is a disaster," I did not quote him. So I was hoping for something more confidential on the Iran-Contra subject that was raging all over town, when I asked him if he was going to resign. The answer was no. And as for those people who said he should have known about the bank funds going to the contras, he said, "I am forbidden by law to be involved. I didn't know about it." If he knew about it he took that information with him when he died a few months later of a brain tumor. It is possible that the tumor had already affected his memory.*

At a small dinner we gave for UN Ambassador Lt. Gen. Vernon (Dick) Walters, he was questioned about UN reaction to the Iran affair. Europeans, he said, told him, "We hope you are not going into

* Whereas House of Representatives Democrats took the position that aid to the contras was a crime, a group of Soviet defectors honored at a party sponsored by the Jamestown Foundation (that aided defectors in America) took the opposite view. Young physicist Dmitri Mikhcycv, who spent six years at hard labor for forming a discussion group at Moscow University, said Americans had to support the contras to help them overthrow the Sandinistas. Stan Levchenko, the famous defector from Tokyo, told me, "There is no other way than to help the contras."

one of your penetential frenzies that paralyze you from exercising the leadership you should be exercising." German Ambassador Guenther van Well, asked what effect it was having on our European allies, replied: "England has pragmatism, France has 'raison d'état' [reasons of state], and Germany has 'Realpolitik.' The American press," he added with a grin, "is so moral." The CIA's director, Bill Webster, smiled when he told me he had the job of using the $100 million Congress appropriated for arms for the contras without being allowed to send any Americans within twenty miles of Nicaragua!*

In May of 1987, George and I went to the biggest private extravaganza I have ever attended. It was given by Malcolm Forbes at his Far Hills, N. J., estate to celebrate the seventieth anniversary of *Forbes* magazine. The late "Malcolm the Magnificent," as he was called in a magazine article, did nothing in a small way. An immensely wealthy advocate of capitalism, he believed that spending on a grandiose scale brought more subscribers to his business magazine. We had been to several parties aboard his luxurious yacht *The Highlander* when it was docked on the Potomac River, and we were among a group of friends flown to New York on his *Capitalist Tool* plane for a dinner cruise around the Statue of Liberty. (The Statue of Liberty was most aptly described during its centennial as "the world's greatest symbol second only to the cross," by Jean Tammenoms Bakker, wife of the former Dutch ambassador, "because it offers a second chance.") But those other Forbes parties were small potatoes compared to the anniversary blast; it drew so many bigwigs by helicopter it took twenty-five minutes just to land. One thousand guests, including 245 chairmen or presidents of corporations, dined in comfort on the lawn under a huge tent. At every woman's place was a small sterling silver bowl from Tiffany (engraved with the most important date in her life) and at every man's place books of *The Sayings of Chairman Malcolm* which encompassed such wisdom

---

* Two weeks before much-admired Secretary of Commerce Malcolm Baldrige died I saw him at dinner at the Italian Embassy where we discussed the contradictory customs of Congress—i.e., accusing Americans of breaking an aid-to-contra law whose restrictive provisions were later lifted by Congress. Mac then sent me a note listing ten laws Congress had made for every American except themselves.

as: "To seduce most anyone ask for and listen to his opinion." (How right he was!) Everybody was given a booklet listing the guests and their table numbers; so if you wanted to talk to Elizabeth Taylor, Mrs. Vincent Astor, David Rockefeller, Beverly Sills, CIA Director Bill Webster, and so on through the list of the rich, famous and elite, you could easily find them. Even Doris Duke, once the richest little girl in the world, was there, seated next to Henry Kissinger—who was now making enough money to speak her language. We danced to Lester Lanin's music and gasped at the most magnificent gesture of the evening—Malcolm presenting a check for $1 million to Elizabeth Taylor for her AIDS research campaign.

The finale of that fabulous fiesta did not come till months later when a handsome engraved silver picture frame from Tiffany's arrived, with a picture of us in it; even later all who had been there received a video of the party from the elaborate preparations months ahead to the sendoff fireworks. What impressed me the most? The garage of eighty or ninety motorcycles our procession passed when following 150 bagpipers into the dinner tent! There was nothing cheap about big, warm, welcoming Malcolm Forbes.

Come fall, Sophia Loren and Luciano Pavarotti starred at an Italian Embassy dinner. Sophia was more strikingly beautiful, more glamorous even than on screen. Her face was unlined, her waist measurement in the midtwenties or lower. How did she look so divine at age fifty-three? "I sleep nine hours," she told me. "I eat half of what they give me. And I don't drink." She had given up smoking four years earlier. To avoid wrinkles, she made no facial grimaces, never frowned—and when she needed to see better she didn't squint, but put on her glasses. So there you have it, girls.

*   *   *

President and Mrs. Reagan's last state dinner, like their first, was for Prime Minister Margaret Thatcher. I was invited again, only this time George was too. It was one of the memorable parties in my life not only because it was bringing the close to an era, but because it was an absolute smash. Besides the president of the United States and First Lady and the next president of the United States and next First Lady, there was "the greatest woman in the world," as Walter Annenberg tagged Britain's prime minister. Political powers, artistic giants, and famed figures from all walks of life filled the state dining room, which was a spectacle of beauty. Centering every table, and above eye level to allow cross-table conversation, was a rounded topiary "tree" of pink roses, each one fresh and perfect. My table was next to the president's. Starting with the table hostess, "Obie" Shultz, and going clockwise around it were: California's Governor George Deukmejian, Betty Beale, "Cap" Weinberger, Beverly Sills, film heart-throb Tom Selleck, Mrs. Tom Wolfe, Librarian of Congress Jim Billington, Lee Annenberg, and one of Mrs. Thatcher's two aides. When Mrs. Shultz sent her gold-crested menu card around the table for signatures—to add to her collection from every such occasion—everybody else at our table did, too, with the exception of Deukmejian and me. I asked Cap, "What would I do with it?" "You might sell it," he replied with a grin. Immediately, the gov and I followed suit.

The governor said even though his state had the sixth largest economy in the world it still had no governor's mansion. That was because Jerry Brown, when governor, wouldn't live in it so it was sold. Weinberger noted that Brown's gubernatorial pad was always referred to as "spartan." "It was our apartment before he took it and it was a lovely apartment," said Cap. "But we had furniture in it. He took it all out and slept on the floor."

Others at the dinner were Mikhail Baryshnikov, Nobel literature prizewinner Joseph Brodsky, artist David Hockney, composer Andrew Lloyd Webber and actress wife Sarah, and still lovely star-of-another-period Loretta Young.

I asked Barbara Bush that evening if she would now go on a shopping spree because as First Lady she would be photographed every time she turned around. "No," she said, adding prophetically, "American women are going to love me." If she meant American women could identify with a white-haired woman who could not fit into a size 10, least of all a size 2 or 4, she was right. In addition, of course, Barbara's relaxed, smiling, easy-to-talk-to ways made her popular with the press who usually portrayed her to the public with the kindness she deserved.

CHAPTER 15

The Place-Card Polka

When Presidents Come to Dinner

I got the idea at breakfast one Sunday in June 1982.

"Let's give a dinner party in the garden," said I.

"Okay, who for?" said George, without looking up from the comic page.

"The president of the United States," I replied in a tone that suggested, who else?

"Why not?" agreed George unfazed. We had entertained the Gerald Fords in our garden when Jerry was House minority leader, again when he was vice president, and finally when he was president. A New Yorker who had been posted in West Virginia, Texas, and New York, George now took Washington life in his stride.

"Whom shall we invite?" I asked, getting down to business.

"Why don't you wait till you know if the Reagans are coming?" replied George, who has a lot of common sense for a man.

I had been reporting on the occupants of the White House since Harry Truman's day, but it wasn't till I heard the funny Vaughn Meader record about the Kennedys that it dawned on me how cooped-up presidential families are in the No. 1 residence. Meader, you recall, mimicked Jack Kennedy's voice to perfection, wondering out loud to Jackie what everyone was doing one night, and wishing someone had invited them out. It was deliciously droll to think of the First Couple, especially a charismatic young pair like Jack and Jackie, not being invited out by their party-giving friends who, in turn, longed for a White House bid.

Though George's main attention was somewhere between "Peanuts" and "Dennis the Menace," he suggested I'd better line up a cook first. (The only thing I have in common with Julia Child is that we were both in the same house at Smith College at the same time. She was funny even then—but if she could so much as boil water in those days she kept it a secret.)

I cleared several summer Sunday evenings with the cook of my choice, and promptly wrote Nancy Reagan to ask if they could come to an informal dinner in our garden on one of those dates. I chose Sunday because all of official Washington is busy on week nights, saving weekends for some private life, and the Reagans spent weekends at Camp David, returning to the White House Sunday afternoons.

It was a good bet. A phoned acceptance for July 18 came a few days later.

By then we had completed our guest list, starting off with the Cornelius Vanderbilt Whitneys—not because their name sounds socially prominent and rich as cream but because they had treated us to marvelous weekend house parties at their homes in Lexington, Ky., Saratoga Springs, N.Y., and at their Deerlands Camp in the wilds of upper New York State. A party for the First Couple was something we could do for them that they might not readily do on their own.

Tennis czar John Gardiner and his wife Monique had also entertained us for several years—at his tennis ranch in Scottsdale, Ariz., the weekend of the Senators Cup Tournament—and had always given us senatorial treatment.

On the home front we had become good friends of Count and Countess Roland de Kergorlay, the European Communities representative to Washington, and his English wife Lavinia. They had wined and dined us elegantly and often but had never set foot in our house. Also we put on our list the former owner of the now defunct *Washington Star*, Joe Allbritton, the biggest banker in town, and his wife Barby; they had invited us to several parties, and put their tennis court at my disposal.

Then there were our close friends in the diplomatic corps, Moroccan Ambassador Ali Bengelloun and his wife Jackie, whom I had been devoted to since their first ambassadorial tour in Washington during the Kennedy administration and visited in Casablanca. Clare Boothe Luce was also a must. She was distinguished as well as glamorous, the best feminine raconteur anywhere, and we had visited her twice at her showplace in Honolulu. We included U.S. Information Director Charles Wick and his wife Mary Jane, even though they saw the Reagans frequently, because they had invited us to the most glamorous parties of the Reagan administration outside the White House.

To carry out my theory that there should be at least one young beauty for the men to feast their eyes on, and a newsman to spark the interest of politicos and diplomats, I added to our list beautiful Alexandra de Borchgrave and her editor-husband Arnaud; and ABC's John Scali and his wife Denise, who had introduced us to the Gardiners. I wound up the list of twenty-four guests with sister Nancy and her husband, Edward Maffitt, a retired U.S. diplomat, and Senator Malcolm Wallop, then single, Republican, and a gentleman—in fact, the grandson of an earl.

If you want to entice a top banana to your house in mid-July in the Nation's Capital, you don't ask him to come in black tie. So I told Nancy Reagan it would be sport shirts for the men with absolutely no jackets or ties.*

Thrilled with the presidential acceptance, I got on the phone and invited all the above. One nice thing about having the president to dinner is that nobody regrets, unless ill or out of town.

With each telephoned invitation I swore everyone to secrecy for

---

* In pre-airconditioned days when people were more conservative and proper about dress, the men would sit in their woolen tuxedos, perspire heavily, and suffer, whether indoors or outdoors. The British government considered Washington a hardship post because of its humid heat. A British diplomat was usually the first to ask if the men could remove their jackets. British diplomats had so much social prestige they could sit at a candlelit table in shirt sleeves without losing their aplomb.

four reasons: One, we had some good friends who were not invited. Two, if it was noised about we would look like a couple of show-offs trying to capitalize on the honor the Reagans were doing us. Three, there was always the possibility that some national or international crisis would cause them to cancel—in which case the more people who knew about it the more egg we'd have on our faces. And, lastly and most importantly, the safety of the president had to be considered.

I told the cook who she would be cooking for but advised her against any leaks whatsoever. I gave her name and the names of three expert waiters to the Secret Service. All had to be checked out first.

Next, I sent out reminders. You never feel quite sure in my home town if the invited will remember the date and hour if it is not written down. Once in a while a hostess will get into such a nervous twit she will send out two! My reminders were our engraved folded cards that read inside across the top: "President and Mrs. Reagan will arrive at 7:30." In the middle I wrote: "Sunday, July 18" and under that: "at 7 o'clock." The lower lefthand corner read: "Men: Sport shirts—No ties." And under that: "Women—Patio costumes." In the lower right-hand corner it said: "To Remind."*

Next, it behooved me to check on the wherewithal to serve such a glittery assemblage. I lined up all our best china and crystal stemware to decide which table would get which pattern. With three separate tables for eight, it was not necessary to have twenty-four matching dinner plates, dessert plates, soup plates, and wine glasses. I had two flowered cloths which I decided to use on tables at

---

* You can write informal reminders any way you choose and ordinarily the partygivers would put "In honor of" in front of the names of their special guests. The reason I did not do so is because we do not honor a president by having him at our house, he honors us. There was a half hour's difference between the two times given because protocol requires that all guests arrive before a chief of state.

I did not send a reminder to the White House. A whole corps of people there knows where the president and his wife are going and the exact time they are due from the minute the engagement is made. Each has an assistant whose duties are to arrange, clear, prepare for, and keep all appointments.

either end of the garden, with a lace-trimmed white one in the middle.

We did not have enough crystal wine glasses in matching sets of eight—without nicks in the rims, that is—to serve the usual embassy complement of three wines. So I settled on white wine for the first two courses and Dom Perignon champagne for the dessert course. I earmarked the eight champagne glasses with hollow stems for the president's table. For Nancy's, I selected our finest and most delicate crystal stemware. The third table would get Waterford crystal.

Fortunately, I had inherited from my aunt, who had the same initials as I, dozens of damask dinner napkins, so all I had to do was fold three sets of eight identical ones.

For the next weeks I went around the house like Sherlock Holmes looking for clues, hunting for dirt, dust, tarnish—anything that might catch the eye of Nancy Reagan, a meticulous housekeeper. The hardest cleaning job to be done was on the big crystal chandelier that hangs from the second floor ceiling over the well of the staircase. The only way to reach it is to stand on a board extending from the top step to the top of a ladder on the landing. George did it; what a sweetheart.

All our silver—flat silver, serving dishes, trays, bowls, candelabra, vases, and ashtrays—was polished; ditto the brasses on the antiques. Everything washable—bedspreads, bathroom rugs, etc.—was washed. By Saturday evening, the house had been cleaned from top to toe, all the food and beverages bought, and the champagne and white wine put in the frigidaire. I was exhausted—so was George—and ready to relax when I suddenly thought I had better check the front door to see if it looked all right. It did not! I shrieked out in anguish, "George! The front door looks poor white!"

My everlovin' calmly said, "That's no problem. I have some black enamel. I'll paint it." So twenty-four hours before our dinner, George put a new coat of paint on the door that would open to the First Couple.

I didn't worry about what to wear. Perle Mesta always wore something old when she entertained and saved her newest and most eye-catching outfits for when she made an appearance as a party guest—she said it doesn't make any difference what you wear when you are the hostess.*

I knew the Secret Service would be around a couple of days in advance. (Only one Secret Service man had checked out my Tracy Place abode when President and Mrs. Lyndon Johnson came to a nightcap party after attending a Women's National Press Club dinner; of course, a carful or more accompanied him to and fro.)

* * *

Back in 1975 when President and Mrs. Ford came to dinner, the president's military aide, a communications expert from the Signal Corps, and four Secret Service men had inspected the premises so discreetly that their visit attracted no attention from neighbors. They asked where the president would have cocktails and where he would sit during dinner. The only change they suggested was that the garden gate, which we keep locked for our protection, must remain unlocked in case the chief executive had to make a sudden escape.

That night, two policemen took up positions in front of our house and were joined by four Secret Service men, two communications specialists, plus two executive protection police. Then the neighbors did get curious, even if they didn't notice the D.C. Fire Department ambulance/rescue van that paused out front before parking around the corner.

How I remained calm, I'll never know. The dinner we planned for the garden had to be moved inside because rain was imminent. A storm would hit us just about nine o'clock, the Signal Corpsmen told us.

So there we were, shortly before our guests were to arrive, moving furniture against the walls so we could set up two tables in the living room. The third table, of course, would be the dining room one.

Incidentally, in pushing the living room furniture out of the way that night we moved the love seat from the fireplace to the glass

---

* I decided on an old favorite striped chiffon blouse with tapered pants that matched the yellow in the stripe. George chose a long-sleeved silky looking sports shirt and light pants—the dress outfit for men in tropical resorts like Jamaica.

doors thus blocking the exit to the garden. The only other way out, besides the kitchen door, was through our bedroom so everybody, including the president, had to go through our bedroom to have cocktails in the garden.

En route, I invited Gerald Ford to take off the safari jacket over his short-sleeved shirt because it was a stifling night. When it was time to leave, Mr. Ford came to the bedroom to retrieve his jacket—only to find nine women, who had just finished their coffee, still in there. He decided to join us and sat on my dressing-table chair, the lone male among women draped around on the bed or sitting on the floor. The White House photographer appeared in time to snap the scene as I observed, "Mr. President, you have your regular cabinet and your kitchen cabinet. Now you have your bedroom cabinet." That profound statement did nothing to change the course of history but I love the photo. Presidents, I have discovered, hardly move without the White House photographer.

Equally memorable was the Fords' departure that night. When they said their goodbyes we went downstairs ahead of them only to find all the dinner guests of Democratic Senator and Mrs. Tom McIntyre of New Hampshire, who lived across the street, waiting outside our door in the rain. They had heard the six advance motorcycle policemen rev up their engines, a clear signal the cavalcade was about to depart. They had witnessed the arrival, and throughout the evening one of their guests, senatorial wife Barbara Eagleton, peeped out of the window to keep abreast of the doings across the street.

I quickly invited them in out of the rain; and after they lined up in the hall, leaving a path for the Fords who were descending the stairs, I suggested they sing something. Jerry Ford was amazed to hear "For He's A Jolly Good Fellow" emanating from the throats of Democratic Senators Alan Cranston of California, Tom Eagleton of Missouri, and Tom McIntyre and their wives, and from Federal Reserve Chairman and Mrs. Arthur Burns and CBS Commentator George Herman and his wife. It was some send-off. As soon as the Fords left we invited the new group upstairs for the second, if brief, party of the evening.

* * *

In 1982, Secret Service men were more nervous. Following the assassination attempt on President Reagan, his protection had seemingly doubled.

The following is a play by play account of what happened when tossing a little, informal Sunday night supper for the prez of the U.S.:

It's Thursday, July 15, three days before our cozy gathering.

9:30 A.M.: Five Secret Service men and one Signal Corpsman inspect our house and garden and then stand out front to study the neighborhood layout. Our next door neighbor, a ninety-one-year-old-woman, nervously calls to find out why a group of male strangers is staring at her house. I explain who they are and why they are there, but extract a promise of secrecy. I didn't know that the men were already ringing the doorbells of all the surrounding houses and asking if one of their ilk could be stationed in their gardens Sunday evening because "an important person" would be in the neighborhood. Of course, everybody knows only the president gets that much protection.

Thursday afternoon two men from the telephone company arrive to inspect the wiring in our house.

Friday, 9:30 A.M.: A telephone man inspects the main phone lines on the telephone pole nearest our house to ascertain if needed circuits are available.

9:45 A.M.: Two telephone men string new wires to our house.

10:00 A.M.: Three Secret Service men, one driving the prototype of the armored presidential limousine, pull up to see if the long car can maneuver our driveway so the Reagans can step out right at our front steps. The long car maneuvers nicely. It then goes back to the White House and returns on a practice run through Rock Creek Park.

10:15 A.M.: Three Signal Corpsmen fill the downstairs bedroom with radio equipment for their command post and connect it to two small antennae outside the bedroom window.

10:20 A.M.: Three more Secret Service men arrive to go over the premises again. Some technical security men also show up to check on everything, including our airconditioning. They ask if there are any outside vents, and explain why. If unguarded, someone could possibly blow poison gas into them. Thank heaven, we have no outside vents! I never realized we were living so dangerously.

10:30 A.M.: A policeman in his car and one on a motorcycle meet in front of the house to discuss Sunday night's parking of cars and motorcade route. A serious conversation ensues: Will the city police or the park police be on the bridges under which the motorcade will pass, if the presidential procession comes via the Rock Creek Park route? The policemen note that if the motorcade should come up Connecticut Avenue instead, men must be stationed on rooftops along the whole way.

By now there are eight men conferring out front near the black presidential prototype limousine, two gray sedans, two police cars, one Signal Corps van, and one motorcycle. Passersby pause and stare. Our neighbors begin inviting friends to spectator parties Sunday night.

10:40 A.M.: The presidential prototype limo and motorcycle take off to make a dry run and settle on the route.

Saturday 9:30 A.M.: The telephone company installs four White House phones—one in my office for the president's use only; one in the command post, i.e., the downstairs bedroom; and two in the downstairs library where, we are informed, five people will remain throughout our party—the president's physician, his military aide, a nurse, a White House press staffer, and an advanceman who checks out everything before the others arrive.

11 A.M.: A Signal Corps warrant officer arrives to test the new phones.

2 P.M.: Three White House staffers, including one from the press office and the advanceman—who turns out to be Mark Hatfield, Jr., son of the senator from Oregon—arrive to look things over and decide where the press will stand for the presidential arrival and departure.

Sunday, 5 P.M.: Ten Secret Service men appear and take up positions everywhere—around the house and in the gardens of all our surrounding neighbors; two Signal Corpsmen take over the command post in the guest bedroom.

5:45 P.M.: Six police cars and two police vans with bomb-sniffing dogs draw up out front. The dogs sweep the house and grounds for bombs. George asks one of the canine cops what happens when the dog sniffs a bomb. "He sits down," was the reply. "Gee, I hope he's not tired," says George. The sniffer isn't tired, but George is, and doesn't have time to sit. He's just been to the Safeway to buy huge bags of ice for the bar and wine coolers.

6 P.M.: The Signal Corps warrant officer comes by to check phones again. These guys leave nothing to chance.

6:15 P.M.: The city ambulance draws up front, but is moved around the corner out of sight after conferring with the Secret Service. What president wants to see an ambulance waiting for him when he sets out for a little diversion?

6:30 P.M.: An NBC crew sets up its cameras across the street.

6:45 P.M.: The advanceman, Mark Hatfield, Jr., takes up his post in the library.

7 P.M.: A carnival atmosphere prevails. A hundred people, including kids and dogs, watch our guests arrive. We should have set up a cold drink concession and rented campstools.

7:15 P.M.: The street is closed to traffic, forcing late arrivals to park a block away and walk.

7:25 P.M.: The Secret Service advises us that the Reagans are now en route in Rock Creek Park and will arrive in five minutes. They ask us not to greet them out front, for safety's sake.

7:30 P.M.: The roar of a helicopter overhead and five motorcycles in front herald the presidential pair's procession. The helicopter sweeps the still-daylight scene with a strong searchlight. Behind the single file of motorcycles comes the lead police car, then the president's limousine, then a long stationwagon full of more Secret Servicemen, followed by a car carrying the president's physician and military aide, the latter clutching the ominous black briefcase; behind them is another car carrying the White House photographer and nurse followed by the CAT car—that's the Counter Assault Team or the Secret Service's SWAT team—followed by two press vans, another ambulance, and more motorcycle police.

Thus began our quiet, mum's-the-word party. It's now about as private as World War II.

George and I decided to stand outside where the Reagans could see us waiting when they turned into our driveway, so they would not think us rude. We were back inside before they got out of the car. But if their protective force did not want them to linger where they could be a target the Reagans gave no thought to such fears. They turned around and waved to the cheering crowd across and up and down the street.

People with cameras got their pictures of Mr. Reagan in his light blue cotton shirt with open neck and long sleeves—the kind worn over slacks in the Caribbean countries. Nancy Reagan had on a picture gown for summer—a cool white seersucker dress with off-the-shoulder neckline, three-quarter sleeves, and full skirt ending in a ruffle, suggestive of moonlight and magnolias.

After they signed our guest book, we escorted them upstairs. The Secret Service showed the physician, the military aide, the nurse, and the staffer (none of whom we ever saw) into the library, where they could watch television and fix themselves cold soft drinks from the bar my thoughtful husband had set up in that room. One Secret Serviceman came upstairs and stood where No. 1 was within his sight all evening.

We introduced our other guests, who were cocktailing in aircondi-tioned comfort in the living room, to the Reagans and promptly supplied the president with his favorite drink, a screwdriver (orange juice and vodka). Nancy, we knew, wanted only Perrier water.

Mrs. Reagan had been in our house before. She came to a small luncheon in early June of their first year. I remember thinking she would find our decor at least within the color schemes she prefers—like her I love the red end of the spectrum—orange, apricot, yellow, and green—and appreciate the antiques I inherited from my aunt, Bess Brownlow. Among the paintings lining the off-white walls of our living room is a flattering portrait of me painted in 1948 by the late Alfred Jonniaux, who had been a portraitist at the Belgian court before coming to Washington to paint members of the Truman cabinet. (It's a pity he did not paint the White House portraits of Harry and Bess Truman. They were done by a little-known artist from photographs and, alas, look it.)

While the Reagans were moving about in this room chatting with everybody, Marylou Whitney, who was at one time an actress and finds an audience irresistible, slipped into a front room to look out the window at the still-gathered crowd. Standing so her white dress could be seen but not her face, she waved magnanimously to the onlookers. I never did discover if they thought it was Nancy Reagan giving them all that noblesse oblige.

All our guests probably thought we were demented when we left our comfortable house to dine outdoors on one of the hottest, stickiest nights of the year, but our flagstone lower terrace looked so pretty and cool, with euonymus growing abundantly, borders of azalea bushes, and masses of pink impatiens. On the upper, tree-bordered terrace, there is more paved flagstone, our small, oval swimming pool, and our white iron chairs and little tables. The whole garden is surrounded by high palisade fencing and trees and shrubbery and is extremely private.

My table was set up close to the big, sliding glass doors to the living room, and George's was at the opposite end, by the glass sliding doors to our bedroom; the third table was in the middle.

The dinner went swimmingly—except for the heat and the humidity; I prayed all the while that the temperature would drop a few degrees. Please, Lord, just a few. Sitting in that same spot one night with Henry Kissinger beside me I had prayed with equal fervor. Then there was that night when it rained for the Fords. Do you suppose somebody up there thought a little humility was needed for balance? At least, I knew Nancy Reagan was almost never too warm. I doubt if anyone ever sees perspiration on her face. And whatever the president was feeling, he showed no discomfort.

In fact, he was such an entertaining guest that nobody at my table could have given the heat a thought. He conducted himself as though he were at the one place in the world he most wanted to be, talking to the group he most wanted to be with. This is Ronald Reagan's remarkable gift of charm, which no other president has matched. No matter what topic was brought up, the world's best raconteur delighted us with one story after another.

He said how much more effective were the love scenes in the movies of his day than in the current films, which show nude couples making love in bed. In the old days, a couple in the same bed had to be dressed and apart. He recalled the shooting of the final scene in a film directed by the noted Ernst Lubitsch, when the latter told the two leads they could go home; he didn't need them. They protested but left. For the last scene, Lubitsch showed a door opening; then a lovely bare feminine arm reaching out to hang a "Do Not Disturb" sign on it. The door slowly closed, leaving to the viewers' imaginations what was going on behind it. It was far more effective and suggestive than the show-all approach of today, noted RR.

This reminded Sonny Whitney of the time he and his cousin Jock Whitney coproduced *Gone With The Wind*. The most memorable line in that film was Rhett Butler's final remark to Scarlett O'Hara—"Frankly, my dear, I don't give a damn." But censor czar Will Hays insisted that the word, "damn" could not be used; they would have to substitute "darn."

Sonny paid visits to Hays' office armed with proof that there was much worse to be found both in the Bible and in Shakespeare. Author Margaret Mitchell, he pointed out, was a southern lady and she had used the word; it would not be offensive to American audiences!

If censorship was carried to absurd extremes then, there is some longing for a little more of it today.

I need not have worried about the food. The president took a second helping of the veal entree and when the dessert came around—vanilla ice cream, fudge sauce, strawberries, and blueberries, all on one tray—and cookies, he took some of everything. Coffee was served at the tables.

When dinner was over, George rose and said what a pleasure it was to have the president and First Lady with us and what an honor they did our house. Then he sat down, forgetting to toast them. He had his mind on my plan to pop up and say something special about Nancy. I stood, and in my usual tactful way, said, "George, you forgot to toast President and Mrs. Reagan! Ha, ha."

I said I had known every First Lady since Bess Truman, and could state that probably no First Lady since Eleanor Roosevelt had come face-to-face with more people who needed help, such as our drug-addicted youth and handicapped children, than Nancy Reagan; and I raised my glass.

George, a little shamefacedly, then stood and asked everyone to join him in a toast "to President and Mrs. Reagan," and those words reverberated softly around the tables.

Mr. Reagan, obviously pleased with my comments about his wife after all the critical harping by the press, rose next. He said when he and Nancy left the White House that evening he said, "Did you ever think we would be going to a Washington party dressed like this?" He noted their pleasure in being there, and thanked us for the party.

When we got up from our tables, I wanted to show the president the upper terrace of our little intown "estate" and our 20′ by 12′ swimming pool, where, I told him, I swam every morning, before breakfast, year round.

The Moroccan ambassador followed us up the steps. A waiter brought up a tray of liqueurs. We were there for only a minute, but it gave Ambassador Bengelloun a chance for a private word with the president, for which he seemed grateful.

When the guests were all back in the living room, chatting up a storm, I crossed the hall to my bedroom and discovered how much cooler it was in there. So I invited Mary Jane Wick and Alexandra and Arnaud de Borchgrave, who were talking together, to come into the bedroom, which they did. Then I went up to RR and said, "Mr. President, wouldn't you like to come into my bedroom? It's much cooler in there."

"That's the best offer I've had all week," he said.

He sat down on the end of our pink-and-white, rose-patterned, bed, flanked by Mary Jane and Alexandra. Into this feminine setting the guests wandered one by one to join RR's rapt audience, draping themselves on the sides of the beds or sitting on the floor, where I was comfortably ensconced at his feet.

George stayed in the living room with Nancy—who was chatting with Clare Luce on the love seat—and the rest of the guests. Eventually, Clare too slipped into the bedroom and joined the foot-of-the-bed group, squeezing in cozily between Alexandra and RR. There was nothing bashful about Clare.

For three-quarters of an hour the president held us enchanted, recounting stories of his prepresidential days. He stood up to demonstrate one anecdote, about a photo of the cast of an Errol Flynn film in which Reagan had a part. Flynn, he said, didn't want any other presentable young man in the front row with him, so young Ronald Reagan was told to stand in the back of the group where he was completely hidden. To counteract Flynn's plans for his obscurity, he unobtrusively stretched first one foot out to scrape up some sand, then another—the president demonstrated smiling broadly—

until he had a high mound. Just as the picture was snapped, he stood
on top of the mound, so that his head popped above the others. It
was captivating to see the leader of the free world acting out a ruse
to compete in an industry just as ruthlessly competitive as politics.

He was in the middle of his tale when Nancy came into the
bedroom to tell him it was departure time. Nancy knew that when
Ronald Reagan was relaxed and had an audience he forgot about
time and the demands of the next day. She learned when he was
governor of California that if he was to keep a healthy regimen she
would have to be the monitor. He finished that story and told one
more before they said their goodbyes and started down the stairs.
Before they stepped out the door they thanked us for the evening.
RR gave me a kiss; George kissed Nancy goodbye. When you come
right down to it, it was like Luciano Pavarotti thanking his dinner
hosts for letting him entertain their guests for free!

With the sound of revved-up motorcycle engines, the neighbors
and their guests again poured out of every house in the area to
witness their departure. They applauded, the Reagans waved goodbye, getting cheery waves in return, as the long caravan slowly
rolled down the street. We rushed back upstairs to hear the comments of our other guests and bid them goodnight, holding back a
few for a postmortem.

We felt it had been a smashing evening. How could it have been
otherwise with the best entertainer in the country masquerading as
president of the United States or vice versa in our modest domicile!

Throughout the party, the White House photographer had
snapped color pictures, which were eventually sent to us. The one
of the president and me had been enlarged and was inscribed, "Dear
Betty—It was a great evening—thank you and warm regards," and
signed "Ronald Reagan." (I suspect he would have written the same
thing if there had been a fly in his soup and gravy spilled on his lap.)
Nancy had inscribed the shot of us together, "Dear Betty—The
trouble is—we never have a good time! Fondly, Nancy."

*   *   *

This chapter would have ended on that note except that President
and Mrs. Reagan came to dinner again in 1986 and once more in
1988. Advanced security measures were even more stringent in '86.

Seven phones were installed. ("Who on earth for?" asked Reagan when I told him.) Everybody had to leave the house while the canine bomb-sniffers checked out the sideboard, the closets, and under every chair. Secret Service people who have to stand are rotated every twenty-five minutes, we learned, to keep them alert. I had planned for the president to be seated in the center of the oval table in the dining room, but was told that would put him in line with the window that looked out on the street; RR was moved to the end of the table, where anyone taking a blind shot through the drawn curtains would miss him.*

In our modest kitchen were five people—the cook, three waiters, and a man from the White House mess who watched every morsel in preparation from 2:00 P.M. on.

Then a lame duck president, Mr. Reagan said the only difference was in the Senate's withholding confirmation of his appointments— holding out for a Democratic president.

He talked about his first kiss on-film. He learned, after planting a real kiss on his costar, that it pushed her cheeks out of shape; his lips should barely touch hers. The camera would be so angled, no one would know. Today, RR told me, a kissing couple "looks as if they are eating their way through."

He told us that he liked his cabinet members to express their opinions, and if they differed to have it out—and then he made his decisions.

This time, George gave a marvelous toast; both Reagans were touched and everybody congratulated him.

Our last dinner for the Reagans took place September 11, 1988, five months before they left the White House. The weather in the garden was perfect that night and the party was one I will never top again in my life—because of what happened after dinner.

By now, the security measures were even more elaborate. For the first time, the bomb-sniffing dog's handler noticed the trapdoor

---

* We dined indoors because it rained again! Seated at the same table were Swedish Ambassador Wilhelm Wachtmeister, dean of the diplomatic corps; Anne Petrignani, wife of the Italian ambassador; Mary Johnston, wife of Senator Bennett Johnston, Louisiana Democrat; my stepdaughter Gretchen Quigley; Mandell Ourisman, who had been our host in Tryall, Jamaica, every winter; and former newsman Charles Bartlett.

leading to our attic which, when pulled down, became a steep stairway. He decided the attic should be checked out so he and the four-footed "nose" did just that. But he forgot one thing: a dog will not come down a ladder. No amount of pulling on the animal's leash could persuade it to try what it knew it could not do. Eventually, the stocky cop got the seventy-six lb. German shepherd draped precariously around his shoulders. Holding him there with one arm, clutching onto the ladder railing with the other, the pair descended, safely if shakily. The dog and I both thought things had been carried too far.

This time, eight men and pretty advance girl Ashley Parker came around to check us out nine days before the party! And five days ahead of time, the telephone men showed up to arrange the installation of six phones, three in the garage where the command post would be and three in the library where the presidential entourage would sit. By now, the Secret Service had a scrambler on a van they could park out front that would provide the president, they said, with secure phone connections to any place in the world.

During preparations, several neighborhood phones went dead. But by now, the neighbors were used to the fuss.

Again Mrs. Herbert Fales, across the street, gave a spectator supper, inviting Ambassador-at-Large Paul Nitze and two former U.S. ambassadors, Robinson McIlvaine and Wells Stabler. When British Ambassador and Lady Acland arrived for our dinner and spied their old friends, the Stablers, across the street they walked over and greeted them. Our block was beginning to look like a neighborhood social.

This time, the presidential caravan, led by six motorcycles, had thirteen cars—including a decoy limo, with flags flying. We served cocktails on our small upper poolside terrace; when I led the president down the uneven steps to the lower terrace for dinner, he held onto the iron railing and mentioned the rickety steps. It was the first sign of age I had ever seen in him.

Conversation at my table, where I had President Reagan on my right and Italian Ambassador Rinaldo Petrignani on my left, flowed easily throughout dinner. At one point I said, "Mr. President, you are often referred to in the media as the most powerful man in the

Free World. Do you feel like the most powerful man in the Free World?"

Reagan responded by simply giving this example of his powerlessness in the face of Congress: "Not a single budget I have ever submitted has been adopted by the Congress. They put it on the shelf and write their own." I couldn't help noticing that every Democratic candidate for president that year called it the "Reagan deficit."

The proximity of Ambassador Petrignani reminded the horse-loving chief executive what all equestrians owe to one Italian cavalryman, Captain Federico Caprilli. It was the latter who originated the forward seat. The U.S. cavalry soon discovered, he said, why the Italians were winning all jumping competitions and copied them.

Reagan also traced the origin of the thoroughbred to King Charles II of England, who imported three Arabian stallions and bred them with English horses. Thereafter he bred only the finest, turning the others into geldings—which was something the Arabs had never done, said RR, who added, "So every thoroughbred horse has some Arabian in him."

In George's farewell toast to Reagan he noted that the president had the press baffled. "They can't understand," he said, "how you perform the world's biggest job with such apparent effortless ease and yet have everything work out so well. They criticized you for calling a spade a spade—as in 'evil empire'—and are confounded when you are invited to address Moscow University students on the advantages of democracy."

When my turn came I gave the prez an inflated globe from the National Geographic Society for his swimming pool, "to keep in touch with foreign countries," and I gave Nancy a marionette that had the face of her husband and boxing gloves on its hands. (Senator John Tower and his Texas lady friend Dorothy Heyser had bought the puppet in London for me to use in some way at our dinner.) When she slipped her fingers in it she could make it throw punches which, I said, was what she had long wanted her husband to do when somebody needed firing and he was too good-natured to do it.

She loved it, and kept it on her hand the rest of the evening.

The real treat for all of us came from the president after dinner.

Following coffee and liqueurs, when I saw everybody standing or sitting, chatting away in twos and threes, I asked Mr. Reagan if he would tell his Errol Flynn story. He shyly agreed, so I clapped my hands to get everyone's attention. I said, "The president has a story I think you'll enjoy hearing."

Standing in front of the mantel in our living room he began with the Flynn story and then continued—as I knew he would—with one amusing tale after another. This time, he talked about his visit to the USSR. He told about getting a complete resumé on Mikhail Gorbachev before their first meeting in Geneva; he knew the Soviet leader had received his detailed resumé, too. So when they were standing together for the first time, Reagan remarked to Gorbachev, "Incidentally, they weren't all B movies."

And he recounted some of the jokes Russian people were telling during his visit there. In one, supposedly visiting a Russian village incognito, he asked the mayor how many villagers had television sets.

"Everybody," said the mayor. "Some houses even have two." How about refrigerators, RR asked. The answer again was "everybody." He then asked the mayor, "Do you know who I am?" "Of course," his honor replied. "You are a CIA agent. Only a CIA agent would ask those questions in a town where there's no electricity."

For the next twenty-five to thirty minutes the Graebers and their guests* had the unique pleasure and honor of having as a stand-up entertainer the president of the United States. We'll never be able to top that. In thanking us again later, Lady Acland said the president should make tapes of his fund of anecdotes for posterity. Antony had one of his uncle's humorous stories and delighted in listening to it.

---

* Anne Petrignani, CIA Director Bill Webster, John Kluge, who had given $1 million to the Reagan Library, and his wife Patricia; David Brinkley and his wife Susan, Kennedy Center Chairman and Mrs. Ralph Davidson, former Ambassador Douglas MacArthur II, Austin Kiplinger of the *Kiplinger Washington Letter* and the *Changing Times* magazine and his wife Gogo; Mary Kay Blount (ex-wife of Postmaster General Blount) who came up from Montgomery, Ala., for the party; Washington divorcees whom we had visited in Aspen and Easthampton respectively— Linda McCausland and Betsy Luessenhop—and our son Bern Graeber.

*   *   *

My husband and I both thought it was the last time a president would come to our house. We had wanted, ever since 1975 when we stayed with George and Barbara Bush in the ambassadorial residence in Peking, to proffer some gesture of thanks. I had retired as a columnist in January of 1989, we had already entertained three presidents, and I wasn't aiming for the *Guinness Book of World Records*.

Then Bill Webster, a friend and fellow Christian Scientist, and Lynda Clugston, a friend and tennis partner, got engaged. I had nurtured the romance for over a year, and promised a dinner in their honor should they ever make up their minds. Their marriage took place October 20, 1990, and they gave me the choice of three dates later that month. After making a list of Bill's associates in official life and the private friends of both, I dashed off a note to Barbara Bush and said the four of us would be thrilled if she and the president could come to dinner any one of those nights. Each had a heavy campaigning schedule, but the First Lady called me a day or two later to say the one night they were both free was Tuesday, October 30th.*

Security precautions for George Bush were positively casual compared to those for Reagan. The Friday before a pretty Secret Service woman came by, took everyone's names, and went over our plans. Early Monday morning two men looked around outside and left; throughout the day only one Secret Serviceman came to our house to review the details. Not till two hours before our dinner did two of them drop by for a few minutes, to reappear with a van and some other men an hour later. No extra telephones were installed. (By now, each car had cellular phones.) No neighbors suspected any-

---

* The Webster's list included Sir Antony and Jenny Acland, Supreme Court Justice Sandra O'Connor and John, lawyer and former Congressman Jimmy Symington and his wife Sylvia, lawyer and former Chief of Protocol Lloyd Hand and Ann, Bill FitzGerald, who gave $1 million to the Washington Tennis Center, and Annelise FitzGerald, also a tennis player, and civic-minded Washington hosts, Bill and Buffy Cafritz. We had ten in the dining room where I sat between the president and Bill Webster, and eight in the living room where George sat between Mrs. Bush and the bride.

thing; there were no spectator parties. No dogs sniffed for bombs, although I learned later one had stuck his nose into every cranny outside. No directions were given as to where Mr. Big must sit at the dining table.

The presidential caravan turned out to be just as long as always and carried the usual entourage—but no Secret Service man stayed on the second floor with his eye on Bush all evening.

Why seemingly so casual for Bush and so careful for Reagan? Can presidents decide how much protection they want? The answer is no, they told me. It's up to the Secret Service. The man in charge decides, based on such variables as the world situation and particular threats received.

The White House photographer—this time it was an attractive young woman—came with the First Couple, but she took only one photograph, of the Bushes and the Graebers in our front hall, and then departed.

The dinner went smoothly. The Bushes couldn't have been more charming or seemed more interested.

Barbara told me that they did not ordinarily go out to a private dinner in someone's house; this was the only time they had done so since he became president.

We felt doubly honored, and so did the Websters. Both Bushes said goodnight to every guest before leaving, which they did soon after dinner. They had just come in from campaigning and were leaving the next day for more appearances, observed Mrs. B.; George Bush needed some rest and she had to take him home.

Two days later I received a handwritten note dated "Hallowe'en 1990," which Mrs. Bush took time to pen though "in haste as I am off for Utah, Kansas & Nebraska." She thanked us for "a great fun evening"—as nice thank-you notes are wont to do—and praised everything, including Bill Webster's choice of "such a darling girl!"

EPILOGUE

Last Waltz

The End of an Era?

Although the Reagan administration had taken social Washington by storm, the decline in Washington's diplomatic and private entertaining became the subject of more and more drawing room talk. "The social activities of today," I wrote in September of 1985, "can't begin to compare with those in the '50s, '60s and '70s." I had only to check my columns of the 1950s to find "seven to 10 major parties given by popular ambassadors in one week . . . 10 private parties in a week or even three private dances on three successive nights—and not debut dances, either. A packed social schedule was the norm before the fashionable and fast young Kennedys gave Washington its reputation as the glamor capital of the U.S.

"There were seven outstanding, moneyed hostesses in the '50s who entertained week in and week out. It was Perle Mesta's heyday when everybody from Dwight Eisenhower, Adlai Stevenson, and Lyndon Johnson to Werhner von Braun came to her parties. Marjorie Post was presiding over elegant dos at her in-town estate Hillwood. Polly Guggenheim was doing likewise at her in-town estate Firenze, now the Italian Embassy." Gwen Cafritz was regularly entertaining VIPs, having gone in for it in a big way when Perle went off as minister to Luxembourg in 1949.

"And there were the more conservative hostesses known as the three B's—Mrs. Robert Woods Bliss, who drew the cultural set to her in-town estate Dumbarton Oaks; Mrs. Truxtun Beale, who held forth in historic Decatur House on Lafayette Square; and Mrs. Robert Low Bacon, whose handsome F Street dwelling has also been preserved." There were Alice Longworth, too, and Mrs. J. Borden Harriman whose dinners were political salons. (When I wrote that column all had passed on with the exception of Gwen, who had retired from the scene and Polly, who was leading a much quieter life.)

Despite the hostess phenomenon, it should be noted that Capital society is, and always was, male dominated. Male government officials or foreign envoys have always given most of the parties. Visiting kings, presidents, prime ministers, foreign ministers, chiefs of staff, and so forth, *cause* the parties. And powerful males make the news at parties. When the president is away the First Lady does not give a formal dinner. When an ambassador is away his wife does not entertain American VIPs at their residence. Not infrequently, the society pages of the Washington papers were dotted with photographs of important men—and only men—at some social function. Through the years, some of my out-of-town papers balked at carrying an all-male picture with my column on their female-dominated society pages. So I had to pull into my photos some woman guest— who frequently didn't even know the men being photographed—in order to satisfy this provincial requirement. Prominent hostesses gained their fame only by the importance of the males they drew to their parties. Power is the name of the game and men—for the most part—have held and still hold that power.

The diplomatic corps—always the main motivators of the party pace—was awash with socially active ambassadors throughout the 1970s. There were France's Henri and Helle Bonnet, then Herve and Nicole Alphand, whose dinners were fabulous and frequently ended up with dancing to records. At one Alphand dinner we all tried to hipswing the hula hoop. Spain's Count de Motrico tossed marvelous New Year's Eve balls and other superb dances that often included flamenco performers. Their superb successors, the Marqueses de Merry del Val, entertained even more often and more amusingly. (The marquesa's favorite dinner game was a better ice breaker than any you'll find in the Arctic. The idea was to take superthin cigarette-paper away from your dinner partner's nostril by sniffing it up. You had to keep it attached to your nose until the person on the other side sniffed it from you. As it is impossible to inhale deeply while laughing the laughter won out.)

There were many other memorable hosts, some of whom I mentioned on earlier pages. But when the Reagans arrived in Washington, embassy entertaining had already dwindled. Most was by Sweden's Count Wachtmeister, Morocco's Bengelloun, Saudi Arabia's Alhegelan, France's François de Laboulaye, and Britain's Nicholas Henderson. In 1985 the major charming entertainment was by Italy's Rinaldo Petrignani and Willy Wachtmeister, with Canada's Allan Gotlieb in third place. Count Wachtmeister believed that entertaining was "indispensable to an ambassador doing his job correctly. Diplomacy is contact. When people come from my country it's important for them to see their opposite numbers, and it's up to me to arrange that. It's much easier if I know them personally, and I don't know them well if they have not been to my house. My government understands the importance of hospitality."

So why does the Nation's Capital no longer scintillate as it once did? What has happened to slow its social pace? Both active and retired residents have been perplexed by the difference between then and now. The most obvious answer, the one that first comes to mind, is the lack of really big hosts or hostesses. To fill that role, one must have the desire—or the need—to play it, the money to realize it, and the judgment to know what is necessary to attract desirable guests. But young modern women are not keen to play a social role. They are more interested in making it in the business world. A young woman reporter who called charming Washington party-giver Buffy Cafritz ended their conversation by asking in a belittling tone, "You don't want to be described as a hostess, do you?" This attitude may have its roots in the 1960s, when even wealthy, social parents couldn't persuade their daughters to have a debut.

And then, Congress, by the early 1990s, had usurped much of the president's power to direct foreign affairs. Ambassadors today find it's more rewarding to lobby on Capitol Hill than entertain presidential assistants or other key figures in the executive branch. For the most part, members of Congress are averse to attending embassy dinners; they figure it won't help them get reelected. And more and more cabinet members are turning down embassy invitations.

"When they won't come, why give a party that just lengthens my day?" observed one European envoy. And in the 1990s, there is the horrific cost of entertaining.

Then, too, benefit parties have burgeoned. They range in cost from $200 or $300 a person to $1,500 or $3,500 (for one seat in the orchestra or a box respectively at the Kennedy Center Honors annual gala). After Washingtonians have shelled out again and again for their own or their friends' favorite causes, they are not so ready to spend more thousands tossing a private bash. And the embassies are plagued every day to lend their big mansions for benefits, because people will more readily subscribe to a function in a prestigious residence they might otherwise never see. Former British Ambassador and Lady Acland were lending their impressive mansion four times a month—and wishing they could call a halt on the demand. The effect has been fewer parties for private friends.

Finally, Washington is more business-oriented today than it ever was. The leading caterer has told me that corporations now give most of the parties they service. And the ease of jet travel has increased the amount of intercontinental commuting. It has also made federal executives so accessible to their foreign counterparts that ambassadors' residences have become free hotels for visiting countrymen, who generally have to be wined and dined—which means less wherewithal for other entertaining.

So there you have it.

The glamorous social life in Washington, which I knew about as a child, when I watched my aunts don their finery, and which I assumed was as permanent as death and taxes, is no longer the same.

Perhaps during the Clinton administration Washington again will become the city in which great hosts and hostesses lead power at play.

Will it ever again be as it used to be?

That's anybody's guess.

Index

28 ~~X~~ DAYS